Finding Common Ground

Finding Common Ground

Governance and Natural Resources in the American West

Ronald D. Brunner,

Christine H. Colburn,

Christina M. Cromley,

Roberta A. Klein, and

Elizabeth A. Olson

Yale University Press

New Haven and London

Quotations in Chapters 3 and 6 from Aldo Leopold, *A Sand County Almanac: And
Sketches from Here and There* (New York: Oxford University Press, 1989), are reprinted
with permission of the publisher.

Printed in the United States of America.

Library of Congress Cataloging-in-Publication Data

Finding common ground : governance and natural resources in the American West /
Ronald D. Brunner . . . [et al.].
    p. cm.
Includes bibliographical references and index.
    ISBN 0-300-09144-3 (cloth : alk. paper) — ISBN 0-300-09145-1 (pbk. : alk. paper)
    1. Natural resources—Government policy—West (U.S.)—Case studies. 2. Commu-
nity organization—West (U.S.)—Case Studies. I. Brunner, Ronald D.
    HC103.7 .F54 2002
    333.7′0978—dc21
                                    2001008611

A catalogue record for this book is available from the British Library.

10 9 8 7 6 5 4 3 2 1

Contents

Preface

This book focuses on the growing problems of governance in the United States and on potential means of alleviating them. The problems are familiar: more single-issue politics and gridlock in Congress, more breakdowns in administrative control and accountability within the executive branch, and more litigation over public policy in the courts—as well as persistently low levels of public trust in the federal government since the 1960s. Relatively few Americans, however, have appreciated the potential of community-based initiatives to help resolve some problems of governance. Such initiatives have arisen during recent decades in response to specific, unresolved issues of local scope in different policy areas nationwide. Some initiatives already have demonstrated their potential by finding common ground on policies that advance the common interest. Nowhere are the problems of governance and the potential of community-based initiatives more apparent than in natural resources policy in the American West, where the federal government has jurisdiction over vast public lands.

The purpose of this book is to help those involved understand and realize the potential of community-based initiatives—both to advance the common interest through innovative policies on particular issues and to contribute toward reforms that adapt governance in the United States to twenty-first-century social conditions. We take the common interest as the appropriate aim of governance in a democracy. From this standpoint, the first chapter documents general problems of governance in natural resources policy and in the contemporary United States, introduces community-based initiatives as responses to those problems, and clarifies the potential of such initiatives as possible solutions. The next four chapters present case studies detailed enough for readers to make their own assessments of these claims and a strategy for proceeding. The case studies are:

- Water management and the Upper Clark Fork Steering Committee in Montana
- Wolf recovery in the northern Rockies
- Bison management in greater Yellowstone
- Forest policy and the Quincy Library Group in northern California

The concluding chapter develops and illustrates the strategy of harvesting experience from these and other cases to make the most of community-based initiatives. For this purpose, we suggest changes in the policies of those most directly involved: participants in community-based initiatives and their supporters, including foundations; interest groups established in and around the federal government; and researchers and educators who advise practitioners on natural resources policy and train the practitioners of the future.

For those concerned about governance in the United States, we clarify how community-based initiatives, along with campaign finance and other options, can bring about reform. We frame contemporary reform in historical perspective, emphasizing the period from 1877 to 1920, when American bureaucracies expanded in response to problems of policy and governance arising from industrialization, urbanization, and concurrent changes in social conditions. In effect, Americans created a new system of governance under the constitutional framework—and may be doing so again, a century later, in response to continuing changes in our society.

For practitioners in natural resources policy, we suggest how community-based initiatives might be utilized. New or emerging initiatives can adapt the experience of "model" initiatives—those that have succeeded in advancing the common interest in circumstances similar to their own. Government officials can rely on successful community-based initiatives to compensate for bureaucratic constraints on their involvement in politics and policy innovation. Environmentalists can encourage community-based initiatives to do what government cannot—propagate the land ethic, as Aldo Leopold urged a half-century ago.

For researchers and educators, we suggest a bridge beyond the remnants of scientific management from the Progressive era to adaptive management, which will require contextual, problem-oriented, and multi-method inquiry. The requisite intellectual tools are not widely known among specialists in natural resources policy, but they are available in the policy sciences—a distinctive tradition that was initiated by Harold D. Lasswell, Myres S. McDougal, and their collaborators in response to the coming of World War II. Since then the tools of the policy sciences have been applied to a vast array of problems in policy and governance. We continue the tradition.

This book culminates a project funded by the Henry P. Kendall Foundation. The project began in June 1998 and sponsored a workshop conducted by the Northern Rockies Conservation Cooperative in Jackson, Wyoming, in September of that year. The workshop included the five coauthors, practitioners involved in the four cases, and other policy scientists and practitioners. The project also supported a policy seminar entitled Governance and Natural Resources at the University of Colorado in the fall semesters of 1999 and 2000. The seminar provided a forum to discuss drafts of chapters and other literature with graduate students from a number of disciplines and with visiting practitioners and scholars. Several working papers were presented at the Policy Sciences Annual Institutes in 1998, 1999, and 2000 at the Yale Law School.

Acknowledgments

The coauthors acknowledge with gratitude the help of many people who have contributed to this book in a variety of ways. We begin with Ted Smith, executive director of the Henry P. Kendall Foundation, who provided encouragement and insightful questions as well as funding. Dave Iverson of the U.S. Forest Service, Don Snow of the Northern Lights Institute in Missoula, and Toddi Steelman, now of North Carolina State University, each read an earlier draft of the entire manuscript and provided many helpful comments and suggestions. So did more than two dozen graduate students and visitors in seminars on governance and natural resources. Marge Brunner volunteered many hours to proofread the manuscript submitted to Yale University Press and the edited copy that came back. At the Press, Jean Thomson Black and Ali Peterson guided the manuscript through the acquisitions and editorial processes.

In the preparation of the manuscript, a number of colleagues and friends helped with encouragement and advice on more than one chapter. These include Andy Willard of the Yale Law School; Gary Bryner, Sam Fitch, Doug Kenney, and Charles Wilkinson of the University of Colorado at Boulder; and Tim Clark, Denise Casey, and Peyton Curlee-Griffin of the Northern Rockies Conservation Cooperative in Jackson, Wyoming. The Cooperative conducted the Workshop on Governance and Natural Resources: New Models for the Twenty-first Century in Jackson, September 2–4, 1998. In addition to the three leaders of the Cooperative and the coauthors, the Workshop included Ed Bangs, Mike Brennan, Wayne Brewster, Dave Iverson, Jay Gore, Michael Jackson, Vanessa Johnson, Brad Kahn, Dana McDaniel, Gerald Mueller, Stephen Lottridge, Bill Noblitt, Steve Primm, Murray Rutherford, Michael Schotz, and Sandy Shuptrine. All participants in the Workshop generously shared their experience and insights.

Many others have contributed to specific chapters. For help on Chapter 2, we thank residents of the Upper Clark Fork River basin who agreed to be interviewed: Joe Aldegaire, Audrey Aspholm, Vivian Brooke, Stan Bradshaw, Jim Dinsmore, Bruce Farling, Bob Fox, Holly Franz, Chris Hunter, Gary Ingman, Dan Kemmis, Ellen Knight, Land Lindbergh, Mike Mclane, Fred Nelson, Jim Quigley, Ole Ueland, Vicky Watson, Dennis Workman, and others who spoke under the condition of anonymity. Both Gerald Mueller and Don Snow were particularly generous in time spent discussing the story of the Steering Committee and related experiences in the West. Charles Wilkinson and Sam Fitch read and commented on an earlier draft.

For help on Chapter 3, we thank Ed Bangs, Larry Bourrett, Tom Dougherty, Hank Fischer, Steve Fritts, Larry Kruckenberg, Curt Mack, and Doug Smith for interviews providing invaluable insights into wolf recovery efforts in the northern Rockies. Ed Bangs was especially ready and willing to answer questions. He also read and commented on earlier drafts of the chapter, along with Tim Clark, Hank Fischer, Doug Kenney, and Roger Pielke, Jr.

For help on Chapter 4, we thank those who took time from their busy schedules for one or more interviews: Jim Angell, Keith Aune, Jim Berkley, Mark Berry, Joe Bohne, Ted Bolling, Wayne Brewster, Ber Brown, Franz Camenzind, Jason Campbell, Jon Catton, Marion Cherry, Mike Clark, Patrick Collins, Peyton Curlee-Griffin, Lloyd Dorsey, Bob Ekey, Matthew Ferrari, Fred Finke, Mike Finley, Harv Forsgren, Arnold Gertonson, Jim Griffin, Anne Harvey, Marty Hayden, Rod Heidschmidt, Jeff Henry, James Holt, Dan Huff, D. Owen James, Robert Keiter, Karen Kovacs, Julie LaPeyre, Pamela Lichtman, Rosalie Little-Thunder, Andrea Lococo, Jim Lyons, Brad Mead, Bill Noblitt, Helga Pac, Mike Philo, Jamie Pinkham, Debbie Pressman, Barry Reiswig, John Russell, Bob Schiller, D. J. Schubert, Paul Schullery, Brian Severin, Bruce Smith, Patrick Smith, Jeanne-Marie Souvigney, Larry Stackhouse, Terry Terrell, Tom Thorne, Heather Weiner, Gloria Wells-Norlin, Louisa Willcox, Chris Wood, and Doug Woody. Tim Clark, John Wargo, and Andy Willard read and commented on earlier drafts.

For help on Chapter 5, we thank the many people who volunteered their time in informal conversations and formal interviews about the case of the Quincy Library Group: Linda Blum, Louis Blumberg, Barbara Boyle, Bob Brezeale, Bill Coates, Rose Comstock, Kent

Connaughton, Jody Cook, Shawn Cosgrove, Doug Crandall, Mike DeLasaux, Neil Dion, David Edelson, Maia Enzer, Steve Evans, Mike Francis, Janice Gauthier, Duayne Gibson, Michael Goergen, Gerry Gray, Anne Heissenbuttel, Steve Holmer, Michael Jackson, Lynn Jungwirth, Bill Lange, Mike Leahy, Mary Mitsos, Tom Nelson, Missy Nemeth, Felice Pace, Dave Peters, Jim Pissot, Bob Powers, John Preschutti, Harry Reeves, Dallas Scholes, John Sheehan, Gary Smith, Karen Steers, Ron Stewart, Dave Stone, George Terhune, Jay Watson, and Michael Yost. Charles Wilkinson, Sam Fitch, Linda Blum, and Elyssa Rosen read and commented on an earlier draft.

Finally, each coauthor warmly acknowledges the congenial and constructive collaboration that made this book possible. Without it, we would have been unable amid competing claims on time and attention to examine as much of the relevant literature—and to explore four cases in such detail—in less than three years. The collaboration proceeded so well because of our shared background in the policy sciences, which helped us clarify rather quickly what needed to be done so that we could get on with it. The collaboration also proceeded so well because of mutual friendship and respect, old-fashioned virtues that we hope to enjoy in comparable abundance in the years ahead.

1 Problems of Governance

Ronald D. Brunner

On the morning of March 6, 1997, just north of Yellowstone National Park near Gardiner, Montana, Rosalie Little-Thunder heard gunfire while participating in a prayer service for the spirits of slain buffalo. It was "a crackling sound, like dead branches snapping," she said. About a mile away she and several others found officials of the Montana Department of Livestock in the snow dressing out the bodies of eight Yellowstone bison they had just shot and killed. Little-Thunder later recalled: "It was like murder in the church parking lot during the service. . . . It was shocking, the disrespect they showed the buffalo." When Little-Thunder asked if she and another Lakota Sioux could pray for the spirits of these bison, she was told to get off the private land where the carnage had occurred and get back onto the road. When she refused, she was arrested for criminal trespass. For the Lakota Sioux and other tribes organized in the Intertribal Bison Cooperative, saving Yellowstone bison—the last free-roaming bison herds in the country— means saving the spirit of the bison. "The buffalo took care of our ancestors for thousands of years, and now it's time to return the favor," said Mike Fox, president of the Cooperative.[1]

At least several hundred and perhaps a thousand bison died inside Yellowstone National Park from snow and ice conditions during that winter of 1996–97, the most severe since 1943—and by one account the most severe since 1902, the year in which Congress ordered the bison rescued from extinction.[2] Another 1,084 bison roaming in search of forage crossed the boundaries of the Park into Montana, where they were shot and killed by officials from the Montana Department of

Livestock and the National Park Service. The officials acted under authority of an Interim Bison Management Plan designed to prevent the transmission of a disease, brucellosis, from bison to the cattle that graze on public and private lands around the Park.[3] Cattle not certified brucellosis-free by the Animal and Plant Health Inspection Service (APHIS) of the U.S. Department of Agriculture are subject to costly restrictions in interstate and international commerce. Mike Gilsdorf, an APHIS veterinarian, argued: "We have our own mandate just like the park has theirs, and ours is to eliminate brucellosis. . . . If we drop our guard and let the diseased bison roam freely out in the countryside, we're inviting trouble."[4]

But shooting free-roaming bison had already brought trouble. "When people describe what's happening here as 'a national tragedy,' I don't disagree with them," said Park Superintendent Mike Finley. "The National Park Service is very uncomfortable with the position it finds itself in. We are participating in something that is totally unpalatable to the American people, and it's something we are not convinced that science justifies." Marc Racicot, governor of Montana, insisted, "We have never wanted this responsibility thrust upon the state of Montana. Our preferred alternative is not to harvest bison, but it is virtually the only option we are left with. . . . Yellowstone has an obligation to take care of its wildlife and it has been remiss." Some stockgrowers were disgusted at the toll of bison, even though they were supposed to benefit directly from this means of protecting cattle from brucellosis. Among them was Delas Munns, whose family has grazed cattle on public land just north of Yellowstone's west entrance for decades. "So many different federal and state bureaucrats are trying to decide what should be done with those park bison [that] it's become a pretty ugly, aggravating situation as far as I am concerned. I'm tired of it."[5] An organized interest group, the Fund for Animals, urged tourists to boycott Montana. "The state of Montana has zero tolerance for buffalo, so we need you to have zero tolerance for Montana," read the Fund's full-page ad in *USA Today*.[6] Two weeks after Rosalie Little-Thunder was arrested, Delyla Wilson was also arrested in Gardiner after splashing rotting bison entrails on Governor Racicot, who was participating in a public meeting on bison management with Agriculture Secretary Dan Glickman and Montana's two senators.[7]

Behind these events are three changes in policy, expressing the different mandates and interests of the Park Service, APHIS, and the state of Montana. This background serves to introduce problems of governance in natural resources policy and other policy areas—it also serves to introduce a potential solution. As we will see, bison management in greater Yellowstone is a microcosm of larger problems of governance in the United States.[8]

A Microcosm

In 1967, the National Park Service acknowledged that management of Yellowstone bison as if they were livestock, that is, intensive management, was no longer appropriate.[9] Instead, they had begun to implement a policy of natural regulation in the expectation that disease and starvation would control the size of Yellowstone's bison herds. But the herds increased, and with the increase more bison crossed the north and west boundaries of the Park into Montana in search of forage, especially during severe winters. In 1985, APHIS declared cattle herds in Montana and Wyoming brucellosis-free. But to protect those herds, APHIS pressured the Park Service to keep bison inside Park boundaries and sought to eradicate brucellosis from all wildlife in Yellowstone eventually. This was an extension to wildlife of its policy of zero-tolerance for brucellosis in cattle. Also in 1985, the state of Montana authorized hunting to help control the bison and to protect cattle. But there was vehement public opposition, especially during the winter of 1988–89, when licensed hunters and state officials killed 579 bison, animal rights activists waged a national campaign against the hunt, and the news media covered these events. In response to public opposition, in 1991 the state legislature revoked authority for the hunt.

Meanwhile, in September 1989, the National Park Service, under pressure, agreed to produce a long-term Interagency Bison Management Plan for greater Yellowstone, together with an Environmental Impact Statement (EIS), as mandated by the National Environmental Policy Act of 1969 (NEPA).[10] A stated purpose of NEPA is "to create and maintain conditions under which man and nature can exist in productive harmony, and fulfill the social, economic, and other requirements of present and future generations of Americans." The rules for achieving this purpose are primarily procedural. NEPA directs "all agencies of the Federal Government" to prepare an EIS when any "major federal actions significantly affecting the quality of the human environment" are proposed.[11] Publication of the draft EIS provides opportunities for public participation prior to decision on the proposed actions. But assessments of NEPA have been mixed. For example, according to one observer, "Exposed to the glare of unforgiving public scrutiny, many short-sighted, uneconomic, and unwise decisions have been derailed [by NEPA]; others have been revised to reflect public concerns and to mitigate foreseeable environmental consequences."[12]

But the same observer also raised concerns that procedural compliance with NEPA has detracted from its larger purposes. Those purposes are not always served by procedural compliance alone. Bison management in greater Yellowstone is a case in point.

When the NEPA process was initiated in September 1989, it was expected to culminate in a long-term Interagency Bison Management Plan in 1991. Instead, state and federal agencies repeatedly postponed the draft EIS and managed Yellowstone bison under a series of interim management plans. Criticism increased from many directions. In 1997, for example, Mike Clark, executive director of the Greater Yellowstone Coalition, concluded, "Our appointed and elected officials have been unable and unwilling to even sit down together and talk meaningfully about the conflict, much less reach agreement."[13] Early in 1998, Governor Jim Geringer of Wyoming stated, "We are no closer to resolution of the brucellosis problem with the different agencies of the federal government than we were ten years ago."[14] The *Bozeman Daily Chronicle* later that year drew attention to the costs: "All that blood in the snow has attracted national media attention and pitted neighbor against neighbor in this area. It has fattened the wedge that divides the ranching industry and environmentalists, groups that in a more rational world would become natural allies. It has cost money, sweat and anguish." The *Chronicle* concluded, "The ten-year shouting match has gone on far too long. It's time to make a decision."[15]

In June 1998, the state of Montana, the National Park Service, and the U.S. Forest Service as lead agencies, together with APHIS as a cooperating agency, released the draft EIS.[16] It listed seven alternatives, all of which called for more research and development of a safe, effective brucellosis vaccine for bison. The agencies' preferred alternative authorized capture and testing of bison north and west of the Park, slaughter of brucellosis-positive animals, quarantine of brucellosis-negative animals, and limited public hunting to keep the number of Yellowstone bison between 1,700 and 2,500 animals. The situation was summed up in a workshop in September 1998: "Where does this leave us? With options from separation of wildlife and livestock for risk management to eradication of brucellosis, and intermediate options like control of the Park boundary and control through hunting. We are caught in a litigation loop—each official plan generates lawsuits. We need extremely high-level politics to intervene to break out of the litigation loop."[17] *Why* "extremely high-level politics" had not intervened was an important but unanswered question. Litigation is indeed a major alternative to the NEPA process when officials or citizens are frustrated within the NEPA process or are excluded from it. There have been at least a dozen lawsuits on bison management and brucellosis in greater Yellowstone since 1985.[18]

The one-hundred-twenty-day public comment period on the draft EIS closed early in November 1998. Of the 67,520 comment documents received, about 70 percent endorsed a Citizens' Plan to Save Yellowstone Bison that had been formulated and promoted by a coalition of conservation groups. The groups took the initiative because they believed that they had been excluded from the formulation of the alternatives in the draft EIS. Following analysis of public comments received, the federal agencies proposed a "modified preferred alternative" for the final EIS. Discussions of that alternative led to an impasse between federal and state agencies and to the federal agencies' withdrawal from a Memorandum of Understanding that had been signed with the state of Montana in 1992 and incorporated into the settlement of Montana's lawsuit against the federal agencies in 1995. The federal and state agencies nevertheless agreed to attempt to resolve their differences through a court-appointed mediator. Mediation in the spring, summer, and fall of 2000 led to a slightly altered version of the modified preferred alternative that is called the Joint Management Plan in the record of decision on the final EIS.[19] The record of decision, dated December 20, 2000, culminated the NEPA process begun more than a decade earlier.

Despite the stated purpose of NEPA and the considerable resources invested over that time, there has been little progress in finding common ground. The Joint Management Plan is less a resolution of the different interests represented by the state and federal agencies than another truce among them—prompted perhaps by exhaustion as much as anything else. Moreover, among the 3,888 who submitted public comments on the final EIS, nearly half objected to the deference given to cattle over Yellowstone's bison. According to the record of decision, "The majority of commentors expressing opinions on this subject (1,800 v. 2) indicated that it should be cattle rather than bison that are moved or managed to prevent contact and possible transmission of brucellosis. Part of the value of the herd to commentors was in its wild and free-ranging nature. Management practices such as capture, testing, slaughter, quarantine, corralling, radio collars, vaginal transmitters, etc. were considered antithetical to the concept of a wild herd by many commentors. Many (1,458) felt that all slaughter should be stopped."[20] Thus the central issue between the agencies' Joint Implementation Plan and a large part of the active public also remains unresolved.

Was there a better alternative, substantively and procedurally? A case can be made that a plan proposed in 1991 by the Bison Management Citizen's Working Group in Bozeman might have avoided much of the divisiveness and expense and made some progress toward a resolution—if federal and state officials had taken the plan seriously.[21] This proposal came closer in several ways to finding the common ground. Procedurally, the plan was the result of more inclusive deliberations by representatives of conservation, environmental, ranching, landowner, wildlife, sporting, and other interests in the greater Yellowstone area. The deliberations, which took place in weekly meetings over several months, were informed by the local knowledge of the representatives and by Native American and technical advisers. Substantively, the members of the Working Group signed off on the plan when they recommended it to the Superintendent of Yellowstone National Park in a letter dated May 15, 1991.[22] They expected the plan to secure the common interest—which included, significantly, preventing brucellosis in cattle *and* maintaining free-roaming bison herds as much as possible. Practically, however, we do not know whether these expectations were valid, because the plan was not implemented, or even seriously considered, by the public officials who were nevertheless in procedural compliance with NEPA. But management techniques like those proposed by the Working Group had already worked around Yellowstone and Grand Teton National Parks in Wyoming. According to ranchers and conservationists living there, Wyoming's brucellosis-free status "is secure now because there is no recent history of brucellosis transmission from wildlife to cattle in [their] counties and because the ranchers in this area protect their cattle through vaccinations."[23]

The bison management problem is a microcosm of larger problems of governance in the United States: the failure to clarify and secure the common interest through specific policies in natural resources as well as in other policy areas. In the American political tradition, it is difficult both logically and politically to justify policies that serve the special interests of the few over the common interest of the many. Contemporary Americans still accept Lincoln's commitment to "government of the people, by the people, and for the people" as a reference to all the people, not the select few. Similarly, Americans still pledge "liberty and justice for all," not for the select few. Under the doctrine of equal rights for all, Americans who demand fair consideration of their own interests cannot legitimately deny fair consideration to other, often competing, interests.[24] This is compatible with a commitment to human dignity for all, as expressed in the Declaration of Independence of the thirteen states of America in 1776 and in the Universal Declaration of Human Rights of the United Nations in 1948. In short: "The ideal of human dignity takes the entire body politic into consideration. It is not a matter of giving a privileged few their freedom of choice but of striking a balance among the claims of all."[25] But the common interest is now increasingly difficult to find within the complex division of authority and control among numerous parts of the federal government with distinctive mandates and jurisdictions, their counterparts in state and local governments, and the nongovernmental groups that lobby and litigate for particular economic, environmental, and other interests. This state of affairs motivates various kinds of initiatives aimed at improving governance and provides a comparative baseline for evaluating them.

The purpose of this book is to assist policy makers in improving natural resources policy and governance from a common-interest standpoint, through inquiry into the practical experience and potential of community-based initiatives like the Bison Management Citizen's Working Group in Bozeman. A community-based initiative is composed of participants representing quite different interests who interact directly with one another over a period of time, in an effort to resolve an issue in the place where they live.[26] Within the broader context of established structures of governance—including interest groups, political parties, government agencies, legislatures, and the courts—the small scale and issue focus of a community-based initiative open up new opportunities for participants to balance or integrate their separate interests into policy that advances their common interest. For example, participants can engage one another face-to-face more easily and creatively, with a minimum of a priori constraints on procedures and outcomes. They can draw more upon local frustrations, knowledge, and leadership, among other resources at their disposal. And they can rely more upon collaborative strategies instead of adversarial ones. But no specific characteristic is clearly necessary or sufficient for the success of any particular initiative, and there is no fixed formula for the success of every initiative. Participants may or may not find a policy that advances their common interest, but the small scale and issue focus mean that they are more likely to accept responsibility for outcomes and to be held accountable by others within and outside the community. Avoiding the consequences of those outcomes, or hiding from others, are not realistic options short of moving out of the community.

If participants in a community-based initiative do succeed in finding a policy that advances their common interest, the initiative can mobilize support as the voice of the people on behalf of that policy within the broader context of governance in the United States. This support is often necessary to acquire formal authority and other resources to implement the policy. In this broader context, a community-based initiative functions as an interest group, but it is one that represents an integration or balance among the multiple interests of a relatively small, place-based community. Thus it is a "multiple-interest group," as distinguished from the conventional "single-interest group."[27] An increased focus on community-based initiatives is justified by their significant potential to provide working solutions to problems of governance in our time. It should be emphasized at the outset, however, that some community-based initiatives will fail to advance the common interest of their own communities or larger communities; that alternatives to community-based initiatives sometimes may be preferred under the common-interest criterion; and that there can be no complete or permanent solution to problems of governance, especially amid changing social conditions that undermine old formulas for governance and generate new problems.

This chapter provides a rationale for the focus on community-based initiatives. The next section develops the concept of the common interest as the appropriate aim of governance in a democracy. Subsequent sections introduce conventional structures of governance in the American experience, review current problems of governance in America, and consider community-based initiatives among other reforms to ameliorate those problems. The chapters that follow elaborate problems of governance and the potential of community-based initiatives as working solutions through four case studies, including the case of bison management in greater Yellowstone. Harvesting experience from these cases and others, the concluding chapter suggests how the potential of community-based initiatives might be realized through changes in various policies—in particular, policies of participants in community-based initiatives and their supporters, interest groups organized in and around government agencies, and the researchers and educators who advise and train the others. These are the principal policy makers we hope to assist in improving natural resources policy and governance on behalf of the common interest.[28]

The Common Interest

In the simplest terms, the common interest is composed of interests widely shared by members of a community. It would benefit the community as a whole and be supported by most community members, if they can find it. By definition, a special interest is incompatible with the common interest. It is pursued by some part of the community for its own benefit, at net cost to the community as a whole.[29] The continuing task of governance—in any community that respects equal rights for all—is finding common ground on policies that advance the common interest. Of course, not all interests are equally valid or appropriate in clarifying the common interest; claims regarding the common interest depend on the specific context; and disputed claims are typically resolved by political means—not by the partial tests of the common interest like those reviewed below. But despite such complications, at least a tentative commitment to the common interest—or some alternative—is logically necessary to provide direction for natural resources policies and governance and to evaluate improvements in them relative to historical baselines. Any alternative commitment ought to be made explicit for consideration by other members of a democratic community.

To develop this notion of the common interest, let us begin with a basic question: What are "interests"? If the interests of community members are misconstrued as carved in stone—indivisible and immutable, like a monolith—the flexibility needed for finding the common interest is not apparent, and the whole notion seems absurd. To illustrate flexibility, reconsider the statement of Mike Gilsdorf, the APHIS spokesman, as an expression of an interest: "We have our own mandate just like the park has theirs, and ours is to eliminate brucellosis. . . . If we drop our guard and let the diseased bison roam freely out in the countryside, we're inviting trouble." This statement demands something of value from Gilsdorf's perspective—that is, the elimination of brucellosis, or zero tolerance of the disease. The value demand is supported by matter-of-fact expectations: Gilsdorf does not expect the elimination of brucellosis to be realized if diseased bison roam freely; presumably he does expect it to be realized through "an integrated strategy of vaccination, testing, and the removal of test-positive animals" as proposed earlier by APHIS officials.[30] Gilsdorf claims that this is an interest shared with others who are identified with APHIS—the "we" in the statement—and not Gilsdorf's alone. Similarly, any other interest may be shared to some extent or not, and it can be broken down into value demands and supporting expectations for evaluation: Is the value demand appropriate in terms of the larger goal values of the community? Are the supporting expectations valid in terms of the evidence available? To what extent is the interest shared? Raising these questions underscores the importance of flexibility in the reconsideration of interests.

Changing circumstances may also lead to the reconsideration of interests. APHIS's core interest in the elimination of brucellosis is no exception. After the bison killings in the winter of 1996–97, the Council on Environmental Quality (CEQ) in the White House began to coordinate the policies of "the federal family" of relevant agencies on behalf of the Clinton administration. Under these circumstances, APHIS accepted a low-risk definition of brucellosis transmission—in effect, the expectation that *some* diseased bison are *unlikely* "to invite trouble" by transmitting brucellosis to cattle. These are bulls, calves, and cows with yearlings roaming on public land after cattle leave their grazing allotments in the fall and before cattle return in the spring. (Brucellosis may be transmitted only through the birthing materials of cows.) Evidently, APHIS officials accepted demands that its policies come into closer compliance with policies of the administration, a demand supported perhaps by expectations that noncompliance could result in budget cuts, loss of jurisdiction, or other costs to APHIS. Like other agencies, APHIS has multiple interests associated with its mandate, including interests in protecting its resource base. When the multiple interests of agencies come into conflict as circumstances change, they provide another basis for flexibility.

Action on an interest may have significant consequences for others, even if the consequences are unintended or indirect. Hence the persons and groups involved tend to take one another into account in formulating their own policies. In other words, they interact—and if they do so with sufficient frequency and intensity, they form a community. APHIS could not easily ignore certain political consequences of its zero-tolerance policy after the CEQ began to coordinate and enforce administration policy. The Park Service could not easily ignore certain unintended consequences of its natural regulation policy after livestock groups and the state of Montana objected, and especially after the state filed a lawsuit. Various citizens also joined the community as bison border crossings, shootings, and other consequences of interim bison management policies in greater Yellowstone became significant for whatever those citizens valued. The formation of a community around an issue does not mean that its members feel good about one another or identify with the community. It means that they are interdependent enough that they find it expedient, if not necessary, to take others into account.[31] When a community forms around an issue, there is a common interest at stake—whether or not members of the community can clarify and secure it through community policy.[32]

At the core of the bison management community are state and federal officials and private citizens in greater Yellowstone who persist in investing more of their time, attention, and other resources in the issue than other people, because they perceive themselves to have more at stake. A job may be at stake for officials and lobbyists paid to represent their employers' positions, for example, and basic moral responsibilities may be at stake for people like Rosalie Little Thunder or members of the Fund for Animals. But there is nothing fixed about the boundaries of the community. Events may activate peripheral interests that are distributed more broadly, inducing other people to interact enough with the core participants to become part of the community, at least temporarily. In this way, the killings of Yellowstone bison by officials in the winter of 1996–97 had the unintended consequence of expanding the community well beyond greater Yellowstone when the news media reported them: people across the United States as well as abroad protested, and the CEQ in Washington intervened and began to coordinate the federal family of agencies through periodic meetings. Similarly, the Citizens' Plan crafted and promoted by the coalition of conservation groups in greater Yellowstone had the intended consequence of expanding the community involved in the issue: the Plan catalyzed the support of about 47,000 people who commented on the draft EIS in 1998.

Expansion of the community around such an issue raises the possibility that the common interest expressed in a policy proposed by the local community may differ from the common interest perceived by larger national or even international communities. Under these circumstances, which of "the people" should prevail? It is often assumed that the larger community should prevail on democratic grounds: if the policy in question affects interests outside the local community— especially the public lands in which all Americans have an ownership interest—then they ought to participate in making the policy decision.[33] But this is clearly an ideal that cannot be realized in practice. Everyone is affected by so many policy decisions, public and private, that no one can possibly participate in more than a small fraction of them. Moreover, not everyone's interests are equally affected by a given policy decision, and not everyone is equally competent to participate in it. So each of us economizes by participating only selectively in those accessible decisions where we have the most at stake and perhaps where we have some minimal competence as well.[34] In short, no democratic association can include all affected interests in its decision process, or even come close; any attempt to do so would lead to coerced participation and gridlock.

Which of "the people" should prevail? No theoretical answer is satisfactory in all cases. "The Principle of Affected Interests is very likely the best general principle of inclusion that you are likely to find," according to the noted political scientist Robert A. Dahl. "Yet it turns out to be a good deal less compelling than it looks." For reasons outlined above, "it seems obvious that the Principle of Affected Interests must be curbed by the criteria of Competence and Economy."[35] There are only pragmatic answers involving multiple forms of democratic association at different scales appropriate to the context. In the first of four pragmatic principles, however, Dahl concludes that "if a matter is best dealt with by a democratic association, seek always to have that matter dealt with by the smallest association that can deal with it satisfactorily."[36] That tends to maximize competence and economy in the making of policy decisions—both important considerations amid the growing number and complexity of issues—if the smallest association does, in fact, deal with the issue satisfactorily. If the smallest association does not, dissidents have the incentive and opportunity to expand the issue by seeking additional support from a larger community. Conversely, if a larger association does not deal with an issue satisfactorily, dissidents in the smaller community also have the incentive and opportunity to expand the issue. This is what the coalition of conservation groups did in 1998, when it promoted the Citizens' Plan to Save Yellowstone Bison in opposition to alternative plans negotiated by representatives of state and federal governments. Issue expansion is an informal supplement to formal mechanisms of democratic accountability, such as elections and bureaucratic controls.[37]

In summary, there is a common interest at stake whenever people who act on their perceived interests also interact enough to form a community around an issue. But their perceived interests may be inappropriate or invalid in some instances, and their interests are subject to reconsideration through evaluation and confrontation with other interests as circumstances change. Hence, there is some flexibility to reconsider their separate individual interests and to find their common interest. The common interest, however, comprises interests shared by members of a community and cannot be taken as fixed or given or assumed. The common interest can only be clarified in the particular context through community decision processes, secured insofar as is practical through community policies, and taken as provisional pending changes in the interests and circumstances of community members. There is no objective or infallible formula for assessing the common interest in the particular context, just as there are no objective or infallible formulas for assessing justice, or the general welfare, or democracy.[38] But there are various partial tests, requiring judgment in applications, that may be used to discipline subjective assessments in particular contexts. Sufficient for present purposes are three tests of the common interest—procedural, substantive, and practical—that are imprudent to ignore and easy to apply.[39]

The procedural test recognizes that inclusive and responsible participation in the decision process serves the common interest. To apply it, consider whether the effective participants (officials and non-officials alike) are representative of the community as a whole. If not, community policy is less likely to reflect the interests of those excluded and is less likely to realize the potential for creative reconsideration inherent in the diversity of interests. Consider also whether the effective participants are responsible, in the sense that they are willing and able to serve the community as a whole, and can be held accountable for the consequences of their decisions. If not, these participants may serve various parts of the community at the expense of the community as a whole—contrary to the common interest. In bison management, the effective decision makers have been federal and state officials who formulate and approve bison management plans under the NEPA process. The litigation loop is evidence that some persons and groups in the civic sector considered themselves underrepresented in the NEPA process, and perhaps excluded from it, even though they also perceived themselves to have a lot at stake—enough to pay the opportunity costs of time, attention, and other resources diverted from interests other than bison management. They have been unable to hold the officials accountable for more than a decade.

The substantive test recognizes that the common interest depends on the valid and appropriate interests of community members. To apply it, consider whether a person's or a group's expectations are warranted by the evidence available. If not, discount the interest as assumed or invalid. An interest in eradicating brucellosis from wildlife in the greater Yellowstone area appears to be invalid if a conclusion of the National Research Council is correct: "It might prove impossible for various reasons to eliminate brucellosis from bison and elk" in greater Yellowstone.[40] An interest in preventing transmission of brucellosis from wildlife to cattle is valid if the experience reported by ranchers and conservationists in northwestern Wyoming is correct. Consider also whether the value demand is compatible with more comprehensive goals. If not, discount the interest as an inappropriate special interest. Zero-tolerance demands are inappropriate—whether for brucellosis in wildlife or for grazing allotments on public lands—if taken literally as demands to be sought without regard to costs in terms of other community values. It is not rational to ignore costs. Advocates of zero-tolerance demands also presume the power necessary to impose those costs on the community as a whole. It is not democratic to do so. Finally, consider whether participants representative of the community as a whole have signed off on a policy, indicating their expectation that the policy serves the common interest. If not, the reasons for rejections may signal a need for improvement from a common-interest standpoint. But the common interest does not require unanimity. "Unanimity is a euphemism for minority veto power, in which the negative decision of one community member enforces policies on all."[41]

The practical test recognizes that the common interest depends upon experience that corroborates the expectations of community members who approved the policy. Even a policy formulated through an inclusive process and accepted by an inclusive range of responsible participants may fail to corroborate expectations that it serves the common interest: like any person or group, the community as a whole may be mistaken about the expected consequences or the value demands integrated into a policy, and the mistakes may become apparent only through the experience that follows implementation of the policy. To apply the practical test, consider the experience that follows implementation in order to identify opportunities for improvements: Where are the remaining opportunities to make participation in the decision process more representative and more responsible to the community as a whole? What interests should be discounted as no longer valid or appropriate? What emerging or otherwise neglected interests should be integrated into the next community policy? As these questions suggest, specific opportunities to advance the common interest are assessed at the margin relative to a concrete baseline in the particular context—and not according to abstract ideals like the principle of affected interests that cannot be realized in any context. It is a matter of improvement, not perfection. Whatever the answers in the particular context, it is clear that the common interest is part of a continuous process of "balancing, accommodating and integrating the rich diversity of culture, class, interest and personality that characterizes the earth-space arena" as a whole, and many smaller arenas as well, including bison management.[42]

These tests are not to be applied mechanically, as if they were necessary or sufficient to assess the common interest.[43] Competent and responsible people can arrive at different judgments about the common interest in a particular context like bison management in greater Yellowstone, even if they apply the same tests to the information available. The most fundamental reason is that each of us is boundedly rational at best: no one has the reasoning capacity and all the information necessary to understand the context completely, completely objectively, or once and for all. Each of us can only make a simplified judgment based on limited perspectives and information.[44] The implication is not to give up the search for the common interest on the fallacious assumption that anything goes if *nobody* knows for sure.[45] "Anything goes" is hardly acceptable policy to those who have much at stake. Furthermore, the implication is not to accept zero-tolerance policy on the fallacious assumption that *somebody* knows for sure. Such policy is hardly acceptable to those who pay the exorbitant costs. Moreover, policy can be improved through inquiry and deliberation, in which differences among various informed judgments are integrated if possible and balanced if necessary in shaping community policy. This is "politics" in the best sense.

The notion of the common interest reviewed above is not merely academic. Something much like it emerged spontaneously from a discussion of the common interest by practitioners in a workshop on governance and natural resources in Jackson, Wyoming, in September 1998. The practitioners represented various professional perspectives, including forestry, environmental studies, law, mediation, psychiatry, and wildlife management. Workshop organizers, including the author, deliberately left the common interest open to interpretation in the letter of invitation: "The purpose of the Workshop is to develop better models for the governance of natural resources, based upon recent experience in selected cases. A better model is one that helps clarify and secure the common interest (not the special interests) of all those who are significantly involved in a specific issue."[46] The discussion occurred just after the summary conclusion, "We are caught in a litigation loop in bison management." This discussion is reconstructed in Figure 1.1 with comments numbered sequentially in brackets and identities disguised in accord with Workshop rules.[47]

At the beginning of the discussion, APHIS's demand for zero risk of brucellosis through eradication of brucellosis from wildlife is described in effect as a special interest: "So long as APHIS imposes their idea of the problem on everyone, no one else can realize their interest" [1]. After some clarification of APHIS's interest, the common interest is defined in the abstract: "It's the intersection of all the individual interests you are talking about" [4]. Moreover, it's "not a thing; it's a journey. It's a discovery process, achieving things communally, not individually. The intersection might be the common interest at one point in time" [5]. Then a procedural test is applied in response to the claim that "the NEPA process is divisive" [5]: "Some interests are excluded. They are assumed to be untrustworthy" [6]. A substantive test is recognized in the comment that "some interests are not valid" [7] and that the validity of interests depends on "what problem needs to be solved" [8]. Unanimity is not required: "There will always be some special interests that cannot be satisfied. You don't need everyone . . . but you

Figure 1.1. Practitioners Discuss the Common Interest in Bison Management

[1] A: Brucellosis is not the problem. The problem is the brucellosis-free stamp. The stamp is controlled by APHIS. APHIS says zero-risk of brucellosis is required for the stamp. . . . So long as APHIS imposes their idea of the problem on everyone, no one else can realize their interest. It's okay for people to disagree on the problem definition and have their own problems.

[2] B: There is some creeping incrementalism here. The administration is cracking down on APHIS. The presence of bison or elk is no longer enough to threaten [removal of brucellosis-free status]. What's behind APHIS's position? They have a successful mechanism [test and slaughter] for eradication of brucellosis from livestock, and they want to be part of completing the job. It was supposed to be completed in 1998. Test and slaughter is technically feasible for wildlife, but you would have to get every infected animal, and it could take 12 years even in a smaller park. Custer State Park went from 3,000 to 600 bison. Will the public accept it? It might cost $30 million a year in Yellowstone National Park.

[3] C: What is the common interest—as opposed to the set of interests that comprise the public interest? Not an eternal truth, but a social construct that evolves over time.

[4] A: It's the intersection of all the individual interests you are talking about.

[5] D: The common interest is not a thing; it's a journey. It's a discovery process, achieving things communally, not individually. The intersection might be the common interest at one point in time. A linear process [like NEPA] doesn't work. When the government opens up an EIS, it's like a jack-in-the-box—people pop up. The draft EIS is a pretense. The NEPA process is divisive.

[6] E: Some interests are excluded. They are assumed to be untrustworthy.

[7] C: The common interest is not the sum of all interests. Some interests are not valid. Who gets to decide which interests are valid and which are not?

[8] A: The common interest doesn't have much meaning outside specific managerial issues. Which interests are valid? Ask what problem needs to be solved. [Then consider which interests can blow up the deal to solve the problem.] If they can blow up the deal, they should be at the table.

[9] F: There will always be some special interests that cannot be satisfied. You don't need everyone from every special interest, but you do need a critical mass or you can't claim that what you are doing is in the common interest. You don't have it if someone can block it.

[10] G: The difficulties come in applying the common-interest concept. For example, who specifically is in a position to block implementation?

[11] H: A's idea of "the common interest" excludes the powerless, voiceless, disenfranchised. [A agrees.]

[12] I: The bison issue will go on and on until the power structure changes. Then it might be solved. [He calls into question NEPA.]

[13] J: People will accept a decision if they feel they have been heard.

[14] K: Power is giving support.

[15] B: The stockgrowers stand hard and fast—theirs is the only way they will accept. The interests involved are unbounded. They include the futures market, and so forth, but global economic interests are largely irrelevant—only a few hundred thousand [dollars per year]. This issue will be decided at the local level. But arguments don't matter, so long as APHIS won't budge.

[16] A: The facts of the case are understood. The problem is that they don't matter. Ranchers have latched on to the bison issue because it's something they can do something about, keeping bison from leaving the Park. They can't control cattle being shipped from Canada or decreasing demand for beef. But the industry thinks it can keep the bison in the Park.

[17] B: APHIS has accepted all of the alternatives in the draft EIS. Montana is no longer afflicted by the conflicting policies of two federal agencies [the Park Service and APHIS]. Now Montana is victimized by veterinarians in other states [who put restriction on imports of Montana beef].

[18] J: The real problem is that Montana stockgrowers feel powerless. [A agrees.]

[19] F: Get the feds out of the room. Give the stockgrowers total control, but don't let them focus exclusively on brucellosis. What if four meetings were scheduled for the Montana stockgrowers to talk about their four biggest problems without feds in the room? They could be required not to talk about bison except in one meeting. Let brucellosis be first. Demonstrate to them that others are concerned about them. Set up a parallel structure outside the existing structure. Don't use the existing one. The existing one may not be working.

[20] A: I agree with F's proposal. But it needs a convenor, and leadership. The problem with this idea is that we need a convenor—someone who can get everyone to come.

Source: See Chap. 1, n. 17.

do need a critical mass or you can't claim that what you are doing is in the common interest" [9]. A practical test comes up in the subsequent effort to identify opportunities for improvement with respect to the common interest, based on assessments of experience to date. "The real problem is that Montana stockgrowers feel powerless" [18]. The proposed solution is: "Get the feds out of the room. Give the stockgrowers total control, but don't let them focus exclusively on brucellosis" [19]. The proposed solution depends on stockgrowers' other interests [15, 16] and on leadership [20].

A significant issue is left unresolved. The first practitioner asserted that participation should be inclusive of all those who can thwart an agreement: "If they can blow up the deal, they should be at the table" [8; see also 9, 10]. But another practitioner noted that this "idea of the common interest excludes the powerless, voiceless, disenfranchised," and the first practitioner agreed [11]. There are expedient as well as principled reasons why the weak and neglected should be included or represented within practical constraints. "The ultimate consequence of tacit nonrepresentation in promotional activities is to create a revolutionary crisis of explosive protest."[48] The short-term consequence may be lawsuits, civil disobedience, and other forms of protest. In bison management, as in other areas, leaders of interest groups organized in and around the agencies often prefer to deal with one another rather than with their constituents. The publication of a draft EIS does little to ameliorate the potential for protest or advance the stated purpose of NEPA if public comments are consistently ignored.

Structures of Governance

Clarifying and securing the common interest through policy decisions is the legitimate function and the criterion of governance in a democracy. Otherwise some interests of the people are arbitrarily excluded as a matter of principle.[49] In any case, communities tend to stabilize structures of governance for making policy decisions in order to provide a degree of efficiency and predictability if nothing else. It is inefficient, and an unnecessary roll of the dice, to decide anew how policy decisions should be made each time another policy problem arises. Structures of governance include such formal and informal institutions as legislatures and political parties, as well as any relatively stable arrangements for making policy decisions in civic (or nongovernmental) groups of any kind. Structures of governance should be evaluated according to their function, and reformed or replaced when they consistently fail to perform that function. At least in the Declaration of Independence it is presented as a self-evident truth that "governments are instituted among Men [to secure certain rights], deriving their just powers from the consent of the governed, That whenever any Form of Government becomes destructive of these ends, it is the Right of the People to alter or to abolish it, and to institute new Government."

This self-evident truth is still applied by Americans, including practitioners in the Jackson Workshop. Recall what was proposed toward the end of the discussion in Figure 1.1: "Get the feds out of the room. . . . Set up a parallel structure outside the existing structure. Don't use the existing one. The existing one may not be working" [19]. It is clear that the common interest in this context is used as the criterion for assessing the existing structure of governance established under NEPA and modified through the settlement of Montana's lawsuit in 1995. It was noted earlier that NEPA's linear process does not work: "When the government opens up an EIS, it's like a jack in the box—people pop up. The draft EIS is a pretense. The NEPA process is divisive" [5]. The common interest is also used here as the justification for an alternative structure in which stockgrowers' multiple interests might be represented more effectively and responsibly along with the interests of others. The existing and alternative structures provide different answers to the constitutive question raised earlier in the discussion: "Who gets to decide which interests are valid and which are not?" [7]. This question is answered by constitutive decisions—in other words, decisions about making policy decisions.

Constitutive decisions are most familiar to Americans through the U.S. Constitution, which merits brief review as background for understanding current problems of governance. The Preamble identifies the most basic and enduring common interest of the people: "We the people of the United States, in Order to form a more perfect Union, establish Justice, insure domestic Tranquility, provide for the common defence, promote the general Welfare, and secure the blessings of Liberty to ourselves and our posterity, do ordain and establish this Constitution for the United States of America." Thus the founders expected to provide for union, justice, and other basic demands of the people through the constitutive decisions that followed in the main body of the Constitution. Articles I, II, and III allocated power to make legislative, executive, and judiciary decisions, respectively, to a Congress that consists of a Senate and a House of Representatives, to a president, and to "one supreme Court" and inferior courts. This separation of powers allows for a system of checks and balances among the three branches of government: for example, the president may veto a bill passed by both houses of Congress, preventing it from becoming a law; but the veto may be overridden by a two-thirds majority vote of both houses. The system was extended in *Marbury v. Madison* in 1803, when the Supreme Court successfully asserted the power to determine the constitutionality of acts of the other two branches. As Madison explained in *The Federalist*, the system relied on the balancing of power to prevent abuses of power, including tyranny of the majority: if a faction pursuing its own interests impinged upon others, the other factions as a matter of self-interest would rise to block it. Thus the common interest is supposed to be served indirectly through the "invisible hand" of competition among factions pursuing their own narrow interests.

Dahl identified an important missing piece in this constitutive formula after summarizing its implications: "What constitutional separation of powers builds into the very center of government are pluralism, rivalry, competition, the representation in the executive and legislative branches of differing and possibly divergent interests, and as a consequence the strong likelihood that president and Congress will press for conflicting policies. What is missing, because the framers did not provide for it, is a constitutional process for readily resolving these conflicts."[50] The missing piece becomes more important as modernization proliferates interest groups and multiplies the number and complexity of issues over which they come into conflict. These issues need to be resolved on behalf of the common interest, which is not limited to preventing abuses of power. The common interest in general also includes various means for establishing justice, insuring domestic tranquility, promoting the general welfare, and the like.

The Constitution also divided powers between the federal government and the states, and made federalism more explicit in the Tenth Amendment: powers not delegated to the federal government are reserved to the states or to the people. The Constitution allocated to the people the power to elect their representatives, who in turn were empowered to make decisions on behalf of the people and to delegate power to officials duly appointed for that purpose. Thus the Constitution established institutions of representative democracy, but it did not entirely restrain the forces of direct democracy. "The government created by the Constitutional Convention had barely begun in 1789 before it began to be reshaped by democratic forces. As George Woods remarks, 'No constitution, no institutional arrangements, no judicial prohibitions could have restrained the popular forces unleashed by the Revolution.'"[51] The electoral college was only the first institution of representative democracy to be transformed to register the popular will more directly. Community-based initiatives are among the more recent manifestations of popular forces, as well as informal means for resolving conflicts. Eventually they might provide the missing piece in the constitutive formula, or some part of it.

The Constitution is the supreme law of the land: in principle all the countless public policy decisions made by Americans since 1789 fall within its jurisdiction. But in practice the Constitution must be elaborated and supplemented through additional constitutive decisions for countless specific policy contexts. For example, as noted above, since 1969 NEPA elaborates how the National Park Service and all other federal agencies must make policy decisions that significantly affect the environment. The Memorandum of Understanding incorporated into the settlement of Montana's 1995 lawsuit against federal agencies further elaborated how bison management decisions in the greater Yellowstone area were to be made, unless the parties withdrew or until they had a long-term plan in place. The Bison Management Citizen's Working Group in Bozeman and its successors established informal structures of governance to formulate their own bison management plans. Such informal and often uncodified constitutive decisions in the civic sector are part of the structure of governance, but not of the government.

Structures of governance help shape but do not determine specific policy decisions. Among other factors, competent and responsible people may overcome some of the limitations inherent in any formal structure of governance. Conversely, any formal structure in the hands of incompetent or irresponsible people can easily fail to clarify and secure the common interest. Certainly many of the countless policy decisions made within the constitutional framework over more than two hundred years have failed by this criterion, but enough have succeeded to sustain public faith in the Constitution as it evolves. Any structure of governance, however, may contribute to a crisis in governance and possible breakdown if it consistently fails to accommodate, through specific policy decisions, the emerging interests created by continuing modernization and other social changes. In general, "Breakdown is not the result of special interests dividing the community, but rather of the particular maladjustments which prevent compromise between these interests."[52] Similarly, crisis is not the result of conflict but of the failure of means for resolving conflicts.

These dynamics are familiar from American history. The Revolutionary War marked the breakdown of the British colonial structure, which had failed to accommodate the distinctive demands and expectations that emerged as the king's subjects increasingly identified themselves with a new American community over the middle decades of the eighteenth century.[53] According to the Declaration of Independence itself, the break arose from a "history of repeated injuries and usurpations, all having in direct object the establishment of an absolute tyranny over these States" by the king of England. First of all, "He has refused his Assent to Laws, the most wholesome and necessary for the public good." The Civil War marked the breakdown of a constitutional structure that could not resolve slavery and related issues. It unleashed democratic forces that abolished slavery through the Thirteenth Amendment (1865), extended citizenship to all persons born or naturalized in the United States through the Fourteenth Amendment (1868), and prohibited denial or abridgement of the right to vote on account of race, color, or previous condition of servitude through the Fifteenth Amendment (1870). Following Reconstruction, structures of governance that had served Americans for most of the nineteenth century were undermined further by industrialization, urbanization, and concurrent changes in social conditions and replaced over several decades by the federal bureaucracy so prominent today. A brief review provides further background for understanding current problems of governance.

During most of the nineteenth century, communications and transportation technologies severely restricted interactions among isolated local communities and effectively dispersed the power to make public policy decisions. According to the historian Robert Wiebe, "The heart of American democracy was local autonomy. . . . Americans could not even conceive of a managerial government. Almost all of a community's affairs were still arranged informally."[54] Political parties and the courts were adapted to the structure of local autonomy and provided for the minimal needs of governance at the national level. Strikingly, even the mobilization of resources for the Civil War depended on the Republican Party: "The great northern war machine was first and foremost a new party machine."[55] But by 1877, the autonomy of local communities had already eroded through the extension of telegraphs, railroads, and other modernizing technologies. These technologies supported organization and operations on larger scales and intensified conflicts between labor and capital, competing capitalists, and populists and progressives, among others. Established elites struggled in the 1880s and 1890s to defend their power positions in the obsolescing structure. Contending elites exploited specific emergent problems to create new institutions, but they "could not sustain support for any effort that threatened to undermine long-established political and institutional relationships."[56]

A new structure emerged rather quickly after the turn of the century. Congress, the presidency, courts, political parties, and local governments were not abolished, of course, but their roles and relationships were transformed as the unmet needs of a changing society supported expansion of the federal bureaucracy. Wiebe summarized "America's initial experiment in bureaucratic order": "By contrast to the personal, informal ways of the community, the new scheme was derived from the regulative, hierarchical needs of urban-industrial life. Through rules with impersonal sanctions, it sought continuity and predictability in a world of endless change. It assigned far greater power to government—in particular, to a variety of flexible administrative devices—and it encouraged the centralization of authority. Men were now separated more by skill and occupation than by community; they identified themselves more by their tasks in an urban-industrial society than by their reputations in a town or a city or a neighborhood."[57] Pressures for reform were expressed in the withering of party machinery and judicial restrictions on action by government, as well as in the Sixteenth Amendment (1913), authorizing Congress "to lay and collect taxes on incomes," and the Eighteenth Amendment (1919), prohibiting the "manufacture, sale, or transportation of intoxicating liquors." Democratic forces were manifest once again in the Seventeenth Amendment (1913), which provided for direct popular election of the Senate, and in the Nineteenth Amendment (1920), which provided suffrage for women.

There was no grand design in this experiment: the new bureaucratic order emerged from a patchwork of specific institutional reforms. The result was "a hapless confusion of institutional purposes, authoritative controls, and governmental boundaries."[58] The experiment was still under way as the nation passed through World War I and into the 1920s. Expansion of the federal bureaucracy accelerated in the 1930s and 1940s to cope with the problems of the Great Depression and World War II, and again in the 1960s in pursuit of the Great Society. "Yet," according to Stephen Skowronek, "the course of institutional development during these more recent decades and the governmental problems encountered in these developments are rooted in this turn-of-the-century departure." These developments "established a new institutional politics at the national level that has proven remarkably resistant to fundamental change.[59]

A structure resistant to fundamental change becomes vulnerable eventually to its own excesses and to changing social conditions. Modernizing technologies are the major factors behind changing social conditions in our time. Through modernizing technologies, "thousands of technical operations have sprung into existence where a few hundred were found before. To complicate the material environment in this way is to multiply the foci of attention of those who live in our society. Diversified foci of attention breed differences in outlook, preference, and loyalty. The labyrinth of specialized 'material' environments generates profound ideological divergences that cannot be abolished, though they can be mitigated, by the methods now available to leaders in our society."[60] For more Americans over successive generations, the material environment common to the nineteenth-century farm has given way to many more specialized environments associated with specialized skills and occupations in cities here and abroad. At the same time, farm environments have become much more differentiated by the deployment of new agricultural technologies.

The effect is to multiply divisions among interests in society and to organize those interests to compete in a more complex society. "Concerted action under such conditions depends upon skillfully guiding the minds of men [and women]; hence the enormous importance of symbolic manipulation in modern society."[61] But effective symbolic politics depend on trust, and trust in central authorities tends to erode as society becomes more complex.[62] Among other things, central authorities find it more difficult to meet public expectations as more agencies and interest groups are organized and able to block each other more often. Citizens find it more difficult to identify the remote officials and non-officials most responsible for policies that affect their interests and to hold them accountable amid the growing number and complexity of issues. Twentieth-century technologies—including airplanes, radio, television, satellites, fiber optics, computers, and the internet—continue to support the proliferation of agencies, interest groups, and complex issues, to interconnect them on a global scale, and concurrently to erode bureaucratic structures and control.[63] As in the nineteenth century, one important effect is to undermine structures of governance adapted to an earlier era.

Current Problems

President Ronald Reagan brought current problems of governance to national attention in his first inaugural address in January 1981. After noting that "the economic ills we suffer have come upon us over several decades," the president delivered a memorable line honed in numerous speeches over nearly two decades: "In this present crisis, government is not the solution to our problem; government is the problem." Moments later he added some reassurance that "it is not my intention to do away with government. It is rather to make it work—with us, not over us; to stand by our side, not ride on our back." He went on to affirm that governance in the common interest is not a matter of government alone. "All of us together—in and out of government—must bear the burden. The solutions we seek must be equitable with no one group singled out to pay a higher price."[64]

President Bill Clinton largely accepted this assessment of current problems in his state of the union address in January 1996: "We know big government does not have all the answers. We know there's not a program for every problem. . . . The era of big government is over."[65] No doubt the president expected his memorable line to resonate with public opinion and therefore to help in his campaign for reelection that year. Public opinion polls show that the proportion of Americans who "think you can trust the government in Washington to do what is right" either "always" or "most of the time" was less than one-quarter throughout the 1990s—down from about three-quarters in the early 1960s. The unprecedented period of prosperity during the Clinton administration dulled the emotional edge of public distrust of the government in Washington, but it did not eliminate it. At the beginning of a new century, it still seems obvious to casual and close observers alike that "Americans have lost faith in the capacity of government to solve the problems that worry them most."[66]

Close observers have described current problems of American government in a variety of overlapping ways. Perhaps the most common is "gridlock," a term that was well established by 1992.[67] It refers to government's inability to act on major national issues, such as health care reform. Gridlock is often but not always a problem in a changing society that undermines old policy solutions and generates new policy problems. Perhaps the most vivid description is "demosclerosis," a term introduced by the journalist Jonathan Rauch to refer to the hardening of the arteries of democratic government: "Government loses its capacity to experiment and so becomes more and more prone to failure. That is demosclerosis: postwar government's progressive loss of the ability to adapt."[68] Underlying gridlock and demosclerosis is the "single-issue politics" cited by Dale Bumpers on retiring from the U.S. Senate after twenty-four years. In his view, single-issue politics emerged in the 1970s from rules that opened committee votes to public scrutiny and from the proliferation of national associations, "right down to the beekeepers and mohair producers." "These groups developed very harsh methods of dealing with those who have crossed them," Bumpers argued. "Suddenly, every vote [now taken in public] began to have political consequences. Congress began to finesse the tough issues and tended to straddle every fence it couldn't burrow under. Consequently, Congress is failing to get its work done. . . . I don't know which was worse: the way the Government was shut down in 1995 or the way we kept it open in 1998." In 1998, Congress kept the government open by folding eight of thirteen appropriations bills "into a $550 billion omnibus bill that was drafted and agreed to not by Congress itself, but by six or eight senior members and a few White House staffers."[69]

Robert Samuelson refers to the growing separation of the Washington political community from the rest of the country as a "disconnect," which he characterized as one of the defining trends of his three decades as a journalist in Washington. This disconnect is partly a consequence and partly a cause of the other problems described above: "Except in token ways, Democrats can't create new programs and Republicans can't cut taxes. Barred from genuine action, politicians become more strident in their debates and more vicious in their personal attacks. They consort mostly with their own 'core constituencies' and sympathetic ideologues, deepening their isolation and illusions."[70]

Similarly, President Gerald Ford characterized modern elections as "candidates without ideas, hiring consultants without convictions to run campaigns without content"—a characterization that drew applause from members of the National Press Club.[71] Thomas Mann of the Brookings Institution summarizes the "Pathologies of the public sector" as "parochialism, special interest influence, [and] bureaucratic layering."[72] More precisely, these are pathologies of governance insofar as interest groups in the civic sector as well as agencies in the public sector are involved.

The structural roots of these problems can be found in the separation of powers in the constitutional formula and in the proliferation of interests organized in and around federal bureaucracies over the past century or more. The data suggest that "agencies come into existence in response to demands for service from politically mobilized segments of society, both inside and outside government."[73] The demands in turn are responses to modernizing technologies that continue to complicate material environments, multiply the foci of attention, and breed differences in interests. The creation of agencies is "spontaneous in the sense that it is governed by the internal dynamics of organizational life rather than by calculations and overall plan. The incessant, uncontrived division and subdivision of work gives many units their start."[74] The subdivision of work also led to exponential growth in the number of agencies of the federal government through at least 1973. In almost every presidential term since 1923, the number of federal agencies created was greater than the number terminated.[75]

The proliferation of organized interest groups in the civic sector also matters. The capacity of government agencies to meet the demands of politically mobilized segments of society depends on the agencies' ability to reassign resources of various kinds. But those resources energize persons and groups to pursue their interests by lobbying government agencies. "In time, a whole industry—large, sophisticated, and to a considerable extent self-serving—emerges and then assumes a life of its own. . . . As it grows, the steady accumulation of subsidies and benefits, each defended in perpetuity by a professional interest group, calcifies government."[76] The number of national associations, most of which lobby government sooner or later, doubled to about 23,000 from 1970 to 1990. Membership in the American Society of Association Executives, founded in 1920, increased sixfold to more than 20,000 during the same years.[77] What the associations do is more important than what they claim or believe, even if they are self-described "public interest" groups rather than for-profit groups. According to Rauch, "All groups, without exception, claim to be serving some larger good, and almost all believe it. And all groups, without exception, are lobbying for more of whatever it is that their members want, generally at the expense of non-members."[78] Whatever their members want is likely to be much narrower than the common interest.

The unintended effect is an increasingly fragmented and dysfunctional structure of governance at the national level. The proliferation of organized groups in the public and civic sectors makes it more difficult to integrate their interests into policies that advance the common interest, even where there is a will to do so. Among other things, the proliferation multiplies the number of contacts and complicates the mutual understanding necessary for cooperation. These difficulties are compounded by substantive and procedural constraints, like NEPA, that cumulate each time an interest group succeeds in protecting or advancing its interests through public law or policy. What is a success for that group may be more bureaucratic red tape for others. On the whole, this complex structure of groups and rules does more to frustrate than to satisfy those involved. A typical response is to adapt their strategies to the structure. Each frustrated group tends to focus on narrower if not zero-tolerance demands in order to maximize the political effectiveness of its limited resources. It tries to compete more effectively for resources from its constituencies with more unequivocal and irrevocable commitments to those narrower demands. And it tends to seek allies among other groups likewise burdened by stronger commitments to narrower demands. If they succeed in constructing a coalition, despite the difficulties, opposing groups are likely to respond to the threat in kind—reestablishing to some extent previous power ratios in the power-balancing process. Thus small changes in policy may be achieved at greater expense, resulting in more frustration all around. The "winners" may not be winners at all in a frank accounting of costs and gains. In any case, under these circumstances, it is not surprising to find more gridlock, demosclerosis, single-issue politics, disconnects, and related pathologies of governance.

Fragmented and dysfunctional structures tend to be replicated in specific policy areas. The major organizations involved in bison management in greater Yellowstone—with their different mandates and jurisdictions and their involvement concurrently in many other issues as well—provide a good example. The U.S. Department of the Interior was established in 1849 with the consolidation of four older offices. "Over the years . . . functions have been added and removed, so that its role has changed from that of general housekeeper for the Federal Government to that of custodian of the Nation's natural resources."[79]

The National Park Service was established within the Interior Department in 1916 with the purpose of "conserving unimpaired the natural and cultural resources and values of the National Park System for the enjoyment, education, and inspiration of this and future generations."[80] Yellowstone is only one of more than 370 national parks, monuments, and other units in that system. In 1939 the Bureau of Fisheries (1871) and the Bureau of Biological Survey (1885) were transferred to Interior to become the U.S. Fish and Wildlife Service, which now manages more than 94 million acres of land and water. In 1946 the General Land Office (1812) and the Grazing Service (1934) were consolidated to establish the Bureau of Land Management, which manages about 270 million acres of public land. Interior's National Biological Survey is also involved in bison management.

The U.S. Department of Agriculture became the eighth department of the federal government in 1889, when the powers and duties of its predecessor were significantly enlarged. The U.S. Forest Service was created in 1905, when the management of federal forest reserves (created in 1891) was transferred to Agriculture. Currently, "As set forth in law, its mission is to achieve quality land management under the sustainable, multiple-use concept to meet the diverse needs of people."[81] It manages 155 national forests, 20 national grasslands, and 8 land utilization projects on more than 191 million acres. Concerns about brucellosis were organized in the Cooperative States–Federal Brucellosis Eradication Program in 1934.[82] APHIS was reestablished by the secretary of agriculture in 1977 "to conduct regulatory and control programs to protect and improve animal and plant health for the benefit of man and the environment."[83] The Agricultural Research Service is also represented in bison management. The federal division of labor is replicated to some extent at the state level, in six agencies in Idaho, Montana, and Wyoming.[84] Bison management in greater Yellowstone is not in itself a major national issue, but at least thirteen federal and state agencies are significantly involved in it.

Problems of coordinating the principal federal and state agencies were acknowledged in the establishment of the Greater Yellowstone Interagency Brucellosis Committee (GYIBC) in 1995, by a Memorandum of Understanding among the governors of Idaho, Montana, and Wyoming and the secretaries of agriculture and the interior. They recognized that "responsible and socially acceptable management of brucellosis-affected wildlife requires effective cooperation, coordination, and sharing of resources among the member agencies and the citizens of the United States."[85] However, as its name implies, GYIBC focuses on brucellosis rather than on free-roaming bison, and effective participation is limited to member agencies. Similarly, the Council on Environmental Quality sought to coordinate the federal family of agencies involved in bison management after the bison killings in the winter of 1996–97. The Council was established within the executive office of the president by NEPA in 1969. "The Council develops policies which bring into productive harmony the Nation's social, economic, and environmental priorities, with the goal of improving the quality of Federal decision making."[86] There is still room for improving decision making on bison management, as indicated by the exorbitant time and other resources invested in reaching a truce among the agencies and by substantial opposition to the Joint Implementation Plan in public comments.

As previously noted, nineteen interest groups formed a coalition to support the Citizens' Plan to Save Yellowstone Bison as an alternative to the interagency plans in the draft EIS in 1998.[87] These groups had been organized over various decades but were activated by their opposition to interagency plans implemented or proposed in the 1990s. Among national organizations, the coalition includes the American Buffalo Foundation and the Intertribal Bison Cooperative, both focused on bison, as well as less specialized groups: Defenders of Wildlife, the National Parks and Conservation Association, the Natural Resources Defense Council, The Wilderness Society, and the National Wildlife Federation. Among regional groups, the coalition includes the Idaho, Montana, and Wyoming Wildlife Federations; the Gallatin Wildlife Association, Montana Audubon, Montana River Action Network, and Montana Wilderness Association; the Jackson Hole Conservation Alliance and Wyoming Water; the Bench Ranch and the Yellowstone Raft Company; and the Greater Yellowstone Coalition, which itself is a regional coalition "formed in 1983 by people concerned about the increasing fragmentation of Greater Yellowstone." It "includes over 7,500 individual and family members, and about 125 local, regional and national member organizations, as well as about 125 business and corporate members."[88] Despite the efforts of these coalitions in the civic sector, the Citizens' Plan remains only an unofficial alternative to the Joint Implementation Plan. An effort to integrate the Citizens' Plan into the official plan might require initiation of another EIS under NEPA or might violate the Federal Advisory Committee Act (FACA), which regulates participation by non-officials in federal policy decisions.[89]

In bison management, in short, participants of all kinds are trapped to a considerable extent in a complex structure of governance that institutionalizes conflict more than it facilitates the integration or balancing of different interests into consensus on policies that advance the common interest. In general, "Federal land management agencies are frequently caught in the middle. . . . Historical missions and practices have been severely eroded by new statutes, and new missions have been charted, but congressional directives often have held out little concrete guidance in concrete situations, and procedural requisites have proliferated. Interests over a wide spectrum forcibly argue that their conception of the public interest should prevail in the circumstances, and all sides are willing to resort to higher forums if dissatisfied with decisional results."[90] Voluminous and often vague congressional directives that respond to a wide spectrum of interests over time force the agencies to make policy in concrete circumstances. The volume of substantive and procedural requisites is manifest in 1,348 pages of closely packed type in Title 16 of the United States Code (1982 edition), virtually all of which is pertinent to the management of public natural resources.[91] It should not be assumed that these voluminous directives are consistent. In natural resources as in other policy areas, "technical rules of law are commonly created in sets of complementary opposites, of highly ambiguous and incomplete reference, to express all pluralistic interests."[92] And the number of pluralistic interests grows with modernization.

The cumulative complexity of this structure undermines one of its principal functions, accountability to "We, the people"—or realistically, those who have enough at stake and enough competence to participate in specific issues. Since the Progressive era at least, all major applications of the administrative management paradigm "emphasized the need for democratic accountability of departmental and agency officers to the President and central management agencies and through these institutions to the Congress," according to Ronald Moe of the Congressional Research Service. "The administrative management paradigm accepted as its fundamental premise that the government of the United States is a government of laws passed by the representatives of the people assembled in Congress. It is the constitutional responsibility of the President and his duly appointed and approved subordinates to see that these laws, wise and unwise, are implemented."[93] But which laws should subordinate officials implement in which contexts when the laws individually or collectively are voluminous, ambiguous, and come in complementary opposites? A case in point is the Forest Service's mandate to manage each of 183 national forests, grasslands, or land utilization projects for multiple uses—outdoor recreation, range, timber, watershed, and wildlife and fish uses. Another case is the complex of directives that applies specifically to bison management in greater Yellowstone and the agencies involved— at least fourteen acts of Congress and eleven Montana laws, in addition to numerous regulations and management policies.[94] And of the many conflicting demands made by interest groups, which ones should officials accommodate, in efforts to avoid litigation if nothing else?

Some officials in the field are immobilized by the expectation that compliance with any particular laws or interest-group demands would leave them vulnerable to many other laws or demands. But other officials who are less risk-averse act on their own best judgment in the particular context, in the expectation that eventual success might justify the actions taken; and that meanwhile oversight by superiors up the line will be sporadic at best, especially if superiors are overloaded with other responsibilities. But in either of these cases, *field officials make the important policy decisions* in concrete circumstances, amid pressures from all sides and above. Thus, as structures of governance become more complex, democratic accountability through the administrative management paradigm becomes more tenuous, and the historical justification for bureaucracy tends to be undermined. That justification included efficiency and equity through the impersonal application of unambiguous rules and goals that minimize discretion by officials and challenges by others. As Mark Sagoff put it, "A bureaucracy may implement clear political goals, but it is hopeless when it tries to resolve what are essentially political disputes."[95] Today, administrative problems tend to be political disputes in that effective solutions depend on the integration or balancing of pressures from all sides and above. The Bureau of Reclamation explained these political realities to its employees: "Today, anyone can delay or even stop your process by lobbying Congress, initiating court action, or rallying grass roots effort to oppose your action. You cannot take away their right to fight. Thus you need to pay attention to their issues and actively seek their participation and consent."[96] But such politicking lies beyond the formal authority of officials who are supposed to implement law and policy, not make them—and often beyond their training and skills in scientific management.[97]

Under these conditions, "The land manager's role is increasingly difficult."[98] That is an understatement. Forest Service chief Dombeck reportedly learned from his predecessor that "the chief of the Forest Service will be in trouble regardless of what he does, so he may as well be in trouble for things of his own choosing." His predecessor's three years in office were "marked by attacks from environmentalists and by hopeless efforts to win the confidence of the agency's old guard, which had openly protested his appointment and sabotaged his initiatives."[99] The chief's job has become vastly more complex with the proliferation of organized interests in and around the Forest Service over the decades. Today's Forest Service is less integrated internally, and more constrained externally, than yesterday's Forest Service.[100] The same can be said about the jobs of other top officials and other agencies, and about the Congress and the White House. Meanwhile, each appointed or elected official, like each citizen, still has only twenty-four hours of time and attention to invest each day and limited competence to cope with the issues of the day. Improvements in managing limited time and attention and voluminous knowledge and information can help. But they cannot fully compensate for problems of governance rooted in complex structures fostered by modernizing technologies.

Constitutive Reform

Problems of governance stimulate demands for constitutive reform in our time, just as they did a century ago. And just as they did a century ago, specific proposals for reform tend to be resisted by those who believe (mistakenly or not) that they have more to lose by risking reform than by defending established structures.[101] No single proposal for constitutive reform appears to be sufficient, given the nature and extent of current problems of governance, although many proposals do merit further consideration if not experimentation. A brief review of major proposals provides some background for considering the history and potential of community-based initiatives, which may be as promising as any other alternative for constitutive reform.[102]

Some proposals for reform attempt to make members of Congress and the president more accountable to the people and less accountable to special-interest groups that buy influence. Specific proposals include tightening disclosure rules and other restrictions on interest groups that lobby, closing loopholes in campaign-finance laws, and imposing term limits on members of Congress. But such reforms address the symptoms rather than the structural roots of governance problems. "If the main problem is in the political structure," as Dahl contends, then "term limits will do no more than change officials while leaving [the structure] still in place."[103] Similarly, within the structure, closing campaign-finance loopholes or tightening lobbying restrictions would not reduce candidates' demand for campaign contributions to win elections or the supply of contributions from special interests to lobby candidates and elected officials.[104] It would merely restrict these activities until they learned once again how to avoid or evade the restrictions. Moreover, there are concerns about the political feasibility of such reforms. For example, in campaign finance there is a "long record of both parties' claiming to support reform only when they can be confident the other side will kill it."[105] In 1997 the House decisively defeated a constitutional amendment to impose term limits on members of Congress.[106] Some congressional candidates who voluntarily made commitments to limit their own terms in office if elected in 1992 or 1994 have abandoned those commitments as the term limits approached. Finally, such reforms raise constitutional issues. First Amendment rights were the basis for a Supreme Court decision that has doomed many proposals to reform campaign finances since 1976.[107] "The ultimate problem with all process reforms is that lobbies are us, and you can't isolate a democratic government from its own society."[108]

Some reforms attempt to make federal officials and agencies more accountable to the Congress and president. Perhaps the most prominent involve performance measures. In 1993, both the Government Performance and Results Act and the National Performance Review led by Vice President Al Gore were based on "the reasonable notion," as the Congressional Budget Office (CBO) described it, that "federal agencies should be able to develop measures of program success, and that these measurements would be useful to managers and other policymakers."[109] In particular, they might be useful in enforcing compliance with law and policy through the federal budget process. However, CBO's review of a broad range of experience concluded that it was not such a reasonable notion after all: "Even if the legislative and executive branches were committed to improving performance measurement and tying those measures to the budget process, two chief obstacles would remain. First, developing measurements that accurately reflect the performance of federal agencies is difficult. . . . Second, there is not enough demand by policymakers to change the way policies are made so that they are more responsive to the measurement of outcomes."[110] A subsequent appraisal concluded that "the biggest difficulty in thinking through the problems of performance management is that reformers and managers alike far too often consider it simply as a problem of measurement."[111] It is also a problem of governance. "The project to revive and modernize government rather than simply shrink it will not be a sterile technocratic exercise."[112]

Faith in government performance measures tends to be sustained by expectations about their use in business. But even in business, management primarily by the numbers is one of the deadly diseases: "The important figures are unknown and unknowable—the multiplier effect of a happy customer, for example."[113] Another deadly disease is the annual performance review for personnel as a basis for resource allocation: "It nourishes short-term performance, annihilates long-term planning, builds fear, demolishes teamwork, nourishes rivalry and politics. It leaves people bitter, crushed. . . . It is unfair, as it ascribes to the people in a group differences that may be caused totally by the system that they work in."[114] Many of the best companies, the visionary companies built to last, do not gauge their performance by the proverbial bottom line. Instead, say James Collins and Jerry Porras, "Profitability is a necessary condition for existence and a means to more important ends, but it is not the end in itself for many of the visionary companies."[115] The dysfunctional consequences of exclusive and automatic reliance on quantitative performance measures were recognized as early as 1956.[116] But they have done little to erode faith in performance measures carried over from scientific management in the Progressive era. In 1922, one advocate referred to the use of performance measures by experts as "The Entering Wedge" to expose "the trading politician and the partisan who has much to conceal."[117]

Demands for constitutive reform are also expressed in attempts to bypass institutions of representative democracy through direct democracy in various forms. Ballot initiatives and referenda are reforms from the Progressive era designed to express the will of the people more directly. Their use is rising, but they are being used more often by single-interest groups and public officials as alternatives to the give-and-take of legislative processes to realize their interests.[118] Citizen-based militias are also rising.[119] In the aftermath of the bombing of a federal office building in Oklahoma City in April 1995, a historian warned: "Not since the era of Southern secession have so many Americans found so little to respect in their political system—to the point where a small but militant minority has vowed to resist that system by any means possible."[120] But violent means are less solutions than symptoms of the many problems of Americans disaffected from their government.

The disaffected Americans who supported Ross Perot in the 1992 presidential election reportedly believed that "America is in deep trouble and knows it, but the system can't do anything about it because of politicians' corrupt and self-serving behavior. Perot's message: The only way to solve such problems is to set aside politics."[121] "Perot seemed to think he could fix it by ordering the special interests to shut up and go away."[122] The possibility of a "strong man" popular solution was not overlooked in Washington at the beginning of the Clinton administration. A former presidential aide projected that if the administration did not make the system work better, "we will have some really angry people out there. . . . We could be looking at Ross Perot as the moderate responsible guy who will be our only hope for stopping some certifiable lunatic who is running ten points ahead of the pack."[123] Not all expressions of direct democracy are constructive.

The rising direct influence of the public is one of the two principal features of the new American political disorder, according to Dahl. It is a problem in the absence of new institutions: "Although public opinion more often directly influences the policies, strategies, tactics, and speech of political leaders, institutions for ensuring that the opinions serving as the views of 'the public' are either representative or well considered have not been created. The *plebiscitary* aspect of American political life has grown, one might say, without a corresponding improvement in its *representative* and *deliberative* aspects."[124] The other principal feature of the new political disorder is the proliferation of conflicting interest groups already emphasized here. It is a problem amid the weakening of political institutions for negotiations "in search of mutually beneficial policies" for the conflicting interest groups and for the general public. Thus one might also say that there is "more *fragmentation* and less *integration*" in the new political order.[125] Problems of governance are likely to grow without more representative and deliberative institutions for resolving conflicts in the common interest.

Such institutions already exist in community-based initiatives. At least the Bison Management Citizen's Working Group in Bozeman, among many others, demonstrated some capacity for the integration of fragmented interests into mutually beneficial (or common-interest) policies through representative and deliberative means. Such small-scale initiatives tend to be discounted as insignificant if they are noticed at all from the center, within the Washington Beltway, or at the periphery of federal agency field offices scattered around the country. Nevertheless, with enlightened innovation, diffusion, and adaptation, community-based initiatives might succeed and multiply enough over time to supply the missing piece in the constitutive formula and to make a difference in resolving current problems of governance. The planning and promotion of many more policies would move down from the federal government and out into the civic sector, leaving established structures of governmental authority and accountability in place but cultivating new ones in local communities where the initiatives succeed. There can be little confidence about the future of community-based initiatives, or established structures of governance for that matter. But in view of growing problems of governance and concerns about the more prominent alternatives for constitutive reform, it is worthwhile to consider the history of community-based initiatives, their potential, and how that potential might be realized.

A comprehensive history of community-based initiatives has yet to be written. But the incomplete history of place-based collaborative groups is relevant to the extent that they overlap with community-based initiatives, a larger category not restricted to collaborative strategies. The history suggests a familiar pattern of political change.[126] Beginning in the 1980s, according to Donald Snow, "numerous groups, far from one another and working in relative isolation, began meeting at about the same time, often with nothing more in mind than the need 'to try something new.'"[127] They were motivated by perceived failures of multiple government agencies to act as stewards of the nation's public lands in the West. The aggrieved parties were narrow-interest organizations and coalitions, such as trade associations, environmental groups, and economic growth councils. Initially they turned to Washington, seeking "relief in the form of new marching orders from Congress or the Administration." What they found more often was gridlock in the struggle for power among factions in federal agencies and in state and sometimes local governments as well: "The war of all against all is fought on every front" in the federal system.[128] "But in nearly every case, collaboration started with an urge somehow to break gridlock, to move beyond a paralyzing stalemate."[129]

But why collaboration, rather than other new things to try? According to Snow, attention was drawn to the potential of collaborative groups. Beginning in the mid-1970s, alternative dispute resolution as applied to environmental issues raised awareness that "in some instances, more effective solutions may grow from the examination of mutual interests among competing parties." In 1982, Daniel Kemmis wrote three influential papers that were intensively discussed and eventually integrated into *Community and the Politics of Place*, published in 1990. The book argued that gridlock "is virtually built into the federal system of government as it was envisioned by James Madison." It also suggested that "breaking gridlock probably must involve a reawakening of the sense of a *res publica*, the 'table' around which we all sit in a democracy."[130] Whatever the sources of collaborative aspirations and techniques, some collaborative groups have failed while others have succeeded. The successes tend to be brought to the attention of other community groups, for possible adaptation elsewhere, through a variety of networks. One network is organized around *Chronicle of Community*, a journal established by the Northern Lights Institute in Missoula, Montana, in 1996. Snow is the executive editor of the *Chronicle* and executive director of the Institute.

The attention drawn to successful collaboratives may have begun to encourage initiatives in hundreds of place-based communities facing similar problems and frustrations in natural resources policy. According to a specialist in Western water policy, for example: "The 1990s have seen a proliferation of 'watershed initiatives,' in which stakeholders from a variety of governmental levels and jurisdictions have joined with nongovernmental stakeholders to seek innovative and pragmatic solutions to the problems associated with resource degradation and overuse. . . . Each watershed initiative is an ad hoc effort tailored to the unique institutional and physical qualities of a particular region."[131] If the early initiatives had no alternative to proceeding alone, in relative isolation, the later ones have access in principle to a growing body of experience through various networks. In any case, there is a new spirit of cooperation in the West in the 1990s, according to Kemmis.[132] The new spirit is based on growing recognition that the old formulas for governance no longer work satisfactorily.

The pattern is not limited to collaborative groups working on natural resources in the American West in the 1990s. Community-based initiatives of various kinds have succeeded in integrating the different interests of small communities into consensus on policies that advance the common interest in other policy areas and time periods as well. For example:

- Amid the energy crises of the 1970s, Davis, California, implemented an innovative passive solar heating and cooling ordinance to reduce energy consumption and costs in new residential buildings. A collaborative strategy was inapplicable: local building contractors vigorously opposed passage of the ordinance. But consensus was reestablished through firsthand experience when contractors learned how to implement the ordinance without adding to construction costs and saw that it worked. This successful community-based initiative attracted national and international attention, including a featured place in congressional hearings.[133]
- Amid controversies over the management of Carson National Forest in New Mexico in 1991, District Ranger Crockett Dumas undertook "horseback diplomacy" to talk one-on-one with traditional Hispanic users of the forest and with organized environmentalists in the area. No group was organized to work out initial differences. But Dumas gained enough trust and insight from community members to end a long history of explosive protests and litigation in his district by 1993 and to develop and implement an innovative plan that served multiple local interests rather than a few large interests. In 1998 this successful community-based initiative won an Innovations in American Government Award.[134]
- Frustrated by a lack of qualified high school graduates for his

expanding high-tech printing business, John Torinus worked with state and local officials and a printers' association to devise a new work-study program for high school students in West Bend, Wisconsin. "The results were astounding. Mediocre students started making the dean's list. After they graduated, Mr. Torinus hired every young apprentice he could. . . . The Wisconsin experiment has spread to other fields: insurance, banking, health, auto technology, electronics, biotechnology, engineering technology, tourism and manufacturing. First, two communities tried this approach; now it's in thirty."[135]

Thus consensus on place-based policies has been achieved without collaboration in a group, in initiatives led by officials and entrepreneurs as well as by other citizens, in other policy areas in addition to natural resources, and in other decades. In view of experiences like these, an exclusive emphasis on collaborative groups tends to divert attention from other kinds of community-based initiatives that may succeed in some circumstances, and to underestimate the potential of community-based initiatives in the aggregate to contribute toward constitutive reform.[136] The search for additional cases is better guided by the common interest and left open to any kind of community-based initiative that succeeds by that criterion.

The general pattern underlying the events described above begins when local people recognize that a pressing policy problem they experience directly might be solved locally. Such recognition may come when they reconceive a national problem as many local ones, or when they perceive the federal government as responsible for the problem or indifferent or incompetent to solve it. In any case, they tend to engage more or less spontaneously in processes of innovation, diffusion, and adaptation in open networks.[137]

- Innovation: As the problem becomes more pressing and more difficult to ignore, people in some communities are likely to reject "do nothing" or other established alternatives in order to try something new. Some communities are more successful in practice than others in alleviating the problem through innovations.
- Diffusion: Through various networks, the successful innovations come to the attention of other communities facing other versions of the same or a similar problem—and do so with sufficient frequency to clarify de facto standards of good practice and to provide field-tested models for meeting those standards.

- Adaptation: Under pressure from leaders or followers to meet those standards, communities that lag behind the innovators tend to select from the more successful models—and to delete and modify selected elements of the models—according to their own unique needs and circumstances.

The gist might be summarized in simpler terms: Necessity is the mother of invention. No one knowingly copies a loser. Nothing succeeds like success. Success in the adaptation process may stimulate a new wave of innovations, so long as the local problems remain important to communities in the network, higher standards and better models are demonstrated and diffused, and other resources necessary for adaptation remain available. Thus successful local innovations may provide the foundation for solving some nationwide problems with little central direction, motivated in large part by persistent local problems left unresolved within established structures of governance.[138]

These processes can malfunction, of course. In the innovation process, for example, claims of success by a community may be hyped or otherwise unfounded, thereby misleading other communities in a network and contributing perhaps to their subsequent failure. In the diffusion process, the dissemination of higher standards or better models may be unorganized, censored, or otherwise restricted, leaving communities in need without reliable information on experience elsewhere to guide them. In the adaptation process, communities may need more than reliable information on de facto standards and models in accessible form. They may need leadership, funds, or authority that are unavailable in some communities. Moreover, enthusiasm for community-based initiatives in general may unwittingly raise expectations so high that disappointments in specific cases become inevitable. Conversely, skepticism about community-based initiatives in general may obscure successes in specific cases that merit diffusion and adaptation.[139] Finally, some agencies and interest groups will perceive successes in advancing the common interest through these processes as threats to their own special interest in maintaining power in established structures of governance. One response may be to coopt community-based initiatives; another may be to resist initiatives indiscriminately, successes and failures alike. With such possibilities in mind, it is not difficult to imagine how community-based initiatives individually or collectively might fail. If they fail, the pressures that gave rise to the initiatives in the first place will not disappear. They will be expressed in other ways.

No one can know reliably or with confidence what community-

based initiatives will contribute over time toward reform of governance. The outcomes of any reform effort become increasingly unpredictable as the time horizon extends into the future, because the outcomes depend on thousands of choices and decisions, each of which
is open to new insight and experience as events unfold.[140] In particular,
individuals and groups may reconceive their interests and redirect
their activities accordingly at any time. Thus the task is less to predict
the course of history than to help shape it toward preferred outcomes.
For the authors of this book, the preferred outcome is to realize the
potential of community-based initiatives, both to advance the common
interest through policies in particular communities and to contribute
toward constitutive reform in America. The preferred strategy is harvesting experience from community-based initiatives as events unfold,
to provide additional insights and information for the consideration
of those private citizens and public officials who will make policy and
constitutive decisions.

The Potential

It is important to be clear about the potential of community-based initiatives, because it has been obscured by various flawed criticisms addressed below. The potential stems from additional opportunities
opened up by the initiatives for resolving place-based issues that are
unique. The bison management issue in greater Yellowstone is not
equivalent to the bison management issue in Custer State Park in
South Dakota, or in commercial bison operations, even though they
share some similarities. Likewise, "watershed management," "endangered species recovery," or "forest management" realistically does not
refer to a uniform issue across contexts but to different issues depending upon the context. Increasingly, such differences must be taken
into account for policy purposes. As Gifford Pinchot and Elizabeth Pinchot put it, "A system that manages work from any distance by setting
uniform procedures and issuing simple orders cannot deal with the
fact that we no longer face a uniform or simple world."[141] The unique-
ness of issues in context is inconvenient for scientific management,
insofar as its scientific components presume uniformity, or its bureaucratic components aspire to standardization.

The additional opportunities opened up by community-based initiatives can be contrasted with those available through agencies and interest groups. Participants in a community-based initiative are relatively
free to seek creative, integrative solutions to a unique issue close to
home; to proceed informally in face-to-face situations with a minimum

of a priori constraints on procedures or substantive outcomes; and to draw upon local resources, including leaders and followers with first-hand knowledge of the issue and significant stakes in resolving it. With those stakes and the small scale comes some degree of responsibility and accountability to the community. In contrast, participants in each government agency or interest group are relatively constrained to advocate solutions that conform to the organization's established procedures and mandate, often in conflict with those of other organizations; to proceed within the formal administrative hierarchy of the organization and the balancing of power among organizations; and to depend on constituencies remote from the issue to sustain the effort—for example, officials in the White House, representatives in Congress, or dues-paying members, as the case may be. Such remote constituencies typically have less information about the particular issue, less time and attention available for it, and less stake in solving it. Responsibility and accountability to the community are much easier to avoid under these circumstances. These disadvantages in finding common ground have been exacerbated by the growing number and complexity of unique policy issues over the past century. Meanwhile, the advantages of community-based initiatives have increased with changes in social conditions.

Nevertheless, the power of a community-based initiative depends on its merits. If it succeeds in integrating or balancing the diverse interests of participants into a policy that advances their common interest, it can legitimately claim to be the voice of the people with respect to the issue at hand, and build upon that success. The voice of the people is difficult to discount or ignore within established structures of governance and within the American political tradition. If it fails in finding common ground, the claims of a community-based initiative are easily dismissed, and the initiative itself is likely to disband voluntarily or to become an advocate of a single interest—and to be recognized as just another conventional interest group. Similarly, the collective power of community-based initiatives in constitutive reform depends on their ability to improve upon successful innovations in policy and governance by diffusing and adapting them to other communities facing similar issues. Furthermore, all of this depends to some extent on the failure of agencies and interest groups in established structures of governance to resolve the growing number of issues faced by Americans close to home, in the places where they live. Such problems are often necessary to motivate participation in community-based initiatives in the first place and to sustain that participation. Significant constitutive reform is not likely to occur among those who perceive existing policies and structures of governance to be working well.

Community-based initiatives also depend, in the end, on the support of agencies and interest groups in established structures of governance. For example, the government agencies that retained fragmented authority and control over bison management in greater Yellowstone effectively rejected the 1991 proposal of the Bison Management Citizen's Working Group in Bozeman simply by ignoring it. More enlightened agencies might recognize the political costs of rejecting proposals that advance the common interest of communities with the most at stake in an issue. More enlightened agencies might recognize the benefits of encouraging such proposals, which can often help agencies economize on the limited time, attention, and other resources available to invest in the decision process. Finally, more enlightened agencies might recognize a principled role in evaluating specific proposals from community-based initiatives—rejecting those that fail to advance the common interest, or fail to conform with duly established laws and policies. Some laws and policies should be called into question, however, when they consistently block proposals that advance the common interest. In any case, community-based initiatives have been selectively incorporated into established structures of governance to compensate for the limitations of those structures, not to replace them. Given the opportunity, community-based initiatives could adapt those structures to the increasing complexity of modern society, by economizing on time and attention and by integrating local competence into policy.

Certain criticisms of community-based initiatives can be addressed from this summary of their potential. First, it is alleged that community-based initiatives are unconstitutional or illegal. According to a professor of law, for example, "The Constitution entrusts the disposition, and regulation, and care of federally owned assets to the national government, not local self-appointed mediators."[142] Moreover, "The statutes . . . nowhere . . . delegate decision-making power to unelected, unappointed citizens at large or interested economic entities."[143] But the First Amendment to the Constitution protects "the right of the people peaceably to assemble, and to petition the Government for a redress of grievances"; and statutes like NEPA specify how citizens and groups are supposed to be empowered to participate in various federal policy decisions affecting the environment. If groups representing environmental, economic, or other single interests are authorized to participate in the management of federally owned natural resources, then community-based initiatives are authorized to participate in all the same ways. In the balancing of power, community-based initiatives are essentially interest groups comprising diverse multiple interests located in a small place.

Second, it is alleged that community-based initiatives are unrepresentative or undemocratic. For example, "Voluntary enlistment in a collaboration cannot assure representation of all who have a legitimate voice (including eastern tourists) nor consideration of all legitimate interests (including future generations)."[144] Neither can voluntary enlistment in single-interest groups individually or collectively assure the representation of all legitimate voices and interests. The principle of affected interests, as argued earlier, is an ideal that cannot be realized in practice. Community-based initiatives, however, are opportunities for some communities, neglected in the balancing of power among national interest groups, to represent their own common interest in policy decisions where they have a lot at stake. That is important from the standpoint of democratic inclusion. "Who elected these people (i.e., the collaborative body)?" asks the chairman of the Sierra Club.[145] It is equally appropriate to ask, "Who elected the leaders of the Sierra Club, or any other conventional interest group?" For both questions, the answer is "their constituents"—defined by shared place in the first case and by shared interest in the second. To the extent that they are informed, both constituencies tend to withhold authority and other support from irresponsible representatives of their interests. Finally, "How do you reconcile the idea that the will of the majority ought to prevail if you set up rules to allow a willful minority (through a consensus rule) to block the will of the majority?"[146] Quite simply, you rely on practical prudence as expressed in the Jackson Workshop: "You don't need everyone from every special interest, but you do need a critical mass or you can't claim that what you're doing is in the common interest" (Figure 1.1 [10]).

Third, it is alleged that community-based initiatives represent an unwarranted redistribution of power. For example: "This redistribution of power is designed to disempower our [Sierra Club] constituency, which is heavily urban. Few urbanites are recognized as stakeholders in communities surrounding national forests. Few of the proposals for stakeholder collaboration provide any way for distant stakeholders to be effectively represented."[147] Conversely, few communities surrounding national forests are recognized as stakeholders in forest management policy by the Sierra Club. The Sierra Club's proposal for zero logging in national forests does not provide any way for local stakeholders to be effectively represented, even though local stakeholders tend to have the most at stake. More important, people can participate only very selectively in the policy decisions that affect their interests. They are empowered to choose whether their own priority interests are best pursued through a conventional interest group or a community-based initiative—but only if they are aware of both alternatives. The criticism of community-based initiatives continues: "Even in places where local environmentalists exist, they are not always equipped to play competitively with industry professionals. There may be no parity in experience, training, skills or financial resources."[148] A distribution or redistribution of political resources is warranted when it consistently serves the common interest of the community, whether the community is local, national, or global in scope. It is unwarranted when it consistently serves special interests, which are not always or exclusively those interests opposed by environmental organizations. A reliable judgment about common and special interests can be made only through inquiry into the particular context.

Finally, some criticisms imply that established and emerging structures of governance are mutually exclusive alternatives for making policy decisions.[149] One professor of law concluded that "the law and its processes, imperfect as they are, are still far preferable to local negotiations as means for resolving resource issues."[150] But there is no need to select one constitutive alternative over the other, once and for all. The beginning of wisdom is to evaluate particular proposals from community-based initiatives through the political process, to support those that are sound, and to reject those that are unconstitutional or illegal, undemocratic or unrepresentative, or otherwise not in the common interest. Machiavelli said it well, on behalf of the people: "The quickest way of opening the eyes of the people is to find the means of making them descend to particulars, seeing that to look at things only in a general way deceives them."[151] If we Americans get down to particulars, open our eyes, and act in good faith, we just might be able to significantly

- reduce the burden on overloaded policy makers in national structures of governance;
- resolve more place-based issues economically, competently, and in the common interest;
- restore some responsibility and accountability to the communities most directly affected;
- accumulate social capital that can be invested in other, larger political arenas;
- and gradually adapt established structures of governance to the realities of our time.[152]

We need not proceed blindly through the process of constitutive reform as we did a century ago. We need not presume that anyone knows enough now to rewrite the Constitution from the top down to solve current problems of governance.[153] We can begin to adapt it to the realities of our time from the bottom up, through the diffusion and adaptation of successful innovations in policy and governance by community-based initiatives.

A Look Ahead

As a step in that direction, the following four chapters present case studies in sufficient detail for the reader to assess problems of governance, the potential of community-based initiatives, and a strategy for realizing that potential. The strategy is harvesting experience, based on the processes of innovation, diffusion, and adaptation, and is presented in the concluding chapter. Each case study focuses on structures of governance and their policy outcomes in a specific area of natural resources policy.[154] The policy outcomes are assessed from the standpoint of advancing the common interest in each context. To the extent that the structures helped advance the common interest, they are considered "models" of governance to underscore the expectation that they worked well enough to be considered for diffusion and adaptation by other community-based initiatives.[155] Finally, each case study addresses the broader significance of the structures and their policy outcomes. Apart from these similarities in focus and scope, the case studies are more or less independent of each other and may be read in any order.

Chapter 2 clarifies by example the potential of community-based initiatives to advance the common interest. Elizabeth A. Olson considers water management and the Upper Clark Fork Steering Committee, a watershed initiative in western Montana led by an expert facilitator from the Northern Lights Institute. The committee worked under a mandate its predecessor sought from the state of Montana to balance beneficial uses of water in the Upper Clark Fork basin through management at the local level. The committee produced a plan that avoided the expense and delay of impending litigation over reservation of water rights, protected existing water rights, and made some progress toward preserving in-stream flow, a neglected but increasingly important interest. The plan was approved by the state of Montana in 1995. The facilitator identified the structural innovation behind this successful effort to advance the common interest: "The emphasis on the local level is the new ground broken by this plan and its goals. Instead of relying on a government agency with limited input from the public, this plan calls for a partnership between local water users and state and federal water managers to strike and maintain a balanced management of the waters of the upper Clark Fork River."[156] This model also demonstrates the possibility of mutually advantageous cooperation between community-based initiatives and established structures of governance. Other cases shed more light on conflict between the two. Conflict can be expected until the advantages of cooperation with community-based initiatives are more widely appreciated.

Chapter 3 clarifies the potential of several different structures of governance in another context. Roberta A. Klein considers wolf recovery in the northern Rockies, a decision made for the most part in Congress under the mandate of the Endangered Species Act and over the opposition of Western livestock producers and their representatives in Washington. Within that national structure, three other structures helped advance the common interest in complementary ways: an advisory committee that failed to resolve the issue for Congress but did generate some useful proposals; an EIS team led by field officials of the U.S. Fish and Wildlife Service that built upon earlier proposals, proceeded rather independently of higher officials, and worked intensively with local communities to mitigate burdens on livestock producers and others; and a program led by a private organization, Defenders of Wildlife, to compensate producers for livestock killed by wolves. The EIS team and the compensation program are community-based initiatives of different kinds that helped accommodate the national decision to valid and appropriate local interests. Local opposition, however, persists—suggesting some room for policy improvements.

Chapter 4 clarifies the potential of community-based initiatives by contrast with established structures of governance that assert exclusive authority and control. Christina M. Cromley presents a comprehensive account of bison management in greater Yellowstone. The details are instructive, especially regarding the protracted and largely futile struggle of federal and state officials among themselves and the unrealized potential of the Bozeman Citizen's Working Group and other community-based initiatives to advance the common interest. Those who were effectively excluded eventually chose to organize against the various interagency bison management plans but still had little influence. Conflict between community-based initiatives and established structures in this case was mutually disadvantageous—at least in hindsight that might have been foresight.

Chapter 5 clarifies by example the potential of community-based initiatives that choose to persist despite opposition by established structures. Christine H. Colburn considers forest policy and the Quincy Library Group, an initiative in northern California led by citizens who vigorously disagreed with one another but nevertheless met in a neutral place, the town library. In 1993, members of the group developed their interdependent interests in the health of the local forests and economy into a Community Stability Proposal for the management of nearby national forests. Rebuffed by the local Forest Service, members of the Quincy Library Group went to Washington to lobby on behalf of their proposal. In 1998, despite the opposition of most national environmental interest groups, President Clinton signed an act of Congress directing the Forest Service to implement an amended version of the original proposal as a pilot project. The interim policy outcomes are mixed so far, but the structure has demonstrated more potential to serve the common interests of both the local and national communities. Taken together, all four cases illuminate the potential for cooperation and conflict between community-based initiatives and established structures of governance.

In conclusion, Chapter 6 on harvesting experience considers how these and other cases might be used to realize the potential of community-based initiatives. For this purpose, it suggests that participants in community-based initiatives and their supporters rely on the diffusion and adaptation of successful models of policy and governance, and beware of certain external threats to further progress. Similarly, the chapter suggests that interest groups organized in and around natural resources agencies support community-based initiatives and their proposals selectively, in those cases where support is warranted from a common-interest standpoint. Selective support may be warranted as a matter of expediency in sustaining the organizations amid changing social conditions or as a matter of principle in accord with the common interest. Finally, the chapter suggests that researchers and educators address the needs of policy makers engaged in adaptive management. Adaptive management goes beyond the remnants of scientific management from the Progressive era, including the contemporary search for scientific generalizations. The primary task is harvesting experience systematically and continuously to improve natural resources policy and governance in particular contexts around the American West on behalf of the common interest.

2 Water Management and the Upper Clark Fork Steering Committee

Elizabeth A. Olson

The Upper Clark Fork River basin, covering 22,000 square miles of southwestern Montana, is a region of extremes. On its trip from Anaconda to Missoula, the river's tributaries roll through isolated wilderness, open farmland, and busy municipalities. The basin is home to the mighty Blackfoot River, a wild and beautiful river immortalized by Norman Maclean in *A River Runs Through It*.[1] Although some reaches of the basin still resemble the pristine trout waters of Maclean's youth, most do not. Today's Upper Clark Fork is home to four Superfund sites, hundreds of miles of dewatered streams, and struggling fisheries. Despite its degradation, the river and its power are in greater demand than ever before. As water travels down the basin, it might be consumed, rafted upon, fished, diverted for irrigation, pushed through hydropower turbines, or simply admired from afar. The human communities of the Upper Clark Fork River basin use the resource in ways that may not appear compatible at first glance. Government agencies, water courts, and community activists are now struggling to solve a perplexing and increasingly common puzzle: how to accommodate the demands of a growing, diverse human population upon a limited natural resource.

Federal and state governments have confronted the degradation of the Upper Clark Fork River with a multitude of studies, projects, and statutes since the 1970s.[2] In spite of the scientific and legal attention given to the river, conflicts surrounding its use and management increased steadily through the 1980s and 1990s. Many of these conflicts pitted environmentalists against ranchers, hydropower producers

Map 2.1. Upper Clark Fork Basin, Montana

against irrigators, and state agencies against conservation districts. The Montana water courts provided perhaps the most popular arenas for confronting problems and forging solutions to water disputes, making for expensive and lengthy management decisions that satisfied the interests of the winners only.[3] In this complex and often confusing system of water governance in Montana, the Upper Clark Fork Steering

Committee emerged as a unique experiment to articulate and incorporate the interests of basin residents into the governance of a scarce natural resource.

This chapter appraises the actions of the Upper Clark Fork Steering Committee, a watershed initiative established in 1991 to solve a resource conflict that was heading quickly toward litigation. The conflict began in 1985, when the Montana Department of Fish, Wildlife, and Parks (DFWP) applied for water rights, called reservations, in the Upper Clark and its tributaries. By 1988, environmentalists, recreationists, sporting groups, irrigators, and hydropower generators aligned themselves either for or against DFWP's application. At the request of the courts and with assistance from the Northern Lights Institute, the reservation applicants began negotiations in 1989 to avoid a contested case hearing. Participants agreed that the hearing would inflict financial and social burdens, and decided to try an alternative process for protecting their interests. In April 1991, this collection of water users approached the Montana state legislature with an unprecedented request. If the state would agree to temporarily close the Upper Clark Fork River basin to further appropriation, the water users would collaborate to find a solution to water allocation problems in the basin. The state granted the group's request, and mandated that the new Upper Clark Fork Steering Committee "balance all beneficial uses of water in the Upper Clark Fork River basin" and "root water management at the local level."[4] After nearly three years of effort, the committee presented its final water management plan to the Montana legislature in December 1994.

In the Upper Clark Fork River basin, the common interest of water users includes three critical substantive components: protecting existing water rights, protecting unallocated instream flow, and augmenting instream flow. Protecting existing water rights means respecting the water rights that have been conferred on certain water users in the basin since the mid-1860s. Water rights owners include ranchers who use their water for irrigation, utilities that rely on it for hydropower production, and municipalities that require it for waste treatment and household or domestic uses. Protecting existing instream flow means keeping whatever water has not been allocated for irrigation and other uses flowing in its natural course. Because most uses requiring instream flow traditionally could not be granted water rights, many of these uses are notably unsatisfied.[5] Anglers and rafters, as well as growing numbers of tourists in the basin, rely on sufficient river levels for recreation. Environmentalists want to preserve the stunning beauty of the basin's peaceful river valleys while protecting the natural ecology, which is valuable to humans and other species. Hydropower producers also support protecting unallocated instream flow, which contributes to fulfilling their legal water rights. Finally, although protecting existing instream flow can help prevent further resource degradation, it is not enough to repair the damage that has already been done. Environmentalists and anglers therefore support increasing instream flow in dewatered stretches to rehabilitate the ecology and aesthetics of the basin.

This chapter tells the story of an interesting watershed initiative, and in doing so, helps improve the governance of water resources by harvesting the committee's experiences for other watershed initiatives and other policy makers. The story is worth telling and appraising because the committee's creative solution addressed the common interest. It drafted a plan that respected existing water rights so that ranchers and industry could continue to depend on their water sources. And it departed from traditional water management mechanisms by improving the opportunity to protect and increase instream flow in ways that can benefit water rights owners. The committee replaced costly litigation with a more appealing alternative, and fostered congenial relationships among historical adversaries, which contributed to greater inclusiveness in the basin's political networks and facilitated tangible changes in resource use. Not all problems in the basin have been solved, and some uses are still threatened under existing conditions. The committee's solution to the allocation dispute nevertheless advanced the common interest. It is highly unlikely, moreover, that as good a solution could have been found within the rigid structure of Montana's water courts or under the time limits and attention constraints of the state legislature. As Audrey Aspholm summed it up: "We haven't changed the world, but those are the changes that are possible. And if you make enough of these little ones then other things can happen too."[6]

Searching for the Common Interest

Gold was first discovered in an Upper Clark Fork tributary in 1852, and soon after water users demanded legal doctrines and political institutions to protect their investments and related interests. The earliest guidelines for water allocation in Montana were the doctrines of prior appropriation and beneficial use. Both doctrines grew out of the common law and were considered by new settlers to be fair guidelines for the just distribution of a limited resource. According to the doctrine of prior appropriation, the water user who was "first in time" would also be "first in right" to use a specified amount of water in a beneficial way. The California Supreme Court formally articulated the doctrine in 1855, clarifying that the first water user on a creek or river had "senior" rights that had to be fulfilled before any later "junior" right could be met. Prior appropriation established a pecking order for water distribution, in which relatively late arrivals in a heavily appropriated watercourse might not have access to water in dry years. In many cases, late arrivals diverted water from another watershed or even another river basin if more local water sources were overallocated.[7]

Prior appropriation might also be understood as an attempt by states and courts to create water policy that reflected the interests of water users at a particular time in the history of the West. At the time that the West was being explored and settled, eastern states continued to rely on the British system of allocating water through a riparian method, which meant that only owners of property contiguous to a watercourse had a water right. Most of the first nonnative settlers of the West were also participants in the gold and silver rushes of the region, and therefore did not favor sharing what appeared already to be scarce water resources.[8] The mining industry required vast amounts of high-pressure water and labor-intensive diversion techniques to extract minerals, which consumed both time and money. If another miner set up a claim on the same watershed and began diverting his share of the water according to riparian rights, the original miner could take a tremendous loss. The doctrine of prior appropriation also suited the needs of farmers and ranchers trying to produce food and forage out of the West's parched landscapes.[9] Whether tending livestock or potatoes, they discovered that the seemingly limitless land around them provided little security. Nature was unpredictable enough without having to worry about a new neighbor moving in and taking the water that ranchers and farmers depended on for their livelihood.

The doctrine of beneficial use also reflected the conditions and demands of new frontier populations. Legally, a water user had to divert water from the streambed and use that water in order to secure water rights. This was because the courts defined "beneficial use" as water uses that were extractive and normally consumptive. Water rights for hydropower production were the most notable exception to the doctrine of beneficial use because hydropower producers could obtain rights to water that remained in the streambed.[10] If a water user did not use all the water appropriated to him, he could lose rights to the unused portion. In other words, water rights owners had to either use it or lose it. Water users quickly learned to divert more water than they actually needed so they might expand crop production or mining operations in the future, resulting in "waste" of the water that could not be used immediately. Between 1914 and 1925, Montana courts determined that beneficial use demanded that the water be used in full and not wasted through poor water management practices. In spite of this and other minor refinements, Montana courts and legislation continued to define beneficial use as extractive and normally consumptive into the 1960s.[11]

Prior appropriation and beneficial use thus appeared appropriate for the temporally and spatially bounded context for which they were written. They protected the relatively fragile livelihoods of Montana's settlers, and they even protected the water demands of the state's native population—at least in theory.[12] But these doctrines were not very accommodating to changing conditions of the land or changing interests of its residents, and also could not be easily enforced on a diffuse population. In short, the doctrines were not always effective in specific situations, especially as more settlers moved into the region.

Informal governing institutions often took over where formal institutions were insufficient, unenforceable, or undesirable for a given season or location. In such circumstances, users themselves were often willing to make informal water allocation decisions as long as their neighbors approved. Although ranchers are quick to caution that these informal institutions are not as established as some would like to think, they remain fundamental to water management in the basin.[13] They also represent the reality of governing the expansive Montana landscape. Even with laws in place to allocate water, the ability to enforce and assess water management decisions is understandably limited. When the state could not make decisions in response to changing conditions or new situations, the water users had little choice but to fill in the blanks themselves. Even hydropower producers established informal, often unspoken agreements about water use with their basin neighbors to allow irrigators with rights junior to utility rights to continue consuming water even when utility rights were not filled.[14]

Informal and formal water management are not mutually exclusive. A typical informal management scenario might consist of three neighbors who share an irrigation ditch deciding to rotate full use of the ditch on a weekly basis, rather than each withdrawing his third of the ditch each day. This works only if all neighbors are satisfied by the agreement and feel that they are benefiting from the arrangement. In contrast, when precipitation declines or the basin enters seasonal low flow periods, these very same neighbors might request the appointment of a water commissioner to control distribution. Mike Mclane of the Montana Department of Natural Resources and Conservation (DNRC) explains that "water users tend to follow the prior appropriation very closely only when water is really low and things are really nasty. The rest of the time, they just kind of get along."[15] These informal arrangements, however, were historically restricted to water rights owners—only those who could prove beneficial use. Thus, like the institutions of prior appropriation and beneficial use, these relatively informal institutions did not factor instream flow users (with the important exception of hydropower producers) into their allocation decisions.

In contemporary Montana, formal and informal management continues to fill in the gaps left by prior appropriation and beneficial use. But they have been insufficient for protecting instream uses that were not consumptive, such as fishing. In fact, the application of prior appropriation by water courts and enforcement by conservation districts resulted in increasingly large amounts of water being removed from Montana's watercourses. In the meantime, the basin had undergone staggering changes. The state's population grew by 10 percent between 1990 and 1996, a drastic increase from barely 2 percent growth in the 1980s.[16] A rebounding economy that increased 4 to 5 percent in the early 1990s is only one of the reasons that people are moving to Montana. Companies in the western portion of the state cite natural amenities and better quality of life as major motivations for locating there.[17] As Montana's urban areas continue to grow, its rural counties are increasingly depopulated. Some family ranches in the Upper Clark basin are no longer profitable enough to employ all the children in the family. If children must find nonagricultural payroll jobs, they will most likely have to leave rural communities in favor of larger municipalities.[18] In the meantime, the non-extractive uses of natural resources, such as aesthetics and recreation, have steadily gained supporters among the immigrants and visitors who recognize the importance of Montana's natural heritage. Instream water users eventually decided that changes in legislation would be critical for protecting fisheries, and for aesthetic and environmental values.

Public confirmation that the doctrines of prior appropriation and beneficial use were not sufficient to accommodate new interests became difficult to ignore during the 1960s. In the logic of prior appropriation, it could do little harm to water users if more water was allocated than actually flowed through a water body; the most junior water rights would only be fulfilled in years of heavy precipitation, but this would theoretically not harm senior rights. As more water was allocated for consumptive uses, however, new and old water users began to recognize that some of the basin's creeks and rivers were drying up from overallocation. This threatened not only traditional instream water uses such as hydropower, but also some things that water users had taken for granted for so long, such as vigorous fisheries and the basin's stunning aesthetics. Today, just as human demands are growing, the Upper Clark Fork and many of its tributaries are appropriated in excess of their true flow. In addition, the quality of water in the Upper Clark reached critical and even hazardous levels as a result of many of the extractive uses that took place throughout the basin, most intensively around Butte and Anaconda.

Montanans could no longer ignore that extractive water use had seriously impaired the condition of many of their rivers, especially the Upper Clark. Residents of the basin faced increasingly frequent reminders that the years of heavy mining, smelting, and degradation of the rivers' banks had reached a critical point in the form of massive fish kills, declining fisheries, and even forced human evacuations and resettlement. In 1981, arsenic and other metallic contaminants were found behind Milltown Dam, and by 1982, the Environmental Protection Agency (EPA) declared the Upper Clark mainstem one of the nation's largest contiguous Superfund sites. The basin also suffered from high concentrations of phosphorus and nitrogen from specific, or point, sources such as waste treatment facilities, and nonspecific, or non-point, sources such as agriculture and domestic run-off. This high nutrient content, which is aggravated by low instream flows, also increased the growth of nuisance algae.[19] Two hundred and fifty miles of the mainstem were so overrun with algae by 1993 that fisheries could not survive in the oxygen-depleted water.[20] The chronically dewatered stretches of the basin likewise could not support fisheries, and the foaming banks of algae-rich waters continue to be unattractive reminders of the state of water resources.

The degraded condition of much of the Upper Clark Fork basin threatened many of the uses that residents felt were important, uses that were relatively unimportant when prior appropriation was established as the legal method of allocation. Anglers and rafters who value the "natural" state of the Upper Clark and other Montana rivers found themselves with limited options for protecting their own interests. Whereas the interests of water rights owners were being protected, those uses that could not be granted water rights were suffering. Those water users without formal water rights could not depend strictly on interpretations made in the Montana water court to protect their interest. After all, the courts were still bound to uphold prior appropriation and beneficial use, the very doctrines that were responsible for damage to instream uses. And although water judges had leeway for interpreting beneficial use, prior appropriation was less flexible. Instream flow advocates realized that they would have to shift their sights from litigation to lawmaking in order to mitigate and even reverse the institutional bias that had degraded their preferred water use.

In the 1960s, water users began promoting their concerns about declining fisheries to their state representatives. The legislature responded gradually by taking action to protect instream flow. The 1965 Stream Protection Act required all state agencies to take prudent precautions whenever agency activities could threaten the health of a stream. In 1969, state representative James Murphy sponsored a bill allowing DFWP to apply for water rights on twelve Blue Ribbon trout streams. These "Murphy Rights" gave DFWP the opportunity to leave water in the streambed for the purpose of benefiting fisheries. Most of the Upper Clark Fork basin had already lost viable trout populations to pollution and dewatering, but two Clark Fork tributaries—the Blackfoot and a portion of Rock Creek—qualified for Murphy Rights. The new water rights on these tributaries granted to DFWP were "senior" enough to actually procure "wet" water, or water that remains in the water body to protect these relatively healthy ecosystems. If the rights were approved for a creek that was already overallocated, the department would own rights in name only, with no physical water to go along with those rights. The Murphy Act was, in a sense, a legislative departure from the traditional definition of beneficial use; the state could now own water that would be put to neither consumptive nor extractive use.

The most critical piece of water policy legislation was the Montana Water Act of 1973. The act modified water quality standards, established mechanisms for enforcing water policies, and mandated that all watercourses go through an adjudication process to eliminate waste. It also created the reservation process, a new provision for allocating water for future uses.[21] Prior to the act's passage, there was a growing fear among water users that neighboring states might be scheming to "grab" Montana water for coal slurries. Montanans did not take kindly to the prospect of water leaving the state for industrial development elsewhere. "We are jealous of conserving our water, keeping our water for our own use," explains committee member Ole Ueland, who at the time was employed by the state's soil and water conservation agency.[22] Ueland suggested to legislators that conservation districts should be allowed to reserve water today for later use. The legislature agreed with Ueland's reservation suggestion, and the final version of the act made provisions for public entities to apply for water rights that would be used in the future.[23] The Department of Fish and Game (later to become the DFWP) could also reserve water with the express intent of leaving the water in the streambed to improve fish habitat.

Reservations seemed like a promising governmental solution to the emerging interests that were not being protected under the existing system, especially those of future populations and instream flow advocates. The Department of Fish, Wildlife, and Parks could apply for water rights and put them to the beneficial use of supporting valuable and struggling fisheries, a functional equivalent to expanding the Murphy Act throughout the state. Furthermore, the reservations carried symbolic weight and were interpreted as a signal from the state that instream flow would be recognized. The statute, however, was too late. Many Montana rivers were already overappropriated by the time the reservation provision was in place and DFWP had completed the studies to support their reservation applications. In overallocated rivers and creeks, DFWP's water rights would be good for only one thing— the opportunity to legally challenge senior water rights holders that appeared to be wasting water. If DFWP could prove to a water judge that water users were wasting their rights and violating beneficial use, then their own paper rights could be filled by that otherwise wasted water.

The reservation process began to be tested in the Yellowstone basin in 1978 and in the upper and lower Missouri River in 1992 and 1994, respectively. The Yellowstone reservation secured two-thirds of Montana's share of the river and today can be regarded as a success to the extent that the Yellowstone has remained free-flowing. Traditional water users, however, were surprised and threatened by the far reach of the reservations as a management tool, and they organized in response. In contrast to the Yellowstone, the Missouri reservations were met with organized resistance from these traditional water users who drew upon political allies at the state level to protect their interests. The Missouri reservation process, which dragged on for nine years, was caught up in costly litigation as irrigators disputed the need for instream water protection and alleged waste of their water rights.[24]

Thus outcomes of the reservations were mixed: although the Yellowstone has succeeded for the time being in shoring up instream flow, it also galvanized traditional water users to resist the processes and derail progress on the Missouri. Because the reservations alone did not improve the department's ability to protect fisheries or degraded habitats on overallocated streams, but gave the department an opportunity to protest water use—to take irrigators who allegedly waste water to court—the process emphasized the divide between traditional water users and nonconsumptive instream water users and their advocates. Like the doctrines of prior appropriation and beneficial use, the reservations had the unintended consequence of strapping state agencies and water users with the high costs and hard feelings of water litigation. In the conservative political climate of Montana, a state agency such as DFWP had little support for taking Montana ranchers to court and faced extreme opposition from legislators and other political powerhouses.[25]

The difficulties and disappointments of the Missouri reservation process did not entirely dissuade DFWP from pursuing reservations on the Upper Clark Fork. Nonetheless, some individuals in the department did begin to recognize that the reservation process could actually impede progress in restoring fisheries, because real improvements would eventually require the cooperation of irrigators. Now retired DFWP employee Dennis Workman, although a strong proponent of reservations, observed that entering into "an adversarial process like the reservation, you never know whom it is that you're battling. At least not well enough to know if you have any common ground."[26] In spite of a growing animosity among irrigators and the legal costs associated with the Yellowstone and Missouri reservations and enforcement, DFWP still considered the statute to be one of the few tools at its disposal that could reverse the damage done by prior appropriation and protect instream water user interests. The department started collecting data for a reservation on the Upper Clark in 1980.

In 1985, DFWP applied for reservations on the mainstem of the Upper Clark Fork and on seventeen tributaries. The Granite Conservation District, representing irrigators of Granite County, also filed for a reservation to construct two storage dams. Montana Power Company countered the Granite request with a legal objection, because more storage would mean more consumptive use and an even greater strain on its already unfulfilled water rights. Trout Unlimited also filed objections to the storage reservations, out of fear that further storage would undermine important fishery restoration efforts. The Department of Natural Resources and Conservation, the agency responsible for administering water applications, determined that a contested case hearing would be necessary to sort out which reservations could be approved in light of the objections. Theoretically, the case could be appealed all the way to the Montana Supreme Court.

The conflict over proposed reservations reflected the greater ideological and legal battles being waged among environmentalists, industry, and irrigators at all scales throughout the basin. Although the DFWP had at one time proposed including Granite's two dam requests in its own reservation request, there was little incentive for the irrigators to accept this concession. Trust between Granite and the department was minimal, and the irrigators believed that the reservation was only the first of many steps by DFWP and conservation interests to revoke or alter their water rights. In truth, DFWP was driven by the conviction that fisheries were going to continue to struggle if fish and wildlife interests continued to be cut out of legal decision-making processes in the basin. Because the doctrine of prior appropriation had given a clear advantage to extractive water users, agency officials believed they needed to be politically aggressive if there were to be any opportunity for fisheries to rebound in the basin. Hydropower producers, who had traditionally sided with the ranching industry on issues of water management, found themselves objecting to the requests of their historical allies.[27] By 1988, the process was moving fairly quickly toward the contested case hearing in which water users would present their support or opposition to DFWP's reservation request.

As the contested case hearing neared, individuals on both sides of the dispute realized that the process might not satisfy the water users' most basic interests, and might simultaneously exert great strain on other things that they valued. Any contested case hearing was guaranteed to be costly in both time and money for all groups involved, and even the most optimistic could not be confident their investment was going to pay off in the end. Although there is some speculation that DFWP was in a good position to win the hearing, it would have many battles ahead if the win was going to make a concrete difference in water management. Most important, those involved in the reservation process knew that they were not fighting for wet water.[28] There were already far more water rights issued than there was actual water in the basin, so even the winner of a contested case hearing would be receiving paper rights at best. Rather than clinging to an adversarial structure, some water users began to seriously consider an alternative for solving their conflict.

The history of water allocation policies is, in sum, a pattern of attempted adaptation to changing water user interests. At one time, prior appropriation and beneficial use reflected the common interest of Montana's population. As that population changed and the unintended consequences of the traditional water management frustrated emerging interests, water users pushed for change. When the water courts were too intractable to accommodate emerging interests, informal and legislative arenas responded with their own solutions for water allocation and previously unprotected interests. The reservation process, however, was more successful at generating hostility and litigation than instream flow. Water users of the Upper Clark Fork River basin eventually rejected existing modes of decision making and shouldered the task of finding common ground in water management.

The Steering Committee Process

The Upper Clark Fork Steering Committee's involvement in planning began when an alternative to the reservation process became politically feasible in the late 1980s. As DFWP and the other applicants moved ahead with the reservation process, environmental and sporting interests met with department officials in Helena. They made a convincing argument that pursuing reservations in the Upper Clark Fork River basin would ultimately create more problems than it would solve if the Missouri process was the relevant precedent. Some DFWP employees recognized that the cost of the former reservations was not just financial, but social and political as well—the cost of destroying working relationships with irrigators. The Northern Lights Institute (NLI) of Missoula, a nonprofit organization dedicated to environmental education and outreach, at that time introduced water users and managers to a new way of making resource decisions.

Northern Lights provided the groundwork for an alternative solution to the reservation dispute. As early as 1984, those working with NLI were considering whether increased conflicts between resource users might be mitigated by including, rather than excluding, disparate interests in the governance of Montana's water. After attempting several collaborative conservation projects in the Missouri and Snake River basins, NLI had the opportunity in 1988 to sponsor a work group on Superfund activities in the Upper Clark Fork River basin. Several environmental and human crises had resulted from the years of heavy metal accumulation from Butte to Milltown Dam, and throughout the basin there was great disagreement on how the cleanup might meet the needs of basin residents, EPA, and the state. The resulting Clark Fork Basin Committee was a novel project, and its crafters and participants were aware of this. Donald Snow, director of NLI, and Dan Kemmis, who was then the project director for the Upper Clark Fork meetings, did not have many models to follow as they embarked on their experiment. Watershed initiatives, community-based initiatives, and collaborative conservation were hardly the buzzwords of natural resource management in the 1980s.[29]

The Superfund discussions lasted only a year—the topic became bound up in formal politics and litigation—but the meetings did create an opportunity for the participants in the reservation process to air their concerns. The Water Allocation Task Force, a subcommittee focused on the future of water allocation, continued meeting after the larger Upper Clark Fork group dismantled. Jim Dinsmore, one participant representing the Granite Conservation District, suggested that the impending reservations were of great concern to ranchers in the basin. Perhaps the Task Force experiment could uncover a less costly way to solve the allocation disputes. After all, the future litigants in the contested case hearing knew that it was going to be expensive and that the results would be "largely a paper victory."[30] By 1989, both irrigators and anglers began to doubt that a costly, time-consuming lawsuit over junior water rights would be the most effective means to resolve their conflict or achieve their individual goals. If the Missouri reservation was any indication of the efficacy of the reservation, their concerns appeared legitimate. The Northern Lights Institute supported the prospect of a diverse group of water users exploring a less costly and more effective solution to the reservation process, and in 1989 it hired Gerald Mueller to facilitate the task force. Mueller recognized the importance of reducing the many complex problems of the basin down to one manageable resource problem, and he agreed that the reservation process might benefit from a collaborative approach.

The task force quickly acknowledged that it would need the legislature's approval to temporarily stop the reservation process and explore the possibility of other solutions to allocation problems. On October 5, 1990, the group began to negotiate closure of the basin to future water rights. Jim Dinsmore suggested that they consider requesting to close the basin to further appropriation, an action that would halt the reservation process without opening the door for increased water rights applications in the interim. The group concluded that in addition to a temporary basin closure, it would ask the state legislature to establish a steering committee to draft a water management plan for the basin.[31] The task force approached the Montana state legislature in May 1991 with their Upper Clark Fork River Agreement. Some members of the legislature were hesitant to pass the bill, but some task force participants with previous experience in the Montana political system convinced the politicians that a temporary closure was a better step to take than moving on to the contested case hearing. The Senate and House agreed to the terms set forth by the Upper Clark Fork Water Allocation Task Force and gave them until the end of 1994 to present a water management plan to the legislature. Through the agreement, the legislature temporarily closed the basin to further appropriation of water rights, pending a report by the legislation's newly chartered watershed group, the Upper Clark Fork River Basin Steering Committee.

Over the next three years, planning and promoting an alternative to the reservation process would prove to be the committee's most significant contributions to formal water policy in the basin. By involving a broad constituency of water users in their discussions from the beginning, the committee effectively promoted its efforts while gaining input from basin residents. Building on the ideas and experience of the task force, the steering committee researched water quality and quantity issues extensively and sought information and participation from residents throughout the basin. Members took field trips, examined existing policy, and funded an economic analysis of water use in the Upper Clark Fork, always keeping track of the fundamental needs of diverse water users. It published the informative *Upper Clark Fork Water News*, a newsletter filled with straightforward articles covering everything from the link between water quality and quantity to water storage and return flows.[32] The committee also kept basin residents in touch through sixty-seven basin-wide and watershed meetings held between 1991 and 1994 that were open to the public. After more than three years of research and creative deliberation, the committee presented the Upper Clark Fork River Basin Water Management Plan to the residents of the Upper Clark Fork River basin. Basin residents had the opportunity to view and comment on the plan in seven meetings that were held between September 27 and October 12, 1994. By the end of this process, the committee felt that it had enough support from basin residents to warrant a trip to the legislature. In December of that year, it presented the final version of the plan to the Montana legislature and Governor Mark Racicot.

As Gerald Mueller readily points out, the Upper Clark Fork River Basin Water Management Plan is not the kind of plan that normally arises from agency or interagency planning efforts. It did not establish baselines, technical procedures, or budgeting guidelines. Instead, the committee's plan was a response to existing water institutions, including, in effect, an amendment of the prior appropriation and beneficial use doctrines. The core of the plan is a continuation and expansion of the original basin closure of surface water rights, a management step that is notably rare in any Western state (Figure 2.1). The committee proposed that the basin closure should preclude further allocation of the basin's surface and groundwater, with the exception of applications for specific uses including groundwater for domestic consumption, livestock water, and Superfund remedies.[33] Whereas the task force's 1991 temporary closure applied to surface water only, basin residents convinced the committee that the basin closure should also include groundwater because many water users had often seen the effect that

Figure 2.1. Central Policy Components of the Upper Clark Fork River Basin Water Management Plan

Basin water rights closure	Closes the upper basin of the Clark Fork and its tributaries to most ground and surface water rights. Exemptions include Superfund remedies, storage, stock water, groundwater for domestic use, and nonconsumptive hydropower generating at existing projects. To be reviewed every five years by the committee. The legislature rejected the groundwater closure.
Water reservations	The water reservations of Granite Conservation District and DFWP are suspended but retain a priority date of May 1, 1991, if the basin closure is ever terminated.
Instream flow pilot study	Authorizes a ten-year pilot study that allows any public or private group or individual to temporarily lease a water right in order to enhance or maintain instream flow for fishery benefit. The committee must report on the success of the pilot study after ten years.
Reauthorization of the committee	Committee members reappointed with several mandates, such as providing a forum for water interests, identifying short-term and long-term water management issues, assessing projects, and reporting periodically to the legislature.

digging a well can have on surface water flows. Where groundwater and surface water are hydrologically connected, digging a well to drain groundwater might deplete the surface flow. The committee agreed that limiting appropriation of surface water might not have the desired outcome if groundwater permits could still be obtained.

Three other important components of the committee's plan would need the legislature's approval in order to be enforced. First, the committee suggested that both DFWP and the Granite Conservation District should be allowed to retain a May 1991 priority date in the event that the closure was terminated. This provision provided both groups the reassurance that they could continue on with the reservation process if future basin communities decide that they want to resume allocating the basin's water. Second, an instream flow pilot program was proposed to encourage temporary transfers of water from extractive use to instream flow in the Upper Clark Fork River basin. Through the pilot program, a public or private group such as DFWP or Trout Unlimited might pay a water rights owner to keep a specified amount of water in a creek or river to benefit fisheries. Once a lease is arranged and approved by DNRC, a rancher can leave irrigation water in a creek rather than diverting it, as long as the change does not harm other water rights owners. Although this instream use could be considered wasteful under the guidelines of beneficial use, the pilot program stipulates that the rancher can maintain ownership of his water rights throughout the lease. Third, the plan suggested that the legislature extend the mandate for the committee and its locally rooted planning process. In addition to reviewing the effects of its plan, the committee foresaw itself providing community services such as educational forums and reports on important yet complex water management issues.

In addition to these central components, the committee endorsed several programs that would contribute to the goal of balancing water use. These projects did not require specific legislation in order to be implemented, but they would demand either financial or material support from the state. A return flow study in Flint Creek and an ongoing wastewater project in Deer Lodge are two examples of projects that would be completed only with the support of the state's legislative and executive branches. The plan also encouraged continued exploration into potential water storage sites throughout the basin and emphasized the importance of establishing communication links between DFWP and water rights owners. It further acknowledged the importance of improving water quality through state programs such as the basin-wide ban on the sale of phosphate detergents. Finally, it offered its support for any future projects that might address nonpoint source pollution in the basin.

The committee planned and promoted its alternative to the reservation process, but the legislature ultimately retained the power to implement and enforce any water policy. Members recall feeling optimistic about their final product, yet they understood that the legislature had no legal obligation to accept their recommendations. "Obviously somebody does have to have authority," explains Jim Dinsmore. "We offer suggestions. And that's probably how it should be. When push comes to shove, those people who have the power want to keep it."[34] The fifty-fourth legislature agreed with the committee's suggestions in S.B. 144 and adopted the Water Management Plan almost in its entirety. It did make one major change by closing only surface water, explaining that a groundwater closure might unnecessarily restrict industrial growth. In response, the committee asked to include an old legal definition of groundwater as water that is "not part of or substantially or directly connected to surface water." The legislature agreed, so that a groundwater developer would have to be sure that drilling a well would not deplete surface water. According to the legislation, the committee must review the basin closure every five years and the leasing pilot program every ten years. If it finds that either component has had adverse unintended consequences on water user interests, both the closure and the leasing pilot program can be terminated. The final version of the Upper Clark bill was passed unanimously in the Senate, and with only three dissenting votes in the House.

After its passage, responsibility for implementing the legislation fell primarily to DNRC. The basin was effectively closed to further appropriation with the limited exceptions listed in the final legislation. The Department of Natural Resources and Conservation evaluates groundwater applications for the basin and determines whether or not they are a part of any surface water body. Although it is difficult to judge conclusively whether waters are connected or not, the department is using the best available science to appraise applications according to the stipulation in the bill. Only 3 of 445 new wells constructed since the plan went into effect have been through this permitting review, which would indicate that some wells are being dug even though they are connected to surface water.[35] But planners in the basin are admittedly more cautious when applying for a groundwater permit than they were before the plan went into effect.[36] The leasing pilot program has gone mostly unused since 1995, with only one lease on Cottonwood Creek actually completed under the committee's pilot program.

Some of the plan's endorsements have moved forward. The Voluntary Nutrient Reduction Program (VNRP), for instance, has since won approval by the Montana legislature. The waste treatment project in Deer Lodge is nearly complete and will divert a third of Deer Lodge's waste effluent away from the Clark Fork and apply it to a historical ranch operated by the U.S. Forest Service. When this project ran into legal difficulties, committee member Holly Franz—representing Montana Power—was able to negotiate a solution that allowed the city to retain the effluent rather than having to dump it back in the river. The Flint Creek return flow study was also completed in December 1997, and it resulted in some interesting findings: sprinkler irrigation or lining ditches with concrete may actually deplete rather than bolster late summer instream flows under certain hydrological conditions.[37] Thus, both major and minor components of the committee's plan have been implemented, but to varying degrees of effectiveness and completeness.

The committee's momentum slowed considerably after the legislature signed most of its plan into law. The legislation remains in place and the basin closure continues to be enforced, but efforts to get involved in another governance endeavor take considerable time—time that many river advocates feel cannot be wasted. Some participants felt that, having written the plan and taken it successfully to the legislature, their work was complete. Other members recognized that beneficial use in the basin was still far from being balanced. Since the plan was completed, the committee has served as a forum for water concerns, amended the membership appointment process, and helped the Tri-State Implementation Council identify test cases for VNRP, Montana's version of the Clean Water Act's Total Maximum Daily Load (TMDL) standards.[38] The committee has also advised the governor's office over a potential conflict between Avista Corporation, a senior instream water rights owner, and junior water rights owners in the basin.[39] The committee is currently collaborating with Dennis Workman to prioritize critically dewatered sections of the Upper Clark that might be improved through cooperation and effort. Although increasing water in these stretches through conservation efforts and leasing would be expensive and time-consuming, there is strong interest in the project among active committee members.

Policy Appraisals

Appraising water policy is one of the most critical, and the most difficult, challenges facing water managers in the West today. As water management grows increasingly decentralized and more communities become involved in watershed projects, the need for sound appraisals is even more crucial. The committee's efforts have prompted independent reviews of its process and policy outcomes by academics and policy professionals who are interested in new approaches to water management. An article by Donald Snow in an issue of the Northern Lights Institute's *Chronicle of Community* and a brief report by Janet Maughan for the Ford Foundation describe the committee's activities and resulting plan with an emphasis on the committee's process and the alternative, the reservation process.[40] A 1997 publication by the National Academy of Public Administration (NAPA) evaluated the committee to "illustrate how community-based initiatives work and how state and federal agencies can support them."[41] All of these articles review the committee's accomplishments positively, contrasting the reservation process in support of their positions. Jennifer H. Smalley concluded in 1993 that the committee seemed to show some potential for finding common ground but, unlike other case studies, reserved judgment about the success of the process until it could proceed further.[42] The committee itself reviews its progress regularly and produces periodic reports to the legislature. The most recent report to the 1999 legislature covered the general state of the basin and introduced new committee projects, as well as funding and spending. It did not, however, make projections about the success of ongoing projects or make suggestions about terminations or revisions to the existing policy.

A visitor to the Upper Clark Fork River basin might gather informal evaluations—sometimes supporting the professional evaluations, sometimes contradicting them—from communities most affected by the closure. In reality, few residents know about or understand the closure even if it benefits them directly or indirectly. Others are skeptical of the glowing appraisals of the committee and its water management plan conducted by NAPA and other professionals. Water managers and wildlife representatives occasionally question whether the committee has really "done anything," often coming to the conclusion that its activities were better than nothing. Then there are people who know exactly what the committee's plan has accomplished—and don't like it one bit. Some consumptive users and instream flow advocates would prefer a contested case hearing and subsequent litigation challenging the committee's solution. Committee members themselves are not always confident that the closure is going to secure a balance among water users, but the prospect of returning to the reservation process is enough to convince them that their alternative was superior. Even if committee members are not entirely confident that the plan will solve basin allocation problems, they are confident that the reservation process was not in their interests. Ole Ueland insists that "if [DFWP] had gone to court and pursued the reservation, there would be no cooperation today."[43]

The central concern of this appraisal is whether the committee's efforts have advanced the common interest of water users in the Upper Clark Fork River basin. As noted in the introduction, the common interest in this case includes respecting existing water rights, protecting existing instream flow, and providing opportunities for augmenting instream flow. The appraisal that follows considers how well the committee's policy has advanced these interests through each component of the water management plan. Using the common interest as the criterion is an alternative approach to "measure" the relative success of the committee's work and turns up some additional impacts not found in existing appraisals.

The basin closure has effectively protected existing water rights and may also be successful in protecting instream flow. Because further appropriation of the basin's surface water is limited to the few uses stipulated in the plan, hydropower producers do not have to face the prospect of more consumptive use taking place upstream from their dams.[44] Irrigators' rights are also better protected by the closure, because more water rights would probably increase their need to challenge someone else's water use in court. In contrast, the contested case hearing would not have been able to prevent junior water rights owners from taking more than their share out in the field unless those users became the subject of litigation. The reservations almost certainly would have led water users back into the courts and the legislature, as they did on the Missouri, to secure their own rights over junior users and combat charges of waste by DNRC. Every new water right is potentially another challenge to existing water rights. The contested case hearing would have respected existing water rights as well, but at greater social and financial costs.

Existing instream flow has also been better protected under the closure than it would have been under the reservation process. The tributaries that were not already overallocated before the basin closure will have a better chance of maintaining their present water levels. The closure does not grant DFWP legal claims to water in the basin, which means that it is not allowed to challenge wasteful users in court as a water rights owner. Had the reservation process continued and had DFWP won the contested case hearing, it would have gained the legal authority to make a call on any rights junior to its 1991 reservation and to challenge senior users on water waste. But having a legal right to take wasteful water users to court is not the same as having the political opportunity or resources to do so. The conservative political climate in Montana would provide the department with little if any support for taking ranchers to court. Likewise, the reservation would not have stopped further allocation of water in the basin. Tributaries that are not overallocated, those that still support healthy ecosystems, could have been appropriated for consumptive use even after the reservations were granted. The effect of the closure is therefore similar to the anticipated outcome of DFWP's reservation request, in the sense that it protects existing instream flows from extractive use. But it could be even more effective, because DFWP's water reservations may not have had the political support necessary to enforce their rights to instream flow.

The closure, then, has contributed significantly toward advancing the common interest. In principle, the basin could have been closed without the committee's work. In practice, however, it would have been much more challenging. In order for DNRC to close a water body, there must be proof that there is "no unappropriated water in the source of supply," a condition that did not exist in all the tributaries of the ba-

sin.[45] And by authorizing the committee to take the initiative in planning and promotion, the legislature freed up strained resources for
other efforts while retaining with confidence the power to dispose of
the committee's final recommendations.

This does not mean that the committee's plan has safeguarded the
Upper Clark. In spite of its accomplishments, the legislation approved
in 1995 might have left some gaps that could impede instream flow in
the long run. The groundwater definition in the legislation stipulates
that groundwater cannot be developed if it is attached to surface water.
Developers continue to claim that the definition alone has forced them
to be more thoughtful before they try to obtain rights to drill. Because
the connection between surface water and groundwater is only beginning to be understood, some permits will likely be awarded that will
have a subsequent negative impact on instream flow. Another consideration is the exemption of domestic use from the closure. If the populations of Missoula, Butte, or Deer Lodge grow as quickly as other Rocky
Mountain municipalities, withdrawals under the domestic use exemption could have more than a trivial effect on instream flow.

The leasing pilot program has not been as effective in promoting
increased instream flow as some water users had hoped. One lease is
hardly enough to begin to repair the damage that has been done to
environmental and recreational water uses. There are several possible
explanations for the poor showing of the leasing pilot program, some
on the demand side of the equation and others on the supply side. Low
interest in leases might be a result of generally high precipitation between 1995 and 2000, which decreased the immediate need for additional instream flow to protect fisheries. But it is more likely that the
complexity and high cost of negotiating leases is preventing organizations such as DNRC and Trout Unlimited from using the provision
more frequently.[46] It is also difficult to provide adequate incentive for
the suppliers, the ranchers, and other irrigators who have water rights.
Quite simply, they need water rights to stay in business. Finally, the
pilot program is largely redundant now that the 1995 statewide leasing
project is under way, which already provides for three leases in the
Upper Clark Fork basin. A drought will be the ultimate test of the leasing provisions, when instream users will be most concerned about leasing extractive water rights and irrigators themselves will be scrambling
for water. The reservation process would not have increased instream
flow unless DFWP had charged that consumptive users were wasteful,
once again an endeavor that would have been unlikely to succeed. The
pilot program has not proven to be a popular mechanism to increase
instream flow, but the program remains in effect with few changes.

These shortcomings may be partly related to two procedural issues: infrequent formal appraisals, and difficulty taking on problems that keep members engaged and active. The committee conducted thorough self-evaluation in the early stages of the planning process, such as checking with basin residents about their suggestions and constantly reassessing the bill's progress through the legislature. But the five- and ten-year basin closure and leasing pilot program reviews are not frequent enough to ensure that the plan's central components are functioning as anticipated or to inform the larger community of its progress. The committee's periodic reports to the legislature occur often enough to trace trends in basin water management, but the reports do not address whether the policies need adjustment or how the committee might improve their effectiveness. Without more frequent and complete appraisals, the committee's success in planning and promotion may have been overcome by actual water management decisions.

Nonetheless, the committee has made some significant steps beyond rules and institutions that support narrow interests, and toward solutions that respect the common interest. The reservation process, with its mandatory contested case hearing, could not be considered to be in the common interest, since all water users were willing to abandon this well-known process for an alternative with uncertain prospects. Although not all committee members or representatives of other interests were satisfied with the water management plan, the vast majority of those concerned participated in shaping it and signed off on the result. The legislature's enthusiastic approval is a signal that the process and the outcome were acceptable to the officials elected to keep the public interest. Such instream uses as aesthetic enjoyment, fishing, and rafting, however, will improve only if the basin community finds an effective way to increase instream flow, and it is possible that the steering committee has resources that have not been fully mobilized for this purpose.

Committee members remain guardedly optimistic about their success. A leasing program alone is not adequate for augmenting instream flow, and permits for groundwater and exemptions will have to be monitored closely to determine if they are going to harm instream flow or existing water rights. Most committee members recognize that their plan cannot balance beneficial uses in the basin, but it might be considered a step toward that goal. Audrey Aspholm, a former councilwoman from Anaconda, suggests that "you get nothing accomplished if everybody stands still and stares at each other. Most people made enough progress to take at least one step. But every little step that you take forward is that much closer to where you need to go."[47] The committee's process, although not perfect and not yet complete, did take important steps toward the common interest that would have been impossible under the reservation process. And this process may have created a new precedent in Montana water management that encourages innovation on behalf of the common interest of all water users.

Governance and the Steering Committee

The committee's approach to governance is one of its most important achievements. The committee's constitutive decisions—or decisions about how it would make policy decisions—were only partially written down and therefore are not as obvious or stable as the constitution for Montana state government. Nonetheless, the committee's approach to governance is a critical factor in its success. An exploration of the committee's more important constitutive decisions provides insight into how it made progress to this point, how it might build on that progress in the future, and how it might inform other watershed initiatives.

The organizers of the committee recognized that the selection of participants would have a significant impact on the outcome of its interactions with irrigators and neighbors in the basin and with legislators in Helena. The actual participants on the committee have changed since 1991, but the criteria for selection are essentially the same ones used by the Northern Lights Institute in organizing the first round of meetings. The selection criteria include: a good understanding of a particular interest in the basin, a firm grasp of knowledge or skills related to water use or governance, and a strong motivation to be a part of the decision process. Committee members active from 1991 to 1995 were also self-described as "community-minded" individuals who felt a sense of responsibility to their basin neighbors. Overall, Mueller emphasized the importance of including any interest that could "kill the deal."

The water allocation decision process in the basin has grown increasingly more inclusive since the reservation process was set aside. When the Water Allocation Task Force initiated planning negotiations on October 5, 1990, eleven people involved in the reservation dispute attended the meeting. By May 1991, when the legislature officially chartered the committee, there were sixteen participants and one facilitator. The legislature set the membership of the committee at twenty-one, a size that Mueller agrees is large enough to accommodate diverse interests but intimate enough to discourage isolation. The 1994 participants are listed in Figure 2.2. An amendment to the legislation in 1997 requires that twelve members be appointed by local organizations, giv-

Figure 2.2. Committee Membership, 1994

SB 144—Committee membership mandates*	Steering committee membership (1994)	Organization or association
Agricultural organizations	Lorraine Gillies	Rancher, Rock Creek Advisory Council
	Eugene Manley	Flint Creek Valley
	Jim C. Quigley	Little Blackfoot rancher
	Ole Ueland	Silverbow rancher
Conservation districts	Jim Dinsmore	Granite Conservation District**
Water user organizations	Jo Brunner	Montana Water Resources Association
	Ronald C. Kelley	Deer Lodge Valley water user
Environmental organizations	Land Lindbergh	Blackfoot River landowner
	Stan Bradshaw	Montana Trout Unlimited
	Bruce Farling	Clark Fork—Pend Oreille Coalition
Local government	Joe Aldegaire	City of Missoula
	Audrey Aspholm	Deer Lodge County Commission
Departments of state government	Gary Ingman	Montana Department of Environmental Quality (DEQ), Water Quality Bureau
	Curt Martin	Montana Department of Natural Resources and Conservation
	Dennis Workman	Montana Department of Fish, Wildlife, and Parks**
	Bob Fox	Environmental Protection Agency
	Tom Beck	State senator and rancher from Deer Lodge
	Vivian Brooke	State representative from Missoula
Industries	Sandy Stash	ARCO
Hydropower producers	Holly Franz	Montana Power Company
	Reed Lommen	Washington Water Power Company

* Some participants could be classified under multiple categories, and some do not fit precisely into the legislative mandate.

** Reservation applicants.

ing local decision makers more say in their representation. The Department of Natural Resources and Conservation is responsible for the remainder of the appointments, but these depend largely on suggestions from the committee.

The interests that should be represented on the committee, as identified in the legislature's bill, are general enough for the actual composition to be adjusted according to the committee's changing emphasis. It was appropriate, for instance, that only one federal employee from EPA was included in the process between 1991 and 1995 because the water is state-owned. If the resource were federally owned, or if the process were engaging a federal issue such as Superfund, the committee would have needed greater federal participation. Even with efforts to be inclusive, there were gaps in the representation on the committee. The Flathead tribes were invited to participate but declined. Also missing from the committee was a representative of the well-diggers who are often aligned with developers in the basin. This oversight may partially explain the failure of the groundwater provision in the legislature.[48]

The participants had diverse perspectives on water policy and management. For this reason, Northern Lights and Gerald Mueller made the deliberate decision to proceed only if the water users themselves were motivated to find an alternative solution. "The idea that there is some large group somewhere that says 'this is good, everybody go do this' is not helpful. The local people have to decide that there is something in it for them, or it's not going to happen," explains Mueller. "We don't do this type of work only because we as Montanans say 'clean water is important to us.' We do this because it's in our interest to do this, because I benefit from it."[49] Even though ranchers and environmentalists had very different opinions about what needed to be done to improve water policy, they were equally concerned about the uncertain outcomes of the reservation process and about the reservations that would be approved. Apart from the certain legal costs, all participants in the contested case hearing knew that their own cause would be set back terribly if they lost. Holly Franz agrees that "everybody on that Committee had something they needed to protect."[50] They knew that the reservation process might not result in efficient or effective protection of water rights or instream flow, and so they were motivated to find an alternative way to solve their disagreements.

Although the basin community and state government representatives were largely motivated to avoid the contested case hearing, committee members themselves were not totally unified behind the alternative of the plan. At least one member was not in favor of the committee's process or its ultimate solution and eventually rejected the plan, believing that the interests of many extractive users would be better served if the process were controlled by the fairly conservative state legislature. The rejection of the plan by one of the committee members was an important reminder to other participants of the resistance that they might face as they tried to obtain the legislature's approval. Committee members believed for the most part that it was to their benefit to be involved. "[We] had folks saying 'hey, I'm better off knowing what's going on here than simply taking an extremely defensive position,'" explains former committee member Land Lindbergh of the Blackfoot Valley.[51] The committee used the diversity of perspectives represented to gauge how well the final plan reflected larger interests of the basin, and to anticipate where problems might arise when the plan was implemented. Had the entire committee been composed of more contentious members, however, it would have had difficulty creating policy that advanced the common interest. As it was, the committee did not abandon its pursuit of the common interest in order to satisfy the demands of one contentious member.

As the process moved on, most participants joined in pursuit of the common interest without abandoning the specific cause that involved them in the reservation dispute in the first place. Although ranchers and environmentalists assigned different priorities to their interests in water, all of their interests would benefit from clean and ample water. Both groups also respected economic realities. "These people are not out there trying to kill fish," says Jim Dinsmore. "Ranchers do care about the resource, and probably more than most people realize. However, you get to a point where you have to make a living. Bankruptcy is not an option either."[52] Instream flow interests discovered that the committee might be a more reliable means of improving the conditions of the river without relying on coercion from the top down. As Dennis Workman recalls, "I thought it was a bad move to get involved with the Steering Committee. I thought that we should go ahead with the reservation. Even with the Yellowstone, I was still in the fighting mode. After I went there I found out that there just might be a better way to work it out."[53]

The twenty-one-member limit ultimately did not prevent others from participating in planning. The committee's process included visiting numerous political arenas and geographic settings, first the Northern Lights Superfund meetings in 1989, then the legislature to request support for its efforts and a temporary basin closure, and back to a less formal setting to plan and promote its solution. By shifting the settings of meetings, the committee facilitated inclusiveness in participation and reinforced motivation while securing support for the committee process and its water management plan. In 1991, committee members decided to establish communication with the larger basin community. It began regular meetings on October 28, usually congregating in Deer Lodge because of its central location in the expansive basin. It also broke into smaller committees in six established watersheds to encourage participation from more local communities. At meetings throughout the basin, there was always at least one committee member identified closely with community residents who could open the meeting and encourage free discussion. Both the larger and the smaller committees met approximately once a month, with the frequency increasing during busy times such as for discussion of the work plan at the end of 1992 and the presentation of the draft plan in September and October 1994.

Once planning was complete and the committee believed that it had enough community support, it had to return to the Montana legislature in Helena. Even as the bill was working its way through the legislature, the committee actively met in the capitol and on its own to be sure that the bill was not tabled and that amendments reflected the interests of basin residents. After the bill passed, the committee resumed meetings with basin communities, although it has not been changing its meeting places as frequently as it did. It has also been content to leave implementation of the plan as legislated to state agencies, emphasizing that the committee's appropriate role is planning and advising rather than enforcement. Membership declined between 1996 and 2001, reflecting how difficult it is to keep individuals involved as other activities make demands on their time. Declining membership might be aggravated by the difficulty of sustaining funds to cover the more mundane costs of the committee, such as postage, photocopying, and even coffee for meetings.

The committee had to identify and develop diverse resources, ranging from the skills of participants to external funding, to succeed. One of the most important resources was political support. During the beginning stage of the initiative, the task force drew support from the overall discontent of water users with the reservation process. Its 1991 trip to the legislature was essentially a request for support to do what state agencies and the legislature did not have the time or resources to do—find an acceptable solution to the reservation dispute. The committee made several critical choices in the use of its support. The most important of these was to deny any committee member a veto over the plan or any other decisions. Granting a veto would have allowed a single member to override the wishes of all other members. The most contentious member on the committee, for instance, felt that it was in his best interest to return to the reservation process. Had he been given veto power, the contested case hearing would have been resurrected against the wishes of state agencies, the state legislature, and the basin's residents. Instead, committee members who shared his interest in water development gradually distanced themselves from his inflexible position in order to make the process work.

Trust, respect, and friendship were additional resources developed through the committee's governance strategies. Mueller was experienced enough to know that committee members would have to begin to respect one another if they were going to make progress toward an alternative solution. For example, Gary Ingman of the Department of Environmental Quality (DEQ) recalls that some committee members were initially skeptical of information he presented about water quality and about the political feasibility of their ideas. As members became more familiar with one another, they began to appreciate the skills and knowledge of Ingman and other participants. Concurrently, through field trips and frequent meetings, they developed friendships that helped build trust in the expertise members brought to the table. Distrust also played a role in moving the committee process along. Irrigators, for example, probably would not have invested so much time if they had trusted environmentalists to look out for their priority interests. A bit of distrust kept the committee members engaged, while trust-building allowed the majority to find common ground on the most important issues.

Some of the committee's resources were not generated by the process itself but were brought in by members or other participants. The diversity of skill and knowledge of participants, for instance, served as powerful policy tools for the committee. State agency employees, such as Dennis Workman, had special knowledge about fisheries habitats and water quality issues that they contributed to the committee's newsletter. Ranchers and former ranchers, including Jim Quigley from Avon and Eugene Manley from Flint Creek, had concrete knowledge of local water conditions and hydrology. Vivian Brooke, a Montana state legislator, contributed to the broad experience that members had with legislative politics. And members had an ample range of communication skills, ranging from Audrey Aspholm's ability to diffuse disagreements, to Stan Bradshaw's and Bruce Farling's lobbying experience, to Jim Dinsmore's ability to converse effectively with the ranching community. If the committee did not have specific knowledge or skills needed for planning or promotion, it recruited advisers from agencies such as DEQ, DNRC, and the U.S. Geological Service, as well as specialists from the University of Montana in Missoula.

Financial support was a critical resource that is still not generated internally, but it is an important component of the committee's governance model. In 1989, Northern Lights applied for grants from the Ford Foundation, the Bullet Foundation, and the Avista Corporation to hire Gerald Mueller as a part-time facilitator and to cover such expenses as travel, room rentals, supplies, publication of the committee's newsletter, postage, and meals or snacks for the meetings. Some participants, including state employees and corporate representatives, were paid by their employers for their work with the committee. Montana Power Company, for instance, compensated Holly Franz for time spent on committee issues. Most committee members volunteered their time and travel expenses. The committee, which now takes responsibility for securing the majority of its funding, is presently supported by a variety of state and federal grant programs.[54] Although the committee's annual expenditure is fairly low, averaging approximately $14,700 from 1996 through 1998, regular funding was essential for retaining the group's facilitator, keeping up mailings, and funding the few projects that required external technical assistance.[55] Unfortunately, the committee has discovered that it is difficult to find continued financial support for its basic operating costs, because most foundations prefer to fund specific projects rather than organizations.

Perhaps the most critical resource for the committee has been Gerald Mueller's leadership. "I'd been exposed to a lot of cookie-cutter facilitators," says Stan Bradshaw, who represented Trout Unlimited on the committee, "people who said 'here is what a facilitator does. Follow these steps and you'll facilitate.' [Mueller] didn't force people into kind words about each other. The first few meetings, if you had to pee on each other's fire hydrants, you did it. Gerald was sensitive enough to understand that people have to stake their ground, even if it's the wrong ground. He let you do that and then moved things along."[56] Mueller also listened. He turned meetings over to local representatives. Most important, he guided members toward understanding what they had in common. "As a facilitator [Mueller] was extremely skilled at keeping that safety net out there and providing lots of opportunities for discussions," says Mike Mclane of DNRC.[57] Through all of the group's arguments, he managed to keep his cool. "I've seen a lot of these facilitator types," explains Land Lindbergh, "and he never got upset. Trust me, he had plenty reason to get upset."[58]

The committee was willing to take some risks, and it made some decisions that could be criticized as empowering some interest groups more than others. Irrigators, for example, had more representatives on the committee than environmentalists did. But the irrigators who participated had less lobbying and legal experience than the nongovernmental environmental groups, and they are also the water users who would eventually have to change their behavior in order to improve instream flow. By sacrificing equality in numbers, the committee was stocked with plenty of water users who could improve the resource. Irrigators felt secure enough to discuss options for increasing instream flow—the very topic that had caused so much controversy in previous efforts to govern water in the basin. In the end, the committee and its policy recommendations gained the support of irrigators where previous attempts to protect instream flow had not. This unequal representation gave irrigators enough power to feel comfortable supporting water allocation decisions that they had previously opposed, and boosted the committee's authority for a critical part of the community in the basin.

With virtually no capacity to coerce its members, and only limited economic resources, the committee necessarily relied on strategies of communication first to develop and then to promote the plan. The committee's resources, fortunately, were sufficient to employ these strategies effectively. Intensive collaboration among themselves and extensive communications with other residents of the basin allowed committee members to identify diverse interests and to incorporate them into the plan as far as possible. This, in turn, simplified the task of persuading those involved to support the plan and built the trust necessary for that purpose. Water users of all kinds agreed that the plan was a better alternative than the costly and uncertain outcomes of the reservation process. Consequently, they did not mount the kind of opposition typically stimulated by innovations in water management after the plan was submitted to the legislature. The plan achieved something that the reservation could not—a win-win outcome through innovation. The collaboration at the core of this strategy requires "cross-fertilization of ideas, education of the group internally," according to Donald Snow. "It is not about compromise. It's about innovation. There are a lot of red herrings about collaboration, and [compromise is] one of them."[59]

The water management plan, the major policy outcome, is only part of the committee's story. Another part is the increase in civic capacity, perhaps the most profound long-term effect of the committee's work and a significant achievement in itself. Civic capacity in the context of the Upper Clark Fork means improvements in the ability of community members to make private and public decisions that advance the common interest, and it includes an ability to organize inclusively for that purpose. In contrast to the concept of social capital, civic capacity emphasizes inclusive participation in community policy decisions; like social capital, it also depends on constructive interactions through social networks.[60]

A number of barriers to constructive social interactions have been breached as a result of the committee's work. Land Lindbergh believes that there is, in addition to ranchers, "a whole new generation of state and federal people that are starting to be much more responsive toward working with the locals."[61] The trust and friendships developed through the committee have helped DFWP chip away at irrigators' negative stereotypes of other water interests. And with the department's involvement, there have been small but concrete improvements in water resources. "We gained a lot of friends out there, and because of that we've been able to do a lot of stream restoration work," says Workman. "Now a biologist can feel safe going to a landowner and asking to talk about the resource."[62] For example, Eric Ryland, a DFWP biologist working out of the Missoula office, took calls from two ranchers in Flint Creek asking for suggestions to improve trout streams that run through their property. Ryland now works with them to improve the streams. Another small but concrete improvement is committee member Jim Quigley's new fish-friendly headgate in a stream on his ranch.

Such increases in constructive interactions have helped open up water management decisions to water users who had been excluded historically. The committee brought instream flow advocates into water management without raising the anxieties of traditional water users during the transition. Gerald Mueller understood that informal access would give instream water users influence "that having a water right will never give you."[63] Irrigators and other consumptive users do not constantly consult instream water users when making water decisions, but now there is greater capacity for mutually advantageous decisions. The committee's continuing project—finding means to increase instream flow in lower stretches of the Upper Clark Fork mainstem—demands a great deal of person-to-person communication among water users and managers, and will demand even more if the project sustains its momentum. Such informal interactions can advance the common interest as much as regulatory action, and perhaps more, under the right circumstances.

The committee deserves a major portion of the credit for increases in constructive interactions among the interests involved. "The point," according to Workman, "is that it does happen now, and it didn't used to happen at all."[64] Through the committee, representatives of different interest groups in the basin shared their resources in pursuit of the common interest. They also recognized the many benefits of keeping the larger basin community involved as shapers of policy, not as merely distant observers or stakeholders. Among other benefits, they uncovered the needs of basin residents who had been largely uninvolved before the committee existed. In contrast, adversarial processes like the Missouri reservation process tend to polarize water users and exacerbate their anger and distrust. The committee's inclusive process had the opposite effect, leaving people in the basin in a better position to resolve subsequent water management issues.

Appraisals of the committee are incomplete without considering the alternatives, governance exclusively through the water court or the legislature. What the committee achieved through the water management plan and in building civic capacity would have been difficult if not impossible to duplicate through a contested case hearing on new water reservations, which was the water court alternative. The reservation process is substantively constrained by water law based on the prior appropriation and beneficial use doctrines. It is also restricted by formal and rigid procedures that favor adversarial strategies, in which resources are hoarded and employed to control outcomes rather than to find common ground. The committee's innovative solutions depended in part on its freedom to set aside such conventional constraints, at least temporarily. "We were able to have some measure of control over the final solution, more than the court process," explains Stan Bradshaw. "With [the committee], you at least have a chance at a win-win situation."[65]

The state legislature had authority to take the initiative on water planning for the basin but lacked the will to do so even after water users in the basin began to consider alternatives to the reservation process. Even if legislators had sufficient will, they would have been much more constrained than the committee in arriving at equivalent outcomes, especially given the substantive and political differences among water users at the outset. The committee's success in devising and promoting an innovative water management plan depended in part on a consistent focus and considerable investments of time necessary for intensive face-to-face communications with one another, extensive contacts with other residents in the basin, and field trips and site visits. A consistent focus and the time necessary for such activities are difficult to find amid the multiple, changing issues that compete for attention in the legislative process even at the state level. Consequently, even under the best of circumstances, it would have taken the legislature much longer to achieve equivalent outcomes. More likely, a legislative plan would have been less inclusive of basin interests and more controversial. The committee found and promoted a plan that advanced the common interest with far greater efficiency and effectiveness than the legislature could have, even if the legislature had been motivated to try.

In spite of its accomplishments, the committee has been relatively inactive since the legislature enacted the water management plan. Perhaps this represents missed opportunities to use the civic capacity, including social networks constructed over the first half of the 1990s to help implement the plan later in the decade. The committee, for example, could be actively encouraging or arranging meetings between consumptive water users in a position to lease water, and others like DFWP or Trout Unlimited who might use leased water to improve instream flow. It could also be appraising the leasing provisions of the plan more frequently, and adjusting strategy or policy accordingly. Neither leasing nor the informal cooperation necessary to resolve remaining water allocation problems can be forced upon consumptive water users. The committee, however, need not restrict itself to policy planning and promotion. If it does, both committee members and supporters might be disappointed in the end. Of course, the committee would not be in a position to choose if it had not achieved enactment of the plan and built civic capacity in the process.

Missed opportunities might also be the result of fatigue among committee members. Participation in a watershed initiative is arduous and intellectually challenging, not to mention time consuming. Moving the meetings around in the basin, arranging field trips and lunches, and allowing the group to forge friendships helped justify the fatigue through the long planning process. Once the legislation was passed, however, and the immediate threat of a reservation hearing was postponed until at least the next basin closure review, many committee members felt that it was time to invest their efforts elsewhere. The committee retained most of its original members through the passage of the plan, but it had significant turnover soon after that. It takes time to bring the new participants up to date on water issues and information, and time to develop new friendships and trust. Fatigue may have driven some members away from the process once the plan was secure. It partially explains why the committee has been slow to take on large projects since 1994.

It should be noted that the committee formed at the height of a long drought in the basin and in response to the projected high costs and uncertain outcomes of the reservation process. Another drought or another crisis in water management might stimulate reactivation of the committee. A much larger challenge to the committee would be to reactivate in the expectation that such crises are inevitable sooner or later, even if the details cannot be reliably predicted, and to devise some contingency plans and maintain the capacity for coping with them. Major changes in policy and in governance are often driven by crises that reveal the limitations of established alternatives, but only if innovative alternatives are available and work well enough in initial implementations to deepen and broaden support.

The Broader Significance

How might the committee's process be understood in the context of Montana water management, and in the broader context of a water-shed management movement that seems to move through cycles of boom and bust? This section reflects on this question and suggests a way to frame discussions on watershed and community-based management that encourages learning from cases like the Upper Clark Fork.

Looking beyond the water management plan, the committee's experience has already contributed to water policy and governance in the Upper Clark Fork basin and in the state of Montana. According to Holly Franz, the committee "turned out to be a very powerful way of diffusing the opposition to [protecting] instream flows" through a statewide leasing program passed in 1995.[66] Gerald Mueller helped the governor's office design the Governor's Consensus Council in 1993 to address a variety of issues. The committee has advised a special board that oversees a citizen advisory group on the allocation of millions of dollars resulting from settlement of a claim against Arco. The committee also advised the governor's office on negotiations between the state and Avista Corporation, and it encouraged the two parties to make the negotiation process more transparent to basin residents. When the negotiations ended without a resolution, the committee encouraged the governor to submit legislation that would establish a basin-wide planning process.[67] The committee also helped initiate a community-based group on conflicts over Georgetown Lake. Some smaller watershed groups in the basin, such as the Blackfoot Challenge, have organized since 1989 and are now wrestling with their own constitutive and policy decisions. In short, the committee has had an impact beyond the boundaries of its own policy process.

The Steering Committee's impact might be even more significant if it capitalized more fully on its experience by focusing on another issue comparable to the water management plan in importance. As Dennis Workman put it, the committee "provided a real good forum to get to know people in the basin that we were going to have to work with if we were ever going to resolve the water issues in the Upper basin."[68] There is no dearth of such issues on remaining and future agendas. Communities in the Upper Clark Fork basin will find it difficult to avoid a host of serious water issues as tourism increases, agriculture adapts to deregulation and other changes in the economy, Superfund clean-up processes continue, and invocation of the Endangered Species Act forces action on habitat protection or restoration. The committee must focus if it becomes involved, unless members can find the additional time, attention, and other resources necessary to proceed productively on more than one complex issue at the same time.

Consider some of the issues that face the basin in 2001. Instream water uses are still threatened in the basin, and it is far from certain that existing policy will be enough to protect them during a drought. Competing for attention will be such related issues as the excessive numbers of recreationists on some rivers, the listing of the bull trout as an endangered species, and the relicensing of hydropower dams on the Clark Fork. Commitments to the Voluntary Nutrient Reduction Program appear to be insufficient to control nonpoint sources of pollution in the absence of a pollution crisis. There is also grave concern about a twenty-year flood or the failure of Milltown Dam that could release large quantities of heavy metals into the river and possibly change the river in ways that could preclude the restoration of desirable aquatic habitats.[69] Although experts generally agree on these negative impacts of a twenty-year flood, they disagree on what the best alternatives are for mitigating these and other negative impacts. But most agree that it is worthwhile to consider how extractive water users might conserve more water, and how to keep that additional water in the stream and make water available for restoring riparian environments and for future clean-up projects. The committee possesses some unique social tools not as readily available in formal government agencies that could play an important role in securing progress toward the common interest.

In a larger context, the Upper Clark Fork Steering Committee has become a significant example of water-user groups that have taken the initiative in response to unresolved water management problems across the country. When traditional structures fail to advance the common interest, in the Upper Clark Fork basin as in hundreds of others, frustrated water users become more receptive to other ways of making water management decisions. "These groups," Donald Snow explains, "are appropriate for changing the relationships between people, and as a result, some real things can happen that would not have happened before. You don't have to agree with them, but you do have to respect them."[70] Among these groups, the steering committee is a case conspicuously successful enough to attract the attention of journalists, scholars, and others interested in understanding watershed initiatives and in disseminating what they learn.

Drawing on a decade or more of experience in various earlier cases, some scholars and legal experts recently have raised concerns about the achievements and potential of watershed initiatives. They caution appropriately that watershed initiatives are not panaceas and they claim that few have achieved documented, on-the-ground improvements in water resources.[71] The recorded history of watershed initiatives is far too thin to assess the empirical basis and significance of such claims, but there are scattered indications that some familiar dynamics might be at work. The early initiatives appear to have attracted a good deal of attention well before there was sufficient time for their efforts to pay off, or for the interim outcomes to be carefully evaluated. Nonetheless, the initial reports of officials and scholars enthusiastic about the promise of watershed initiatives appear to have been picked up by journalists who sometimes resorted to Old versus New West clichés to tell the story. Such hype unwittingly sows the seeds of failure: it creates unrealistically high expectations for watershed initiatives to meet, and it provides premature or otherwise undependable information that is used in efforts to meet those expectations. Doug Kenney writes, "Despite the efforts of numerous investigators critical research focused on the western watershed movement still lags woefully behind the level of experimentation and promotion."[72]

In any case, it should not be forgotten that innovations generally tend to fail simply because they are innovations. It takes time for problem solving by trial-and-error to reduce failure rates and build upon the successes. Meanwhile, failure rates support skepticism and perhaps even political backlash that may inappropriately discredit the successes or the process as a whole. Failure rates should not detract from the significance of the successes, especially the early successes, or the wisdom of building on them. The Upper Clark Fork Steering Committee is one of the early successes in the watershed movement.

The committee's experience clarifies the main role of watershed initiatives in the management of water resources, and it demonstrates the feasibility of that role at least in the Upper Clark Fork basin. The committee's role was to integrate and balance diverse interests in the basin in order to develop a plan that advanced the common interest and at the same time satisfied the broader interests represented by legislators in Helena. For reasons already reviewed, that role could not have been duplicated by either a contested case hearing in water court or by the legislature itself, which nevertheless retained authority and control over water policy. The limitations of these traditional structures of governance become especially apparent when it is understood that the problems addressed by the committee were in some respects unique. The Upper Clark Fork basin differs from all other basins in many physical, ecological, and social details relevant to finding common ground, and these details are subject to change on various time scales. Realistically, policies that accommodate such differences depend on proceeding from the bottom up, through watershed initiatives, rather from the top down, as has been the case traditionally.

This role is essentially political and should be recognized as such. Science and scientific advisory groups are not adequate substitutes. Vicki Watson of the environmental studies program at the University of Montana agrees that many of the issues in the Upper Clark Fork River basin are not scientific. "A lot of times it's not a scientific issue, it's a political issue. We have a lot of scientific information, and the question now is what we ought to do."[73] That is primarily a question of policy and politics. There is no scientific consensus, for example, on the minimal amount of water needed to maintain a fishery in Upper Clark Fork tributaries or other rivers in the West, but there is a high degree of certainty that a dewatered stream will not support fisheries. That is sufficient to move on to the political problem of finding common ground on policies that accommodate what is known, by scientists and nonscientists alike, about the physical, ecological, and social details of any basin. Perhaps Montana's DFWP recognized the difference between policy and political issues on one hand, and scientific issues on the other, when it hired "human dimension" specialists to join its traditional rosters of biologists.

The committee's experience also suggests that successful performance of this role depends on motivation sufficient to sustain an initiative over several years of collaboration and communication, and the freedom to set aside traditional constraints temporarily in order to find innovative solutions. These conditions are not likely to be met by state initiatives to establish or manage watershed groups statewide from the top down. Oregon's Watershed Health Program, for example, requires that watershed councils develop a plan to assess the condition of a watershed and implement that plan.[74] Such programs need to be evaluated as carefully as initiatives taken by residents in a watershed. Meanwhile, it should be recognized that there is a difference, in responsibility and accountability if nothing else, between an initiative taken by residents in their own watersheds and a statewide initiative from state officials. It should also be anticipated that there will be efforts to reduce watershed initiatives to traditional roles in support of scientific management by central authorities, which would compromise the potential of watershed initiatives to advance the common interest in ways that traditional structures cannot duplicate.

The means employed by the Upper Clark Fork Steering Committee to achieve significant innovations in water policy and governance do not represent a formula to be generalized to all watershed initiatives. Among other things, not every basin needs to be closed to new reservations. Moreover, the committee's experience provides no guidance on what to do if established authorities reject an initiative's request for planning authority or an initiative's plan. In the Upper Clark Fork case, the state legislature accepted both—wisely, it turned out. But the committee's policy and constitutive decisions advanced the common interest in the Upper Clark Fork well enough to be considered models by other watershed initiatives. Such initiatives "are place-specific, time-specific, issue-specific, people-specific," argues Donald Snow. "Do they have some commonalities? Yes. But . . . just as natural ecology of forests differ, you have to attune yourself to the diverse ecology of politics."[75]

The doctrines of prior appropriation and beneficial use served the common interest when they were originally conceived and implemented, but they have not been flexible enough to accommodate the new water interests that have emerged in recent decades. Irrigators have traditionally relied on water courts to reaffirm historic rights to consumptive uses of water, just as environmentalists have more recently turned to the courts to enforce federal regulations like those in the Endangered Species Act or the Clean Water Act. But adversarial proceedings are often expensive, slow, and insensitive to context, leaving water users frustrated with traditional structures for making decisions.

Watershed initiatives might provide innovative solutions to difficult water management problems in many places concurrently. The Upper Clark Fork Steering Committee advanced the common interest in its basin by planning and promoting a water management plan that was superior to the uncertain but certainly costly outcomes that were projected to emerge from a contested case hearing over reservations in water court. During the process, the committee shared knowledge and skills while developing new channels of communication, trust, and friendships. With exceptional leadership, the committee used such resources effectively enough to earn the legislature's support for the water management plan. The policy outcomes have not entirely balanced beneficial water uses in the basin, but they advanced the common interest more than what would have been possible through the water courts or through the legislature acting on its own.

More policy and constitutive appraisals are needed to guide the continuing evolution of particular initiatives and the watershed movement as a whole. It is important to disseminate information on the experience of successful initiatives like the Upper Clark Fork Steering Committee, and to build on those successes through adaptations in similar contexts elsewhere. Progress on a wider scale will also depend on leadership by elected and appointed officials who are willing and able to work with watershed initiatives to help advance the common interest. In this case, legislators in Helena and employees of the Department of Fish, Wildlife, and Parks like Dennis Workman, in addition to the committee members, are models to emulate.

3 Wolf Recovery in the Northern Rockies

Roberta A. Klein

We reached the old wolf in time to watch a fierce green fire dying in her eyes. I realized then, and have known ever since, that there was something new to me in those eyes—something known only to her and to the mountain. I was young then, and full of trigger-itch; I thought that because fewer wolves meant more deer, that no wolves would mean hunter's paradise. But after seeing the green fire die, I sensed that neither the wolf nor the mountain agreed with such a view.
—Aldo Leopold, *A Sand County Almanac*

Aldo Leopold, one of the foremost wildlife biologists, experienced a transformation in attitude toward the wolf that anticipated a recent shift in societal attitudes. Once viewed with hatred and fear, the wolf was nearly eradicated from this country with a fierceness that many now find hard to understand. Nevertheless, to some Westerners the wolf still represents a threat to the traditional Western rural lifestyle. To others, however, the wolf has become a positive symbol of nature and the last vestiges of wilderness and wildness. And this is the problem: The wolf is largely a symbol. "Wherever he goes, whatever he does, he is burdened with a heavy load that we have laid on him—all our images of him, our dreams, our fears, our stories."[1] This chapter examines the clash of those symbols in the late twentieth century—and the various structures for decision making used to resolve the clash—as the federal government paved the way for the gray wolf's return to the northern Rockies.

The gray wolf (*Canis lupus*) was classified as an endangered species under the Endangered Species Act of 1973 (ESA). The act requires the secretary of the interior to develop and implement recovery plans for

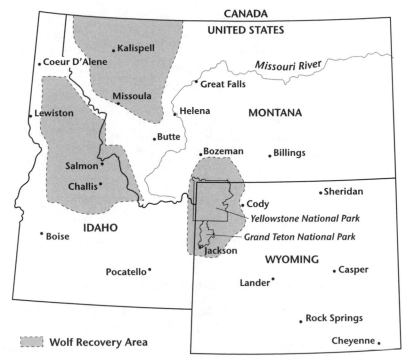

Map 3.1. Northern Rockies Area

the conservation and survival of endangered species. Pursuant to this mandate, the U.S. Fish and Wildlife Service (USFWS), an Interior Department agency, developed a plan for the recovery of gray wolf populations in three areas in the northern Rockies: northwestern Montana, central Idaho, and Yellowstone National Park (Map 3.1). The plan originally defined recovery as ten breeding pairs in each of the three areas for three successive years.[2] It was later revised to define recovery as a total of thirty breeding pairs distributed throughout the area for three successive years. Under this plan, the federal government introduced sixty-six wolves to Yellowstone National Park and central Idaho in 1995 and 1996. At around the same time, wolves were migrating on their own from Canada to northwestern Montana. Early in 2001, wolves were well on their way to reaching the recovery goal. Depredation of livestock by the wolves has been less than expected, and livestock producers have been compensated for the losses that they have suffered, if it has been verified that the losses were due to wolf depredation. The recovery program nevertheless remains controversial.

Various structures exist for making natural resource policy decisions, including those prescribed in the National Environmental Protection Act (NEPA) and other environmental laws, and in litigation under those laws. Several additional structures involved in planning and implementing the return of wolves to the northern Rockies also merit attention: a congressionally mandated advisory committee, a gray wolf recovery team led by employees of the USFWS, and a program established and led by Defenders of Wildlife to compensate livestock producers for wolf depredations. The recovery team and the compensation program are community-based initiatives, but different from the Upper Clark Fork Steering Committee (Chapter 2) or the Quincy Library Group (Chapter 5). The recovery plan and its implementation sought to advance the common interest of the community, which includes people living in the vicinity of wolf recovery as well as people outside the region. From a common interest viewpoint, the plan was an improvement over the status quo, although valid concerns remain.

Historical Search for the Common Interest

Since the 1800s, this country has had a series of national policies regarding wolves and their prey. Each policy can be viewed as an attempt, within a changing context, to advance the common interest pertaining to wolves. And each policy gave way to a new policy as the unintended adverse consequences of the old policy became apparent, new interests emerged, and nature took its course.[3]

Before the European colonization of North America, the wolf had one of the widest distributions of all land mammals. It inhabited most of the North American continent, including the Yellowstone area. Lewis and Clark reported that wolves were abundant when they passed through Montana in 1805–6. Before the creation of Yellowstone National Park in 1872, different animal populations lived in the Yellowstone habitat. Their numbers were kept in check by natural processes that included wolf depredation.[4]

As European settlement of the West proceeded in the mid–nineteenth century, the customary policy of the time permitted the indiscriminate killing of wildlife. This policy was supported by a prevailing philosophy that presumed human domination of and mastery over nature and natural resources. To compound the problem, early North American settlers brought with them a hatred of wolves that had developed in Europe, particularly England. Farmers viewed wolves as thieves that robbed them of their livelihood. Wolves were also associated with evil and the devil for many reasons, including their "elusive, watchful, nocturnal habits," and their transmission of rabies.[5]

The popularity of wolf pelts in the 1850s and 1860s resulted in unrestricted wolf hunting. In 1880, Yellowstone Park superintendent P. W. Norris reported that "the value of [wolves'] hides, and their easy slaughter with strychnine-poisoned carcasses have nearly led to their extermination."[6] Indiscriminate killing of millions of bison, elk, and other ungulates that were prey for wolves also severely depleted the populations of these animals.

Gradually, new interests emerged, challenging the indiscriminate killing of wildlife and calling for the preservation of nature. Congress created Yellowstone, the world's first national park, in 1872 and prohibited in principle "the wanton destruction of fish and game" within the Park.[7] Market hunting of big game animals continued in the Park for several years after its creation, however, because Congress did not provide enforcement against poaching, and employees of the Park killed big game animals for food. The media and other concerned interests successfully promoted protection of the Park's wildlife. The poaching ended after Congress sent the U.S. Cavalry into Yellowstone in 1886. The cavalry also fed the elk, drove them back into the Park, and erected a fence to keep them in. Elk began to multiply, even though they had almost been eradicated from the United States by the end of the nineteenth century. There were more than 35,000 elk within Yellowstone by 1914.[8]

The new policy of protecting wildlife did not apply to wolves and other predators. Few people apart from game conservationists supported the protection of wolves at the time. In fact, an organized constituency called for their eradication. As millions of deer, elk, and other wolf prey were killed, wolves turned to livestock for food. Some livestock producers in the northern Rockies claimed average losses of 25 percent of their calves to wolves in the late 1800s and succeeded in convincing state legislatures to enact bounties for wolves.[9] Nearly 30,000 wolf bounties were claimed between 1895 and 1917 in Wyoming alone.

Not satisfied with the states' efforts to eradicate wolves, livestock producers turned to the federal government for help. The U.S. Biological Survey (predecessor to the U.S. Fish and Wildlife Service) was created in 1885 to promote research on wildlife and economics. Under pressure from livestock producers, Congress turned the Biological Survey into a predator control agency. By 1914, Congress had appropriated funds for the destruction of predators, including wolves, on public land.[10] Killing wolves was now the official policy of the federal government. This policy advanced the dominant interest in settling Western lands and raising livestock before there was any significant interest in protecting predators.

Wolf sightings in Yellowstone rose sharply in 1912, around the time that elk numbers were rebounding. The cavalry had generally resisted demands to kill predators in the Park. Then the first officially documented wolf killing in Yellowstone occurred in 1914. After the National Park Service assumed responsibility for Yellowstone in 1918, the Biological Survey and the livestock industry pressured Park employees to continue to kill wolves. This persisted despite the Service's Organic Act providing that "the fundamental purpose of the [national] parks . . . is to conserve . . . the wild life therein and to provide for the enjoyment of the same in such manner and by such means as will leave them unimpaired for the enjoyment of future generations."[11] Park officials justified their control of wolves with the argument that wolves were "a decided menace to the herds of elk, deer, mountain sheep, and antelope."[12] Park officials also felt responsible for preventing the Park from becoming a breeding ground for predators that would leave and cause problems for the nearby livestock industry. At least 136 wolves were killed within the Park between 1914 and 1926. By the 1930s, wolves—whose populations once numbered in the thousands—had been eradicated from the West.

Scientists' attitudes toward wolves began to change in the 1920s and 1930s with improved understanding of the role of predators in ecosystems. One incident in particular gave biologist Aldo Leopold insight into the danger of overcontrolling predators: the success of a predator control program on the Kaibab Plateau in Arizona led to an explosion in the deer population. As they depleted vegetation and encountered several harsh winters, thousands of deer died. Another wildlife biologist, Adolph Murie, conducted a study in Yellowstone and discovered that predators did not cause the decline of antelope, bighorn sheep, and white-tailed deer, as Park officials believed. Instead, inadequate winter range caused the decline. Biologists began to realize that the Park's predator eradication policy had given elk a competitive advantage.[13]

The public's attitude toward wildlife was continuing to evolve as well, due in part to the near extinction of such species as the whooping crane and the trumpeter swan. As a result of new scientific understanding and public sentiment, an organized constituency arose to demand an end to the government's predator control program. The common interest was no longer secured by widespread destruction of predators. Rather, it needed to be redefined to accommodate these rising interests. In the early 1930s, a variety of conservation and hunting organizations such as the American Society of Mammalogists, the New York

Zoological Society, and the Boone and Crockett Club pressured the government to cease unnecessary predator control. The Park Service responded by banning use of poisons in national parks, except in very narrow circumstances. For the wolf population, however, this act was largely symbolic. Wolves already had been eradicated from the Park, and predator control continued outside the Park.

Because of the policy of protecting elk in the absence of predators, the elk herd in Yellowstone continued to grow. A game conservation committee on which Theodore Roosevelt served recommended that the Park kill a certain number of elk every year to balance the population with the food supply. In the mid-1930s, the Park adopted a management policy that authorized rangers to regulate elk numbers by methods that included shooting the animals within Park boundaries. Between the mid-1930s and mid-1950s, Park officials killed as many as 900 elk each year. In late 1961 and early 1962, Park officials shot 4,300 elk within six weeks. The shootings were broadcast on the nightly news and stimulated a public outcry. In response, Secretary of the Interior Stewart Udall established a committee, chaired by A. Starker Leopold, to review the situation. In its 1963 report, "Wildlife Management in the National Parks," the Leopold Committee recommended continued reductions in the elk herd, but also encouraged control through natural predation whenever possible.[14]

George Hartzog, director of the Park Service, agreed to stop the shooting of elk within the Park in 1967, after Senator Gale McGee of Wyoming held hearings on the issue in response to public pressure from hunters who wanted to hunt elk themselves and from environmentalists and animal lovers. In accordance with the Leopold Committee's recommendation that the national parks should provide a "vignette of primitive America," the Park Service in 1968 implemented a policy called natural regulation. The new policy assumed that elk numbers would be controlled by limited food supplies, predators, and other natural forces within the Park, and by public hunting outside the Park. The policy was flawed in at least one respect, however: the wolf, an important natural predator, was missing from the Park. After implementation of the new policy, elk numbers grew steadily from slightly over 3,000 in 1968 to 21,000 in 1987–88.

Natural regulation remains controversial. Critics claim that it is a politically motivated policy lacking a sound scientific basis, which has allowed elk to overrun the Park and destroy its vegetation. Scientific or not, natural regulation set the stage for the next step in the search for the common interest pertaining to wolves.

Wolf Recovery Plans

Although Americans have been interested in wildlife conservation since at least the Progressive era, the environmental movement that emerged in the 1960s emphasized the protection and recovery of endangered species. Congress responded initially by passing the Endangered Species Preservation Act in 1966. Then Congress strengthened its protections with the Endangered Species Act of 1973. The act's expressed concern was that economic growth and development were causing a number of species to become extinct, and it requires the secretary of the interior to develop and implement plans for the recovery of endangered and threatened species. The wolf was listed as an endangered species in 1974. Thus, ESA helped force the issue of wolf recovery in the northern Rockies. Failure to act would leave the federal government vulnerable to claims of noncompliance with the law.

Yellowstone managers began to consider wolf reintroduction as early as 1967. In 1971, an assistant secretary of the interior met with Yellowstone officials to discuss wolf restoration. One of the first orders of business was to attempt to confirm the numerous reported sightings of wolves in Yellowstone. The Park contracted with biologist John Weaver to determine whether the sightings could be verified. Over a twelve-month period, Weaver traveled on foot, skis, and snowshoes inspecting trails, ridges, and streams for evidence of wolves. He broadcast taped and human-imitated wolf howls. He placed baits of road-killed ungulates and canid scent at several locations and monitored them with time-lapse cameras. And he spent thirty hours in flight searching for wolves. But he found only two sets of tracks and heard only one series of howls that may have been from a wolf. No wolves were photographed at the bait sites, nor were any observed in the aerial flights.[15]

Weaver found that although up to ten canids may have occupied areas near the Park around 1970, it seemed unlikely that these animals were a population of pure wolves that had survived over the years or migrated from Canada and Montana. He could not rule out the possibility that wolves had been surreptitiously released, but he believed their chances for survival would be slim. He also considered, but could not verify, whether hybridization was responsible for the sightings. Weaver concluded that the evidence did not show a viable wolf population in the Park and recommended restoring wolves to Yellowstone through reintroduction.[16]

The Northern Rocky Mountain Wolf Recovery Team was created in 1975 to develop a plan for wolf recovery. It was one of the earliest teams formed under ESA. An employee of the Montana Department of Fish and Game headed the original recovery team, which included representatives of other relevant state and federal agencies and the National Audubon Society as well as a University of Montana professor who had studied wolves. Its first plan, released in 1980, presented a vague timetable for restoring wolves by 1987. Wayne Brewster, the endangered species program supervisor for Montana and Wyoming, appointed Bart O'Gara of the Montana Cooperative Wildlife Research Unit to lead the team in 1981. Brewster also added biologist John Weaver. These appointments helped revitalize the team and diversify the perspectives represented. So did the participation of Joe Helle, a sheep rancher; Hank Fischer from Defenders of Wildlife, an environmental organization; Timm Kaminski, a wildlife biologist; and Renee Askins, an environmentalist.[17]

The Wolf Recovery Team released a much more specific plan in 1985, amid growing public interest in wolf reintroduction. A study found that Yellowstone visitors, by a margin of six to one, thought wolves in the Park would improve the experience. Other polls showed support for wolf recovery.[18] The team's new plan recommended natural recovery of wolves in Montana and Idaho and reintroduction of wolves in Yellowstone under the "experimental nonessential" provision of ESA. This provision permits the USFWS to promulgate rules governing the management of introduced populations in a more flexible manner than ESA would otherwise permit. The team narrowly approved reintroduction by only one vote. Opponents of reintroduction were concerned about its political feasibility and believed that, given enough time, wolves would return naturally on their own, which, they argued, would be more acceptable to the public. After much controversy and delay, the USFWS acting regional director approved the plan in August 1987.[19]

While the government moved forward with recovery plans, wolves were finding their own way back to the northern Rockies. Canadian provinces had ended their wolf eradication campaigns in the late 1960s, allowing wolf numbers to begin to grow in Canada and prompting some to disperse south to the United States. Researchers at the University of Montana began searching for wolves in Montana in 1973 and finally spotted a lone female in Glacier National Park in 1979. By 1986, researchers verified the first wolf reproduction in more than fifty years in Glacier. This was another critical event: wolves were repopulating the northern Rockies, and those that migrated on their own, rather than those that were introduced by the federal government, would enjoy ESA's full protection. In the following year, wolves killed five cows and nine sheep in northwestern Montana, causing much local controversy.

Meanwhile, in 1985, National Park Service director William Penn Mott, Jr., had already suggested compensating livestock producers for losses caused by wolves. Mott told Hank Fischer, from Defenders of Wildlife: "The single most important action conservation groups could take to advance Yellowstone wolf restoration would be to develop a fund to compensate ranchers for any livestock losses caused by wolves. Pay them for their losses and you'll buy tolerance and take away their only legitimate reason to oppose wolf recovery."[20] Fischer convinced the organization's board of directors to compensate Montana livestock producers on an experimental basis and then evaluate the results to determine whether to make the fund permanent. Defenders of Wildlife raised $3,000 from private sources and sent a check to the producers who had lost livestock, substantially reducing the controversy. The board of directors later authorized creation of a permanent Wolf Compensation Trust, financed entirely by private donations.

In 1988, the USFWS established another interagency team to manage the northwestern Montana wolves. (This was separate from the Wolf Recovery Team formed earlier to develop a recovery plan.) Wayne Brewster hired wildlife biologist Ed Bangs to lead the management team, which included a secretary and three other USFWS biologists. The program had four primary purposes: radio collaring a few members of each pack to monitor the status of the wolf population; controlling wolves that attacked livestock; conducting research on wolf ecology; and educating the public about wolves. What Bangs learned in leading this program would carry over into later stages of the wolf recovery process and contribute to its success.

After the USFWS signed off on the plan of the Wolf Recovery Team in August 1987, Mott, a supporter of wolf recovery, suggested that the next logical step would be preparation of an environmental impact statement (EIS). The National Environmental Policy Act requires that an EIS be prepared whenever any "major Federal actions significantly affecting the quality of the human environment" are proposed.[21] The Wyoming congressional delegation met with Mott, USFWS head Frank Dunkle, and other federal officials to persuade them to stop the reintroduction of wolves. Soon after the meeting, Mott made a public statement supporting wolf reintroduction. This prompted Representative Dick Cheney of Wyoming to write to the secretary of the interior, Donald Hodel, stating his staunch opposition to reintroduction of wolves in Yellowstone. Hodel pressured Mott to announce that reintroduction was on hold pending the Wyoming delegation's approval. Dunkle stated publicly that he would fight wolf reintroduction in Yellowstone, despite the fact that his agency had recently approved the plan.[22]

Ordinarily federal agencies do not need congressional approval to prepare an EIS; Congress usually allows agencies broad discretion in this area. In this case, however, wolf supporters were forced to lobby Congress to initiate the EIS process because the Wyoming delegation had persuaded the administration not to proceed with wolf reintroduction. The response of the congressional delegation was to block funding for an EIS.[23] This tactic proved to be successful for several years.

In 1987, Utah congressman Wayne Owens introduced a bill to require the National Park Service to reintroduce wolves to Yellowstone. That bill failed. But in June 1988, the House passed an appropriations bill that included $200,000 for a Yellowstone wolf reintroduction EIS. The counterpart appropriations bill in the Senate lacked funds for an EIS. In the conference committee to resolve such differences, Senator James McClure (R-Idaho) reached a compromise with the House to appropriate $200,000 for the Park Service and USFWS to conduct a study called *Wolves for Yellowstone?* instead of an EIS.

Again in 1989, the House voted to appropriate funds for a wolf reintroduction EIS. Senator McClure again blocked the appropriation. He succeeded in having the appropriations bill amended to prohibit any expenditures on a wolf reintroduction EIS. Instead, Congress appropriated $175,000 for more studies on the issue. The first two volumes of the studies came out in May 1990 and generally supported wolf recovery. In 1990, the House once again appropriated funds for an EIS, and the Senate once again blocked the appropriation.

Meanwhile, an aide to Senator McClure, Carl Haywood, had attended meetings of the Wolf Recovery Team. McClure eventually became concerned that if wolves naturally migrated into Idaho, they would be entitled to the fullest protection under ESA. McClure knew he could not get ESA repealed, so he proposed a plan on behalf of his rancher constituency to reintroduce wolves but to afford them less protection than if they had naturally migrated into the reintroduction area.[24] His bill called for the introduction of three pairs of wolves into both Yellowstone and a portion of Idaho, and removal of the wolf from the endangered or threatened species list in areas outside the reintroduction zones. The bill died. By this time McClure knew he had to persuade livestock producers to accept wolf recovery as inevitable and to become involved in shaping how that would happen.[25]

Then director of the USFWS, John Turner, a Republican from Wyoming, was searching for a pragmatic solution to the stalemate.[26] He proposed creation of a Wolf Management Committee to resolve the issue, and McClure helped push the proposal through Congress. Congress directed the committee to develop a wolf reintroduction and management plan for Yellowstone National Park and central Idaho that represented a consensus agreement, and required that at least six of the ten committee members support the plan. Congress set a deadline of May 15, 1991, for completion of the task.

The Wolf Management Committee met between January and April 1991. It was composed of six members representing state and federal agencies, two representing conservation interests, and one each representing the livestock industry and hunting interests. K. L. Cool of the Montana wildlife department organized the other state wildlife agencies and the livestock representative to create a voting bloc that he controlled.[27] Cool insisted that wolves be removed from the endangered species list in Montana, Idaho, and Wyoming, except in national parks and wildlife refuges, before reintroduction could proceed. One of the other state agency directors felt it would have been political suicide for him to take a position at odds with Montana's or Wyoming's, and that his state legislature would overrule him if he did.[28] The conservation representatives, however, would not agree to any recommendation that required amending ESA. Committee members refused to budge from their initial positions after several months of discussion.

Despite their differences of opinion, the committee members came close to a consensus solution. John Mumma, the committee's Forest Service representative, submitted a proposal at the April 1991 meeting that was acceptable to all but the livestock representative. Under the Mumma proposal, the experimental population area would be extended into Montana except for the area immediately around Glacier National Park; state and federal agencies would share management responsibilities; Congress would provide funding for development and implementation of the management plan; a subcommittee would be established for information and education purposes; and landowners would be permitted to shoot wolves caught preying on livestock, though they would be required to report any livestock killings within a certain time limit and produce physical evidence of depredation.

By the next meeting, outside pressure had been applied to committee members, the consensus had disappeared, and the committee once again was deadlocked. The USFWS submitted a proposal that would establish an experimental population area including Idaho, Wyoming, and most of Montana, and grant states primary management of wolves. The proposal would have required that Congress pass legislation removing most Montana wolves from the endangered species list and would have allowed livestock producers to shoot wolves on sight, whether or not they were preying on livestock.[29] The environmental representatives voted against the USFWS proposal, but it garnered the requisite number of votes in the committee and was sent to Congress.

The day after the committee's proposed plan was delivered to Congress, Senator Quentin Burdick (D-North Dakota) and Representative Gerry Studds (D-Massachusetts) stated that they opposed the plan because it would violate ESA. These members of Congress chaired committees that had oversight responsibility for the endangered species program.[30] Other Democratic congressmen serving on key committees wrote to Secretary of the Interior Manuel Lujan voicing strong concerns about the plan. Defenders of Wildlife launched a campaign to defeat the plan. The USFWS did not push the plan because many people in the agency felt it "stretched the ESA too far."[31] Congress did not act on the recommendation of the Wolf Management Committee.

By this time James McClure had retired from the Senate, and no other senator from Wyoming, Montana, or Idaho served on the Appropriations Committee. Although members of the congressional delegation from the region complained about wolf reintroduction, and all six senators from the region signed a letter opposing funds for an EIS, they did not work hard at this point to stop the EIS from going forward. Ed Bangs believes the regional delegation had become convinced that wolves were migrating back to the northern Rockies on their own, and further delay would only reduce management options.[32] Consequently, Congress finally approved funding for an EIS in November 1991.

Although no decision on reintroduction was made before completion of the EIS, Bangs assumed that it would be the likely outcome of the EIS process: the issue had been debated for twenty years, and it was unlikely any new information would come forth.[33] Furthermore, Congress stated in an appropriations bill in October 1992 that it expected the preferred alternative to come out of the EIS process would be "consistent with existing law," which precluded alternatives that would require amending ESA to lessen the wolf's protection.[34] Approval of EIS funding was effectively the decision on recovery of wolves in the northern Rockies. After that, the question was not so much whether wolves would be brought back, but how.

Preparation of the EIS began in the spring of 1992. The USFWS chose Bangs to lead the Gray Wolf Interagency EIS Team. The EIS team emphasized public involvement throughout the process, starting with issue scoping. Scoping is "a process for determining the scope of issues to be addressed and for identifying the significant issues related to the proposed action."[35] In April 1992 the team sponsored twenty-seven "issue scoping open houses" in Montana, Wyoming, and Idaho, and an additional seven outside the region. Participation was open to anyone interested. More than 1,730 people representing diverse interests attended the open houses. With this public input, the team identified thirty-nine issues, including concerns about controlling depredations on domestic livestock, compensation for livestock losses, impacts on big game populations, hunting, land use restrictions, human safety, private property rights, animal rights, wolves that already lived in Yellowstone and Idaho, federal subsidies, management responsibility for wolves, and the local economy.

Later the EIS team developed five alternatives and summarized them in a brochure mailed to numerous people and inserted into several thousand Sunday newspapers in Wyoming, Montana, and Idaho. The five alternatives were

- reintroduction of experimental wolf populations in Yellowstone and central Idaho, the preferred alternative
- natural recovery, or the "no action" alternative
- proposal of the Wolf Management Committee's majority
- reintroduction of fully protected wolves
- the "no wolf" alternative

The team then held twenty-seven alternative scoping open houses and six public hearings to identify means of addressing the issues.

The draft EIS was released in July 1993. In preparing it, the team consulted with the USFWS, the National Park Service, and the U.S. Forest Service, as well as the wildlife departments of Montana, Idaho, and Wyoming. The EIS team presented the draft EIS to thirty-one groups, including Defenders of Wildlife, the No-Wolf Option Committee, Eastern and Western Wyoming Resource Providers, the Nez Percé tribe, Rotary and Lions Clubs, Chambers of Commerce, Kiwanis, the Farm Bureau, People for the West, the Audubon Society, and Montana Stockgrowers. More than 1,000 people attended these presentations. Almost 1,500 people attended sixteen hearings on the draft EIS that were held in the three affected states as well as in Salt Lake City, Seattle, Washington, D.C., and Denver. Copies of the draft EIS were sent to federal and state agencies and officials, Native American tribes, local officials, businesses, and organizations ranging from the Wyoming Woolgrowers to the Sierra Club. The secretaries of interior and agriculture signed the record of decision on the wolf recovery plan in June and July 1994, respectively.

Congressional and legal requirements circumscribed to some extent the influence of public input on the alternatives developed, as well as the final choice of an alternative. Council on Environmental Quality

(CEQ) regulations require that all environmental impact statements consider a "no action" alternative.[36] In this case "no action" meant natural recovery, that is, relying on wolves to migrate to Idaho and Yellowstone on their own, rather than through reintroduction by government agencies. In addition, Congress prescribed that the recommendation of the Wolf Management Committee be considered as an alternative.[37] Congress also directed, however, that the preferred alternative be consistent with existing law.[38] The EIS team included these options to present a broad range of alternatives. According to Bangs, the team also included the "no wolf" alternative to comply with NEPA and to show the public that it had examined one of the main alternatives supported by public comments.[39]

The final EIS rejected the "no wolf" alternative because it would not allow wolves to fulfill their ecological role in the northern Rockies and it would require new legislation to amend ESA. The natural recovery, or "no action," alternative was rejected because it could have taken up to thirty years for full recovery with less management flexibility to resolve local concerns. The EIS team expected that under this alternative wolf populations would reach recovery levels in the three areas at very different times: 2002 in Montana, 2015 in Idaho, and 2025 in Yellowstone. Wolves could not be removed from the endangered species list until recovery goals were met in all three states, which meant that Montana could have wolves above recovery levels for many years before control could be turned over to the states. Having the three populations recover at around the same time was an important reason for not relying on natural recovery in Idaho.[40] Costs of wolf management under the natural recovery alternative would be $10–15 million, compared with slightly less than $7 million for the preferred alternative. The EIS team's final decision was a compromise among its members to "carve out that middle ground among the polarized public comment— minus the hype."[41]

The plan's goal was to achieve wolf recovery in and around Yellowstone, central Idaho, and Montana by the year 2002. It authorized the capture of approximately thirty wolves in southwestern Canada for three to five years and their transport to Yellowstone and central Idaho for release. Subsequent releases were to be modified depending on what was learned during previous years. Natural (or non-reintroduced) wolf populations in Montana were expected to recover at about the same time as those in Yellowstone and central Idaho. The plan classified the reintroduced wolves as an experimental nonessential population. The rules for managing this population contain the following provisions:

- Landowners may harass any wolf in a non-lethal manner at any time.
- Livestock producers may kill or injure any wolf caught in the act of killing or harming livestock, provided such incidents are immediately reported and livestock freshly wounded or killed are evident.
- Livestock producers on public lands may receive permits allowing them to take (kill) wolves under certain conditions.
- Governmental agencies may relocate or kill wolves that have attacked livestock or domestic animals.
- Land use restrictions on public lands are allowed to control intrusive human disturbance within one mile of active den sites between April 1 and June 30.
- Except in national parks and wildlife refuges, no land use restrictions are permitted after six or more breeding pairs are present in a recovery area.
- Nonselective control (poisons) may not be used to control predators in areas occupied by wolves.
- States and tribes may relocate wolves to other areas if wolf predation is negatively affecting local ungulate populations at unacceptable levels, as defined by the states and tribes.
- Unintentional, nonnegligent, and accidental taking by the public pursuant to otherwise lawful trapping or other recreational activities, or any taking in self-defense or in defense of others, will not violate ESA provided any such incident is reported within twenty-four hours.[42]

The plan encouraged but did not require state and tribal wildlife agencies to lead wolf management outside national parks and wildlife refuges by entering into cooperative agreements with the USFWS. The plan provided no federal compensation for livestock losses caused by wolves. Finally, the plan provided that after a minimum of ten breeding pairs were documented for three years in each of the three recovery areas, the gray wolf would be proposed for delisting—that is, removal from the endangered species list. The USFWS later revised this standard to allow delisting when a total of thirty breeding pairs were distributed throughout the area for three years. Monitoring to ensure wolf populations did not again become endangered or threatened would continue for five years thereafter. At that point the states or tribes or both would assume authority for managing wolves and the federal government's involvement would terminate unless wolves were relisted under ESA.

To implement the plan, the federal government had wolves radio-collared and trapped in Alberta in late 1994 and early 1995. Shipment of wolves to the United States began in January 1995. Release of the wolves, however, was blocked temporarily by a court order arising from a lawsuit filed by the Farm Bureau. The Sierra Club Legal Defense Fund (later renamed the Earthjustice Legal Defense Fund), the National Audubon Society, and other environmental groups also challenged the legality of the wolf reintroduction program in a separate lawsuit. Both groups of plaintiffs contended that reintroduction of wolves under the "experimental nonessential" provision of ESA would be unlawful because there were naturally occurring wolves already in the release areas, and the reintroduced wolves therefore were not "wholly separate geographically from nonexperimental populations of the same species" as required by ESA.[43] Although the Farm Bureau wanted to prevent reintroduction, the environmental plaintiffs sought more protection for the reintroduced wolves.

On January 12, 1995, the court lifted its order and government officials released seven wolves into acclimatization pens in Yellowstone. Agency officials released another four in the Idaho wilderness two days later. The Yellowstone wolves were "slow released," meaning they were held in acclimation pens for slightly over two months before release. The central Idaho wolves were "quick released" or released immediately without being held in pens. The government released twenty-nine gray wolves in central Idaho and Yellowstone in 1995 and an additional thirty-seven in these areas in 1996.

The USFWS was unsuccessful in its attempts to turn over wolf management to the states. Montana, Idaho, and Wyoming drafted wolf management plans, but all were abandoned for lack of sufficient public support. In Wyoming, for example, the wildlife department released a draft wolf management plan outlining five management alternatives. The agency held seven public hearings and received more than 3,400 written comments. It ultimately recommended that the state have very limited involvement in wolf recovery and management before delisting because of a lack of consensus on how the state should manage wolves. Most livestock producers wanted the right to shoot any wolves leaving Yellowstone, while many environmentalists wanted management to be based on wolf behavior rather than numbers. The agency felt it got "beat up," by livestock producers for even considering involvement and by environmentalists for recommendations that were "too strict."[44] In August 1997, the governors of the three states announced they would not be directly involved in wolf management until wolves were delisted. As of late 2001, Idaho and Montana were in the process of completing post-delisting management plans. Wyoming, however, had not yet started on a plan. The USFWS will not propose delisting until all three states have wolf management plans in place that the USFWS has approved and that would reasonably assure wolves would not become threatened or endangered again.

The Nez Percé tribe of Idaho participated in the EIS process on the assumption that the state and the tribe would co-manage Idaho's wolves. When the state did not become involved, the tribe prepared a wolf management plan and has been managing the Idaho wolves since 1996 under a cooperative agreement with the USFWS. Tribal members support the wolf management program and have made personal contributions to make up for shortfalls in USFWS funding. The tribe works with livestock producers to manage problem wolves that kill livestock. It also notifies livestock producers if a wolf enters their property, and provides information about wolves to anyone who is interested. The tribe's biologist believes that local citizens would perceive USFWS control of the program as the equivalent of "the feds shoving this down our throats" and would shut their doors. He believes that not having the federal government involved diffuses a lot of anger about the program.[45]

On December 12, 1997, a federal judge issued his ruling in the consolidated Farm Bureau and Earthjustice lawsuits. He agreed with the plaintiffs' argument that the reintroduced wolves could not be designated as an experimental nonessential population under ESA because lone wolves existed in or could disperse into the experimental area, and he ordered the removal of all reintroduced wolves. The order was stayed pending appeal.[46] On January 13, 2000, the Tenth Circuit Court of Appeals unanimously reversed the Wyoming district court, ruling that the wolf recovery plan did not violate ESA.[47] The losing parties did not seek further review in the U.S. Supreme Court.

Bangs and his Montana-based team, the Nez Percé tribe, and Yellowstone National Park monitor wolf numbers in the three recovery areas, and they manage and control wolf populations as well. Control efforts include relocating or killing depredating wolves. In 1999, for example, the government killed nineteen wolves in "control actions."[48] The team also participates in outreach and research. Meanwhile, Defenders of Wildlife continues compensating livestock producers for wolf-caused losses through its Wolf Compensation Trust fund. Under the trust, landowners who sustain a suspected loss from wolves may contact the state game warden or the federal wildlife services agency. A trained biologist conducts an investigation, and if he or she can verify wolf depredation, notifies Defenders of Wildlife. Hank Fischer then contacts the livestock producer directly and provides compensation shortly after receiving the report. County extension agents help Defenders decide fair market value when there is a difference of opinion with the landowner.[49]

Wolf numbers have greatly increased in the northern Rockies since reintroduction, as documented below. Consequently, in July 2000 the USFWS proposed to reclassify gray wolves in Idaho, Wyoming, and Montana from endangered to threatened. The experimental nonessential status of wolves in Yellowstone and central Idaho would remain, and a rule would extend similar control measures to the entire Western population, which includes Colorado, Oregon, Utah, Washington, and portions of Arizona and New Mexico. The agency, however, has not yet proposed delisting of the wolf in the northern Rockies.

Policy Appraisals

The USFWS has conducted several appraisals of the wolf recovery program, and the report for 2000 is the most recent.[50] The *Rocky Mountain Wolf Recovery 2000 Annual Report* covers monitoring, research, outreach, and livestock depredations and management. In addition, a USFWS Web site provides regularly updated reports on the wolf program.[51] Data are available on the numbers of wolves and packs in each of the three areas at the end of 2000 (Figure 3.1).

The USFWS announced in September 2001 that a thirtieth breeding pair had been located in Idaho, bringing the wolf populations to the minimum level to begin the three-year countdown to delisting. Populations in northwestern Montana declined in 1997 and 1998, and recovered somewhat in 1999 (Figure 3.2). The number of breeding pairs in northwestern Montana has remained at five or six for the past four years (Figure 3.3).

Wolf control in response to livestock depredation was a leading cause of death for wolves in northwestern Montana in 1998 and 1999. According to the 1999 annual report, nine out of fifteen wolf mortalities

Figure 3.1. Wolf Numbers and Packs—End of 2000

Recovery area	Number of individual wolves	Number of packs producing pups
Yellowstone	177	13
Idaho	192	9
NW Montana	64	6

Source: USFWS, *Rocky Mountain Wolf Recovery 2000 Annual Report.*

Figure 3.2.   Trends in Wolf Populations by Recovery Area and Year's End

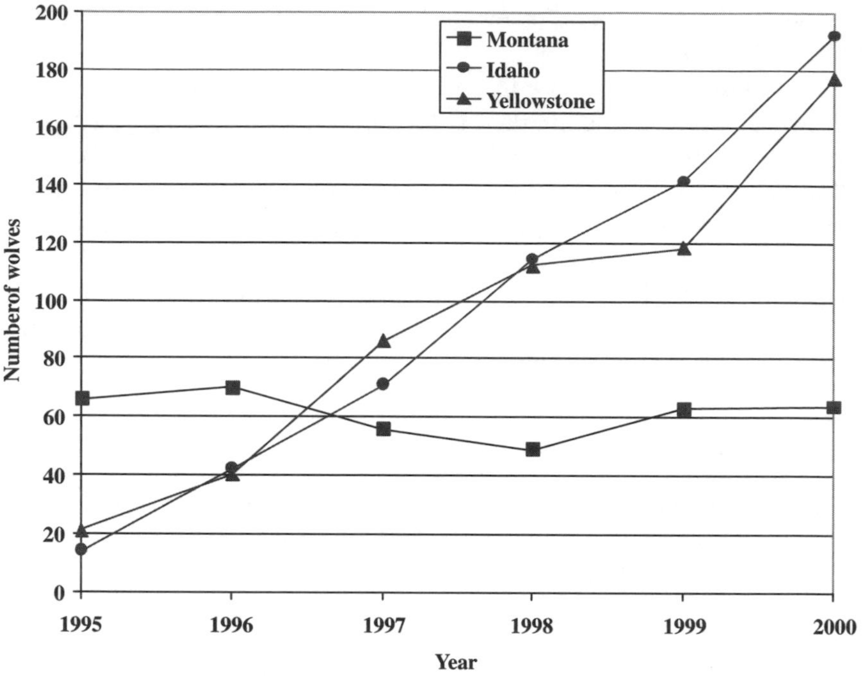

Source: USFWS, *Rocky Mountain Wolf Recovery 2000 Annual Report.*

in northwestern Montana that year occurred in response to livestock depredation. Livestock losses and resulting control efforts declined in 2000. Wolf depredation in Yellowstone and Idaho has been lower than predicted in the EIS for a fully recovered wolf population (Figure 3.4). The 2000 report concedes that some wolf-caused losses will be undetected. Whether confirmed losses represent a large or small portion of actual losses is the subject of much controversy. The USFWS and others conducted a research program (the Diamond Moose Calf Mortality Study) to try to determine the true extent of livestock losses to wolves. To give the wolf depredation figures some context, the 1998 appraisal observed that Montana livestock producers suffered annual average losses of 142,000 sheep and 86,000 cattle to all causes, most unrelated to depredation.[52]

Because of limited space in the two reintroduction areas, the USFWS has predicted that wolves will move outside of Yellowstone and the public lands in central Idaho as their populations continue to grow. As that occurs, more wolf management will be required because there will be more conflicts with humans and livestock. The agency

Figure 3.3. Trends in Breeding Pairs by Recovery Area and Year's End

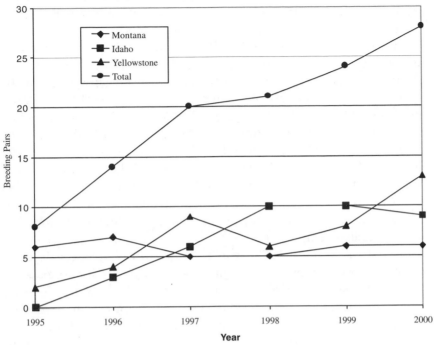

Source: USFWS, *Rocky Mountain Wolf Recovery 2000 Annual Report.*

Figure 3.4. Projected and Confirmed Depredations, 1987–2000

Recovery area	Projected average annual depredation from a recovered population (100 wolves)	Actual average annual depredation	Total confirmed depredation
NW Montana	Not provided in EIS	6 cattle, 5 sheep	83 cattle, 63 sheep
Yellowstone	19 cattle, 68 sheep	3 cattle, 23 sheep	19 cattle, 139 sheep
Central Idaho	10 cattle, 57 sheep	8 cattle, 26 sheep	46 cattle, 154 sheep

Sources: USFWS, *Rocky Mountain Wolf Recovery 2000 Annual Report* (confirmed depredations); USFWS, *The Reintroduction of Gray Wolves to Yellowstone National Park and Central Idaho* (projected depredation rates).

Note: Wolves have been present in Yellowstone and central Idaho since 1995, but in Montana since 1987.

thought that livestock producers might have greater tolerance for non-depredating wolves if problem wolves were controlled by lethal means.[53] It did not address how well the general public will tolerate increased killing of wolves by government agents.

The 1998 appraisal by the USFWS concluded that enforcement of ESA prohibitions against the illegal taking of wolves has been successful. At that time, only twelve wolves had been illegally killed in the experimental area, and six of those cases had been resolved. In Montana, nine wolves had been illegally killed and four of these cases had been resolved. Fines were imposed and one person served six months in prison. Two wolves were legally killed by livestock producers who saw the wolves attacking livestock and reported the shootings within twenty-four hours. The 1999 appraisal reported another illegal killing, and two wolves were found dead in Idaho in late 2000. As of late 2001, at least nine Idaho wolves appear to have been killed by Compound 1080, a deadly chemical.

From 1973 through 1998, wolf recovery in the northern Rockies cost slightly over $10 million, in figures not adjusted for inflation. Some of this cost may have been a result of delay and of the unnecessary congressional studies that served as a substitute for action on an EIS. Although the EIS estimated that a recovered wolf population in Yellowstone alone could generate up to $23 million annually in economic activity, none of the appraisals evaluated whether wolf reintroduction has produced any increases in tourism or spending.

Defenders of Wildlife reports the status of its Wolf Compensation Trust on its Web site. By December 2000, the organization had paid a cumulative total of approximately $144,000 to livestock producers in Montana, Idaho, and Wyoming for verified or probable wolf depredations (Figure 3.5).

To what extent has the wolf recovery plan, as written and implemented, succeeded in advancing the common interest? Procedurally, all the major interests were represented before Congress and the USFWS at key points in the decision process. Congress balanced the interests involved and, by funding the EIS, effectively decided that wolves would return to the northern Rockies. In many respects, the "no wolf" interest was defeated at that point. The USFWS further balanced national and local interests in developing the recovery plan through the EIS process, and later through implementation of the plan. Bangs and his staff, the Nez Percé tribe, Yellowstone National Park, and other government officials continue to serve the diverse interests, both by protecting wolves and by relocating or removing wolves that cause problems for local citizens. Those environmentalists and livestock pro-

Figure 3.5. Payments by Defenders of Wildlife, 1987–2000

Wolf population	Total depredation	Total compensation
Yellowstone	145 sheep, 26 cattle, 18 other	$43,909
Central Idaho	188 sheep, 63 cattle, 3 other	$55,898
NW Montana	68 sheep, 89 cattle, 2 other	$44,156

Source: Defenders of Wildlife's Wolf Compensation Trust, www.defenders.org/wolf-comp.html.

Note: Payments in Montana began in 1987; payments in Yellowstone and Idaho began in 1996 (there were no depredations in these states in 1995, the year of the initial releases). These figures vary somewhat from the USFWS's figures (figure 3.4) because the USFWS includes only confirmed depredations by wolves. Defenders of Wildlife's figures include all incidents for which compensation was provided, including probable but unconfirmed depredations, as well as injured and missing livestock.

ducers who felt their interests were not adequately represented could and did resort to legal action in the courts.

Substantively, the wolf recovery program satisfied an interest in returning wolves to the northern Rockies that is shared by majorities in the region and by larger majorities nationwide, as well as by many environmental organizations.[54] The interest in wolf recovery is valid because wolves were returning to the region on their own. It is appropriate because ESA mandated the protection and recovery of wolves. The plan did not satisfy the interest of those environmentalists who opposed reintroduction of an experimental population in Idaho on the ground that some wolves had already migrated there on their own. This position was not supported by the federal appeals court's decision that ESA permits reintroduction of experimental populations even though lone wolves (rather than breeding populations) exist in an area.

The interest in avoiding the adverse financial effects of wolf reintroduction on livestock producers has been satisfied to some extent. Defenders of Wildlife provides compensation in verified or probable cases of wolf depredation, and the government relocates or removes problem wolves. This is a valid interest; wolves do kill livestock and such losses hurt livestock producers financially. The plan did not satisfy the interest of some livestock and other local groups that wanted removal of the wolf from ESA's protection and generally unregulated killing of wolves by the public. This interest is inappropriate in view of the overwhelming public opposition to a return to the days of widespread wolf eradication. This interest is also incompatible with more comprehensive interests authorized in ESA, including protection and recovery of endangered species in general and wolves in particular. Although concerns about financial losses from depredation are valid, they are insufficient to warrant blocking the larger interest in wolf recovery, especially when the government relocates or removes problem wolves and Defenders of Wildlife provides compensation for known or suspected wolf depredations. Finally, the plan largely satisfied the interest of local landowners in avoiding the imposition of new land use controls through wolf reintroduction, because the action required hardly any additional controls.

The plan did not satisfy the interest of those who supported natural recovery rather than reintroduction of wolves. This interest is not incompatible with the overall goal of wolf recovery, although federal biologists think recovery would have taken much longer if it had relied on natural migration of wolves rather than reintroduction. The biologists also believe that fewer conflicts with humans result from reintroduction because wolves tend to settle in the protected or remote areas where they are located, such as national parks and wilderness. The 1998 USFWS appraisal found reintroduced wolves had a lower rate of human-caused mortality than wolves that migrated on their own because they were released in remote areas.[55] A comparison of population figures in the three wolf recovery areas supports the agency's expectation: the naturally migrating Montana wolf population has not had the kind of rapid growth experienced by reintroduced populations in Yellowstone and Idaho (Figure 3.2). Natural recovery, however, might have done more to advance the interest of local citizens in minimizing federal government involvement in local issues.

Most, though not all, environmental groups have signed off on the wolf recovery plan. The National Audubon Society, originally a plaintiff in the lawsuit challenging the wolf program, realigned itself with the federal government in the appeal from the district court's decision. The National Wildlife Federation, Defenders of Wildlife, Wyoming Wildlife Federation, Idaho Wildlife Federation, and Wolf Education and Research Center appeared as intervenors on behalf of the federal government. Filing briefs in support of the government's wolf reintroduction program were the Environmental Defense Fund, World Wildlife Fund, Wildlife Conservation Society, Izaak Walton League, Idaho Conservation League, Wolf Recovery Foundation, Center for Marine Conservation, National Parks and Conservation Association, and the Nez Percé tribe. The Predator Project, Sinapu, Gray Wolf Committee, and Friends of Animals opposed the government's position in the appeal.[56]

None of the other livestock industry groups joined the Farm Bureau's lawsuit or filed a brief on behalf of its position, although the

National Cattlemen's Beef Association passed a resolution in 1998 supporting legislation to delist the wolf under ESA and efforts to prevent further reintroduction of wolves to Yellowstone and other areas. Some livestock producers and groups have even expressed grudging acceptance of the plan. A livestock industry publication described the Farm Bureau's lawsuit as a threat to the "workable coexistence" that had developed among ranchers, environmentalists, and wolves.[57] Montana rancher Leo Hargrave said wolves are not that big a deal, and he urged his fellow Montanans to learn to live with wolves and work together on the issue.[58] Hank Fischer reports that livestock producers often tell him they don't mind having wolves around as long as they leave livestock alone.[59] Illegal killings are few, indicating that local citizens have accepted the plan to a degree. Still, opposition to wolf recovery reportedly remains strong in some areas. The Idaho legislature overwhelmingly passed a resolution in 2001 demanding that wolf recovery efforts in Idaho be discontinued immediately and that wolves be removed by whatever means necessary. Although unanimity is not necessary to advance the common interest, continuing opposition to the policy—provided it is based on valid and appropriate interests—suggests that there may be room for improvement from a common interest standpoint.

As implemented in practice and documented above, the wolf recovery program is meeting the main expectations established when it was approved. Of course this might change as wolves continue to multiply and disperse. Some adjustments in the program have already been made in light of experience. For example, the original recovery goal of ten breeding pairs in each of the three states was modified in response to concerns that delisting could not occur if there were twenty or thirty breeding pairs in two states, but fewer than ten pairs in the third state. Biologists felt the old recovery goal was not biologically meaningful and could have led to a highly fragmented wolf population.[60] If and when the recovery targets are met, the current policy will have to be adjusted by delisting wolves and turning their management over to the states.

From a common interest viewpoint, the wolf recovery plan was an improvement over the status quo. It recognized and attempted to balance the valid and appropriate interests of environmentalists and the general public in wolf recovery against the interests of livestock producers for control of problem wolves, compensation for losses, and limited land use control. Although natural recovery may have provoked less initial opposition than reintroduction, it would have taken years longer for wolves to return to Yellowstone and central Idaho on their own, and could have resulted in more conflicts between humans and wolves. Natural recovery also could have prolonged federal control over wolves. Opponents of federal government intervention, ironically, now have an interest in expediting progress toward delisting so that management can be turned over to the states sooner. On balance, the recovery program in place appears to be preferable to the natural recovery alternative

Structures of Governance

At least four structures of governance were directly involved at some point in bringing the wolf recovery program this far. The overall structure is established in national environmental laws, especially the National Environmental Policy Act and ESA, and includes those interested in or responsible for implementation of such laws. Working within this overall structure, not instead of it, were three more specialized structures that merit attention: the Wolf Management Committee, a congressionally mandated advisory committee; the Gray Wolf Interagency EIS Team that developed a plan through the EIS process; and the Wolf Compensation Trust, a program led by Defenders of Wildlife. The latter two are community-based initiatives, but each is a different kind than we have previously discussed.

These four structures were interrelated. The Endangered Species Act mandated that the federal government recover wolves or face the possibility of sanctions for noncompliance. The National Environmental Protection Act required that an EIS be prepared before approval of a wolf recovery plan. Power-balancing politics in Congress produced a stalemate over funding for an EIS. In an attempt to break this stalemate, Congress created the Wolf Management Committee. The plan recommended by the committee majority was unacceptable to environmentalists and thereby failed to gain support in Congress. The committee's failure to produce a viable plan, however, opened the way for congressional funding of an EIS that allowed the recovery process to go forward. The Gray Wolf Interagency EIS Team included the committee majority's recommendation as one of the alternatives in the draft EIS and incorporated elements of the committee's work into the recovery plan eventually selected. The EIS team worked closely with local communities in an attempt to minimize the adverse impacts of wolf recovery. The Wolf Compensation Trust was established in response to the natural migration of wolves into Montana, but it compensates for depredation by reintroduced wolves as well. This program was not specifically authorized or prohibited by law. It worked in parallel with the Wolf Management Committee and later the Interagency EIS Team, and it further ameliorated the adverse impacts of the wolf recovery program in local communities.

Concerned that species of fish, wildlife, and plants had become extinct, or were in danger of it, and recognizing that these species had "esthetic, ecological, educational, historical, recreational, and scientific value to the nation and its people," Congress enacted ESA "to provide a program for the conservation of such endangered species and threatened species."[61] The act requires the secretary of the interior, or another cabinet secretary if appropriate, to list plant and animal species if they are endangered or threatened. It generally prohibits any person from taking an endangered species, where "taking" is broadly defined to include harassing, harming, hunting, shooting, and killing.[62] It also requires the secretary to "develop and implement plans for the conservation and survival of endangered species and threatened species," unless the secretary finds "such a plan will not promote the conservation of the species."[63]

Within the Interior Department, the USFWS is responsible for administering ESA and developing recovery plans to promote the conservation and survival of endangered species. In developing recovery plans under ESA, the secretary "may procure the services of appropriate public and private agencies and institutions," as well as other qualified persons. Recovery teams are not subject to the Federal Advisory Committee Act.[64] Before the approval of a recovery plan, the secretary must provide public notice and an opportunity for public review of the plan and must consider "all information presented during the public comment period."[65] The secretary is required to cooperate with the states to the maximum extent practicable.[66] Nevertheless, the USFWS alone is authorized to approve a recovery plan.

Congress can influence how ESA is implemented by increasing or reducing funding to the agencies involved, as illustrated by the protracted struggle to fund an EIS for wolf recovery. Congress also can amend ESA, as it did in 1982 by adding the experimental nonessential provision to facilitate recovery of endangered species such as wolves. These decisions are outcomes of the competition among different interests in the balancing of power in Congress and in other political arenas. A minority interest can sometimes exert extraordinary influence over the implementation of ESA and other laws if a sympathetic member of Congress has a seat on an appropriate committee, as was the case in wolf recovery.

Interest in wolf recovery in Yellowstone preceded ESA, but the act helped force the issue in the northern Rockies. Wolves were listed as endangered, and ESA generally requires that the secretary develop a recovery plan for endangered species. Failure to act could have made the government vulnerable to claims of noncompliance with the law. Citizens can sue to have courts order compliance if the secretary fails to fulfill his or her duties under ESA, and sometimes ESA's mandates are carried out only after this occurs. And sometimes the mere threat of a lawsuit is enough to compel compliance. The courts, in any event, are supposed to interpret the laws rather than balance competing interests as a legislature would.

In the National Environmental Policy Act, Congress declared "a national policy which will encourage productive and enjoyable harmony between man and his environment; . . . promote efforts which will prevent or eliminate damage to the environment and biosphere and stimulate the health and welfare of man; [and] enrich the understanding of the ecological systems and natural resources important to the Nation."[67] The act requires all federal agencies to provide, for "major Federal actions significantly affecting the quality of the human environment," a precise statement about the environmental impact of the proposed action.

Regulations specify NEPA procedures in more detail. A lead agency supervises preparation of the EIS. Other federal agencies involved with the decision or having special expertise may participate in the process and are called "cooperating agencies." The lead agency is required to invite the participation of affected federal, state, and local agencies, tribes, and other interested persons and to determine the scope of significant issues to be analyzed in the EIS. The lead agency, working with cooperating agencies, prepares a draft EIS and obtains comments from affected governmental agencies, tribes, and the public on the draft. The final EIS must respond to public comments, present the environmental impacts of the alternatives, and circulate to interested parties and agencies. Throughout the process the agencies preparing the EIS must make diligent efforts to involve the public by providing notice of hearings and meetings and of the availability of documents, by holding or sponsoring public hearings or meetings when appropriate, and by soliciting information from the public.[68]

The National Environmental Protection Act provides the framework for citizens to comment on decisions such as the reintroduction of wolves. Unlike ESA, NEPA's requirements are procedural, not substantive. "NEPA itself does not mandate particular results, but simply prescribes the necessary process. . . . Other statutes may impose substantive environmental obligations on federal agencies, but NEPA merely prohibits uninformed—rather than unwise—agency action."[69] Citizens may obtain court review of an agency's decision concerning preparation of an EIS. Courts are often asked to review agencies' compliance with NEPA's procedures.

Consider next the Wolf Management Committee (WMC), the first of three specialized structures that merit attention in this case. When Congress established the committee, it specified that the ten members should include representatives of federal and state agencies as well as representatives of livestock, hunting, and environmental groups, the primary nongovernmental interests involved. The environmental members volunteered, while many of the other members were appointed by their agencies. Western members of Congress opposed to wolf recovery influenced some committee appointments. Committee members' perspectives on acceptable outcomes were inflexible from the outset. The environmental representatives, for example, were unwilling to support amendments to ESA, while representatives of state agency and livestock interests insisted on delisting the wolf.[70] Congress appropriated $375,000 for the WMC and its technical staff to work over the early months of 1991 toward a recommendation by the May 15 deadline. Congress specified that a recommendation required only simple majority support, that is, six of the ten committee members. The environmental representatives did not have enough influence to block or significantly amend the plan eventually recommended by the majority. But they did have enough influence in Congress to ensure that the majority's plan went nowhere. The committee nevertheless contributed to the Interagency EIS Team, which incorporated elements of the majority's plan and the Mumma proposal in the final wolf recovery plan.

The Wolf Management Committee was an advisory group rather than a community-based initiative as defined in Chapter 1. It was composed mainly of state officials and federal officials at the regional level representing primarily the interests of their respective agencies, rather than the interests of communities in and around the three recovery areas. The committee sometimes met in cities some distance from the recovery areas, such as Cheyenne and Denver. Perhaps the major factors contributing to the committee's failure to find a consensus plan were the inflexibility of the members' initial perspectives on acceptable solutions and a lack of incentives to balance or integrate their differences into a consensus plan.[71] In one member's assessment, the agency representatives were more worried about their positions than about finding solutions.[72] The need for only a simple majority made it easier to recommend a plan but more difficult to find a consensus. In addition, a consensus plan may have been thwarted by the inability to amend ESA, a substantive constraint, and by procedural constraints including the limited time available to meet the deadline.

Next there was the Gray Wolf Interagency EIS Team, led by Ed Bangs, which developed the recovery plan through the EIS process. Bangs's team included representatives of the USFWS, National Park Service, Yellowstone National Park, U.S. Forest Service, and Idaho Department of Game and Fish. Several other federal and state agencies and institutions participated in preparation of the EIS through technical review or content analysis teams.[73] The EIS process was also open to thousands of citizens and organizations through issue and alternatives scoping and through public comment on the draft EIS. Several of the USFWS representatives had worked together in the wolf management program in northwestern Montana after Bangs was appointed to lead that program in 1988. He and his colleagues tested and shaped their perspectives on wolf recovery through experience in the field.

Bangs's perspective is that wolves are "no big deal." "They don't attack people, they don't create land-use restrictions, they don't hurt the economy, they may eat livestock, but only a little," and "they're attractive and most people like them."[74] He nevertheless made it clear that he had no qualms about killing wolves if necessary to solve a problem. He told sportsmen's groups that he had killed plenty of wolves and that, too, was no big deal, but there was "a big fine for killing wolves and [he] hoped they wouldn't do it." He also told conservation groups that wolves would need to be killed or relocated if they attacked livestock.[75] Bangs's balanced views about wolves left him able to integrate into a plan the diverse interests of the public participants in and around the recovery areas.

The numerous public participants in the process had a wide range of perspectives, from the technical (how to manage wolves) to the philosophical (the role of humans in nature). At one extreme were those who felt that ESA should be repealed, or that at least a finding should be made that wolves are not endangered; that private citizens should be allowed to kill wolves; that compensation should be provided for livestock depredation; and that the states rather than the federal government should manage wolves. At another extreme were those who believed that reintroduced wolves should receive full ESA protection; that the federal government rather than the states should manage wolves; and that livestock producers should have to share public land with wildlife, including wolves. Local citizens sometimes felt that outsiders had too much influence, while outsiders sometimes felt locals had too much influence.

The EIS team decided initially to hold informal, unstructured, face-to-face meetings or "open houses" to allow members of the public to speak informally with government biologists. Experience in the man-

agement program in northwestern Montana had demonstrated that local citizens are more open to new information when they associate the
wolf recovery program with a person. This experience included nearly
three hundred presentations on wolves to more than 11,000 people in
local organizations over a three-year period. These events allowed local
citizens to link the program to specific persons, which helped foster
an atmosphere of trust even amid disagreement. They also allowed the
biologists to hear first-hand what concerned local citizens about wolf
recovery. The EIS team, including veterans of the earlier program, preferred open houses that allowed them to talk personally with everyone
who attended. The purpose of the open houses was to disseminate information to the public and obtain input back from it. The team scheduled the open houses within a short time frame in each local area so
that media reports would be less likely to bias attitudes and attendance.
It wanted one-on-one conversations to take place in a nonhostile, non-
intimidating environment.[76]

Some local interests were not satisfied with the low-key, back-and-
forth nature of the open houses, so they pressured their representatives
in Congress to insist on holding formal hearings where people could
publicly vent their anger.[77] The Congressmen in turn demanded that
Interior Secretary Manuel Lujan order the EIS team to hold public
hearings in addition to the open houses. Director John Turner of the
USFWS argued that more hearings would be a waste of taxpayer
money, but Lujan nevertheless capitulated.[78] Thus after the open
houses the EIS team held six public hearings. Although Bangs and the
EIS team insisted that the EIS process was not a voting contest, supporters of wolf recovery "got out the troops," outnumbering opponents
at the hearings by more than four to one. The strategy of the local
opponents backfired, and their attendance at later hearings declined
markedly. Bangs concluded that having open houses first was a good
idea, because many more people became educated and personally invested in the process during open houses than if there had been a
"shouting match" in hearings at the outset.[79]

The EIS team had considerable resources, in addition to the experience gained earlier in the program in northwestern Montana. Congress
appropriated $348,000, and the USFWS provided funding for the three
affected states, the Forest Service, Animal Damage Control, and the
University of Montana to participate in the process. In addition, the EIS
team sought and achieved considerable autonomy to conduct the EIS
process. Bangs agreed to lead the team only if he could work independent of higher-level officials in the USFWS.[80] While the team asked
for input on occasion, and USFWS officials made some suggestions,

the team made most of the decisions about how the process would be run. Bangs believes his superiors went along with his demand for independence at least in part because they thought the EIS process would fail due to federal politics. (Lujan's intervention on the hearings issue may be an example of what they had in mind.) They did not want to be closely associated with the expected failure, so they left the EIS team alone for the most part. The team nevertheless made interagency communication a high priority so that upper-level managers in all the affected agencies were well informed and never surprised.[81]

The outcome of the EIS process satisfied those who wanted wolves returned to the northern Rockies as quickly as possible. It also satisfied, to some extent, those who sought control over wolves. It did not satisfy those who wanted reintroduced wolves to be fully protected under ESA, or those who did not want wolves recovered at all. The Farm Bureau claims that while a few livestock producers may have gone along with the final plan, no livestock organization officially supported it. Additionally, the Farm Bureau holds that the rules allowing the public to shoot depredating wolves are part of the government's "marketing plan" and are too strict to be of much use to livestock producers.[82] The attorney for the Earthjustice Legal Defense Fund objected to the translocating of wolves to Yellowstone and Idaho—it was seen as an example of the human need to control nature.[83] Clearly the EIS process was not entirely successful in integrating the interests of all participants.

Participation in the EIS process might have appeared more exclusive in the later stages, when livestock interests threw in the towel after they were outnumbered at the hearings and then passed up subsequent hearings. These interests were not excluded, however. They simply chose not to participate when they realized they were outnumbered. The Farm Bureau complained that its views were ignored, but the Wyoming district court specifically found that the Farm Bureau's comments and concerns were addressed in the EIS process and resulting rules. Although most participants have learned to live with the outcome, those who felt especially deprived resorted to litigation. Public comment did influence some aspects of the final recovery plan, within the constraints established by Congress. Because of strong public sentiment, the EIS team decided to allow more private control of wolves— but not on public land.[84] An additional nine minor changes were made to the preferred alternative in response to agency and public comment on the draft EIS.

The Gray Wolf Interagency EIS Team can be characterized as an agency-led community-based initiative. The team was constrained under various substantive and procedural directives from Washington, which forced the issue after wolves began migrating naturally into northwestern Montana. But within those constraints, the team arranged to proceed more or less independently of superiors in the USFWS to find a plan that accommodated the diverse interests of people with the most at stake in and around the three recovery areas. It discussed the issues with these people face-to-face, and often one-on-one, during numerous open houses. Many participants in the open houses took polarized positions. Some focused on generating publicity, raising funds, being martyrs, or going down fighting. Some sought more to influence members of the EIS team on behalf of one interest than to accommodate multiple interests. Bangs wondered how much listening actually occurred during the open houses.[85] The team members nevertheless understood first-hand the diverse interests of the people most affected and did their best to balance those interests when they decided on the final recovery plan. Bangs and some other members later took responsibility for the program's implementation.

Was this agency-led model of governance responsible for outcomes in the wolf case? A decision-making structure alone cannot determine an outcome, but in this case it certainly contributed. Compared with its counterpart in bison management in greater Yellowstone (Chapter 4), the Gray Wolf Interagency EIS Team was much less handicapped by institutional fragmentation. The team operated under the authority and control of a single agency, the USFWS, which enjoyed a relatively clear legal mandate and exclusive jurisdiction over wolf recovery. This superseded conflicting state and local laws. The USFWS also enjoyed support at the national level for recovery of the wolf. Once the power struggle in Washington was resolved, the team proceeded relatively independently under the USFWS's mandate, jurisdiction, and support for recovery. In addition, the members of the team knew and trusted one another and worked well together, as some of them had already done in an earlier wolf management program. Much of the team's success can be attributed to Bangs's perspectives, strategies, and leadership skills. But even these considerable resources probably were not sufficient without the timely return of wolves on their own, and without widespread support for wolf recovery nationally and to a lesser extent within the northern Rockies.

The fourth structure involved was the Wolf Compensation Trust, a program established and managed by Defenders of Wildlife, with effective participation by others. Hank Fischer, who administers the program as the organization's representative in the northern Rockies, is a practitioner of collaborative decision making. He organized a trip to Minnesota for livestock industry leaders from the northern Rockies to discuss how wolves were managed in that state. He proposed compensation for the producers who lost livestock to wolves in northwestern Montana in the summer of 1987. And he is now involved in a collaborative effort to restore grizzly bears to the Selway-Bitterroot ecosystem. A collaborative strategy on behalf of the common interest is authorized in the trust's charter "to reimburse ranchers in the Northern Rockies for verified livestock losses caused by wolves," and thereby "to [help] eliminate a major factor in political opposition to wolf recovery and to shift the economic burden of wolf recovery from livestock producers to those who support wolf reintroduction."[86]

Fischer makes a point of having an extended conversation with every livestock producer who claims compensation from the trust. He also sends a letter to each producer soliciting suggestions for improvements in the program. Fischer evaluates each suggestion to assess whether it can make the program more responsive to legitimate claims by livestock producers but not more vulnerable to exploitation. He takes meritorious suggestions to the board of directors, which then decides whether to revise the trust's policies.[87] On at least two occasions the program was altered in response to suggestions. It now pays 50 percent for suspected but unconfirmed losses; it also pays fall market value for calves or lambs killed by wolves in the spring or summer. In addition to direct compensation for losses, Defenders of Wildlife works with livestock producers to reduce the likelihood of depredation by buying electric fencing, sharing in the cost of guard dogs, or purchasing hay so a producer can feed cattle at a different location.[88]

Fischer reports that the program is promoting greater tolerance. Two of three livestock producers he talks with tell him they "do not mind having wolves around," and some insist that depredating wolves be given another chance as long as the trust provides compensation for any losses.[89] Some livestock industry groups that oppose wolf recovery criticize the program, claiming that the number of confirmed wolf kills represents only a small percentage of actual kills. There are also environmentalists who would like to eliminate livestock grazing on public land and who believe the compensation program handicaps conservation in the long run. They liken it to paying polluters for cleaning up their own dirty air. Satisfaction of these special interests ("no wolves" in the first case and "no grazing on public land" in the second) would compromise the common interest, which includes tolerance for wolves and compensation for financial losses resulting from wolf recovery.

The trust has made progress in accommodating these valid and appropriate interests and therefore in advancing the common interest. It is unknown, however, whether the trust will continue after delisting. The states may then assume responsibility for compensating livestock depredation losses caused by wolves.

The trust is a community-based initiative of another kind than that discussed elsewhere in this book, unilaterally established and administered by a single private organization. It does, however, include effective participation by livestock producers who claim compensation for losses to wolf depredation, officials who must verify wolf kills, and environmentalists who contribute to the fund. Because it is not a governmental program, it can operate under relatively few substantive and procedural constraints. It relies primarily on face-to-face meetings with individual livestock producers, both to compensate them for losses and to find ways to prevent future losses in the same areas. It also takes suggestions from livestock producers on ways to improve the program by collaborative means. The participants are close enough to the consequences of their decisions that it would be difficult to avoid responsibility for them.

The structure of the trust as a privately funded and unilaterally established program may account for a significant degree of its success in advancing the common interest in this case. It does not have to rely on traditional power-balancing politics to secure an annual appropriation—funds that many in government and the environmental movement would oppose because of concern about expanding governmental liability for wildlife-caused damage. Rather, it allows wolf recovery supporters to "put their money where their mouths are" by ameliorating the financial losses of those who have the most to lose from wolf recovery. In addition, it has the flexibility to respond to the legitimate concerns of livestock producers. Defenders of Wildlife has not used the program to advance its interests at the expense of other competing interests. Acting instead in good faith, the organization seeks to include multiple interests in the decision-making process, and to integrate those interests into its decisions. The trust's experience demonstrates that community-based initiatives are not always dependent on governmental institutions to implement policies developed outside government. It also shows that the framework of existing laws allows community-based initiatives to advance the common interest on their own, in the absence of specific authority from Congress, other legislatures, or the courts.

A modest restructuring of the trust to include occasional face-to-face meetings among all participants might be an improvement from a common interest standpoint. This might, for example, stimulate more creative solutions to the problem that not all wolf depredations can be verified and compensated. Defenders of Wildlife is already addressing this issue by drawing on its experience working with livestock producers on projects aimed at preventing conflicts between wolves and livestock. The group launched a program called the Proactive Carnivore Conservation Fund to help pay for aversive measures such as livestock guard dogs, scare devices, electric fencing, and hay for drawing livestock away from wolves. According to Fischer, this program shows that "conservationists are not trying to get rid of ranchers. Livestock will remain part of the landscape . . . and predators will remain part of that landscape. The idea is to resolve conflicts."[90] The fund is also engaged in a cooperative research project with the USFWS, USDA's Wildlife Services, the Turner Endangered Species Fund, and the University of Montana to investigate the use of dog training collars to teach wolves not to attack cattle.[91]

Broader Significance

Would a more conventional community-based initiative have done a better job of advancing the common interest than the complex of governance structures actually involved in wolf recovery? Hank Fischer thinks so, because people who live, work, and recreate in wolf habitat would have had more opportunities to talk across different sides of the issue.[92] Also, the outcome of wolf recovery left some participants believing that they had lost. Such perceptions in one case can have unintended negative effects in other cases. The outcomes of wolf reintroduction as seen by some participants may have hardened lines of division on bison management in greater Yellowstone. On the bison issue, John Varley, chief scientist at Yellowstone National Park, stated that some livestock producers and politicians "did not like us winning the wolf issue and they are determined not to lose this one."[93] Finally, neither livestock producers nor environmentalists can be sure that they have enough influence to push their interests through power-balancing processes in Washington. Similarly, courts cannot be relied on to rule in one's favor, as the Farm Bureau learned in this case. Although its plan may have closely resembled the plan now in place, a more conventional community-based initiative may have increased the perception of participants that they had arrived at a "win-win" solution. Community-based initiatives in general, however, are not likely to realize their potential if one side has significant advantages over the others, or if they are perceived as an easy way out by agencies focused on other problems.[94]

Whether a more conventional community-based initiative can facilitate endangered species recovery efforts is being tested now with grizzly bears. In the early 1990s Defenders of Wildlife joined with the National Wildlife Federation and timber and labor interests to address grizzly bear recovery in the Bitterroot region of Idaho and Montana. The coalition agreed that grizzlies should be restored but their impacts should be minimized. The groups all cosigned a letter to the congressional delegations of Montana and Idaho requesting funds for an EIS. In contrast to the wolf case, the delegations supported the request, and the USFWS received funding to start the EIS process in 1995 (the year wolf reintroduction began). The coalition submitted a joint proposal to reintroduce grizzlies as an experimental population, with a locally based team of citizens and agency officials responsible for managing the program. In 1997 the USFWS selected this proposal as its preferred alternative.[95]

Although this may appear to be the optimal approach to finding common ground, the EIS took longer than expected to complete. Senator Conrad Burns of Montana had language added to the 1999 Interior Department appropriations bill forbidding the federal government to spend any money on grizzly reintroduction for a year. Local support for grizzly reintroduction reportedly declined. As with wolf recovery, some local citizens oppose reintroduction because they fear the bear and dislike the federal government.[96] Some environmentalists are no more supportive. Fischer thought that once environmentalists forged a consensus with industry and labor, politicians would flock to their support.[97] That did not happen.

The USFWS completed the EIS in November 2000. It selected the preferred alternative under which the agency will introduce a minimum of twenty-five grizzly bears over five years into the Selway-Bitterroot and Frank Church–River of No Return Wilderness under the experimental nonessential provision of the Endangered Species Act. A citizen management committee will oversee the effort, as recommended by Defenders of Wildlife and its coalition.[98] Within a few months of this decision, however, the state of Idaho sued to halt the reintroduction plan, arguing that it threatens visitors to the area and ignores the state's sovereignty.[99] After the election of President George W. Bush and his appointment of a conservative secretary of the interior, Gale Norton, the USFWS proposed withdrawing the plan to reintroduce grizzlies.[100]

It is too early to judge whether community-based initiatives of the kind involved in grizzly recovery will be an improvement, from a common interest viewpoint, over the structures involved in wolf recovery. Early lessons suggest that the approach in the grizzly case resulted in less political opposition to the initiation of an EIS, but subsequently encountered other high-level political obstacles similar to those encountered in wolf recovery. An approach like that taken in the grizzly bear case nevertheless may help alleviate some of the local opposition that continues in the wolf case.

The outcomes of wolf recovery efforts so far have been an improvement over the status quo from a common interest viewpoint, given widespread public support for the recovery of endangered species in general and wolves in particular. Although achievement of wolf recovery in the northern Rockies is within sight, it took almost thirty years after wolves were listed, it came at great cost, and it has not satisfied all the valid and appropriate interests involved. Depredations have been low but are rising as wolf numbers increase. Although Defenders of Wildlife has compensated livestock producers for many wolf kills, an unknown number of kills are not compensated. Whether Defenders will continue its program after delisting is unclear. Government "removal" (killing) of problem wolves provokes fierce opposition from some wolf recovery supporters. The states will assume responsibility for wolf management after delisting, yet the Idaho legislature has called for the removal of all wolves from the state. The effects of the struggle may have left some self-perceived losers bitter enough to harden lines on other issues in the region.

Outcomes in the wolf case depended on human efforts and wolf biology. Wolves are good dispersers with relatively high reproduction rates and are very adaptable—they need no change in habitat to thrive. The traditional structures of governance, acting slowly and inefficiently, set the stage for reintroduction to occur. The community-based initiative led by Bangs and his EIS team crafted a recovery program that attempted to mitigate many of the adverse impacts of reintroduction and natural recovery on livestock producers and others in and around the three recovery areas. The team's relative independence from higher authorities, its emphasis on interacting person-to-person with citizens in the recovery areas, and Bangs's leadership and communications skills all contributed to the outcome. The Wolf Compensation Trust led by Defenders of Wildlife was a community-based initiative of another kind that helped build tolerance for wolves by compensating livestock producers for verified wolf kills.

Wolves are now among the "charismatic megafauna" in the American West—a beautiful species that has gradually come to symbolize over the past three decades the value of nature's wildness to the public. By learning from efforts to reintroduce wolves, grizzly bears, and other species, we can develop governance structures and strategies, train leaders, and gain other resources sufficient to satisfy more of the local and national interests affected by implementation of ESA.

4 Bison Management in Greater Yellowstone

Christina M. Cromley

"For the benefit and enjoyment of the people" are the words engraved on the grand arch welcoming visitors to the northern entrance of Yellowstone National Park. This phrase expresses an ideal established with the Park in 1872 that Yellowstone and its unique natural resources should be managed in the common interest, the interest of all the people. One of those resources, the bison, is depicted on the seal of the U.S. Interior Department and on the badge worn by its employees in the National Park Service. Under the policies of recent decades, however, the management of Yellowstone bison has become controversial because bison continue to do what made them a legend in American folk songs and a symbol of the Wild West—they roam. The persistence of management controversies suggests a failure to realize the common interest more than a century after the Park's creation. The bison now symbolize a discrepancy between the ideal and the political reality.

When they roam out of the Park, bison enter into jurisdictions of the U.S. Forest Service, state livestock departments, state wildlife and game agencies, and private landowners. The presence of brucellosis in bison led the U.S. Animal and Plant Health Inspection Service (APHIS) to claim authority in bison management as an extension of its mandate to eradicate this disease from cattle herds. Through a 1995 court decision, APHIS gained authority to participate with other agencies in developing a long-term bison management plan. Each agency involved has specialized mandates, policies, and jurisdictions that tend to bring it into conflict with other agencies and interest groups. Some agencies have mandates to protect livestock, for example, and others to protect wildlife. Such conflicts have led to extensive litigation involving brucellosis in wildlife and bison management around greater Yellowstone. Settlements of the lawsuits have granted power over wildlife to judges, established win-lose situations, excluded nonlitigating parties, and cost a great deal in dollars and time. Some decisions have been made by officials far removed from the scene of action, and sometimes those directly affected have been excluded from working with officials. This fragmented structure of governance is an obstacle to managing bison in the common interest.

The problem is primarily a matter of politics and governance. It is *not*, for several reasons, merely or essentially a problem of brucellosis. First, the organism causing the disease is transmitted only through birthing materials, so females of calf-bearing age are theoretically the only potential threat to the cattle from bison. They migrate out of the Park only in the winter, when most cattle that graze in the Yellowstone area are nowhere near the Park. And only about 2,000 head of cattle graze on public land around the Park in other seasons, generally after the brucellosis organism in birthing materials has been killed through exposure to the elements. Thus the risk of brucellosis transmission is very slight because of the small numbers of bison and cattle involved and their separation in time and space. Second, measures for the management of this risk, apart from separation, have been unofficially tested in practice by ranchers around Jackson, Wyoming, just south of Yellowstone. There cattle graze next to bison on allotments inside Grand Teton National Park.[1] The experience of Jackson-area ranchers over several decades demonstrates that vaccination of cattle effectively prevents brucellosis. There is, however, no safe and effective vaccine to prevent brucellosis in bison. Third, in spite of the small risk combined with effective risk management measures, Montana state officials insist that in the spring, just before cattle return to grazing allotments outside the Park, the only acceptable policy is to haze, remove, or capture and test for brucellosis *all* bison that leave the Park, and to slaughter those that test positive—including bulls and calves—even though a test-positive result may indicate either resistance to the disease or infection by it. The problem, then, is largely political and represents an inability to resolve policy differences among participants involved in the fragmented structure.

Advancing the common interest in this context means finding a consensus on management alternatives that integrate the two major interests in conflict: protecting livestock producers by minimizing and containing the risk of brucellosis transmission from bison to cattle, *and* protecting wild, free-roaming bison herds in Yellowstone from inten-

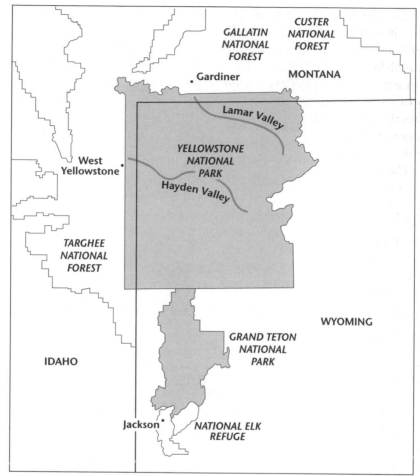

Map 4.1.   Greater Yellowstone Area

sive management measures that would reduce them to livestock. These interests are broadly supported and officially accepted as goals in the draft Environmental Impact Statement (EIS) released by federal and state agencies in June 1998 and in the final record of decision released by federal and state agencies in December 2000.[2] The management alternatives, however, in the draft EIS and in the final record of decision fall short of securing these goals, as detailed below—despite the risk management measures unofficially tested in the Jackson area that would meet both goals if applied across greater Yellowstone.[3] The search for a consensus is complicated by the geographic and social context seen in Map 4.1. Greater Yellowstone covers 19.9 million acres, most of which are owned by the federal government (69 percent). The rest are owned by Indian reservations (4 percent), states (3 percent), and private citizens (24 percent). It includes two national parks, Yellowstone and Grand Teton, six national forests, three federal wildlife refuges, five "gateway" communities, and thirteen counties in three states.[4]

Bison management in greater Yellowstone is a problem of politics and governance, and the common interest is the appropriate criterion for assessment. We begin with an overview of the historical context, turn to a description of and appraisals of the policy process that has failed to solve the problem, and then consider the fragmented structure of governance that accounts partly for the policy failures. We conclude with policy and structural alternatives to advance the common interest.

Historical Context

The ideal of managing national parks in the common interest has not been directly challenged over the past century. But policies that attempt to advance the common interest have changed in response to the unintended consequences of past management policies and because of external factors, including success in the control of brucellosis in livestock, the rise of environmentalism, and advances in the science of ecology. This section outlines the historical evolution of Park management policies, and related policies, as they pertain to contemporary bison management.

Approximately 40 to 75 million bison once roamed the United States, but the population was reduced to a few hundred animals by the late 1880s.[5] Many factors contributed to the demise, but buffalo hunting and demand for buffalo products figured prominently.[6] Some historians also allege that U.S. Army officials tried to exterminate Indians by destroying their subsistence base, the bison.[7] Once it became apparent that buffalo might become extinct, some states passed legislation—usually too late—to prevent further hunting of buffalo. People nationwide owned domesticated bison, but one of the last wild herds lived in the area that became Yellowstone National Park. Although officials established the Park to protect the area's unique geothermal features, they soon began to recognize the Park's potential as a wildlife sanctuary. By 1883 they prohibited hunting in the Park but did little to enforce the prohibition. Poaching continued within Park borders.[8] Public pressure to protect Yellowstone's bison increased in 1894 after national publicity about the arrest of a bison poacher. Congress passed H.R. 6442, or the Lacey Act "to protect the birds and animals in Yellowstone National Park, and to punish crimes."[9] Penalty for violating the act was $1,000 or two years in jail. Thus the nation decided to protect the remnant wild herd, which in 1895 numbered only two hundred.[10]

Protecting Yellowstone's bison remains an interest of great emotional significance for many Americans. Bison symbolize one of the country's first conservation success stories, in the country's first national park and in the gemstone of the national park system. Native Americans also identify their troubled history with the near extinction of bison, which provided subsistence and still remain a strong component of many tribal cultures. Some Native Americans feel their cultural survival depends on the survival of wild buffalo. A tribal elder from South Dakota, Rosalie Little Thunder, could compare the significance of bison only to money, the god of today.[11] Bison also remind conservationists and other Americans of the potential for special interest groups—including buffalo hunters, poachers, the railroad, possibly the army, and others who prevailed in the nineteenth century—to destroy a natural resource. This interest in protecting wild bison in Yellowstone, however, can be realized through practical alternatives that do not compromise other valid and appropriate interests, especially the interest in protecting livestock from brucellosis.

Early management of Yellowstone bison was part of a policy that sought to protect "desirable" animals—mainly herbivores such as bison and elk—from poachers, predators, and winter mortality through intensive management techniques.[12] Officials purchased domestic bison and established a captive herd in 1902 while continuing to protect the wild bison.[13] Managers fed bison, separated calves, castrated bulls, and sponsored roundups and stampedes for tourists.[14] The corralled herd increased from 21 to 44 by 1905, and to 147 by 1911.[15] Managers began to set target populations to maintain the maximum number of ungulates given range conditions. The techniques used to maintain a target bison population included shooting, live shipment to Indian reservations and zoos, and capture and slaughter.[16] These intensive techniques were adapted from ranch and range management techniques developed for cattle, and they kept bison inside the Park.

From the 1930s to the 1960s, however, the Park gradually shifted policy away from intensive management techniques. Ecologists came to understand that protecting Park wildlife required protecting the natural processes of which they are a part, rather than managing intensively for a single species such as bison. This reflected and reinforced a larger evolution of thought, in which managers and the public began to see scientific expertise as a necessary part of the search for any sound natural resources policy. Advocates of scientific management claimed it was an alternative to the politics of special interests. Since then science has become more influential in the management of natural resources, including bison, but not all of the influence has been so constructive. On occasion science has been misused to delay decisions on the pretext that more scientific studies would resolve policy issues; to justify rather than inform prior political positions; and to devalue local knowledge based on trial-and-error experience as complementary to scientific knowledge in informing policy decisions.

Meanwhile, as policy gradually shifted within the Park, events outside would eventually complicate debates over managing the Park's resources. In 1916, a committee formed within the U.S. Livestock Sanitary Association to address the brucellosis issue and continues today as the Brucellosis Committee of the United States Animal Health Association (USAHA), a professional association of veterinarians. Federal and state governments became involved in 1934, forming the Cooperative State-Federal National Brucellosis Eradication Program to rid livestock of brucellosis. Working together, the U.S. Agriculture Department, state livestock departments, and livestock producers have made progress in eradicating brucellosis from domestic cows, where it can cause abortions, infertility, reduced milk production, and a retained placenta—and in doing so, devastate ranchers economically.[17] Protecting livestock producers from the problem of brucellosis is a valid and appropriate interest within the strong agrarian tradition, particularly in the West, that values ranching as part of the American cultural heritage.

By 1960, however, with brucellosis infecting fewer domestic herds, the Brucellosis Committee of the USAHA began to view the disease in bison and other wildlife as a threat to eradication efforts.[18] This brought into conflict the interest in protecting livestock from brucellosis and the interest in protecting wild Yellowstone bison from domestication. In an early response to the concerns of the veterinarians and allied interests, in 1962 Yellowstone Park officials began capturing bison, testing them for brucellosis, and sending positive reactors to slaughter. This program was terminated in 1964, however. Park researchers claimed it could never end because only 75 percent of bison could be captured. Capture also changes the wild behavior of bison. Furthermore, removing all positive reactors would reduce herds to dangerously low numbers and eliminate the genes of dominant females who teach historical habitat use patterns.[19] Budgetary constraints also influenced the program's termination.[20] In short, it was decided that an extensive and expensive capture and testing program in the Park would not eliminate brucellosis but would threaten the wild bison herd.

By 1966, public pressure and a changing ecological understanding of wildlife led to the Park's natural regulation policy. This policy mandates that managers depend more on natural conditions, such as winter starvation, than on human actions to control wildlife populations. By 1967, the new natural regulation policy, the increasing role of science in management, and strong public opposition to wildlife population control in the Park—in particular the slaughter of thousands of elk—led to the termination of all human reductions of wildlife populations in the Park.[21] The bison herd numbered 397 at that time and stayed within Park borders.[22] There was little initial increase in the bison population, but by 1968, bison began moving toward Park borders. A border control policy and other attempts to deter the migrations, including cattle guards and fences, failed to end the migrations in the 1970s and early 1980s. Debate continues over explanations for the migrations: increasing populations due to the natural regulation policy, herd memory, and easy-to-travel snowmobile trails are among the possibilities. Whatever the explanations, the migrations seemed inevitable without a return to intensive, ranchlike control of Park bison.

The gradual return to these more intensive management techniques began about 1985, when APHIS granted Montana and Wyoming a brucellosis-free status. This assures buyers that cattle from the states are disease-free, subjecting producers to fewer costly regulations and increasing the cattle's marketability in interstate and international commerce. The livestock industry began to demand that Yellowstone and Grand Teton National Parks eradicate brucellosis from bison to maintain the brucellosis-free status.[23] (Grand Teton, adjacent to Yellowstone National Park on its southern border, also contains a herd of brucellosis-infected bison.) Yellowstone officials initially did little to control migrations of or brucellosis in bison, arguing that the risk of transmission to cattle is too small to warrant handling the wild animals: there were (and are) no documented cases of the transmission of brucellosis from bison to cattle in the wild. Livestock interests, frustrated by Yellowstone's refusal to meet their demands, turned to the state veterinarian and to the Montana Department of Fish, Wildlife, and Parks (DFWP). At the request of the state veterinarian, state game wardens from DFWP shot eighty-eight bison that wandered into Montana in the winter of 1984–85.[24] These actions were the first direct and intensive control of Park bison by state agencies, and they set the stage for policies to manage border crossings in the future. Although methods have varied, all policies recommended or applied by agency officials since then have involved killing bison.

The Decision Process

In 1985, the first attempt to develop a plan for bison management by the Park and DFWP failed because of interagency conflicts.[25] The Department of Fish, Wildlife, and Parks responded to bison migrations like a game agency, one that manages wildlife by killing game animals with public hunts and other methods. As a state agency, it is responsive to the interests of ranchers. The Park, in contrast, seeks to protect Park resources. As a federal agency, it is accountable in principle to national officials and ultimately to the national public. The different mandates of agencies with some jurisdiction over bison management make coordination among them difficult. Officials are often loyal to their own agencies, through personal preference or through inducement or threats from superiors, even amid interagency coordination efforts. Thus far, no agency-mandated policy has realized the potential to advance the common interest.

The difficulties of advancing the common interest through interagency coordination alone show up in a recurring pattern: bison exiting Yellowstone National Park are killed indiscriminately or after testing for brucellosis, under written or unwritten public policy. In response to the killing, members of the public protest in various ways— by appeals to legislators or others, by filing lawsuits, by developing citizens' alternatives to official policy, or even by acts of civil disobedience. In response to public protests, public officials make superficial changes in policy, setting the stage for repetition of the pattern. The result is heightened frustration all around, which leads to repetition of the pattern as long as participants are unable to make significant changes in public or private policies.

In 1985, after the killing of bison that winter, the Montana state legislature responded to public protests and to pressure from hunting groups by designating bison a game animal. Under this superficial change in public policy, hunters joined officials from DFWP and killed fifty-seven bison outside the Park in the winter of 1985–86.[26] The public protested once again. Few considered shootings by hunters an improvement over shootings by officials; in either case, the outcome for bison was the same. Some considered hunting bison no more sporting than shooting a couch; bison normally do not try to evade or attack the threat represented by the hunter. The Fund for Animals, an animal rights group, sued the Park for allowing bison to migrate into Montana just to be shot.[27]

After the bison killings in the winter of 1988–89, public protests erupted again. Many readers will recall televised images of Yellowstone in flames the summer of 1988, and the resulting ghost forests.[28] The flames subsided when rain came in the fall, but only after burning about a million of the Park's 2.2 million acres.[29] The massive fires, a drought, and a harsh winter made it difficult for bison and other ungulates to find forage the following winter. Few animals died in the flames, but officials from the Montana DFWP and hunters killed 579 of 900 bison from the Park's northern herd that crossed the border in search of food.[30] This generated more complaints to the governor of Montana, Stan Stephens, than any other issue.[31] People compared the hunt to a firing squad and to the slaughter of buffalo in the nineteenth century. A National Wildlife Federation employee said the killing shows "the livestock industry flexing its muscle," suggesting that the balance of power was tipping in favor of livestock interests.[32]

By 1989, the principal state and federal agencies were all frustrated with a situation that served none of their primary interests. Moreover, the Montana DFWP and Department of Livestock (DOL), the National Park Service, the U.S. Forest Service, and APHIS could no longer avoid one another. So they sought to reach an enduring solution to bison management problems through development of a long-term plan.[33] Officials from the Park and DFWP developed the first Interim Plan and Environmental Assessment (EA) in 1990 and released it to the public for comment in 1991. The agencies received 319 public responses.[34] In spite of public concern over bison killings during the previous five winters, the plan called for public hunts, state sharpshooters, and the capture of calves. The plan allowed Park officials to help kill bison outside the Park, reflecting pressure from livestock groups and state officials on Park officials to accept responsibility for protecting livestock by controlling bison. Park officials believed that helping Montana outside the Park was better than killing bison inside the Park, and that such a strategy might reduce demands to control the herd inside the Park. They were less able—or less willing—to argue, as they had done in the 1970s and 1980s, that the risk of transmitting brucellosis from wildlife to cattle was minimal.

Frustrated by the performance of agencies on this issue, a Bison Management Citizen's Working Group was organized in Bozeman, Montana, in 1990 under the leadership of Leroy Ellig, a retired regional supervisor for DFWP. The group included landowners, ranchers, hunters, conservationists, and retired agency personnel, with agency officials and a tribal member serving as advisers and consultants.[35] They did more than critique the current Interim Plan of the agencies. They developed an alternative to protect wild bison and livestock through risk management measures that included separation of bison and cattle in time and space and vaccination of cattle. After all group members approved the plan in 1991, it was submitted to the agencies, which treated it as just another response to the Interim Plan and not as a step toward a common-interest alternative.[36] Consequently, state and Park officials continued killing bison under a revised 1992 Interim Plan. However, because of bad publicity, the Montana state legislature outlawed the public hunt of bison. This was another superficial change in public policy that failed to address the underlying political or structural problems. Meanwhile, by 1994, the bison population peaked at 4,200 animals, the highest since the nineteenth century.[37]

At the same time, livestock and veterinary interests refocused on bison management and asserted their influence. The professional veterinary association, USAHA, that includes the Montana and many other state veterinarians as members, issued five brucellosis resolutions in 1995.[38] One resolution stated the expectation that brucellosis in and overpopulation of bison and elk threaten cattle. Together with the Western States Livestock Health Association, composed of seventeen Western state veterinarians, USAHA pressured APHIS to downgrade the status of states that allowed wild bison to roam after exposure to brucellosis.[39] Even though USAHA is not an official policy-making body, it is respected enough to be highly influential. Subsequently, APHIS threatened to revoke Montana's status without a scientific or legal basis. The Montana state legislature also changed the primary authority for managing bison from DFWP to DOL—an agency with a mandate to "protect the health and well-being of the livestock industry and economic well-being of ranchers" and without previous experience or responsibility in wildlife management.[40] Thus the perspectives of livestock management became more influential in the management of wild bison that roam outside the Park and into Montana.

In 1995, governor of Montana Marc Racicot sued APHIS and the National Park Service out of frustration over increased attention on brucellosis, pressure from state veterinarians outside the region, unresolved conflicts in federal policies, and threats from APHIS to revoke Montana's brucellosis-free status.[41] He alleged that the state was harmed because the Park failed to prevent bison migrations into Montana and because APHIS threatened to downgrade Montana's status based only on the presence of diseased wild bison in the state. This lawsuit resulted in a settlement agreement in November 1995, signed by Racicot, assistant secretaries of agriculture and interior, the Galla-

tin National Forest Supervisor, and the vice president of the Royal Teton Ranch, a private landowner adjacent to the Park and an intervenor
for Montana.[42]

The agreement prevented APHIS from downgrading Montana's status as long as the state complied with the Interim Plan.[43] The agencies
were directed to follow a revision of the 1992 Interim Plan, developed
as an Environmental Assessment (EA).[44] The agencies had to revise the
EA and the Interim Plan to protect livestock through additional bison
management, limit bison mortality, and allow themselves more time
to prepare an EIS for a long-term plan.[45] In effect, this formalized the
policy, initiated in 1984–85, of controlling bison that leave the Park by
lethal means. The agreement specified that the National Park Service,
the U.S. Forest Service, and the state of Montana co-lead an EIS in
cooperation with APHIS. It also gave DOL the power to decide which
bison can enter Montana. This essentially consolidated control over
the development and implementation of policy.

The agencies released a draft EA and Interim Plan in December
1995. It directed the agencies "to provide spatial and seasonal separation of bison and domestic cattle in order to maintain Montana's brucellosis class-free status, while permitting the bison herd within the
park to fluctuate, to the maximum extent possible, in response to natural ecological processes."[46] The agencies received 260 comments from
state and federal agencies, Native American tribes, organizations, and
individuals. A member of the 1991 Bison Citizen's Group remarked
that "a lot of politics and positioning has occurred . . . and are driving
. . . interests apart."[47] Much of the controversy centered on the allow-
ance of capture facilities inside Park boundaries for the first time, indicating the Park's acceptance of more responsibility for protecting livestock through control of bison and changes in the Park's conception
of allowable (or perhaps necessary) actions under its own natural regulation policy. Respondents complained that the low risk of brucellosis
transmission did not warrant capture facilities and test and slaughter
for bison, and that approval of a capture facility within Park boundaries grants DOL authority within the Park. Furthermore, blood tests
for brucellosis in live bison cannot distinguish between infection by
and resistance to brucellosis. Tissue samples, which can be taken only
from dead bison, are necessary to determine if an animal is infected.
Respondents also complained that the plan omitted consideration of
tribes, did not provide adequate compensation for agricultural interests, and used capture and slaughter of wildlife in all alternatives. In
spite of public opposition, the National Park Service approved the plan
in 1996.[48]

Like the Fund for Animals in 1991 and Governor Racicot in 1995, organizations that felt excluded from the decision-making process sought to change policy decisions through the courts. In particular, they sued to halt the application of the 1996 Interim Plan.[49] They argued that a slaughtering program *inside the Park* violates the National Park Service Organic Act, which requires protection of Park wildlife. They also argued that it could have negative environmental consequences, thereby violating NEPA. Judge Charles Lovell heard the case and ruled in favor of the defendants. This was not surprising, because he presided over the 1995 settlement agreement directing the agencies to follow the Interim Plan. The plaintiffs appealed the ruling. In May 1999, the Ninth Circuit Court of Appeals issued a one-sentence judgment upholding Lovell's "reasonable" ruling.[50]

Frustration over bison management peaked in the winter of 1996–97. That year, bison faced the most severe snow and ice conditions in the Park since 1943, forcing them to migrate to lower elevations outside the Park for forage.[51] State and park officials shot 1,084 bison between November 1996 and April 1997.[52] A capture facility was operated *within* the Park near the northern entrance. Another 300–400 bison died in the Park from the harsh winter conditions. Some management actions that winter deviated from the 1996 Interim Plan. Heavy snows prevented the use of a proposed trapping facility outside Yellowstone's western boundary, so DOL established a shoot-to-kill policy there. On the northern boundary, the 1996 Interim Plan proposed capturing and sending to slaughter all bison approaching the border. As increasing numbers of bison approached the border, the Park began testing bison and sending only test-positive bison to slaughter in order to minimize bison deaths.[53] Such deviations from written policy underscore DOL's interest in killing bison to protect ranchers, and the Park's interest in minimizing lethal control of bison.

These events provoked a national public outcry. Thousands of newspapers, magazines, and television and radio stations covered the shootings, reporting bloody scenes at the capture facilities and the sale of stacks of bison heads, hides, and meat.[54] People once again compared the killings to the nineteenth-century slaughter. Citizens, livestock interests, conservation groups, and others wrote letters to the Park. State veterinarians in Alabama and Oregon placed restrictions on cattle from states around Yellowstone. The national publicity also complicated the issue by involving members of more agencies and higher-level officials.

Top officials felt they needed to provide at least an appearance of making changes. Meetings occurred among officials in Washington,

D.C., including Interior Secretary Bruce Babbitt and Agriculture Secretary Dan Glickman.[55] Governor Racicot met with President Clinton. Senior administration officials, including Secretary Babbitt, discussed the issue with Montana's congressional delegation.[56] Proposals from these talks met with criticism from all sides. In addition, the White House Council on Environmental Quality (CEQ) initiated meetings, dubbed "the federal family" meetings, to coordinate officials from the Washington offices of the National Park Service, the U.S. Forest Service, and APHIS. All of this once again was restricted to interactions among agency officials.

Frustrated by the agencies' handling of the issue and believing their interests were not being addressed, a group of ranchers, conservationists, and hunters in Jackson Hole, Wyoming, wrote a letter to the Clinton administration in January 1997, in the midst of the crisis. They requested that APHIS stop threatening to downgrade the state's brucellosis-free status. Ranchers in Jackson Hole, they noted, had been running cattle next to bison for more than thirty years with no outbreaks of brucellosis. They concluded that the risk of transmission is low and that cattle vaccination combined with separation of cattle and bison make the risk almost zero. The real risks, they said, "are the proposals originating from and/or driven by APHIS and the unfounded premise that brucellosis poses a real threat to man and beast." The letter urged the officials to "recognize the common ground which exists" and to "concentrate your management efforts on non-lethal and non-invasive methods of minimizing that already insignificant risk of disease transmission rather than concentrating on the eradication of brucellosis via the lethal and costly methods now being proposed."[57] The most direct response by APHIS was to force Wyoming ranchers to submit to a station review of their brucellosis-control measures. The review involved thousands of dollars in brucellosis-testing costs for Wyoming ranchers. In February 1997, however, APHIS did respond positively to pressure from other federal agencies and the federal family meetings. It acknowledged that a state's brucellosis-free status cannot be revoked unless there is an uncontrolled outbreak of brucellosis. In other words, the mere presence of bison with brucellosis was no longer adequate grounds for APHIS to threaten or penalize a state's livestock producers. Nevertheless, Montana officials continued to haze, shoot, or capture and slaughter virtually all bison crossing into Montana.[58]

In February 1998, APHIS scientists developed a definition of low-risk bison in response to public pressure, the federal family meetings, and a request from DOL director Larry Peterson. The definition, accepted by all federal agencies, identifies as low-risk those bison that cannot emit birthing materials containing the organism that causes brucellosis.[59] The low-risk definition also endorses temporal separation of bison and cattle, because transmission can only occur if they come into contact.[60] The U.S. Forest Service altered cattle grazing allotments to give the Montana state veterinarian authority to prevent cattle from entering allotments until thirty to sixty days after bison return to the Park for the summer, minimizing the potential for contact. These alternatives, according to Patrick Collins, director of legislative and public affairs at APHIS, "protect Montana . . . and minimize the need for lethal control of bison."[61] Nevertheless, Montana state veterinarian Arnold Gertonson wrote to APHIS and to other state veterinarians rejecting the definition because other states could still place sanctions on Montana cattle, even with a brucellosis-free status for Montana.[62] In response to Gertonson, APHIS officials reported they had pressured veterinarians from other states to lift sanctions on Montana cattle— sanctions without a scientific or legal basis.

On June 5, 1998, Yellowstone National Park, the state of Montana, and the U.S. Forest Service finally released the draft EIS and Interagency Bison Management Plan for public comment.[63] Most of the strategies de-emphasize risk management in favor of handling and manipulating bison rather than cattle and moving toward zero tolerance for test-positive bison. All alternatives call for more research and the development of a vaccine for female bison to reach the objective of "the eventual elimination of brucellosis in bison." Vaccination for cattle, however, is only encouraged in each of the seven alternatives.[64] All alternatives include boundary control by agencies and capture and testing, with provisions to slaughter infected animals and to give uninfected animals to tribes or put them on public lands. All but one of the seven proposed alternatives would establish special management areas where the bison exit north and west of the Park, with varying degrees of tolerance for bison. The agencies proposed to keep the bison population between 1,700 and 2,500 animals, to increase killings as the number approaches 2,500, and to minimize lethal strategies as the number approaches 1,700. These numbers are not explicitly justified by scientific studies or by practical experience. The preferred alternative also provides for limited public hunting.

The interagency agreements on the draft EIS and on the long-term plan were only temporary, however. By December 1999, in a letter to Governor Racicot, the federal agencies sought to revise the plans to "allow for tolerance of bison outside the Park as opposed to unnecessary killing of bison." They also wanted to withdraw from the 1992

Memorandum of Understanding that formalized interagency negotiations on a long-term bison management plan, and to proceed without Montana in issuing a final EIS. In justification for this action, the federal agencies' letter cited Montana's "unreasonable objections" to the federal proposal.[65] Once again the agencies returned to Judge Lovell's court to settle the dispute. Although federal agencies retained legal authority to terminate the memorandum, they nevertheless agreed to meet a request by Judge Lovell and continued negotiations for seven more months. They finally produced a record of decision and Joint Management Plan one year later, signed by officials from the U.S. Forest Service, the Department of Interior, the U.S. Animal and Plant Health Inspection Service, and the state of Montana. In the record, the agencies state that the plan "is not intended to be a brucellosis eradication plan," but it "sets forth actions to address brucellosis within the bison herd."[66] The plan requires hazing, capture, testing, and lethal control of bison, sets herd limits for bison, and requires vaccination of cattle grazing next to Yellowstone's borders. It also sets a longer-term goal of vaccinating the Yellowstone bison herd against brucellosis using a remote delivery system.

Policy Appraisals

Looking back over roughly a decade and a half of bison management in greater Yellowstone, it is difficult to argue that the common interest has been served. Few of those directly involved have been satisfied with the decisions of the courts or agency officials. There have been repeated public protests, acts of civil disobedience, and demonstrations, including a Native American spiritual journey to Yellowstone in honor of the buffalo. There have been at least twelve lawsuits.[67] About 70 percent of more than 67,000 public comments on the draft EIS supported a Citizens' Plan to Save Yellowstone Bison over the agencies' alternatives. Four other nonofficial plans were proposed, in addition to the Citizens' Plan: Plan B from the Alliance for the Wild Rockies; the Bison Alternative from the Fund for Animals; the U.S. Animal Health Association Alternative; and Alternative Eight from the Fort Belknap Indian Community Tribal Government.[68] And although a record of decision has been reached among agencies, public controversy over the Joint Management Plan outlined in the record continues. These are among the major indicators of widespread frustration with bison management in greater Yellowstone.

Conservationists and others argue that intensive management techniques prescribed in the 2000 Joint Management Plan—hazing, bait-ing, capturing, testing, and slaughtering bison—are not suitable for managing a wild, free-roaming herd.[69] Moreover, the goal of maintaining a wild herd is incompatible with the goal of eradicating brucellosis from wildlife through these intensive techniques. Blood tests are unreliable because a test-positive result may indicate either resistance to brucellosis or infection by it. No safe, effective vaccine currently exists to protect test-negative bison from contracting brucellosis. And not all bison or the thousands of elk in the area can be rounded up for testing and vaccination. Intensive management techniques also fail to meet the goal of protecting livestock producers. Among other things, these techniques maintain the perception that brucellosis in bison is reason enough for other states and countries to impose sanctions on Montana cattle, and they shift attention away from the producers' success in eradicating the disease from cattle in the state. The intensive management techniques also divert resources from more serious threats to the livestock industry.

These methods are employed despite evidence that the risk of transmission remains minimal, even with increased bison migrations. Only one study shows brucellosis transmission from bison to cattle, but it was conducted in an artificial, highly controlled setting.[70] Many dispute the relevance of the study and argue that there have been no documented cases of brucellosis transmission from bison to cattle in the wild. Ranchers in Jackson Hole cite the thirty years they have grazed cattle near bison, with no outbreaks of brucellosis, as evidence of minimal risk. As further evidence of minimal risk, others cite no outbreaks of brucellosis after the intermingling of cattle and bison outside the Park following the fires of 1988.[71] The only known method of transmission is through birthing materials. Yet DOL plans to continue to capture, test, and kill bull bison and other bison that cannot possibly emit birthing materials. Additionally, bison migrate out of the Park in large numbers mostly in the winter, when snow covers forage in the Park. The majority of ranchers do not graze their cattle outside the Park in the winter.

The economic stakes involved in transmission are rather small, although this, too, is disputed. Only about fourteen ranchers graze around 2,000 head of cattle near Park borders. About 45 percent of those 2,000 cattle graze on public land, generating only $5,000 per year in revenue for the U.S. Forest Service.[72] Hope Sieck, associate program director of the Greater Yellowstone Coalition, expressed concern about the millions of dollars expended for these few cattle and for little revenue.[73] In spite of such concerns, the high expenditures are likely to continue under the Joint Management Plan. The counterargument is that brucellosis can decrease the marketability of all cattle in greater Yellowstone. Therefore, claimed former state veterinarian Clarence Siroky, "any discussion of brucellosis . . . must include the total inventory and economic value as well as the value of infrastructure of the cattle industry in Idaho, Montana, and Wyoming."[74] The total inventory was valued at $773 million.[75] Although maintaining the economic health of the livestock industry is a valid interest of ranchers, it is not necessary to eradicate brucellosis from bison to do so. More important than the "correct" numbers, the dispute signals a lack of trust among participants, an inability to reconcile their differences, and the intense threat ranchers feel to their livelihood—all of which intensifies debate and complicates the search for the common interest.

Livestock and other interests argue that important underlying issues are left out of the draft EIS and record of decision. The Park's policy of natural regulation is one of them. A Montana rancher said, "I'm not a proponent of culling but they at least need to address it and work with the surrounding states if they don't want to cull in the Park."[76] Hagenbarth Livestock stated that "the 'natural regulation' management policy practiced by YNP does not exempt them from their responsibility of being a good neighbor."[77] Clarence Siroky said, "The impact upon Montana, Wyoming and Idaho was never figured as part of the 'natural' equation."[78] Wyoming governor Jim Geringer and agriculture director Rob Micheli see overpopulation of wildlife and failure to vaccinate them as problems.[79] Department of Livestock officials feel that the "laissez-faire [natural regulation] philosophy" results in populations of bison and elk that are too high.[80] Native American groups also argue that the idea of self-regulated wildlife populations diminishes the importance of hunting by the Bannock, Nez Percé, and other tribes for centuries in and around the Park.[81] "Natural" processes of regulation included humans.[82] Supporters of natural regulation point out that the policy does not prohibit culling outside the Park. Whether or not one believes the natural regulation policy to be ecologically sound, it is controversial.

These persistent controversies are costly in various ways. The Department of Livestock's involvement in bison management, including hazing, testing, and slaughtering, cost it about $95,000 through mid-February 1999 of that fiscal year. This is a substantial fraction of DOL's annual expenditures. The U.S. Department of Agriculture also approved $225,000 in federal funds to operate the capture facility.[83] The Park Service has paid for personnel to assist in killing bison, to operate a capture facility in Park borders, and for preparation of the draft EIS. Under the Joint Management Plan, the Park plans to continue paying for such intensive management techniques as capture and testing. The station review by APHIS in Wyoming cost ranchers thousands of dollars for testing. Lawsuits filed by livestock groups, states, conservation groups, tribes, animal rights groups, landowners, and agencies were all expensive, and they continue to contribute to the polarized atmosphere. The controversies also drain another precious resource, human energy. Personnel burnout and turnover, high levels of frustration, and feelings of powerlessness and mistrust among nearly all participants are some of the results of the contentious atmosphere. Less obvious long-term costs should be considered as well. Mistrust, for example, will make it more difficult to find common-interest solutions to problems in bison management in the future.

Tensions among agency officials may have been ameliorated somewhat by such interagency efforts as the Greater Yellowstone Interagency Brucellosis Committee, the federal family meetings in Washington, and repeated interagency EAs and EISs.[84] These interagency efforts, however, give an appearance of coordination that is misleading. Agency officials often remain loyal to agency mandates that contribute more to gridlock than to finding common ground. In addition, different agencies pursue their own policies in bison management, with the Montana DOL and state veterinarian holding predominant power. The Department of Livestock continues to operate under its own definition of the risk of transmission and to haze, shoot, or capture and test all bison that roam into Montana. The Park made some concessions to intensive management within its borders but continues to prefer its natural regulation policy. And APHIS has made some concessions on the definition of risk and on sanctions. But on the whole, it is difficult to see enough movement toward common ground to justify the costs of the interagency efforts. Meanwhile, members of the public who expect to influence bison management through the interagency EIS process have been disappointed if not alienated. The EIS process in principle involves citizens, but in practice the agencies seldom incorporate citizen input from the official public comment period into official management alternatives. Lawsuits are expected to be an inherent part of the EIS process, no matter what the official decisions. This expectation, based on experience, reduces the incentive to incorporate citizen input.

Formal assessments have done little to improve the decision-making process in bison management because they have focused on technical or scientific issues and have given little attention to political issues. Interior Secretary Babbitt commissioned a study of brucellosis by the National Research Council (NRC) in 1997. In 1992, Senator Alan Cranston commissioned a study by the U.S. General Accounting Office (GAO) of the transmission of brucellosis from bison and elk to cattle. In 1997, the Subcommittee on National Parks, Historic Preservation and Recreation of the Senate Committee on Energy and Natural Resources commissioned a similar study from GAO, which in turn called for more studies.[85] Although such studies add information, any side in the political controversy typically can and often does use them selectively to reinforce rather than reconsider its position. The NRC study in 1997, for example, concluded that "neither sufficient information nor technical capability is available to implement a brucellosis eradication program in the [greater Yellowstone Area]." Two pages later, it also concluded that "it is likely brucellosis can be eliminated from [Yellowstone National Park] without loss of large numbers of bison or loss of genetic diversity."[86] Calls for more scientific studies continue. But the state of Montana found existing knowledge adequate to pressure APHIS into withdrawing threats to downgrade the state's brucellosis-free status; and later APHIS found information adequate to urge other states to withdraw sanctions from Montana's cattle. These were political accomplishments, not scientific ones, demonstrating the subordination of science to politics.

Some small successes should not be overlooked. As noted above, Montana officials and later APHIS officials have helped protect Montana livestock producers by reducing the threat to downgrade the state's brucellosis-free status and reducing the threat of sanctions imposed by other states. Ranchers have succeeded in protecting their herds from brucellosis, amid various government actions and inaction. The lack of transmission of brucellosis in Jackson Hole, despite intermingling of bison and cattle, indicates the effectiveness of prudent ranching practices, including vaccination. It also indicates the limited potential for transmission, especially in winter. Moreover, citizens' groups have invested time and other resources in finding common ground, especially the 1991 Bison Management Citizen's Working Group in Bozeman and the coalition of ranchers, conservationists, and hunters in Jackson Hole in 1997. In addition, the 1998 Citizens' Plan to Save Yellowstone Bison was endorsed over the interagency alternatives in most public responses to the draft EIS.

Structures of Governance

Fragmented structures of governance in large part account for the failure to clarify and secure the common interest through a long-term bison management policy. The structures encourage officials to serve their own agency's specialized mandates, policies, and other interests as if these were the equivalent of the common interest. If the officials do not, they may be subject to penalties. Consequently, each agency with partial jurisdiction over bison management tends to come into conflict with other agencies and with interest groups in the private sector. Interactions among them are loosely organized through the EA and EIS processes established by the National Environmental Policy Act (NEPA). However, the political power necessary to force an integration of various factions into policy that advances the common interest either does not exist or has not been used to any significant extent in a decade and a half.[87] Thus, Montana does not accept APHIS's definition of low-risk bison; the federal government has not imposed it on Montana; and no government has banished critical interest groups from the arena.

In the state of Montana, DOL and allied veterinarians hold predominant power over bison management. The Montana Board of Livestock formulates policy for DOL, directs its operations, and hires both the executive director of DOL and the state veterinarian. The seven-member board is appointed by the governor, and includes producers of livestock, swine, dairy cattle, sheep, and game. Veterinarians act as advisers to the Board of Livestock, DOL, and ranchers, much as conservationists rely on natural scientists as advisers.[88] Veterinarians have experienced "a high degree of frustration," according to former Montana state veterinarian Clarence Siroky, because "the State Veterinarians and the livestock industries in all fifty states are committed to the eradication of brucellosis," but "their authority does not extend to within park boundaries, the [last] source of infection" in the intermountain region.[89] Veterinarians in other states have threatened sanctions against Montana cattle and have encouraged APHIS to revoke the state's brucellosis-free status. Montana rationalizes its zero-tolerance policy for infected bison as necessary to avoid such sanctions. The state also refuses to approve bison management proposals that are unacceptable to the state veterinarians and the USAHA.

Regardless of the intent of Montana officials, it should not be assumed that the policies of Montana veterinarians and DOL do in fact "protect the health and well-being of the livestock industry and economic well-being of ranchers" as mandated. Whatever else a policy to eradicate brucellosis from bison does, it harms the Montana livestock industry by focusing attention on the brucellosis issue and inflating the perception of risk among potential buyers outside the state. It also costs the Montana ranchers who fund DOL about $100,000 annually. Moreover, it should not be assumed that progress of the policy to eradicate brucellosis from cattle can be extrapolated to wildlife. The eradication of brucellosis from wildlife is a different matter biologically, given the lack of an effective vaccine for bison and the presence of brucellosis in thousands of elk as well as bison.[90] It is also a different matter politically so long as most citizens do not regard elk, bison, and other wildlife as livestock and protest when large numbers of wildlife are killed.

The Greater Yellowstone Interagency Brucellosis Committee (GYIBC) was created in 1990 after a task force of cattlemen, sportsmen, and representatives of state agencies "recognized that eradication of brucellosis in the GYA was desirable" and recommended it. Missing from task force discussions were conservationists, federal agencies, tribal representatives, and landowners. The goal was "to fulfill the needs of state agencies relative to brucellosis in wildlife."[91] Evidently, the needs of other groups, public and private, with respect to related issues were relatively insignificant to the task force, if considered at all. In 1995, the governors of Wyoming, Idaho, and Montana and U.S. interior and agriculture secretaries signed the Memorandum of Understanding that established the GYIBC.

All agencies that have some jurisdiction in bison management now have voting representatives on the GYIBC executive committee. Included are the directors of the state wildlife agencies of Montana, Wyoming, and Idaho; state veterinarians or directors of agriculture for the three states; the Wyoming state director of the Bureau of Land Management; one regional forester from the U.S. Forest Service; the Region 6 director of the U.S. Fish and Wildlife Service; the director of the Rocky Mountain Region of the National Park Service; and a designated representative of APHIS. Nonvoting members include representatives of the National Biological Service and Agricultural Research Service.[92] The GYIBC's official goal is the eradication of brucellosis from greater Yellowstone by the year 2010. This official goal presumes that the necessary technology, funds, and political support now lacking will become available. The GYIBC was originally conceived to coordinate the planning and implementation of policies relevant to the official goal. Instead, it has become a means of coordinating information on brucellosis and keeping member agencies informed of related issues.[93]

The GYIBC's policy is to leave its meetings open to the public but to exclude representatives of the public from the committee itself. The agencies have concluded that the Federal Advisory Committee Act (FACA) prohibits a public representative.[94] Most meetings include an opportunity for members of the public to make comments. The comment period, however, occurs at the end of meetings, when many GYIBC members are leaving and attention is dwindling. The effective exclusion of citizens was evident during a GYIBC meeting in May 1999. The governors of Montana, Wyoming, and Idaho and Assistant Secretary of Interior Don Berry attended to discuss future strategies and the possibility of expanding the role of the GYIBC to include policy recommendations and implementation. Members of the public also attended but were prevented from asking questions or making comments before the officials left.[95]

The GYIBC has not moved the policy process much closer to finding common-interest solutions. This is not surprising in view of the rather exclusive membership, the official goal, the lack of resources, and the policy regarding public participation, as well as policy differences among its members. As its name implies, the GYIBC institutionalizes brucellosis as the main problem, if not the only one; its name also suggests that the agencies alone are authorized or otherwise competent to find a solution. Thus the GYIBC helps institutionalize conflict with those in the private sector who perceive problems besides brucellosis and aim for solutions that address underlying issues, and who have enough at stake to remain active participants. These groups include, ironically, the ranchers and others in Jackson Hole who considered the threat of overregulation the problem and advocated the vaccination of cattle and their separation from wildlife as proven low-intensity management solutions.

At the national level, the White House Council on Environmental Quality became involved to coordinate the federal family after the shooting of more than a thousand bison in 1997. Weekly meetings occurred for several years among federal officials and scientists in the Washington offices of APHIS and the U.S. Forest Service, both in the Agriculture Department and the National Park Service in the Interior Department. The meetings gave the agencies an "opportunity to talk about ways to get away from the thirty years of bad history" on this issue.[96] The federal family meetings have led to changes in APHIS. Agency veterinarians maintain a "disease control perspective" and were once viewed as villains in this issue.[97] Partly as a result of the federal family meetings, APHIS withdrew threats of sanctions in the absence of a brucellosis outbreak and developed the low-risk definition for bison. Also partly as a result of these meetings, the USFS altered grazing allotments to allow for temporal separation of cattle and bison. The USFS, however, maintains a low-profile role in the process because it is mandated to maintain habitat, not to manage wildlife.[98] As discussed above, the federal policy changes have resulted in little difference in practice because Montana rejects them and maintains control over bison management in greater Yellowstone.

Similarly, other efforts to coordinate have had little effect in practice. Washington officials involved in bison management circulate interoffice memos and meet informally.[99] Western governors and members of Congress pressured federal officials, typically on behalf of livestock interests in their states. Top officials such as Governor Racicot and President Clinton and secretaries of the interior and agriculture met sporadically. Insofar as such efforts take place behind closed doors, it is difficult for outsiders to determine who might be held accountable for the lack of coordination. Finally, as noted above, the EIS process has done more to polarize the issues between public agencies and private interest groups than to advance the common interest through policy. Frustrated by interagency bison management alternatives, and effectively excluded from the structures through which those alternatives are devised, private interest groups seek other means to make a difference in bison management policy. Lawsuits are an obvious choice, because there are plausible grounds in law for almost any interest group with enough funds to challenge official decisions. Whatever the courts may decide in a particular case, they exclude nonlitigants who nevertheless may have an important stake in the issue, and they provide little room for integrating or balancing the competing claims of litigants. In one case, as discussed, the court assumed authority and considerable control to oversee the revision and implementation of interim plans. Interest groups and officials have also appealed to legislators, state and federal, for legislation on the issue. In 1995, for example, the Montana state legislature transferred to DOL authority over bison that have been exposed to brucellosis and enter Montana.[100] Also in 1995, Senator Burns of Montana introduced a bill to require the National Park Service to eradicate brucellosis from Yellowstone bison. The bill proposed testing, culling, vaccination, and relocation of bison as well as keeping their numbers below the "optimum population."[101] The bill was not passed. Livestock groups in particular have been able to secure some of their interests through legislatures or the courts, but this is not equivalent to advancing the common interest.

The Bison Management Citizen's Working Group in Bozeman was an attempt to clarify and secure the common interest in 1991. It is worth recapping here the structure and outcome of this and other community groups' efforts to contrast it with the agency-led initiatives described above. The group included a local rancher, a member of the Montana Wildlife Federation, a member of the Greater Yellowstone Association of Conservation Districts (a now-defunct livestock group), members of The Wilderness Society and the Greater Yellowstone Coalition, retired employees from the Montana DFWP and the USFS, and a local landowner. Agency officials from DFWP, APHIS, Yellowstone National Park, and the USFS served as technical advisers; a member of a tribal organization was also consulted.[102] The group attempted to be inclusive of the interests involved, which is consistent with a procedural test of the common interest. The group's ground rules, however, excluded any party that demanded zero tolerance for any bison outside the Park or zero tolerance for any lethal control of bison. Extreme positions were not tolerated. Animal rights organizations elected not to join the group under these ground rules. The group met once a week from March to May in 1991 to develop a plan for bison management, with the intent of "satisfying diverse interests and management perspectives."[103]

The members were able to work through their policy differences and agree on a plan for submission to agency officials. When all members accepted the plan, it passed a substantive test of the common interest. The objectives were "to maintain a self-sustaining population of wild bison within Yellowstone; to protect local livestock by reducing the potential for transmission of *Brucella abortus* [the organism causing brucellosis]; and to reduce the potential for bison-human conflict and property damage caused by bison outside the park."[104] The plan called for tolerance of bison on land outside the Park, but it allowed for trapping, testing, and transportation of migrating brucellosis-free bison to tribal lands, other public lands, and back into the Park. It left some flexibility for the agencies to work out the details. The intent was to address the demands of participants to protect ranchers, bison, and landowners but not the zero-tolerance demands of participants outside the group. The plan remains a good start toward a common-interest solution, one that minimizes the potential for transmission of brucellosis while protecting the wildness of the Yellowstone bison and allowing for control of any bison that cause property damage or endanger human safety. But the plan cannot pass a practical test of the common interest unless it is implemented by the agencies.

Citizens in Jackson Hole also attempted to clarify and secure the common interest in 1997. They included Jackson area ranchers, the executive directors of the Jackson Hole Conservation Alliance and the Greater Yellowstone Coalition, and the president of the Wyoming Wildlife Federation, a hunting organization. As noted, these citizens drafted a letter together and sent it to President Clinton, Secretary of Interior Bruce Babbitt, Secretary of Agriculture Dan Glickman, and Governor Geringer of Wyoming. They wrote, "While we share your concern for protecting the 'Brucellosis Free Status' of Wyoming, we think it is secure now because there is no recent history of brucellosis

transmission from wildlife to cattle in Teton, Park and Sublette counties and because the ranchers in this area protect their cattle through
vaccinations." They also wrote that the Wyoming Game and Fish Department has policies to keep elk off private cattle feedgrounds and
would do the same for bison if the need arose, eliminating the potential
for the transmission of disease. The letter recommended "non-lethal
and non-invasive" techniques of control but did not make detailed recommendations (beyond spatial separation and cattle vaccination), because the signatories believed the problem was adequately addressed
through current management practices, at least in Wyoming. The techniques were less intensive than those recommended by the Citizen's
Working Group in Bozeman, but the objectives and methods were otherwise similar. They acted partly to show that the Jackson community
can resolve such issues without heavy-handed government intervention.[105]

In a separate effort, citizens in Jackson also worked with area agencies to devise a management plan for the bison herd in Jackson Hole,
where circumstances are more challenging in some ways than in Montana.[106] The Totem Studies Group formed after citizens became frustrated with bison management in the area, around 1995. The group
included unaffiliated citizens, conservationists, agency personnel,
county commissioners, educators, Native Americans, members of the
agricultural community, and scientists. Their goals included improving bison management in the common interest and building relationships among community members.[107] They engaged in deliberations to
overcome political differences in the EIS process. And they gained the
support of agencies with the authority to implement a plan: Wyoming
Game and Fish, the U.S. Fish and Wildlife Service in the National Elk
Refuge, and the National Park Service in Grand Teton National Park.
Portions of the group's Jackson Hole Bison Management Plan were
incorporated into the agency-led Environmental Assessment and Long-
Term Plan. It called for risk management measures to prevent the
transmission of brucellosis. Although participants in the Totem Studies Group recognized room for improvement in the plan, they believed
the working relationships and trust they had developed would allow
adaptation and change as new needs and insights arose. Thus the plan
represented progress with respect to procedural and substantive tests
of the common interest, but not the practical test: the Fund for Animals
successfully blocked implementation. The group nevertheless helped
change perceptions about citizen participation in the U.S. Fish and
Wildlife Service and Wyoming Game and Fish. One official of Wyoming Game and Fish, for example, claimed his agency had a break-

through when it recognized that early involvement by citizens can help agencies envision the common interest.[108]

Private interest groups formed a coalition to develop the Citizens' Plan to Save Yellowstone Bison in Montana in 1998. The plan was submitted to the agencies during the NEPA process to provide an alternative to the interagency draft EIS, to meet the demands of the coalition's sixteen conservation and tribal organizations and three businesses, and to protect Montana's cattle.[109] The 1991 Citizen's Working Group and the 1998 coalition are not directly related, and the coalition was less inclusive. But the leadership abilities of Jeanne-Marie Souvigney, a member of the 1991 Citizen's Working Group, have been cited as instrumental in developing the plan.[110] Souvigney and others consulted with agency officials at all levels. The plan received 47,599 endorsements in public comments on the interagency draft EIS, partly because of promotion efforts by the National Wildlife Federation and the Intertribal Bison Cooperative.[111]

The Citizens' Plan recommends special management areas on public land where buffalo would roam with minimal intervention. It proposes a scientific determination of minimum and maximum herd size, using such strategies to manage the herd size as live removal to tribal lands and a public hunt. To ensure that only brucellosis-free animals would be relocated, the plan recommends building a "pasture-type bison health certification facility."[112] It also recommends an interagency/tribal/public cooperative team composed of wildlife professionals to advise managers. It advises changing the time or location of Forest Service grazing allotments to maintain separation of bison and cattle. The plan would prohibit hazing or capture of bison on public lands absent of cattle, unless the herd's population exceeds the maximum. It recommends that Montana and other states accept the federal low-risk definition, address brucellosis in elk, encourage ranchers near the Park to vaccinate their cattle, and make a land exchange outside of Yellowstone's northern border a priority.

The federal government is already implementing several of these alternatives. In August 1999, the government signed a land exchange deal with the Church Universal and Triumphant to secure 7,800 acres outside Yellowstone's northern boundary where bison migrate in search of winter forage. This land also provides habitat for elk, deer, antelope, bighorn sheep, wolves, and grizzly bears.[113] The exchange allows for nonlethal bison management options outside the Park. In addition, the Forest Service has already altered grazing allotments to allow the Montana state veterinarian to prohibit cattle from entering public land before bison return to the Park for the summer, thereby minimizing the risk of brucellosis transmission. Finally, APHIS has encouraged Montana to accept the federal low-risk definition. Whether these changes make a difference, however, will depend on the state, which retains control over the implementation of bison management policy in Montana. Judging from the Joint Management Plan in the record of decision, not much will change in the short run.

Although the Citizens' Plan to Save Yellowstone Bison includes alternatives that may help achieve the goals of maintaining a free-roaming herd and protecting cattle, a number of important interest groups failed to support it. Why? Attempts in 1998 to bring ranchers into the discussions failed, perhaps because the issue was so contentious and because the major demands of livestock organizations, if not individual ranchers, were already being met.[114] Leaders of the livestock producers had little reason to come to the table. Since 1990–91, when agencies began formal efforts to coordinate and the inclusive Citizen's Working Group formed in Bozeman, interests have polarized further and Montana has gained more control. The less-inclusive 1998 Citizens' Plan was developed in a more divisive climate that tended to estrange groups that were once closer together. No agency or interest group is monolithic, however. Within the agencies, conservation groups, livestock associations, tribes, and hunting groups are members still willing to meet with members of opposing groups in search of common ground. With better leadership they might be able to overcome the fragmented structure of governance and succeed.

Policy and Structural Alternatives

The goals of the draft EIS, as discussed, are to "maintain a wild, free-ranging population of bison and address the risk of brucellosis transmission to protect the economic interest and viability of the livestock industry in the state of Montana."[115] There are various alternatives to meet these goals—policy alternatives for minimizing the risk of brucellosis transmission to protect livestock producers, policy alternatives for protecting wild, free-ranging bison, and structural alternatives for governance, which have broader significance for natural resources policy in the American West.

Minimizing the risk of brucellosis transmission to protect livestock producers is a valid and appropriate goal. It includes preventing other states from placing sanctions on Montana's cattle and preventing brucellosis from re-infecting Montana's cattle. The reduction of Montana's class-free status could cost the state's livestock industry as much as $27 million for testing, according to an industry estimate.[116] The attempt to eradicate brucellosis from wildlife, however, will not assure Montana's class-free status or prevent sanctions. On one hand, "total eradication of brucellosis as a goal is more a statement of principle than a workable program at present."[117] On the other hand, the attempt reinforces the perception that brucellosis in wildlife is a valid justification to impose sanctions. Given Montana's position in the fragmented structure of governance, it will take better leadership in Montana's state agencies and among livestock producers to change the focus to risk management. The alternatives available include adoption of the federal definition of low-risk bison, changes in Forest Service allotments to ensure separation of bison and cattle, and vaccination of cattle against brucellosis. Wyoming's experience is instructive. It has maintained its brucellosis-free status despite four outbreaks.[118] And the experience shows that containment depends on how a producer handles an outbreak.[119] For a state to lose its class-free status, an outbreak with undetermined origin must occur, it must be uncontrolled, and a second outbreak must occur.[120] The Animal, Plant, and Health Inspection Service cannot legally pull Montana's status if an outbreak occurs from infected bison, as long as it is handled appropriately. Better leadership could portray eradication of brucellosis from the state's *cattle* herds and management of the negligible risk of transmission as successes for Montana and its ranchers.

Conflicts over the control of resources would remain, however, even if brucellosis were completely eradicated. Many ranchers view bison migrations as another sign of their loss of control to an "environmental agenda." Livestock officials claim that before the passage of NEPA in 1969, "resource industries dominated the use of federal lands." Now the costs of grazing leases, restriction of private property rights, and multiple uses of national forests indicate a change in priorities on federal lands. Bison outside the Park also compete with cattle for forage. There is a feeling that "the economic importance of agriculture to rural counties in the western states is often not recognized."[121] Few groups wish to see ranchers pushed off their land because of bison, but some believe that if Montana pushes for zero tolerance of bison, others will demand zero tolerance for ranchers on public land. A range war on public lands would likely result in loss of leasing rights for ranchers. Neither zero tolerance for bison nor zero tolerance for grazing cattle on public lands is consistent with the common interest, and grazing by both bison and cattle can be accommodated.

Moreover, there are greater threats to the livestock industry than roaming bison. As of 1995, only four firms controlled 81 percent of the meatpacking industry.[122] This concentration of buying power enables the meatpacking industry to sustain artificially low prices paid to live-stock producers. Large quantities of imported livestock, especially from Canada, are also of concern to producers.[123] Discrepancies be-tween U.S. and Canadian animal health inspection procedures, includ-ing brucellosis testing requirements on U.S. exports to Canada, are one issue.[124] Finally, demand for beef products is declining. Ranchers' abil-ity to absorb the costs of grazing leases, brucellosis vaccines and tests, and other costs of doing business in the West are related to the market-ability of cattle and the prices paid for them.

To address more pressing threats to the industry, resources might be redirected away from the eradication of brucellosis in wildlife and toward risk management measures, and additional resources might be sought. Such programs as the U.S. Market Access Program and the Foreign Market Development Program could be used to market U.S. beef as brucellosis-free.[125] A portion of federal and state funds currently spent on an unworkable program to eradicate brucellosis from bison might be reserved to pay for additional testing, vaccination, and other costs associated with potential outbreaks. It would be cheaper to vacci-nate the 2,000 head of cattle that might intermingle with bison than 100,000 head of wild bison and elk, especially because no safe, effective vaccine (or method of administering it) currently exists for wildlife. The National Wildlife Federation also has offered to pay to vaccinate cattle around Yellowstone. Many ranchers near Yellowstone already do vaccinate cattle.[126] Vaccination of cattle is effective not only in pre-venting outbreaks of brucellosis, but also in giving more control (and more responsibility) to those most directly affected by potential out-breaks—the livestock producers.

Alternatives also exist to address the perceived risk of transmission, which may be different from the actual risk. As discussed, APHIS con-vinced other state veterinarians to lift unjustified sanctions against Montana cattle and agreed to defend Montana against such sanctions in the future.[127] The agency has ensured the continuation of these ef-forts. Under the settlement agreement, APHIS agreed not to down-grade the state's brucellosis-free status "based on the presence of bison migrating from YNP into Montana," if the state complies with the In-terim Plan.[128] The Joint Management Plan also includes a statement that "implementation of the Joint Management Plan will not cause APHIS to downgrade Montana's brucellosis class-free status."[129] To fur-ther protect the class-free status of Montana cattle, APHIS could also provide assurances that they will not pull Montana's status if a rancher handles an outbreak appropriately and that APHIS will pressure other states to lift unjust sanctions.

Another major goal of bison management is to maintain a wild, free-roaming herd. The Park's natural regulation policy made some progress toward achieving this goal: bison populations are up and bison are reestablishing their former ranges. Maintaining the wildness of the herd, however, will require attention to the unintended consequences of the policy, including expansion of the political arena and the dispersion of control over bison management decisions beyond the Park Service. Some changes in the natural regulation policy are already occurring. The Park's practice of capturing and testing bison inside the Park and the proposed population limits in the draft EIS, for example, challenge the natural regulation policy.[130] It is time to ask how these changes will affect the wildness of bison and how that wildness can be maintained, while addressing the potential adverse consequences of natural regulation for other valid interests in the community. One zoologist suggests a need for an assessment of both ecological carrying capacity, based on available wildlife forage, and "social carrying capacity," based on complaints arising from wildlife-human interaction but not necessarily measured.[131]

A recommendation to reexamine the natural regulation policy is not a recommendation to return to ranching in Yellowstone National Park. The general public would not accept such a policy. Most of the public accepts natural fluctuations in wildlife populations and differences in the standards appropriate for national parks and cattle ranges. Scientists support the idea of the Park as a baseline against which more intensively managed resources outside the Park can be compared.[132] Evaluations of the natural regulation policy, however, have focused on its ecological effects inside the Park.[133] Few assessments consider its social and political effects outside the Park. So establishing a population range might be appropriate now that bison populations have increased. Such alternatives as hunting by Native Americans and shipping calves to tribes and other public lands are means to regulate bison populations that are consistent with current proposals. Some control of bison populations exercised within the Park might sustain wildness better than capture of all bison that exit the Park. It might also return more control over bison management to the Park.

A reassessment of natural regulation might also address the misplaced faith in, and burden on, science to resolve differences in management policy. Many identify value conflicts as the root cause of the problem of policy differences but then call for more science as the solution. But scientists, apart from policy scientists, are supposed to avoid policy differences in political arenas and not consider values beyond hard data. Thus, although science can inform policy decisions, "it is not a substitute for decision making."[134] Management decisions, for example, must be made now, even in the absence of a safe and effective vaccine for bison. But if and when such a vaccine is developed, it would still take many years of effort and great expense to eradicate brucellosis in bison, and policy differences would not disappear because administration of the vaccine would compromise wildness in the herd. Misplaced faith in science also devalues trial-and-error experience in the field. When separation of bison and cattle and vaccinations of cattle have proven effective in practice, there is little to be gained by deferring decisions pending completion of more scientific studies. Often we know enough without further studies to make an informed policy decision, while recognizing that new insights or experience will warrant changes in the policy.

To the extent that policy differences persist because of the fragmented structure of governance, structural alternatives are also in order. Some conservation groups and ranchers already agree that the NEPA process in bison management has become more contentious and that discourse is needed to resolve differences among the multiple interests involved. One rancher leasing land outside the Park said, "It's politicized from the very beginning. . . . It's who's got the most pull." Consequently, he argues, "there's a need for informed public discourse."[135] Some agency officials also seem interested in discussing the issues with citizens.[136] Thus from various sides of the debate, there may be enough support for an initiative to institutionalize discourse on bison management among representatives of the multiple interest groups and agencies involved. The precedents to build on include the initiatives taken by several groups in the Jackson area in the latter half of the 1990s and by the Bison Management Citizen's Working Group in Bozeman in 1991. A new community-based initiative might monitor implementation of the Joint Management Plan and continue to work with agencies to suggest changes. Agencies would have to consult with lawyers to avoid violations of the Federal Advisory Committee Act (FACA), but FACA does not preclude citizens and agencies working together. Such collaboration could in the long run reduce the need or desire to litigate. For more than token improvements in bison management to occur, a civic science is needed that allows for citizens and scientists to work together to monitor, evaluate, and contribute knowledge to decisions. Adaptive management need not be restricted to scientific advances in biophysical knowledge alone, as suggested in the agencies' Joint Management Plan.

A new community-based initiative would have an opportunity to build on the 1998 Citizens' Plan to Save Yellowstone Bison. Recall that it was endorsed over the interagency alternatives by a large majority of public comments and that it includes provisions consistent with those developed by earlier and more inclusive groups in Jackson and Bozeman. The discourse should include representatives of livestock, conservation, and tribal interests as well as landowner and agency perspectives. It might be facilitated by the Northern Lights Institute, which played an important role in the success of the Upper Clark Fork Steering Committee (see Chapter 2 of this volume) and other community-based initiatives.

Involving multiple interest groups in the development of policy alternatives through a community-based initiative could be an improvement in the long run—even from a narrow agency perspective—over soliciting and rejecting citizens' comments on exclusively interagency alternatives in the NEPA process. In a community-based initiative, officials could retain vital roles in planning, promoting, and authorizing policy alternatives and in implementing, evaluating, and eventually terminating them. Officials could also gain more access to the information and political support they need, both internal and external, and they could even take the lead in organizing the community. Most officials, however, lack the training and skills needed to coordinate across agency mandates and deal with increasing numbers of interest groups. They are more often prepared to proceed within the narrow mandates and jurisdictions of their respective agencies. For the short term in bison management, these limitations may be overcome by reassigning exceptional agency personnel. (This is typically easier during or immediately after a crisis, such as the severe winter of 1996–97, when demands to respond are high.) For the long term, and beyond bison management, it is time to rethink the traditional training and skills developed for the management of natural resources in the twentieth century. New skills can be taught in workshops and in schools for natural resources professionals to exploit the potential of community-based initiatives for finding common ground in the twenty-first century.

The bison case demonstrates the need for new structures in the governance of natural resources in the greater Yellowstone area. Since the Park's inception in 1872, the aspiration to manage Park resources in the common interest, "for all the people," has not changed. But changes in Park policy have affected ecological conditions, increasing wildlife populations and migrations. As bison cross over Park boundaries, they alter politics and governance, drawing more interest groups with more diverse interests into bison management. Current structures of governance, largely agency-led and controlled, have failed to find policies that advance the common interest within these more complex conditions. The problem of bison management is not primarily one of brucellosis or science or economics, but rather one of politics and governance.

Alternative structures of governance such as community-based groups in Jackson and Montana led to the development of plans that could advance the common interest. These plans call for risk management over the eradication of brucellosis in wildlife. Agencies, however, have failed to capitalize on the plans and have continued largely on their own. The situation may seem intractable, but common-interest solutions are possible with better leadership willing to take some risks. Montana needs to back down from its demand for zero tolerance of brucellosis in bison if it wants to protect livestock producers rather than merely assert control over natural resources policy. Citizens need to continue working with others who have opposing values to find common-interest solutions. Agencies need to be more open to such alternatives. Only through changes in the rigid structures and political interests in place can livestock producers and a wild, free-roaming herd of bison be protected over the long run.

5 Forest Policy and the Quincy Library Group

Christine H. Colburn

Forestry policy has long been a contentious issue in the United States, pitting the culture and livelihoods of many Americans against the conservation values of others. Lives have been threatened, and indeed, bullets have been fired over the issue. It was not uncommon around 1990 to see stuffed spotted owls strung up by loggers, or environmentalists strapping themselves to trees in the Pacific Northwest—both potent symbols of protest and tension. A new alternative has gradually emerged in forest management, however: community-based forestry. Citizens in forestry-dependent towns have begun to come together to search for common ground.

One such town is Quincy, California. In 1992, environmentalists, loggers, community leaders, homemakers, and others in this small, timber-dependent community came together in the only neutral ground they could find—the town library. In 1993, the Quincy Library Group agreed on a Community Stability Proposal for the management of two national forests and part of a third in the surrounding area, and they submitted it to the Forest Service. When the service did not accept the proposal, however, the group took it to Congress. The bill directing the Forest Service to implement the proposal on a pilot basis sailed through the House in July 1997 with a vote of 429 to 1, and it passed as a rider on the omnibus appropriations bill. On October 21, 1998, President Clinton signed into law the Herger-Feinstein Quincy Library Group Forest Recovery Act. The Forest Service has only begun to carry out the pilot project prescribed in that act. With a few exceptions, envi-

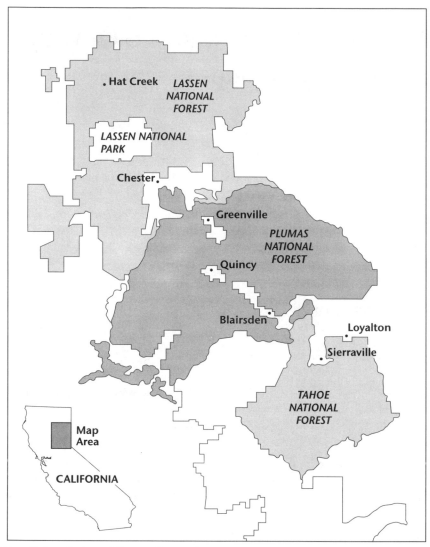

Map 5.1. Quincy Library Group Area

ronmental organizations have been outspoken in their opposition. Timber advocates have been quietly supportive. The Clinton administration held it up as a model to be emulated. Although the Quincy Library Group is only one of hundreds of citizen groups organized around forest management policy, it stands out because it achieved passage of legislation at the national level, where the issue remains highly controversial.

Setting the Stage

The story of forest management in the Quincy area is both one of rela-tionships developing among the parts of a community—including but not limited to people—and one of a series of policies that attempt to find the common interest. As the community evolved, a policy that at one time advanced the common interest became obsolete because of factors both related and unrelated to the policy at hand.

Where the lively town of Quincy, California, now stands, at one time there was nothing but vast pristine forest inhabited by the Maidu, Washo, and Paiute Indians. In the spring of 1850, however, major change came to Quincy. The area was flooded with gold-seeking set-tlers, whose mining camps soon lined the once-tranquil streams of the Feather River watershed. In their frenzy to find gold, the settlers rav-aged the riverbeds, rerouted streams, dug ditches along the banks, and essentially transformed the land for generations to come. Logging first came to the area as a service industry to miners, who used wood not only to develop their mines, but also to build their homes, schools, churches, and businesses. Ranching came early to the Quincy area as well, providing meat and dairy products for miners. Ranchers, miners, and loggers generally were free to use the land as they chose to, unfet-tered by federal or other regulation. At that time, the federal govern-ment's policy was to foster an entrepreneurial spirit in extractive indus-tries as a way to provide incentives to settle the West.[1] This policy reflected the common interest of the time, allowing ranchers, miners, and loggers to pursue their goals, while also serving the national goal of Western expansion.

Mining remained the largest industry in the area for fifty years after the initial rush, but it dropped off dramatically around 1900 when most miners left the area. Mining was soon replaced by large-scale logging. After construction of the transcontinental railroads was complete, around the turn of the century, timber companies could ship lumber all over the country.[2] Previously, only enough timber to meet the needs of local communities was harvested, but once markets across the coun-try were accessible, the timber industry, along with Quincy, grew rap-idly. As a result, a large portion of the Tahoe National Forest was har-vested, and currently the Tahoe is dominated by second-growth stands of timber about eighty to ninety years old.[3] The Plumas and Lassen National Forests met similar fates.

Trains brought tourists as well, and consequently, a thriving tour-ism industry emerged. Local entrepreneurs quickly established resorts and lodges to house fishermen, hikers, and sightseers. Passenger trains continued to run along the Feather River Route until 1970, but now the line is used only for freight traffic. Nevertheless, tourism remains an important industry in the area and has been expanded to include golfing, antique shopping, windsurfing, and more.

Policy shifts as well as modern technology have had a significant impact on the Quincy area. Today, Quincy is surrounded by three national forests: the Plumas, the Lassen, and the Tahoe, all established by President Theodore Roosevelt in 1905. Although their establishment as national forests marked a change in administration, the emphasis on timber production remained constant. This position was consistent with ongoing federal policies that encouraged settlement of the West by supporting natural resource industries. Federal law dictated that the first purpose of national forests was to protect watersheds, a policy adopted in response to growing demands from farmers for reliable sources of irrigation water. The second purpose was to produce commercial timber.[4] These dual functions marked the beginning of the Forest Service's long history of attempting to balance multiple and sometimes competing interests.

The philosophy of the Forest Service in its early days was aptly expressed by Gifford Pinchot, the first chief: "All the resources of forest reserves are for *use*, and this use must be brought about in a thoroughly prompt and businesslike manner, under such restrictions only as will insure the permanence of these resources." More succinctly, he said, "To grow trees as a crop is forestry."[5] National forest management continued to be singularly guided by these principles until the 1970s. As the Forest Service developed, it emphasized timber sales and harvests, as well as fire science and silviculture, all under the overarching purpose of growing trees as a crop. Even so, it was not until World War II—when the demand for wood rose sharply—that the Forest Service began extracting substantial volumes of timber.[6] Before the war, the Forest Service "could make its cut from 'easy' lands—highly profitable stands that would jeopardize few recreational or environmental values. There simply was no basis for any controversy."[7]

Clearcutting became the dominant method of logging during the 1970s, provoking a torrent of criticism from the environmental movement. This was heightened by the fact that more outsiders, many of them environmentalists, were moving to Quincy. David Brower, a national environmental leader, and others founded the Friends of the Plumas Wilderness in the Quincy area. It was not only the environmentalists who were opposed to clearcutting, though. Loggers, too, were against it because the technique replaced high-skilled jobs with low-skilled, low-paying jobs.[8] Furthermore, employees at small logging companies were especially hard hit. Many local companies could not bid on timber sales because the jobs were too big. Former logger Jim Wilcox asserts that clearcutting never produced the bonanza for small local operators that it did for industry giants.[9] The Forest Service policy, which privileged clearcutting as the preferred method of harvest, no longer reflected the common interest. In fact, it represented neither the interest of environmentalists nor that of local timber workers.

The environmental movement was gaining momentum at the national level, too. Congress passed the National Environmental Policy Act (NEPA) in 1969, and the National Forest Management Act (NFMA) in 1976. NEPA requires federal agencies to complete a "detailed environmental impact statement" (EIS) before all major actions "significantly affecting the quality of the human environment." The EIS must assess the environmental impacts of the proposed action and evaluate alternatives to it. The law combined with its implementing regulations also requires federal agencies to provide a draft EIS and to offer the public and other agencies opportunities to comment. Although NEPA included some substantive provisions, too, the provisions that compelled action were the procedural ones.

The National Forest Management Act heralded a new era in forest management: one that called for regulation of timber extraction and protection of nontimber forest values. It aimed, in effect, to bring Forest Service management policy back in line with the common interest. NFMA restricts clearcutting but does not prohibit it. The act mandates that timber cuts are performed in a way that allows for the protection of streams and soils, and it requires the Forest Service to provide for "diversity of plant and animal communities."[10] NFMA also created new planning procedures, including requirements for extensive public input, increased scientific research, consideration of all resources (not just timber production), and interdisciplinary decision-making teams (rather than those made up exclusively of foresters). Although environmentalists were initially delighted with the passage of NFMA, it was rarely invoked in its early years, and for the most part business continued as usual in the Forest Service. The act was an attempt by Congress to re-align Forest Service policy with the common interest, but in practice, the Forest Service continued to operate under an unwritten policy prioritizing commercial timber harvest over other interests.

Back in Quincy, environmentalists were dissatisfied with the extractive priority and concerned about unsustainable harvesting of old growth trees. In response, three members of the Friends of the Plumas Wilderness came together to work on a plan. They were Michael Jackson, an environmental attorney from Quincy, Michael Yost, a forestry professor at Feather River College, and Steve Evans, a Sierra Club leader.[11] The three men walked most of the land in the Plumas National Forest to see firsthand which areas had already been cut, where there were riparian zones, salmon and owl habitats, and remaining stands of old growth that deserved special protection. They received expert advice throughout the process from The Wilderness Society, the Sierra Club, and the Natural Resources Defense Council (NRDC). "We basically protected all the land we could—streams, roadless area, old growth—and then told the computer to thin the remaining (roaded) forest heavily," said Yost. "We were trying to show there was volume out there."[12] In their plan, they proposed that thinning be done with "group selection," a technique that clears small areas ranging from about one-tenth of an acre to two acres. The openings created are large enough to allow in enough sunlight to regenerate a variety of species, but small enough to allow the surrounding trees to reseed the openings naturally. In 1986, they submitted their plan, the Conservationist Alternative, for consideration in the Plumas National Forest planning process.

The planning process mandated by NFMA directs the Forest Service to develop a Land and Resource Management Plan (LRMP) for each national forest and to revise it every ten to fifteen years. Regulations require that an EIS, subject to public comment, is developed. After the Friends of the Plumas submitted their plan, Plumas Forest Service officials developed a draft EIS but included a modified version of the Conservationist Alternative, called the Amenity Alternative, rather than the version developed by the Friends of the Plumas. The public comment period on the draft EIS inspired widespread and passionate participation from local residents. While the Friends of the Plumas Wilderness were advocating adoption of the Amenity Alternative, the Plumas Sierra Citizens for Multiple Use were banding together to press for greater emphasis on timber extraction. In the words of one member, "The more commodity production is emphasized the better the economic health of Plumas County."[13]

On April 29, 1986, the Forest Service held a public hearing. "Loggers in hardhats and work boots joined business people in dress shirts and coat jackets to jam [the hearing] and demand maximum timber harvests on the Plumas National Forest."[14] Businesses in Quincy closed for two hours that afternoon to show support for a forest plan that emphasized timber extraction. A parade of logging trucks, backhoes, fuel trucks, and pickups adorned with streamers rolled through the streets of Quincy, displaying banners proclaiming "forests forever—

for everyone." Supporters of Citizens for Multiple Use were heavily represented at the hearing, repeatedly urging the Forest Service to consider the local economy.[15]

The Plumas National Forest finalized its long-term plan in 1988 and did not adopt the Amenity Alternative. Forest Service officials explained that they rejected it because the success of group selection, a new technique, was uncertain. They also said this type of management would require foresters to travel in and out of the forest frequently, impacting the soils more than traditional management techniques. In the "preferred alternative," adopted by the Forest Service, clearcutting was the dominant harvesting method, and group selection and single-tree selection were to be used only on an experimental basis in a limited area. The preferred alternative also allowed a slightly larger timber harvest than the Amenity Alternative.[16]

Environmentalists believed it subordinated their interests to timber interests. The Friends of the Plumas Wilderness and the other environmental groups decided to appeal the plan with legal help from the NRDC and the Sierra Club. The lengthy appeal challenged the legality of the Forest Service plan on a variety of grounds, including inadequate protection for spotted owls and other species, concerns about water quality, and allegedly unsound data. But three or four years later, the Forest Service still had not acted on the appeal.[17] The Washington office eventually reported that the plan was not in violation of the law, and the appeal was denied.

During this period, evidence was mounting that forest management practices in Washington and Oregon were threatening the viability of the northern spotted owl. The Forest Service, therefore, was violating the National Forest Management Act, which requires the agency to provide for diversity of plant and animal communities. Congress had refined NFMA regulations in 1979, elaborating the approach by which the Forest Service was to protect species diversity under the act. The 1979 regulations required the service to identify indicator species that would act as surrogates for a given animal or plant community as a whole. If the indicator species was healthy, according to the theory, so was the community. The northern spotted owl was chosen to be the proxy for ancient forests.[18]

The Forest Service released its proposed management guidelines on the spotted owl in 1986. It generated 40,000 letters from industry members and environmentalists alike. The timber industry was concerned that the proposal would cost thousands of jobs by prohibiting logging on huge tracts of land. Environmentalists feared that the plan was inadequate to protect the viability of the spotted owl and predicted that the owl might survive only twenty-five years under the plan as written. The service released final spotted owl guidelines in 1988, which provided for more protected land than had the 1986 guidelines. Lawsuits swiftly proliferated until forests in the Pacific Northwest were virtually shut down. Also in 1988, the Seattle Audubon Society and other environmental groups sued the Forest Service in what has been called "the most far-reaching" suit of the period.[19] They claimed that the 1988 spotted owl guidelines violated NFMA and NEPA. A federal district judge granted a preliminary injunction on 135 timber sales in 1989, and a year later, the decision was upheld in the *Seattle Audubon* case.[20] Forests in the Quincy area were not directly impacted by this decision because they did not include northern spotted owl habitat. But the California spotted owl (a related species) did range in the forests surrounding Quincy, and consequently timber companies in California feared a shutdown similar to the one occurring in the Northwest.

Meanwhile, timber sales all over northern California were on the decline. On the Plumas National Forest they went from 205 million board feet in 1987 to 120 million board feet in 1991. Similar trends were occurring in the other two forests surrounding Quincy.[21] The decline was due in part to the efforts of national and local environmental groups, who, like the Friends of the Plumas Wilderness, were fighting timber sales at every stage of the process. Michael Jackson and another environmental activist from Quincy, Linda Blum, were heavily involved in these appeals and litigation. Concurrent and significant decreases in Forest Service personnel due to budget cuts meant that fewer timber sales could be managed. This combination of factors left the lumber mills in and around the area struggling to keep afloat. The situation in Quincy had changed, and Forest Service policy no longer accommodated the interests of timber workers, environmentalists, or the local community.

During this period the Forest Service was on shaky ground, concerned that its management practices in California might have been in violation of NFMA. "We immediately went into a huddle," said Ron Stewart, regional forester at the time.[22] State and federal officials held joint meetings and decided that a team from the U.S. Forest Service would conduct a biological analysis. The team was charged with producing the California Spotted Owl (CASPO) report, which would provide guidelines for forest management consistent with protection of the owl.

In the midst of growing tension within the Forest Service, in 1992 Bill Clinton was elected president. The Clinton administration brought new appointees to high-ranking positions in the Department of Agriculture and the Forest Service. With new leadership came a shift in focus—at least at the top—from a Forest Service that emphasized timber production to one that emphasized ecosystem management and conservation. The new administration called for a dramatic decrease in timber sales. As a result of this shift, combined with environmental legislation and litigation, the logging community in Quincy was hard hit. "We were literally crashing the economy of this area," said Wayne Thornton, the supervisor of Plumas National Forest at the time.[23]

Bill Coates, Plumas County supervisor, was concerned about the situation in Quincy and the other rural communities he represented, as well as about Sierra Pacific Industries, the timber company that dominates Plumas and Lassen Counties and the company that had supported his political career. In Plumas County, like many counties in the West, a portion of the revenue raised through timber sales on public land is allotted to the county government to compensate for loss of revenue that would come from property taxes if the land were privately owned. Timber receipts consequently represent a significant portion of school and road budgets for Plumas, Lassen, and Sierra Counties. The federal government owns 75 percent, 54 percent, and 59 percent, respectively, of the land in these counties.[24] Coates and others were fearful they could not sustain their schools, hospitals, roads, and other services. They were also concerned about the poor health of surrounding forests and the associated threat of severe wildfire.

Local environmentalists were not content with the situation, either. Their central strategy—trying to stop logging by filing administrative appeals—was cumbersome and only partly effective. It demanded extensive research of every logging site and detailed written documentation. The appeals typically resulted in delays of logging but not termination. This is largely because environmental advocates often gain the greatest leverage in courts through procedural attacks, and the judicial remedy for a procedural attack is generally to remand the case and order compliance with proper procedures. Local activists were struggling to maintain their labor-intensive strategy. Linda Blum said, "As a grass-roots activist, I couldn't keep it up. It wasn't sustainable activism."[25] Tensions between loggers and environmentalists in Quincy were mounting to frightening levels. Spikes were driven in trees scheduled to be cut, sugar was poured in gas tanks, and bullets were fired into the window of Michael Jackson's law office. Nobody was satisfied with forest policy in the Quincy area, and the situation seemed to be deteriorating. The Quincy Library Group emerged from the growing dissatisfactions of area residents and eventually sought to advance the common interest over these dire circumstances.

Common Ground and Battleground

In November 1992, Plumas County Supervisor Bill Coates did something unprecedented: he called environmentalist Michael Jackson in an attempt to find a way out of the timber wars. "All right, we're through," he said. "We've got to do something new. Will you meet with the mill owners?"[26] Jackson agreed and met with Coates and Tom Nelson of Sierra Pacific in the hope of finding some common ground. Against the backdrop of dramatically declining timber harvests, the Conservationist Alternative proposed by the Friends of the Plumas in 1986 looked more attractive to Quincy-area timber workers. In the 1980s, the plan's levels of harvest had seemed low relative to average harvest levels, but in the context of 1992, the same levels seemed high. Coates, Nelson, and Jackson used that alternative as a starting point for their discussions.

At first, they held private meetings in the back of Jackson's office, but they soon opened the meetings to other interested environmentalists and industry representatives and met in the public library. This group became the Quincy Library Group. One environmentalist said of the first meeting: "I remember being quite nervous about [it] because I didn't have any idea who these timber people were . . . and there had been a lot of animosity in town up to that time. There was a real tension in this community, between the timber industry who felt like all the jobs were being taken away from them, and the environmentalists who felt like they weren't getting any protection for the roadless areas and the riparian zones. . . . So the first meeting was really pretty tense."[27] But right away, the different interests in the group realized that they had some things in common. They agreed that they didn't want the town to "dry up" or turn into a resort town.[28] They discovered that the environmentalists were not opposed to all timber cutting and that the timber workers wanted to preserve parts of the forest, too. The group decided early on to expand the landbase in the plan beyond the boundaries of the Plumas National Forest. They chose to include the Lassen National Forest and the Sierraville Ranger District of the Tahoe National Forest because these were also important sources of timber for the industry in and around Quincy.[29]

While citizens were coming together in Quincy to address issues of forest health in California, momentum was building in the nation's capital to gather more scientific background. In 1993, Congress authorized funds for a "scientific review of the remaining old growth in the national forests of the Sierra Nevada in California, and for a study of the entire Sierra Nevada ecosystem by an independent panel of scientists."[30] The purpose of the report was to advise Congress, not to prepare a plan or recommend alternatives. The team was directed to assess what was known and judge the implications of that knowledge for meeting the goal of "protecting the health and sustainability of the Sierra Nevada while providing resources to meet human needs."[31] The outcome was the Sierra Nevada Ecosystem Project (SNEP) report, which would later be used to justify arguments of the QLG's proponents and opponents alike.

The QLG completed the Community Stability Proposal in the summer of 1993. The plan relied on three management strategies. The first was a system of group and individual tree selection in order to "provide an adequate timber supply for community stability and to maintain a relatively continuous forest cover." The second was implementation of fire and fuels management objectives recommended in CASPO "in order to achieve stability in the [eco]system." The third was a watershed restoration program and network of riparian habitats in managed areas "in order to protect fisheries and watershed health." The proposal sought to develop these strategies on "the broadest landscape possible," but "sensitive areas such as roadless areas, Scenic River corridors, and riparian areas would not be scheduled for harvest." Then group members summarized their shared interest: "In general, we believe that the implementation of these strategies will expand the existing landbase available for timber production beyond that currently 'zoned' for timber production but that environmental effects upon this expanded landbase will be greatly reduced. The intent of these strategies is to create a forest that will more closely mimic the historic natural landscapes of the Sierra, while protecting and enhancing recreational opportunities."[32]

Once the plan was complete, the QLG placed an ad in the town newspaper, the *Feather River Bulletin*, inviting the public to an open meeting in the town hall to discuss the plan. That meeting drew by various accounts 150 to 250 people, but the group itself has since stabilized at about 30.[33] During the meeting, Bill Coates and Michael Jackson described the plan and held a question-and-answer session. At the end, they asked, "Does the community think we should continue in this effort?" The response was overwhelmingly positive. Only a handful expressed reservations or opposition. These critics—two environmentalists and three from the timber industry—opposed the plan for substantive, procedural, and personal reasons. Some, for example, felt the landbase was too large; others found the style of interaction at QLG meetings to be abrupt or even "hostile."[34] But with such widespread popular support, the QLG decided to move forward with its plan.

As a self-initiated citizen group, the QLG itself had no authority to implement the proposal. It had to convince local Forest Service officials, who did have formal authority, to adopt their plan. The Quincy Library Group presented its plan to the supervisors of the Plumas, Lassen, and Tahoe National Forests. The group recommended that the plan be carried out for five years while the regional EIS for CASPO was being prepared, decided, appealed, and litigated. It was assumed that after five years, guidelines established by the CASPO EIS would be implemented on each forest, replacing the QLG plan. Members of the QLG expected the Forest Service to embrace the plan and welcome this unified request in place of conflicting demands that often led to appeals and lawsuits.

Only some officials in the Forest Service were supportive; others, however, were reluctant to stray from the tradition of scientific management. In a message to employees dated January 9, 1994, Lassen Forest Supervisor Leonard Atencio stated his position. "We have been involved with the QLG for almost one year. One of my expectations did not occur. I really thought they would dissolve by now. . . . We have had several discussions on the forest regarding this group. I have heard the concerns and agree with everyone, this group is not going to be easy to work with. I also agree that this group *does not have the answers either*. I also agree that this group doesn't have the expertise they claim. We have heard what the Clinton administration's desire is, to increase opportunities and partnerships with communities in solving problems. The Chief and Regional forester have stated they want to increase public involvement. With this emphasis from management I want to restate my commitment to continue working with the QLG."[35] The consensus that the experts ought to make the management decisions, with approval from higher-level officials, echoes scientific management.[36] In spite of the "emphasis from management," the forest supervisors did not implement the plan. So the QLG went to their immediate superior—Ron Stewart, the regional forester at the time—with a request to direct forest supervisors to accept the Community Stability Proposal. Stewart told them that he could not do so without a public process and that the QLG proposal would be analyzed as one alternative in the CASPO EIS process. Stewart did, however, instruct the forest supervisors to implement aspects of the proposal that were already consistent with existing plans. The supervisors balked, though, complaining that they did not have adequate funding to do so.[37]

The Quincy Library Group decided to go to Washington, D.C., to lobby higher-level Forest Service officials and members of Congress to increase funding to the national forests in the Quincy area so that the proposal could be implemented. In early 1994, Quincy residents George and Pat Terhune heard Michael Jackson and Bill Coates on the local radio station, soliciting donations from the community to help pay for the trip. Later that day, the Terhunes saw Coates and Jackson at the bakery and offered to help finance the trip, but before they left, Coates and Jackson had convinced them to go as representatives of the community.[38] The Terhunes became part of a delegation of forty-three that traversed Capitol Hill to persuade Congress to appropriate funds to facilitate implementation of the QLG plan.

They met with members of appropriations and other relevant committees, as well as with Jim Lyons, then assistant secretary of agriculture, and Jack Ward Thomas, then chief of the Forest Service. Coates had gained substantial experience lobbying through various leadership positions in the National Association of Counties, and he believed that the most powerful lobbying groups were those representing three interests. In Washington, he organized the QLG members into parties of three, paying close attention to the composition of each group—a timber representative, an environmentalist, and a community member. Rose Comstock, a member of Women in Timber and the QLG, said, "It's been great to go into a Congressional office—a Democrat who I would've never been able to speak to before—but I [could] because I was with Linda Blum. She and I sat together and were able to convey [our goals] to these people, who were astonished that we were together, that we agreed on anything, and [that we were] two women representing both points of view. That was a rush—an adrenaline rush!"[39]

The trip seemed successful. Lyons told group members that he supported the QLG model and that he had the commitment to make it work. The Forest Service notified the QLG in November 1994 that $1 million had been identified, from carry-over fiscal year 1994 funds, to be used for activities consistent with the QLG proposal. This figure represented approximately 2 percent of the entire budget of the three national forests and was substantially below the $28 million estimated by the forest supervisors to be required for full implementation of the QLG plan.[40] A year later, Secretary of Agriculture Dan Glickman announced a $20 million allocation of funds to begin implementation of the QLG recommendations in fiscal year 1996. Already existing in the local national forest budgets was $15.3 million, and Glickman promised an additional $4.7 million.[41] Forest Service officials generally welcomed the increased appropriations secured by the QLG, but agency employees did not always see eye-to-eye with the group. Local Forest Service employees interpreted Glickman's announcement to mean that $15.3 million would go to their regular programs, and only $4.7 million would be spent on implementation of QLG recommendations.[42] Members of the QLG believed that $20 million was intended to go to projects they recommended, and they began to grow frustrated with the local Forest Service.

The group was still waiting for consideration of its full proposal as an alternative in the CASPO EIS process. A draft EIS was released on February 6, 1995, with one alternative based on the QLG proposal. "But QLG viewed this alternative as a misrepresentation and misuse of [its] Proposal, and considered it more like a poison pill than a legitimate example of the QLG forest management strategy."[43] This only added to the frustration of QLG members. In response to public comment, the draft was revised and the CASPO team was prepared to release it in August 1996. But the draft was criticized for failing to take into account newly available science, especially the information available in the SNEP report. The day before release of the report was scheduled, the secretary of agriculture called for a review of the science by a Federal Advisory Committee.[44] After a long and drawn-out bureaucratic process, the Forest Service chose to redirect its attention to development of the Sierra Nevada Conservation Framework, in an effort to address management policy related to the California spotted owl as well as other priority issues in the Sierra Nevada. At that point, the Forest Service expected to finalize the framework no sooner than August 1999. For members of the QLG, the prospect of enacting the Community Stability Proposal through the CASPO EIS process did not seem promising.

Another factor was the Salvage Rider. Enacted by Congress in 1994, it allowed the sale of timber that was dying or dead due to fire or insect damage in national forests. In a significant move, Congress made these sales immune from appeal and litigation. Soon after passage of the rider, the Barkeley Fire burned in a salmon habitat area of the Lassen National Forest. The area was designated for protection under the QLG proposal, but not under the existing Forest Plan. The forest supervisor, Leonard Atencio, scheduled the Barkeley timber sale over the protest of the QLG. It was clear that the local timber industry's response would be a crucial factor in determining whether the QLG would continue or disband. If timber companies, desperate for timber, decided to bid on the sale even though the area would be off-limits to logging under the Community Stability Proposal, they would compromise the group's hard-earned trust. The QLG held an emergency meeting, and members reaffirmed their commitment to the agreement. Not a single timber company bid on the sale. This restraint by the timber representatives in the group demonstrated their resolve, consolidating members' trust of one another.

By 1996, members of the Quincy Library Group had exhausted their patience with the cumbersome process of the Forest Service. "We just got frustrated," said Nelson. "By this time we'd developed a lot of trust; we'd been together for years. We went and lobbied and got [the Forest Service] money, and it still wasn't working."[45] The group decided to take a different approach: urge Congress to pass national legislation directing the Forest Service to implement their plan. Representative Wally Herger, their local congressman, agreed to sponsor a bill in the House, and Senators Boxer and Feinstein of California sponsored one in the Senate. After numerous meetings, informal discussions, hearings, and a floor debate, in July 1997 the House version of the Quincy Library Group bill, H.R. 858, passed by a vote of 429 to 1. The turning point came when Representative George Miller (D-CA) decided to support the QLG bill after it was amended to affirm that "nothing [in this Act] exempts the pilot project from any Federal environmental law."[46] Many members of Congress followed Miller's lead on environmental issues, so the bill gained votes after he signed on. The final version incorporated more than fifty changes in the bill initially introduced by Herger.

In the Senate, however, the bill did not move so swiftly or smoothly. National environmental groups had mobilized their opposition by the time the bill reached the Senate. Though Senator Boxer had initially been a strong proponent of the Quincy Library Group and the bill, she removed her name as sponsor after national environmental groups intensified pressure, threatening to run a Green Party candidate against her in 1998 if she continued to support the group's efforts.[47] She later placed a hold on the bill. Even though Senator Feinstein maintained support of the bill, Boxer's hold stopped all action in the Senate for at least six months.

In contrast, Republicans in both Houses were eager to back the QLG bill and claim it as a victory for local control. Newt Gingrich, Larry Craig, and Helen Chenoweth all publicly praised the group and encouraged others to follow the lead of the QLG. For many Republicans in Congress, their timber constituency is more important than the environmental interest groups.[48] And beyond the battle between these groups, the bill was mainly inconsequential for most members of Congress because it had no direct impact on the areas they represent. Republicans had little to lose and much to gain from supporting the bill.

The issue eventually became embroiled in a web of imaginative deal-cutting and power moves as it was tacked onto various environmental bills, removed, and reattached to other bills. Ultimately, senators circumvented Boxer's hold by passing the QLG bill as a rider on the omnibus appropriations bill. President Clinton signed the appropriations bill on October 21, 1998, and the Herger-Feinstein Quincy Library Group Forest Recovery Act became law.

The act directs the secretary of agriculture to implement the Quincy Library Group Community Stability Proposal as a pilot project on the Plumas, Lassen, and Tahoe National Forests. The proposal is defined as "an agreement . . . to develop a resource management program that promotes ecologic and economic health for certain Federal lands and communities in the Sierra Nevada area." It provides for three management activities: construction of fuelbreaks, group and individual tree selection, and riparian protection and restoration. Although the act does direct implementation of the QLG proposal, it does not do so without qualification; a number of exemptions and rules were added to the original version of the proposal to answer critics in Congress and gain their support. The act does require that an EIS be prepared "in consultation with interested members of the public, including the Quincy Library Group." An independent scientific panel is directed to "review and report on whether, and to what extent, implementation of the pilot project . . . achieved the goals stated in the Quincy Library Group Proposal, including improved ecological health and community stability." Here again, the act requires that the report be prepared with members of the public, "including the Quincy Library Group."[49]

The story does not end with passage of the law, though. It remains to be seen whether in practice the outcomes will advance the common interest as envisioned in the act. When the bill became law, the QLG established a committee to focus on issues related to implementation of the act. The Pilot Project Consultation Committee, or P2C2, monitors Forest Service actions, communicates with Forest Service employees, and urges action consistent with the intent of the original Community Stability Proposal. The committee holds regular meetings attended at times by Forest Service officials.

The Forest Service, too, instituted organizational changes to support the QLG act. Before the bill became law, the agency set up coordinating structures and allocated personnel and money to carry out parts of the QLG plan. After the act passed, the Forest Service re-allocated twenty-seven employees to work in positions related to conducting the pilot project. An interdisciplinary team was appointed to prepare the

EIS required by the act. A position was created to oversee implementation of the QLG act and pilot project. Dave Peters, pilot project manager for the act, says, "One of the reasons I was selected to do this job is that there was a belief on the part of the [selection] committee that I have good rapport with people in the QLG." On whether the selection committee was right about this assessment, Peters says, "It varies from week to week. Sometimes I do; sometimes I don't."[50] Peters attends all QLG meetings and initially attended all meetings of the P2C2.

On December 21, 1998, the Forest Service published a notice of intent to prepare an EIS for the QLG act, and on June 11, 1999, the draft EIS was published.[51] In it, Forest Service officials attempted to develop two alternatives that closely reflected the respective interests of the two groups that had contributed the most thorough, detailed comments earlier: the Sierra Nevada Forest Protection Campaign and the Quincy Library Group.[52] Other comments were incorporated as elements of various alternatives. Ultimately, though, the agency had to choose one alternative and reject all the others. The record of decision for the final EIS was signed on August 20, 1999. The Forest Service chose an alternative that closely followed the QLG act but included an added mitigation measure to prohibit any thinning of timber or harvests in spotted owl habitat.[53]

Fifteen appeals were filed at this stage, including one by the QLG itself. The group appealed the decision in an attempt to remove the mitigation measure, which would dramatically reduce the area eligible for construction of fuelbreaks. They believed that the viability of the spotted owl—the very thing the mitigation was designed to protect—would be threatened because of the increased likelihood of fire. Furthermore, the theory behind the proposed system of fuelbreaks would not be effectively tested on a landscape scale, as intended in the QLG proposal and the act. The QLG also challenged the decision because, they alleged, the Forest Service did not adequately consider the social and economic effects of imposing the mitigation measure. People would lose jobs because of lower timber harvests, and county governments would suffer from reduced forest reserve revenues.[54] The other appeals were filed by various environmental organizations. Many of these groups sought withdrawal of the decision to implement the QLG project. They were concerned that the decision would result in considerably higher levels of logging, that watershed and riparian areas were vulnerable, and that wildlife habitat areas were not adequately protected.[55] The regional forester, however, affirmed their original position by rejecting all appeals, and forest supervisors began to execute the

five-year pilot project as redefined by the record of decision. At the
same time, as required by the act, the Forest Service began to monitor
implementation of the pilot project.

The QLG also created its own monitoring plan to complement the
Forest Service plan, as part of a project launched by the Lead Partnership Group and Forest Community Research. The monitoring project
set out to observe real-life outcomes of the pilot project, including both
economic effects and impacts on forest health. The QLG also hoped
to bring stakeholders together to "trust and verify" management activities. They made a specific effort to include distant stakeholders.

Meanwhile, in January 2001, the EIS for the Sierra Nevada Conservation Framework (SNCF) was finalized. The framework amends management plans for eleven national forests throughout the Sierra Nevada range, including the three affected by the QLG act. It replaces
the CASPO interim guidelines and consequently is expected to restrict
implementation of the QLG pilot project.[56] Specifically, about 10 percent of the planned fuelbreaks called for in the pilot project will not
be constructed because the spotted owl strategy in the framework prohibits such treatments in certain areas. Similarly, not all of the group
selection proposed in the pilot project will be allowed. About 5,000
acres of group selection (rather than 8,700 acres) will, however, be permitted through a special exemption.[57] The QLG is likely to appeal the
decision in an effort to have the pilot project implemented as intended
at the time of the QLG act final EIS.[58] Environmental groups are generally supportive of the framework, although it remains to be seen
whether they, too, will choose to appeal the decision.[59] The impacts of
SNCF on the implementation of the QLG pilot project are uncertain
at the time of this writing.

Policy Appraisals

Each proposed or authorized plan for forest management around
Quincy was appraised and adapted to new circumstances, by somewhat different participants, in a continuing evolutionary process. In
July 1993, the Quincy Library Group unanimously approved its Community Stability Proposal, an adaptation of the Conservationist Alternative of 1986. Adapting that proposal, the Congress reconciled H.R.
858 and S. 1028 in the Herger-Feinstein Quincy Library Group Recovery Act signed by the president in October 1998. And by adapting the
pilot project prescribed in that act, the Forest Service selected its preferred alternative in the EIS process in August 1999. The service began

to adapt that plan through the Sierra Nevada Conservation Project, which established a management plan for eleven national forests in the region in January 2001.

Members of the Quincy Library Group continue to believe that without the Community Stability Proposal and its successors, the area would be worse off. Residents would have lost their jobs and abandoned Quincy, and businesses, schools, and hospitals would have closed down, leaving only a skeleton of what was once there. Some believe that the community would have sought tourist dollars in desperation, transforming the character of Quincy and replacing jobs connected to nature with jobs serving people. Some are worried that inaction would have resulted in further deterioration of the local forests and perhaps led to catastrophic fires. And yet another concern is that community instability would have disrupted family stability. As George and Pat Terhune reported in 1998, "It was generally felt that if this effort failed, all parties would suffer great losses."[60] Local community leaders and residents have mostly supported the Community Stability Proposal and its successors since the town meeting in July 1993. Like members of the QLG, they understand their vulnerability to the management of the surrounding forests and are strongly motivated to act on behalf of the economic and ecological health of their community. They are not in a position to tolerate gridlock, as some lobbyists and officials in the nation's capital have been.

Local timber interests have supported the Community Stability Proposal and its successors from the outset. Their representatives, as members of QLG, helped negotiate the proposal. National timber corporations and professional organizations initially opposed the bill in Congress, but they have supported it since the elimination of a provision granting exclusive rights to local timber companies for timber harvested under the bill. Local ranchers were initially apprehensive that the riparian restoration provisions in the QLG bill might infringe on their grazing and water rights in the national forests. Riparian zones are important to them for grazing as well as for watering cattle. They were satisfied, however, when a provision was added to the Senate bill protecting against undue adverse effects on grazing permittees, and when the State Water Resources Control Board certified that the pending legislation would not affect water rights.[61] Two local environmental groups have supported the Community Stability Proposal and its successors from the outset: Friends of the Plumas Wilderness and the Plumas Audubon Society, the local chapter of the national organization. Their members also helped negotiate the proposal as members of QLG.

They believe that because they live in and around these particular forests and have depended on them for years, they are qualified to participate in the development of management plans.

Local support for the Community Stability Proposal and its successors is, of course, not unanimous. The Plumas Forest Project is a small group that split off from Friends of the Plumas Wilderness soon after the QLG formed. This group is aligned with regional and national environmental groups in opposition to the QLG's efforts.[62] Some say they felt excluded from the QLG meetings by a "hostile" environment. In the town meeting attended by a few hundred people in July 1993, three people aligned with timber interests and two aligned with environmental interests opposed the Community Stability Proposal. A coalition of fifty-two business leaders from the larger area around Quincy urged the Forest Service to reject the preferred alternative in the draft EIS in August 1999. "We're a tourism economy now," said Paul Jorgenson, owner of an oriental rug store in Nevada City, California, "and people come up here to see trees standing, not on the ground."[63]

Substantive appraisals by Forest Service officials in the Quincy area have been mixed at best, judging from their initial refusal to implement community-based proposals in 1986 and 1993, and from their words and deeds since then. As discussed, early in 1994 Lassen Supervisor Leonard Atencio agreed with his colleagues that "this group [QLG] *does not have the answers either.*"[64] Also in 1994, Plumas Supervisor Wayne Thornton noted that he needed money to execute the QLG proposal but that his budget for Plumas had been cut by $11.9 million (about 40 percent) since 1992. In that time Plumas lost about 150 full-time positions. A spokesman for Ron Stewart, who was then regional forester, concurred that "the very things that led the Quincy Library Group to meet in the first place are the very things that are limiting our ability to respond."[65] Undersecretary of Agriculture Jim Lyons had a different explanation. "I was part of the [1994] dialogue (along with former Chief Jack Ward Thomas) that said to the local forest supervisors, 'work with them.' But you had a couple of forest supervisors who were more focused on process than solution. What I had in mind would have been a little more responsive and timely. I wanted them to test what the group had in mind—reduce fire risk, reduce fuel loads. . . . The problem was an agency that was so stuck on process it couldn't solve a problem."[66]

By 1997, when H.R. 858 and S. 1028 were pending in Congress, Plumas Supervisor Mark Madrid looked ahead to the real work and to the financial implications. "The meat is going to be in the EIS," he said. "Our analysis shows it will generate income over the long term. But we will need start-up money." Lassen Supervisor Kent Connaughton looked favorably on passage of the bill as a validation of relatively clear priorities by Congress. "It simplifies my life," he said. His staff had already been "at work for a year on the QLG's general approach to fire control."[67] In a sign of acquiescence if not support before the QLG act, the Forest Service created a position for one employee to act as liaison with the QLG and to coordinate efforts among the three national forests involved.[68] Since the act, an office of about two dozen employees has worked with QLG and others on issues related to the prescribed pilot project.[69] Little of the pilot project has been implemented, however.

After Representative Herger introduced H.R. 858 at the end of February 1997, national environmental groups and their regional and local allies significantly escalated their opposition. They objected largely on procedural grounds: activists in California offered in April 1997 to "work collaboratively" if QLG would "kill the bill."[70] Their substantive appraisals have been concerned primarily with the health of the forests and hardly at all with the economic health of the communities that depend upon them. These interests repeatedly object to the volume and location of logging, and to the use of untested methods on too vast a scale.

Many groups claimed that the QLG bills would double the volume of logging at the expense of forest health. In testimony on S. 1028 in 1997, for example, the legislative director for the Sierra Club, Debbie Sease, cited "Office of Management and Budget estimates that by the second year of the program, logging would at least double current levels. There is no scientific justification for this radical increase in logging on these forests."[71] Louis Blumberg of The Wilderness Society says, regarding 1997, that "conservative estimates indicate that the levels would at least double, and therefore far exceed the level estimated to be sustainable under the forest plans as amended by the CASPO policy."[72] A coalition of environmental groups in early 1999 repeated the claimed doubling in public comments on the draft EIS to implement the QLG act. They alleged that the resulting effects "have the potential to result in serious environmental degradation, including adverse impacts to wildlife species viability, water quality, and soil health."[73]

The location of the logging allowed has also been criticized. Sease, in her Senate testimony, alleged that "the bill allows logging in ancient forests and key watersheds identified in the SNEP analysis, the most current science available."[74] Another environmentalist backed this claim in 1998: "At the time the agreement was made, [the QLG] thought that they were going to get all the old growth and roadless areas out, but new information from the Sierra Nevada Ecosystem Project found that there's 67,000 acres of old growth that are in the timber base, and there's also several roadless areas that would be entered as well."[75] Environmental groups generally support the January 2001 SNCF decision to protect more of the disputed pilot project locations from logging.[76]

These groups have also claimed that the QLG bill mandated the use of untested methods on too vast a scale. Sease stated that "the bill is a vast experiment with inadequate scientific justification."[77] The QLG bill, said the Audubon Society, "allows Sierra Pacific Industries to conduct a large-scale, taxpayer funded, 350,000-acre experiment, which requires intensive logging, when their hypothesis is untested and many experts agree that it will probably have an effect opposite of the one intended."[78] The fuelbreaks are likely to increase the threat of fire, the society argued, because they will allow more sunlight into the forest and stimulate the growth of more dense vegetation, which is susceptible to fire. "It's being cast as a pilot project, but in fact, the scope and duration are enormous. It could have significant environmental impacts on water quality and wildlife habitat," said David Edelson of the Natural Resources Defense Council.[79] After the bill became law, The Wilderness Society argued that the scale of the project ought to be "appropriate to the task." The Wilderness Society continued, "Experience shows that the most successful efforts are relatively small and focused on a particular project."[80]

More environmental groups might have supported the Community Stability Proposal or its predecessor before the QLG went to Washington to lobby Congress. Recall that The Wilderness Society and the Natural Resources Defense Council were deeply involved in development of the Amenity Alternative in the mid-1980s. Since then, however, the environmental community has been able to demand more, thanks to the spotted owl decision and other policies restricting logging, and to claims of new scientific knowledge. In the view of one lobbyist, it might not have been a bad agreement in the context of 1993, "but given the scrutiny that the timber program is under now and the knowledge that we have about the need to protect old growth and roadless areas, I just don't see it as being an adequate agreement. Even to [implement] it administratively. And to legislate it is just not something we can sit by."[81]

These appraisals are relevant but incomplete: the common interest is not limited to the health of the forests in question. In the local community, representatives of the diverse interests included in the Quincy Library Group unanimously approved the Community Stability Proposal, which included measures "to promote forest health, ecological integrity, adequate timber supply and local economic stability."[82] All but five of the few hundred who attended the town meeting in July 1993 consented as well. In the national community, members of the House voted all but unanimously for H.R. 858, and members of the Senate Committee on Energy and Natural Resources recommended unanimously that the Senate pass S. 1028.[83] The act prescribes a pilot project to implement the modified Community Stability Proposal, defined as "a resource management program that promotes ecologic and economic health for certain Federal lands and communities in the Sierra Nevada area."[84]

Members of both the Congress and the local community clearly expected the act and the earlier proposal to advance the interests of the diverse constituencies they represent. Their support provides evidence for the claim that the substantive common interest of both local and national communities includes the ecologic and economic health of the area. Indeed, the Community Stability Proposal was an attempt to "reflect the fact that a healthy forest and a stable community are interdependent; we cannot have one without the other."[85] From this standpoint, the following appraisal considers the extent to which the continuing evolution of proposed and authorized forest management plans has advanced the ecologic and economic health of the area. The point of reference is not an abstract ideal community, but the baseline ecological and economic health of the area in late 1992, when Coates, Nelson, and Jackson began the conversations that led to the Quincy Library Group.

The effects of proposed, authorized, and actual logging on forest health in the Quincy area are disputed. The Sierra Club's demand for zero logging on national forests is based on the expectation that logging is detrimental to forest health, and the condition of the forests around Quincy warranted no exception. The QLG believes that the poor condition of most of the forests around Quincy in 1992 was a result of clearcutting and other kinds of mismanagement over the decades. It also believes that group and individual tree selection and thinning in such areas are necessary to achieve "an all-age, multi-story, fire-resistant forest approximating pre-settlement conditions" and a forest hospitable to the spotted owl.[86] The Quincy community, unlike the Sierra Club, is betting its own stability on the belief that its understanding is correct. It should not be *assumed* that environmental interest groups alone act on behalf of the natural environment, or that all logging or thinning is detrimental to forest health. These are empirical questions best resolved by experience on the ground in a particular context.[87]

The volume of logging authorized is actually much less than the doubling claimed by critics. In the area in question, "the total harvest was more than 400 million board feet every year from 1984 until 1992."[88] In fiscal years 1992 through 1996, the comparable average volume offered for sale was 246 million board feet per year, according to figures provided by Forest Service Deputy Chief Ron Stewart in October 1997, which correct earlier figures provided by the Congressional Budget Office and often cited by critics. Stewart estimated that "potential timber outputs" generated by S. 1029, "if fully funded with additional revenues, would not double but would remain consistent with the outputs" in fiscal years 1992 through 1996.[89] The potential timber output authorized in the Forest Service's management plan in August 2000 was 286 million board feet per year. The actual timber output is much less. A report from Quincy one year after the pilot project officially began cites, "No logs have been cut for lumber. None of the 200,000 acres targeted for fire protection has been cleared of brush and small trees."[90] The pilot project cannot improve or harm forest health until it is implemented.

Forest health depends upon protection of areas that are in relatively good condition. The Quincy Library Group claimed its bill protected all but 11 percent of the late-successional old-growth acreage delineated in the Sierra Nevada Ecosystem Project Report, the same report cited by the critics.[91] Senator Feinstein stated that the Senate Energy and Natural Resources Committee went further, "providing report language directing the Forest Service to avoid conducting timber harvest and road construction in late-successional old-growth areas." Feinstein also claimed that some areas were misidentified as old-growth in the report. "The Quincy Library Group has looked at some of these areas on the ground and found that some not only have no old growth, but in one instance there are no trees at all [because] the area is under Bullards Bar Reservoir." A scientist agrees that "the magnitude of the classification errors shown in this report indicates that it would be dangerous to attempt detailed site-specific prediction of forest structure . . . directly from the maps" in dispute. Even authors of the SNEP report cautioned that "databases and maps should not be utilized for local management purposes without additional ground-based measurements."[92]

The effects of untested management methods on forest health are unknown, of course, until they are field-tested over a period of some years. This is recognized explicitly in the Community Stability Proposal and the QLG act. Preliminary results from the field in 1999 suggest that the Defensible Fuel Profile Zones (or DFPZs) in the QLG pilot project may be effective in reducing the risk of catastrophic fires. "In a three-year period before Congress approved the full plan, the three national forests logged and cleared brush from 63,000 acres using the system advocated by the Quincy Library Group. Wildfires last year and this summer that raced through other parts of the forest slowed and cooled when they hit these treated areas, leaving large old-growth trees standing."[93] Some critics of the QLG's "untested" methods support a different set of untested methods authorized in the Sierra Nevada Conservation Framework.[94] It would be constructive for the critics to participate in the QLG's all-party monitoring project to help resolve uncertainties about the effects of management methods through observations on the ground.

The risks to forest health and other interests from the use of untested methods can be reduced in principle by downscaling the "experiment" in the field. In practice, however, the appropriate scale of the field experiment varies with expectations about the appropriate risks, costs, and benefits. As noted, environmental critics tend to believe the area open to timber harvest and thinning in the pilot project is much too large. Other environmental critics consider the area too small. One critic, for example, claims that "science says you've got to look at a whole ecosystem. But what the Quincy proposal does is say 'well, let's just forget about that and look at part of the system.'"[95] Like their opponents, members of the Quincy Library Group cite the SNEP report to justify the scale of the pilot project. Michael Yost, who teaches forestry at Feather River College in Quincy, contended at the end of 1997 that "the current bill is guided by more than good intentions. It is based on good science. The scale of the plan at two and a quarter national forests is landscape size—just right, according to SNEP scientists."[96] Most environmental critics support the SNCF plan that includes the pilot project area within a much larger area—eleven national forests across the entire Sierra Nevada.[97] The appropriate scale is a political variable, not a scientific one.

Mark Sagoff aptly diagnoses the problem and outlines the alternative: "Science cannot determine the public interest. . . . The public itself, through a representative and deliberative process, must make out where its interest lies."[98] The public has done so in the Community Stability Proposal and in successive plans. Within the constraints of environmentally sustainable management, the QLG scaled its proposal to provide enough timber volume to support the economic stability of the surrounding community. The QLG has deliberately underemphasized this justification, though, because it is not politically popular. (Economic justifications had not helped the timber industry earlier in the Pacific Northwest.) The economic health of the community is nevertheless a more reasonable defense of the scale than ecosystem science. But this defense only works politically where the goal of advancing the common interest is accepted, which is not everywhere. "It's easy to take the moral high ground when you don't live in these communities," explained Tom Nelson of the QLG. "It's tougher when you have to face these people every day."[99]

Has the Community Stability Proposal and its successors advanced the common interest in the economic health of the pilot project area? Thanks to the QLG act, the community is in a better position to stabilize the local economy through timber harvesting and thinning. But the authorized amounts were cut back in the management plan to administer the pilot project in August 1999, and again in the January 2001 SNCF plan. And even the authorized amounts are far from realized. A year after the pilot project began, Frank Stewart, a member of the QLG, concluded, "We've received absolute zero—zilch."[100] According to the same report from the area, no timber has been cut under the pilot project, and "the eight California counties promised $2.3 billion in economic benefits for five years are still waiting for the first dime."[101] At the beginning of 2001, Sierra Pacific Industries closed its Loyalton sawmill in the Quincy area. By February, the closing appeared to be permanent, leaving about a hundred workers without jobs. "We had every hope that it would be temporary," said Ed Bond, a spokesman for SPI, "but the Forest Service's Sierra Nevada Framework has virtually put a stop to implementation of the Quincy Library Group plan."[102] The company had invested millions of dollars to retool the mill to process the small-diameter logs expected to be harvested under the QLG plan. Contributing to the decision to close the mill were lumber prices at their lowest levels since the mid-1990s, reflecting large volumes of lumber imported from Canada, New Zealand, and Chile.

It is reasonable to conclude from the information available that the Quincy Library Group is now in a much better position to realize the common interest of both local and national communities in the pilot project area. The QLG act and its continuing support from most of the community and Congress are significant achievements. The results of their efforts so far, however, have demonstrated only modest gains in the community's ecologic and economic health over the poor conditions of 1992—and that is mostly through indirect impacts from the construction of fuelbreaks and from budget increases for the national forests in the area. The direct effects of the pilot project cannot be reliably assessed until it is implemented by the Forest Service. For now, at least, it is clear that the QLG's efforts have fallen far short of the goals envisioned in 1993.

This mixed appraisal is consistent with those of QLG members. In 1998, the Terhunes concluded that "on the one hand, QLG has not achieved its original goals, because five years have elapsed and QLG's suggestions have not yet been fully implemented, even on a trial basis. On the other hand, QLG has seen its goals and suggested methods of forest management strongly vindicated, because during those five years the Forest Service has moved slowly but steadily toward the management theory and practices that QLG promotes."[103] In 2000, the QLG's all-party monitoring project found similarly mixed economic and ecological results of the Forest Service's management of the pilot project one year after it formally began. Monitoring found that "some treatment prescriptions had inherent problems in meeting wildlife management and wildfire management objectives and that, in some places, prescriptions were being incorrectly applied." But monitoring also found several "examples of good forest management, identified and agreed upon by both the Forest Service and the Quincy Library Group."[104]

To the extent that the effort has fallen short of its goals in practice, where does the responsibility lie? Part of the responsibility lies with the Forest Service. Some have even suggested that the Forest Service is intentionally trying to sabotage the project.[105] Several members of Congress wrote to Forest Service Chief Mike Dombeck in March 1999, criticizing the agency for the slow pace of the EIS to implement the QLG act and suggesting that some of the delay was intentional. The letter also questioned the wisdom of recent decisions to cut staff on the Plumas National Forest: "We are concerned that these staff reductions contravene the priority that Congress has placed on successful implementation of the QLG project, particularly in view of the $8 million increase in appropriations Congress has provided for that purpose. Region 5 should revisit its staffing priorities to ensure that Plumas N.F. is equipped to meet its statutory obligations." The letter also expressed concern over reports of specific forest management programs undertaken in the QLG area that appear to contradict, in some instances, the intent of the QLG act, and in others, the letter of the law. As written, it claims one ranger district reportedly "has devoted staff to working on projects in *watersheds that were expressly designated as off-base or deferred from timber harvest by the QLG plan and the law*, in effect committing staff to work on projects arguably prohibited by the Herger-Feinstein law."[106] The Forest Service may have made some adjustments

in response to the letter. At least one congressional staffer "saw a re-
newed commitment from region five to make sure that the Forest Supervisors and the EIS Team were implementing the act in good
faith."[107]

Even so, forces beyond the control of the Forest Service in the pilot
project area cause delays and limit employees' ability to carry out the
project. Budgets for managing forests in the area have increased but
still come up short of the funds required for the pilot project. Restrictions imposed first by the habitat mitigation measure in the QLG final
EIS, and then in the SNCF final EIS, make it difficult for forest supervisors and rangers to find locations where the QLG strategies can even
be put into action. The SNCF EIS is nearly incomprehensible in places,
and Forest Service personnel are left trying to decipher its meaning,
while all around them, disgruntled citizens are preparing appeals to the
decision.[108] The larger problems of governance discussed in Chapter 1
are clearly manifest in the implementation of the QLG act.

The QLG Model

Structures for making decisions help shape policy outcomes, and the
QLG act is no exception.The Quincy Library Group can be described
as a model of governance within the larger structure involved, and that
structure can be appraised and critiqued from a common-interest
standpoint.

The Quincy Library Group stabilized at about thirty participants
after the town meeting in July 1993. They are employees of Sierra Pacific Industries and Collins Pine, county supervisors, an environmental
lawyer, a biologist, a retired airline pilot, a forestry professor, moms,
dads, husbands, grandparents, business owners, and more. Most are
residents of Quincy, though a few live in neighboring towns. Participation is voluntary—members are not appointed by QLG, though some
members have actively encouraged others to participate. One member,
Rose Comstock, took the initiative to assume the role of unofficial liaison and representative for ranchers, because the demands of raising
cattle made it difficult for them to attend the meetings.[109] Michael Jackson invited representatives of regional environmental groups in San
Francisco. Some chose not to participate because their work, the location, or the timing made it hard to do so. Others avoided the meetings
because they felt uncomfortable with the direct, confrontational, and
occasionally heated interactions that characterized some QLG meetings. Still others simply did not like meetings.[110] The choice to participate or not is an expression of priorities, a way to vote with our feet.

Nevertheless, participation continues to be inclusive of most parts of the community and open to outsiders. And many outsiders have participated in meetings—visiting scholars, members of other community-based initiatives, people seeking endorsement from the QLG, scientific experts, and others.

There have been a few exceptions, however. The group did not include Forest Service officials in the first few meetings because they believed their presence might revive old hostilities and divert attention from efforts to find common ground on a proposal. But after their third meeting, the group described their working proposal to Plumas Forest Supervisor Wayne Thornton.[111] Now, almost every meeting is attended by Forest Service officials "who make valuable contributions to the discussion; but they are not members, and they do not participate in QLG decisions."[112] The Federal Advisory Committee Act arguably precludes official participation in QLG decisions; at least it can be used to block official participation where there is a will to do so. But Forest Service officials do gather information for the agency and contribute information on such topics as silviculture and Forest Service planning processes and goals. Another exception occurred on March 30, 1999, when the group voted unanimously to close some of its meetings to certain environmentalists who had interrupted and inhibited the Pilot Project Consultation Committee and allegedly misrepresented its work.[113]

Members participate in the QLG for a variety of reasons that are not always obvious from their positions in the community or their identifications with environmental or timber interests. Several members quoted in the *Feather River Bulletin*, explaining why they are involved in QLG, are examples.[114] Harry Reeves identified himself as an "outdoor sports enthusiast." "Traditionally the environmental movement has been most effective at stopping things. QLG is unique in that we have zeroed in on ways to turn things around and use government, business and community resources to constructively improve the management of our forests. I see this as a positive opportunity to make things better rather than to simply make things 'less worse.'" Robert Meacher, Plumas County supervisor and local business owner, "became involved because I wanted to make sure that the small logger was represented. I was also concerned about the local economy and the threat of fire danger." Paul Harris, a representative for the Union of Industrial Workers, "viewed the QLG as a workable plan to help resolve the issues that lead to the timber shortages as well as the fire and environmental problems. The work force that I represent is and has been directly affected by the issues that the QLG has been addressing." Biological specialist Michael Kossow explained that "I'm involved with the QLG for my family. It's hard to have family stability unless you have community stability. I was part of the problem—now I want to be part of the solution." Community stability was identified early as a shared concern. It helped open the way for members to understand and accept other interests in the community. Tom Nelson summed it up in his 1997 Senate testimony: "We discovered that we all care deeply about the stability and well-being of our communities, our forested surroundings, and the legacy we leave to our children and grandchildren. Moreover, we found that we share a common concern for the very real and very ominous risk of catastrophic wildfires within these forests which surround our communities."[115]

Meetings are generally held in Quincy, though occasionally in neighboring communities. Often they last all day. There is no regular schedule, but meetings tend to be held about once a month, depending in part on activities in the Forest Service and in Congress, and on strategic choices faced by the group itself. Meetings were held to formulate comments to submit to the Forest Service during the EIS processes for CASPO, the QLG act, and SNCF. Other meetings were held to decide changes in strategy or to attend to specific interests affected by the QLG proposal, such as the ranchers' interest in preserving water rights and grazing access.

The QLG's strategies for making decisions evolved over time as a matter of necessity. In the initial meetings, it was not uncommon for shouting matches to erupt, or for an impassioned participant to storm out of the room in a cloud of rage. Discussions were sometimes heated and emotional, sometimes cool and rational. Although the original members of the QLG felt that it was important to put all the issues on the table—including emotional and controversial ones—they also focused on areas of agreement right away. When the shouting got out of hand, Nelson says, "we'd all smile and say 'now there's an issue we need to table.' We never said from the beginning that we'd collaborate on every issue that came up. That gave us an out."[116] In many cases, the group returned to the tabled issues after passions had cooled and more trust had been built.[117]

The group set its agenda together. Decisions were made by consensus, but the real work was in the discussions. Votes were usually taken only after it was clear that a consensus or near-consensus had been reached. Generally, Coates led the meetings, but there was no official facilitator. They got along without one, says Linda Blum, because they "figured out a way to ask each other 'what the hell do you mean by that?'" In one meeting, Blum was expressing concern over the impact of grazing on spotted owls, and another QLG member was incredulous.

"How do *cows* affect *owls?!*" she asked. Blum explained that when cattle trample the ground, they destroy the habitat of the owls' prey, thereby removing a food source for the owls. "This is a place where you can ask questions like 'how are cows and owls connected?'" said Blum, "and someone will answer."[118] One key was "a willingness to tolerate intemperate statements about the issues, but not about each other."[119] These strategies proved effective for developing solidarity, consensus, and cooperation among group members.

Group members had to learn additional strategies in the larger structure of governance. They originally believed that the Forest Service would accept and implement a plan if environmentalists and loggers both accepted it. (Forest Service employees had played these two groups against each other, explaining to each that the contradictory demands of the other blocked management actions.) When they presented this idea to Wayne Thornton, Plumas Forest supervisor, he liked it. "It looks like we're all going to be singing from the same songbook," he said.[120] But such words were seldom corroborated by deeds, and the QLG proposal was given little further attention. The members eventually understood that a legislative solution was necessary because an administrative solution was not likely. As Michael Yost explained in 1997, "After working eleven years with the national environmental organizations [on the Conservationist Alternative] and four years with the QLG [on the Community Stability Proposal], the best option is now to seek a legislative solution—an exercise of our First Amendment rights."[121] When members went to Washington to lobby Congress, they provoked opposition and support from a much broader range of participants, but at the same time, national environmental groups began to claim that the QLG was exclusive. One strategy used in Washington was lobbying in groups of three—an environmentalist, a businessperson, and another member of the community.

The QLG might have appeared, by some standards, disadvantaged, in Quincy and especially in the larger structure. They were not wealthy. As individuals, many members were struggling to make ends meet.[122] As a group, they had no funding initially, and they still have no bank account. They had little security. Their jobs were threatened, and they were exposed to catastrophic wildfires, a constant source of fear in and around Quincy. Moreover, the social climate was hostile in the early 1990s, with tensions between environmentalists and timber workers at an all-time high. But a situation that could have deteriorated further became an asset instead. As residents recognized that their separate interests depended on cooperation with others, they became motivated to find common ground in the QLG. This led to enormous investments of time and energy in their shared cause. For many people, like Rose Comstock, there was plenty of energy available: "I was one of those loggers [in the Northwest] with my husband, traipsing around trying to find a job. I guess when you know how that is you do anything to. get away from it. You don't have a home, you don't have a paycheck, you don't know anything. You've got a hundred bucks in your pocket for gas and you don't know where it's going to take you. You've got four kids in the car, [and you're] trying to figure out how you're going to feed them. You're just destitute. . . . That was the driving force for me."[123]

As time went on, members of the group began to trust one another and build new friendships. Nelson explained how: "We were perfectly honest with each other from the start. We show respect for each other too."[124] They also developed new knowledge and skills. George Terhune, for example, applied his math and analytical skills to teach himself some technical aspects of fire ecology and fire prevention. Yost was already an expert in fire ecology by education, and he taught the group some of the fundamentals. Blum earned the nickname "NEPA Goddess" as she developed her extensive knowledge of NEPA, NFMA, and other aspects of the legal framework.[125] When Blum pointed out that NFMA regulations require the Forest Service to consider socioeconomic impacts, three women who worked for the timber industry became interested. They met in Blum's house, where they pored over the regulations with Blum pointing out the relevant language. "They learned a lot," Blum said.[126] The trust, knowledge, and skills the QLG members achieved on their own were an important basis for the respect and political support they later received from others.

The group also had ideological assets to broaden its base of support and help foster respect, much like civil rights groups did in the 1950s. For many, the QLG represented government by the people in an ideal form. It took part of the timber wars out of courtrooms and into conference rooms, just as President Clinton urged in Portland in 1993. Republicans and Democrats alike could embrace it. And any powerful group that opposed this symbol of "we the people" risked the appearance of being a tyrant in the eyes of the public. An editorial in the *San Francisco Chronicle* in June 1997 noted that the group was "fast gaining legendary status on Capitol Hill as a rare symbol of civility and collaboration."[127] Not many single-interest groups are portrayed in the same favorable light.

The assets and strategies of the QLG turned out to be sufficient to win nearly unanimous support for the act on Capitol Hill, but insufficient so far to implement the pilot project on the scale prescribed.

Whatever the ecologic and economic outcomes in the community turn out to be, it is clear that the QLG has accepted the responsibility to work on behalf of their community; otherwise, the group would have disappeared long ago, as Leonard Atencio expected. It is also clear that the QLG has been held accountable to other interests through the larger structure of governance; otherwise, the Community Stability Proposal would have been accepted intact and already completed after five years.

Is the QLG model of governance a success? Part of the answer is yes, insofar as it contributed to substantive policies that advanced the common interest. Another part of the answer depends on whether the QLG contributed to more inclusive, representative, and responsible participation in forest policy decision making locally and nationally, compared to the structure that was in place before the group began to emerge in 1992. Recall that in that year, the Quincy community was essentially collateral damage in the larger timber wars fought in re-gional and national arenas—a victim little noticed by the major com-batants until the QLG emerged to represent the community directly. Nearly a decade later, the QLG still represents the community in forest management decisions, but other interests have not been excluded. Rather, when they have chosen to participate, other interests have done so through the larger structure of governance—particularly through Congress, the courts, and planning processes in the Forest Service. A comprehensive summary of evidence supports the position that the QLG succeeded by procedural as well as substantive criteria. It is, how-ever, worthwhile to address claims to the contrary.

The principal claim advanced by critics is that the QLG and its Community Stability Proposal failed to meet democratic standards of inclusive participation. Sease of the Sierra Club testified that "the QLG plan has never received broad-based citizen input."[128] Timothy Duane, a professor of environmental planning and policy at Berkeley, con-cedes that the QLG proposal met his standards of democratic inclu-siveness, but "only within the community of place known as Quincy; they are violated when non-local communities of interest are consid-ered. It is clear that the QLG proposal would affect many parties out-side of Quincy, many of whom have not been equal participants in the negotiations."[129] Blumberg and Darrell Knuffke of The Wilderness Society wrote: "The broader national interests, as well as the interests of the land itself and those of future generations must be represented. They were absent in the Quincy process. The Forest Service and envi-ronmentalists from outside the area were specifically excluded from the outset."[130] Such claims are based on an unrealistic criterion unfairly applied, and on selective and misleading use of the evidence available.

The criterion is that all interests affected by a proposed policy should be included in the planning process *at the outset*. This is an extreme form of the principle of affected interests, discussed in Chapter 1 as a criterion that does not get us very far because it cannot be met by any democratic association. Imagine just the physical difficulties of transporting representatives of all affected interests to Quincy and packing them into the local library or the town hall from the beginning. Imagine further the political difficulties of forcing them to set aside their own priorities in order to attend every meeting. The larger structure of governance provides for the representation of remote interests through institutions of representative democracy. That burden of responsibility cannot be placed on the Quincy Library Group: no single form of democratic association is adequate for democracy in a modern society.[131] The criterion is unfairly applied unless the critics acknowledge that their own organizations—the Sierra Club, The Wilderness Society, and Berkeley—have not included from the outset all the affected interests, internal and external, that might be affected by their planning activities.

Representatives of environmental and other groups were, in fact, part of the process throughout. Local environmental groups participated in the Quincy Library Group and in the town meeting at the outset; nearly all supported the proposal, but a handful did oppose it. Representatives of regional environmental groups negotiated with QLG in the spring of 1997 in an attempt to block the group's pursuit of a legislative solution. Sease, Blumberg, and other members of national interest groups testified in congressional hearings on S. 1028 and participated in other ways as well. They lobbied members of Congress, influenced Senator Boxer's decision to put a hold on S. 1028, and expressed their opposition in letters, op-ed pieces, and full-page newspaper advertisements.[132] Members of Congress who represent environmental interests (including George Miller) in addition to many other interests overwhelmingly supported H.R. 858 and S. 1028 in votes on the House floor and in the Senate Energy and Natural Resources Committee. National environmental interest groups were not excluded; they simply lost the key votes on their own turf in Washington. These groups nevertheless made significant changes in the bills as they moved through the legislative process, and they could also do so later in the pilot project through EIS processes. Perhaps the most powerful participants of all were Forest Service officials in the Quincy area. Most officials rejected the Community Stability Proposal and its predecessor, and through EIS processes made the decisions that substantially modified the pilot project as prescribed in the QLG act. The interests allegedly excluded from the QLG process were actually included, along with local interests in Quincy. Few decision processes in forest policy have gone so far toward democratic inclusiveness.

The QLG is responsible for opening forest policy decision processes to more inclusive participation in the Quincy area and (to the dismay of environmental groups) in Washington. The group, however, is not responsible for shortfalls in participation arising from choices by critics or others who have declined opportunities to participate in its meetings or in the monitoring project. Such choices are an expression of these individuals' priorities, not the QLG's. Nor is the QLG responsible for the behavior of its critics or opponents. It was Senator Boxer—not the QLG—who, under pressure from environmental groups, prevented a vote on S. 1028 by the full Senate. Furthermore, a report on the all-party monitoring project concludes that "despite their participation in meetings and field trips, environmentalist participation proved limited and generally negative. . . . Their focus was—and remains—on blocking implementation of the QLG plan. Nonetheless, the Quincy Library Group hopes that before their plan is fully implemented, environmentalists will engage constructively, participating in reviewing monitoring protocol and results."[133] The QLG's hopes are more responsible than the reported behavior—whether the standard of responsible participation is a good faith effort to find common ground, respect for the rule of law, or even expedient self-interest. Environmental critics have a self-interest in staying involved in the monitoring project to prove their point through observations on the ground—if they do, in fact, believe the pilot project prescribed by the QLG act is detrimental to the health of the forests.

A second claim is that the QLG act undermines existing law and policies, particularly environmental ones. The Audubon Society, for example, claimed that both S. 1028 and H.R. 858 would predetermine the outcome of the NEPA process if enacted. "They tell the Forest Service to go through the motions of public participation, but mandate that the final result must be the QLG's plan or some version of it."[134] Barb Cestero, a collaborative conservationist, also criticized the QLG for circumventing existing environmental laws. "Rather than amend existing forest management plans pursuant to NFMA, QLG sought congressional direction on management. It is in this circumvention that Quincy fails to meet the lesson that constructive collaboration should occur within existing law and policy."[135] Such claims are based on criteria that amount to blind defense of the status quo, and again on selective and misleading use of the evidence available.

It is certainly important to respect the existing framework of law and policy, but it is equally important to modify that framework at the margin—at least until all of the people and their elected representatives are satisfied that we have it right. The First Amendment to the Constitution acknowledges "the right of the people peaceably to assemble, and to petition the Government for a redress of grievances." The body of the Constitution prescribes how the laws may be changed. It is therefore inappropriate to use the existing framework to inhibit the exercise of basic rights by the people, or the exercise of legislative powers by the Congress. One of the critics, Duane, concurs that "existing laws are not sacrosanct and deserve reconsideration through new legislation. The critical question is whether or not any law allows for or precludes the achievement of social, economic, and ecological objectives"—all of which are typically relevant to advancing the common interest in particular contexts.[136] The stimulus for change often comes from conflicts within the existing framework of law and policy, as alleged by the Audubon Society in this case. Such conflicts tend to proliferate with modernization, as shown in Chapter 1, and initiatives like the QLG are promising additional means of resolution.

The evidence is clear that few in the Quincy area were satisfied with the management of local national forests under existing law and policy when the QLG emerged to exercise the basic right of the people to petition for a redress of grievances. Congress made the QLG act consistent in principle with the existing framework of environmental law. One provision—that "nothing [in this Act] exempts the pilot project from any Federal environmental law"[137]—was necessary to reassure George Miller and other members of Congress who represent environmental interests. Whether this reassurance in principle was denied in practice is an empirical question. It is not known whether NEPA or NFMA was compromised by the local Forest Service officials who interpreted the QLG act. It is known that the substance of the QLG act was compromised in the EIS processes.

The problem is that conflicts within the existing framework tend to be resolved by local Forest Service officials in the Quincy area, not by the Quincy Library Group or by those formally superior to field officials—in the agency, the White House, or Congress. Local Forest Service officials are, in effect, making law and policy, because conflicts have not been resolved by their superiors and despite their superiors' interest in the Quincy case. Early in the process, President Clinton,

Secretary Glickman, Undersecretary Lyons, and the Forest Service chief publicly supported the Quincy Library Group and directed local Forest Service officials to work with it. Some of this "support" may have been insincere, perhaps a means of letting local officials take the heat for opposition to the QLG.[138] After four years of attempting to work out an administrative solution with local officials, the group sought a legislative solution in Congress.[139] In their March 2000 letter, Senators Feinstein, Craig, and other members of Congress charged that the Forest Service had openly and willfully defied the intentions of Congress in the QLG act. The QLG has challenged the local officials' implementation of the QLG act and probably will challenge their SNCF decision. It appears at least that local officials are not accountable to their appointed or elected superiors or to the QLG.

A third claim is that the QLG violated certain rules for collaborative processes. The assertion is advanced by both proponents and opponents of collaborative conservation.[140] One of the proponents, Cestero, argues that the QLG failed because it violated certain "keys to constructive collaboration" applied as rules. "What may have begun as a place-based attempt to resolve local forest management issues evolved into a 'collaborative advocacy group' that lobbied Congress to pass its particular plan over widespread opposition. Along the way, the QLG hit many of the land mines inherent in local decision making over public lands, and as a result, it is not a positive model for place-based collaboration."[141] The reference to "widespread opposition" overlooks widespread support for QLG bills in Congress, as evidenced by floor and committee votes. This view also rules out an interest-group role in national politics for those involved in constructive collaboration.

Acceptance of such rules for collaborative processes is entirely voluntary; they are certainly not binding on the QLG or any other group. However, the application of these rules has no warrant in the practice of democracy. The Constitution, for example, requires consensus among the branches of government to enact legislation and pass judicial review, but it also recognizes conflict in the separation of powers. Both conflict and collaboration can be constructive in advancing the common interest, depending on the context. The application of such rules has no place in rational policy inquiry, either. They are examples of goal displacement. For Cestero, "the bottom line" is that "constructive collaborations work toward improving conservation and finding creative ways to meet local economic and social goals."[142] Cestero loses sight of these goals, however, when she focuses attention on collaboration—first as a means to achieve these goals, but ultimately as a goal in itself.

Cestero does not consider whether the QLG advanced those sub-stantive goals; she considers only whether the QLG complied with her rules. This is not rational, unless conformance with the rules infallibly achieves the substantive goals, and there are no other means to achieve the goals. Otherwise, a substantive appraisal of QLG's efforts is in or-der, and collaborative means of achieving the goals should be com-pared with other means, including conflict. The QLG could not make much progress in "improving conservation and finding creative ways to meet local economic and social goals" so long as local Forest Service officials rejected its proposal. We know, because the QLG tried for sev-eral years. Short of giving up, the group had no realistic alternative to seeking a legislative solution as an interest group in Washington—where it made progress, even though it has not yet achieved the goals in the proposal. If constructive collaboration rules out an interest-group role in national politics, then those who accept the rules cannot achieve the local goals in Cestero's bottom line where field officials are closed to outside proposals. Collaboration is capitulation in such con-texts.

It is impractical to address all claims that the QLG failed or suc-ceeded on procedural or substantive grounds. But perhaps enough has been done here to demonstrate that the criteria employed are not al-ways justified, the evidence available and relevant to the criteria is sometimes overlooked or ignored, and formal or effective responsibil-ity for successes and failures is sometimes misplaced. The common interest in natural resources policy must advance, but without more careful assessments of the Quincy Library Group, the politics of the appraisal process will continue to obscure the significance of the group's experience, and these politics will continue to mislead the pol-icy makers involved.

The Broader Significance

The significance of the precedent being set by the Quincy Library Group does not stop at the borders of Plumas, Lassen, and the Sier-raville District of Tahoe National Forest. But what is the precedent so far? The evidence reviewed in this chapter demonstrates that:

- A community-based initiative can clarify the common interest of the local community in forest management issues through the development of a policy proposal.
- A community-based initiative can effectively advocate that

proposal in Congress and in the process reconcile the proposal
with the common interest of the national community.

- Enactment of such a proposal may be insufficient for effective
field implementation, despite continuing support in Congress
and the administration.

There is nothing unique about the first demonstration: other initiatives in community-based forestry have done the same. There is no
evidence, however, that a proposal from any other community-based
initiative has prevailed in Washington, after rejection by officials in the
local area, and over the opposition of interest groups established in
Washington. Thus the QLG precedent appears to be unique. As such,
it could be significant in adapting governance in America to twenty-
first-century social conditions—especially if local Forest Service officials decide to implement the pilot project, and it proves itself in the
field. Neither the precedent nor its significance has been entirely determined.

What will come of the QLG precedent over time is uncertain, but
the important factors shaping its future can be identified. The first is
the persistence of the Quincy Library Group and its supporters. Without this, the efforts begun late in 1992, if not earlier in the Conservationist Alternative, probably cannot succeed. In view of the group's past
efforts and their improved position through the QLG act, however, they
are not likely to give up. The second factor is the direction taken by
local Forest Service officials. On the one hand, their words have
stressed cooperation with the QLG almost from the outset. Consider
a memo about the QLG to employees of the three national forests affected by the Community Stability Proposal from their supervisors and
the regional forester in January 1994: "It is vital that we embrace this
cooperation if we expect to continue as an effective and respected land
management agency. This is a new process—a new way of doing business, both internally and externally. . . . The Forest Service will be
judged by how well we are able to shift to a new way of doing business.
Let's strive to make the judgment favorable."[143] On the other hand, the
deeds of these officials and their successors over the years have not
matched the professed aspiration to learn a new way of doing business
or to earn a favorable judgment for the Forest Service.

Under these circumstances, the third important factor is oversight
by appointed and elected officials in Washington who have supported
the pilot project as an important experiment in forest management.
With the end of the Clinton administration, many of the appointed

officials have moved on, but a core of supporters remain in Congress, including Senators Boxer, Craig, and the other members who pressured the Forest Service in March 2000 to implement the act. The outcome may depend on their ability to apply more pressure more often and to find appropriations for the management program authorized in the act. It is not possible for officials in Washington to intervene (and to do so effectively) in field decisions on a large scale, given the multitude of field decisions and other issues competing for their time and attention. But it is possible and prudent to intervene in significant cases like the QLG, where there are indications that the intent of Congress has been misinterpreted or ignored and where selective intervention could make a significant difference.

Although future outcomes are uncertain, preferences from a common interest standpoint are relatively clear. These are that the QLG and its supporters in the local Forest Service, in Washington, and elsewhere enforce implementation of the pilot project prescribed in the QLG act and demonstrate the effectiveness of the management program through improvements in the ecological and economic health of the area. Realization of these preferences would begin to spread the expectation that it is better to cooperate with those community-based initiatives that appear to have clarified the common interest rather than reject their proposals out of hand. Representatives of traditional interest groups, at least, would have some doubts that they can prevail, or do so at reasonable costs to themselves. It is generally preferred that proposals to advance the common interest of particular place-based communities are seriously considered as a matter of standard practice and are assessed by tests of the common interest, including procedural, substantive, and practical tests. To the extent that this preference is realized, it will not always be necessary to legislate such proposals or enforce their implementation in the field.

Hundreds of other community-based initiatives have formed and will continue to form in response to dissatisfactions with the management of the national forests and other nearby public lands, where residents have more at stake than other citizens. Some have and will continue to look to the Quincy Library Group as a model to adapt to their own circumstances. The group has been relatively successful, and because of conflicts surrounding it, relatively visible. Others, no doubt, have been deterred from using the QLG as a model by misleading appraisals that have been allowed to stand. How far the QLG precedent will travel, and where it will be adapted, remains to be seen. Community-based initiatives in forest management will come together to diffuse and adapt information among themselves about successful innovations like the QLG, and they will educate others about such initiatives.

The QLG is part of a wider association, the Lead Partnership Group (LPG), which is a consortium of bioregional watershed and community-based groups from northern California and southern Oregon. These groups include representatives of the timber industry, environmental groups, and other citizens who "desire an increased role in resource management decision making—not local control, and seek to improve the well being of local communities within their areas of focus."[144] The LPG was created in October 1993 in response to a surge of interest in collaborative groups and a dearth of understanding or guidance from resource professionals. The group aims to provide federal agencies with recommendations about partnerships and appropriate collaborative strategies. To further this aim, in October 1995, the LPG hosted the Roundtable on Communities of Place, Partnerships and Forest Health, to "[explore] ideas for collaboration between the national environmental community, the forest products industry and community groups."[145] More recently, the LPG and its member organizations have been conducting pilot projects to study different approaches to monitoring. They have developed a set of "lessons learned" to share with other community groups, federal agencies, and Congress.[146]

Two conservation organizations, American Forests and the Pinchot Institute, have been pioneers in facilitating community-based forestry. Gerry Gray of American Forests described his organization's role this way: "Rather than be a group speaking as an advocate for certain kinds of issues, we try to build trust with different local groups and with different national interests—both environmental and industry interests—to say that we are going to be a conveyor of information and a bridge." The aim, Gray says, is "promoting dialogue to help connect people," in order to encourage discussion and raise issues.[147] The Pinchot Institute provides three central services—meeting, convening, and facilitating; research and policy analysis; and leadership development—in program areas including sustainable forestry. Like American Forests, it does not take positions on policy issues, but brings together people with divergent views to talk through the issues and if possible discover common ground.

It remains to be seen how and how much the Quincy Library Group will impact the future of natural resources governance. Some things, however, are clear already. First, the QLG arose from local dissatisfaction with the status quo. Late in 1992, when the QLG began to emerge, few in the community were satisfied with the policy outcomes largely imposed through remote decision processes. Second, the QLG was able to clarify the common interest by attending to all interested parties insofar as practical and by focusing on areas of agreement in the local community. As an interest group competing in Washington, it also reconciled the Community Stability Proposal with national interests as far as possible. Third, to the extent that implementation of the pilot project prescribed in the QLG act—and others like it—actually succeed in advancing the common interest, both the Forest Service and the environmental movement face critical junctures in their evolution. Much will depend on whether they choose selective cooperation or conflict on all issues. Leadership could make the difference.

Governance in the United States was transformed profoundly between 1877 and 1920, and the current system is no more permanent than the one it replaced. The task is not to defend the present distribution of authority and control as a matter of reflex, but to reflect on those innovations that might contribute to clarifying and securing the common interest under changing social conditions and to build upon those that work. Perhaps through building on successful innovations— and the Quincy model so far is an important one—we can create a new system of governance better adapted to our time.

6 Harvesting Experience

Ronald D. Brunner and Christine H. Colburn

What might be done to realize the potential of community-based initiatives, both to advance the common interest through policy in particular communities and to contribute toward constitutive reform in America? Whatever that potential may turn out to be, the pivotal factors in realizing it (or not) will be the policies implemented by the people and organizations most directly involved. This chapter focuses on the policies of participants in and supporters of community-based initiatives, organized interest groups in and around the agencies affected by such initiatives, and researchers and educators who converge on such initiatives.[1] The purpose is to suggest policy changes that are principled as well as expedient from the standpoint of those most directly involved. Policy changes are expedient when they help sustain an organization; they are principled when consistent with larger goals, including the common interest. For this purpose, the strategy is harvesting experience from the preceding cases and from other sources.

Community-Based Initiatives

Participants in community-based initiatives directly engage one another over a period of time in an effort to resolve their differences over an immediate issue. They proceed within the distinctive opportunities and constraints of a place-based community. They are more likely to succeed if their actions are informed by the experience of other community-based initiatives. It is not necessary for any new or evolving initiative to reinvent the wheel or to repeat mistakes given the wealth of experience already gained by others. But what experience should be harvested, and in what forms, to be most useful for participants and supporters in the innovation, diffusion, and adaptation of successful community-based initiatives?

There is evidence that harvesting experience works better for practical policy objectives when it focuses on models—in this context, innovative models of governance in narrative or story-like form—rather than on generalizations in the form of rules, principles, or maxims.[2] A model of governance summarizes and integrates experience relevant to the main constitutive questions. These questions have been answered one way or another, implicitly or explicitly, by every community-based initiative that has contributed to policy decisions. The same questions will be answered in the evolution or design of each future initiative. The following questions are illustrative, not exhaustive, of each category:

1. Participants. Who should participate in what decisions by the initiative? With what qualifications? By what mode of selection?
2. Perspectives. What policies are to be sought by the initiative? What interests of participants are relevant to those policies?
3. Situations. How should interactions among participants in the initiative be organized? How should interactions with others outside the initiative take place?
4. Resources. Who should be given authority to make what decisions within the initiative? What other resources (for example, funding, knowledge, skills) should participants be authorized to obtain?
5. Strategies. How should participants be authorized to use resources to influence policy outcomes? With what limits? By what methods?
6. Outcomes. What mode of deciding should be authorized? What decisions may be affected?
7. Effects. For what intended or unintended effects of the policy decisions should participants be responsible? Who should hold the participants accountable?[3]

Answers from the four cases are summarized below for participants in community-based initiatives and for their supporters. A case-specific narrative can retain information on the significance of each answer to the above questions, in the context of the model as a whole and in its larger context.

In contrast, a generalization across cases must eliminate differences in context. From a common-interest standpoint, for example, it makes sense as a general rule to select participants who represent different interests in the community. But the general rule says little about coordinating the selection of participants with a perceived problem in order to distinguish between relevant and irrelevant interests; with situational factors, including distance, that facilitate or preclude face-to-face interactions among potential participants; with the resource needs of the initiative, including participants' skills; with the strategies available to acquire missing resources and to shape policy outcomes; with the prospects for consensus on policy outcomes; and with the arrangements for accountability for policy outcomes—all of which depend further on the larger context of the initiative. A generalization that begins to accommodate interdependencies like these becomes a statement about a particular case very quickly. Because of interdependencies like these, a model in narrative form tends to be easier to understand for practical purposes of application than a list of generalizations.[4]

The strategy of harvesting experience can be illustrated by summarizing answers to the main constitutive questions in the models of governance from the four case studies and by considering each model within its larger context.[5] The Quincy Library Group, the Upper Clark Fork Steering Committee, and certain initiatives of other kinds are also models in the normative sense and are worth considering for adaptation: compared to the structures of governance otherwise available in the northern Sierra or in western Montana at the time, the Quincy Library Group and the Steering Committee each succeeded well enough in advancing the common interest to motivate and inform community-based initiatives elsewhere, as did the Gray Wolf Interagency EIS Team led by the U.S. Fish and Wildlife Service, and the Wolf Compensation Trust led by Defenders of Wildlife. Of course, these are not the only models of governance. Additional models covering more experience are needed to expand the range of field-tested alternatives for community-based initiatives now and in the future. There is a continuing need for harvesting experience because there is no fixed formula for success and because the larger contexts are subject to change.

As detailed in Chapter 5, the Quincy Library Group succeeded in agreeing on the Community Stability Proposal in July 1993, and in gaining broad support for the proposal from the larger community in and around Quincy. Various components of the group's structure contributed to this policy outcome. It was open and inclusive, through self-selection of participants representing many different local interests, but also through efforts by some participants to invite or represent ranchers, small-business loggers, and other missing groups. Forest Service employees were initially excluded, however. Participants shared the expectation that a precipitous decline in logging threatened the stability of their community, jeopardizing its ecologic and economic health and leaving the area vulnerable to catastrophic forest fires. Without specific authority or formally appointed leaders, they sought to develop consensus on a plan for community stability by meeting in the local library and similar neutral places beginning in November 1992. They drew primarily on their own time, energy, and other personal resources over subsequent months and years, and they developed the mutual trust, shared knowledge, and diverse skills necessary to succeed. Members insisted on putting all issues on the table but deferred relatively intractable issues to focus on areas of potential agreement; they tolerated intemperate statements about issues, but not about each other; and they decided by vote, but only after consensus (not necessarily unanimity) on an issue had been achieved.

Congress passed and President Clinton signed the Herger-Feinstein Quincy Library Group Forest Recovery Act in October 1998. This policy outcome would have been unnecessary if supervisors of the Plumas, Lassen, and Tahoe National Forests had originally accepted and implemented a version of the Community Stability Proposal as the Quincy Library Group had expected. When local supervisors refused, the group went to Washington to lobby Forest Service officials and members of Congress on behalf of a bill to carry out their proposal as a pilot project. Nearly unanimous passage of a bill in the House in July 1997 fueled the opposition of national environmental organizations. Opposition from official and unofficial sources seemed to intensify solidarity and cooperation within the group and attract additional support for the group as the voice of the people in the Quincy area. At the same time, progress in gaining allies at the national level seemed to reinforce the group's perseverance. Progress also depended on the group's ability to acquire and use the political knowledge and skills necessary to participate effectively in the power-balancing process in Washington, and these were in addition to what was necessary for finding common ground in Quincy. Part of the strategy was to accept some changes in the bill in order to move it forward. By October 1998, the Quincy Library Group Act had passed many of the same procedural and substantive tests of the national interest as the National Environmental Policy Act had in 1969. However, while NEPA advanced environmental interests in competition with other national interests, the Quincy Library Group Act seeks to advance the common interest of the people in the Quincy area. The struggle to implement the pilot project continues.

Group members have ample reason to continue to act responsibly, because they cannot avoid the direct consequences of their actions. Few
participants in the regional timber wars have taken any responsibility
for the collateral damage done to the Quincy area in the early 1990s,
in the form of deteriorating ecologic and economic conditions and the
growing risk of catastrophic fire.

Chapter 2 examines the Upper Clark Fork Steering Committee,
which found widespread support in the basin for its draft Water Management Plan in a series of public meetings in September and October
1994. Various components of this community-based initiative contributed to this outcome. Participants in the steering committee were first
invited by facilitators from the Northern Lights Institute in 1991 to
represent all interest groups in the basin powerful enough to kill a deal
on water allocation. Participants were later selected by facilitators to
represent different interest groups under a mandate from the state legislature and to bring to the committee knowledge and skills relevant to
resolving the main issues. With a few exceptions, participants expected
high costs and uncertain outcomes from a contested case hearing over
water reservations and were therefore open to the committee as an
alternative. Committee members interacted with one another about
once a month, on field trips and in public meetings in a central location. The committee and subcommittees also met with residents in different watersheds in the basin. The group had authority from the state
to devise a plan and modest funds from private sources to hire a facilitator. It was able to move forward without undue constraints from external supporters under the leadership of an exceptional facilitator,
Gerald Mueller, and to build mutual trust and respect as it proceeded.
The committee turned the diversity of members and basin residents
into a key resource for shaping proposals and evaluating their political
feasibility. But no one had a veto.

In December 1994, the committee brought a bill to implement the
final plan to the Montana legislature, where representatives of other
communities and interest groups had opportunities to participate. In
the only major change, the legislature exempted groundwater from the
basin closure, but limited the exemption to groundwater not connected
with surface water. The committee met in the state capital to lobby the
bill and monitor its progress, using the legislative skills and experience
that particular members brought to the committee. A remarkable part
of the story is that the Water Allocation Task Force, the committee's
predecessor, sought authority for the committee from the state before
the members were formally appointed and began working. State officials, in turn, recognized the committee and eventually its Water Man-

agement Plan as assets for improving water policy in the basin, and not as threats to their control over water policy in the state. The relatively smooth integration of the committee's work into state water policy through this collaborative strategy is one reason why the committee is less notorious than the Quincy Library Group. But both the steering committee and the Quincy Library Group proceeded through established structures of governance in which they functioned primarily as planning bodies and then as interest groups that lobbied on behalf of their plans. Legislatures and elected executives in both cases retained authority to reject, modify and enact plans as policy.

As discussed in Chapter 3, wolves were listed as an endangered species in 1974 under the Endangered Species Act, but a policy to fulfill that mandate to recover wolves in the northern Rockies was effectively blocked until November 1991. At that time senators representing Western livestock producers in the Senate Appropriations Committee relented and allowed the appropriation of funds for the mandatory Environmental Impact Statement under NEPA. Thus, wolf recovery in the northern Rockies was a policy made through established structures of governance in Washington. Continuing opposition, based on the valid and appropriate interests of some livestock producers, indicates room for policy improvements from a common interest standpoint. Nevertheless, there is experience worth harvesting from three organizations that contributed toward reducing the burden on livestock producers and helped advance the common interest, especially during implementation of the policy.

First, the ten-member Wolf Management Committee was an advisory committee established and funded by Congress in 1990.[6] The group lost its opportunity to shape policy directly when the majority imposed a last-minute plan on a minority, the two environmentalists. It was easy enough for these two to block the plan by appealing to representatives of environmental interests in Congress. The power of an advisory group, like a community-based initiative, evidently depends upon integrating diverse interests into a consensus—which tends to minimize the influence of an appeal to a larger community and might eliminate altogether the need for such issue expansion. The committee shaped policy indirectly by devising proposals that were later adapted by the wolf recovery team in the field.

Second, the Gray Wolf Interagency EIS Team, under the leadership of Ed Bangs, was a community-based initiative of another kind. The team was constrained to reintroduce wolves under various procedural and substantive directives from Congress, but within those constraints it made informal agreements to operate relatively free of directives from superiors in the Fish and Wildlife Service. In the field, the team welcomed regular participation in its meetings by representatives from livestock producers and other interest groups and actively sought input through interaction with the public at numerous open houses and hearings. Thus the EIS process may be open to participation by non-officials in practice as well as in principle, and the outcomes may help advance the common interest of local communities through the implementation of national policy decisions. Perhaps it helped that recovery teams under the Endangered Species Act are exempt from the Federal Advisory Committee Act (FACA) of 1972.

Third, the Wolf Compensation Trust, established to compensate producers for livestock killed by wolves, is a community-based initiative of still another kind. It was created and funded by Defenders of Wildlife but served the interests of both livestock producers and Defenders alike, as well as the Fish and Wildlife Service. The leader, Hank Fischer, states that "Defenders has made changes in its program over the years in response to concerns raised by livestock producers."[7] Such programs may be reconceived as community-based initiatives of another kind and multiplied by interest groups to help carry out national policy decisions in the common interest of communities with the most at stake. Such programs are also at least partial exceptions to the generalization that community-based initiatives must work through government agencies.

Chapter 4 looks at participants in bison management in greater Yellowstone who have not been able to find common ground through the established structure of governance. Conflicts have not been resolved in the Joint Implementation Plan of December 2000 despite the resources invested over a decade or more. These include conflicts among the agencies that controlled the EIS process; conflicts between the agencies and many of those who provided public comments, including supporters of the Citizen's Plan to Save Yellowstone Bison; and conflict over the management of bison as wild animals or as livestock. In this case, the structure of governance established under national legislation (including NEPA) provided government of, by, and for contending agencies and certain allied interest groups. It is not apparent that they have accepted any responsibility to the community, or that the community can hold them accountable for the failures of bison management policies in the 1990s.

The Bison Management Citizen's Working Group in Bozeman in 1991 and its successors were missed opportunities to begin to resolve in the common interest such costly conflicts. What could the Bozeman group have done differently? Not much, so long as certain agencies were able to insist on a zero-tolerance policy to eradicate brucellosis from wildlife in Yellowstone, to dominate other agencies in the EIS process, and to exclude citizen groups from the formulation of alternatives in the EIS process. Under these circumstances, members of the Bozeman Citizen's Working Group had no better course of action than to participate in coalitions that opposed official plans and policies in court and in the court of public opinion. (Evidently, the expected payoffs of sustained lobbying in state capitals or in Washington on behalf of the 1991 plan or subsequent plans were insufficient to justify the expected costs.) What could the agencies have done differently? They could have reconsidered their own interests. It would have been expedient early in the EIS process to recognize their interests in minimizing the resources invested in sustained conflict. In retrospect, there was little gained by their investments. It would have been expedient to open up the EIS process to the Bozeman group's plan as a point of departure for advancing the common interest.

Participants in community-based initiatives and their supporters are advised to select among successful models of governance and adapt them to their own contexts. Models that work help sustain the efforts of participants by reinforcing the expectation that community-based initiatives can work, depending on the context—an expectation that is realistic insofar as it is based on carefully harvested experience. Successful models also provide guidance on how to make the most of those efforts: each model is useful insofar as it clarifies constitutive decisions—about participants, perspectives, situations, resources, strategies, outcomes, and effects—and policy decisions that were sufficient to advance the common interest. The more models there are available, the more likely it is that any given initiative will find more than one model suitable as a basis for its own efforts, and a menu of characteristics from other models worth considering if not incorporating selectively. The intent is to make decisions informed by experience, building on successful models. These models tend to eliminate failures from the flow of intelligence by diverting attention from them. Failures may "poison the well" in the places where they occur, but they need not deter initiatives and continuing innovation elsewhere. Removing failures, as well as building on successes, accounts for much of the progress in problem-solving processes that are naturally or deliberately based on trial-and-error.[8]

Community-based initiatives must also be aware of certain threats to their success. Consider three of the more significant ones. First, there is a threat that various general formulas, or recipes, or lessons distilled from experience will be *mis*applied to deter the rise of community-based initiatives, or to inhibit continuing innovation by them. David Getches has discovered that "few groups get far without the clear focus, committed participants, leadership, and sound structures that I found in all those [successful watershed-based initiatives] that I reviewed." Sound structures include broad representation, acceptance of ground rules by all participants, decision making by consensus unless it inhibits the effort, a neutral facilitator, and linkages with outsiders, both to obtain resources and to influence government decision-making processes. "Some groups may have relative strengths and weaknesses in these areas, but it is fair to say that a dearth in any one of the four areas can be fatal."[9] In practical applications, such general formulas tend to become maxims. The weak form is a warning: beware of proceeding without a clear focus, committed participants, leadership, *and* sound structures. The strong form is an injunction: do not proceed without any of them. If a successful model clarifies what to do in particular, such maxims clarify in general what *not* to do. As researchers distill additional formulas, recipes, and lessons from a growing body of experience, however, they tend to multiply the requisites for success. Consequently, it may appear foolish to proceed at all, because it is less likely that all the requisites can be met in any particular context. Community-based initiatives appear in the aggregate to be reasonable only in those rare contexts in which all the requisites are met at the outset.[10]

There are several reasons why it is not prudent to rely on formulas incorporating requisites like a clear focus, committed participants, and leadership. Leadership, for example, is not one requisite but something that comes in many forms, no one of which is necessary for success. Effective leadership was exercised by a public official (Ed Bangs) in the wolf management context, by an expert facilitator (Gerald Mueller) in the Upper Clark Fork context, and collectively by officials and non-officials without special expertise in mediation in the Quincy context (Bill Coates, Michael Jackson, and Tom Nelson initially, and later others including Linda Blum, Rose Comstock, and Pat and George Terhune). We do not know what other forms of leadership might succeed in a given context without trying them. It is also difficult to assess leadership in advance of trying, because effective leadership depends not only on the personal qualities of leaders but also on followers and other factors in the context.[11] Moreover, any relationship between a set of general requisites, ingredients, or lessons on the one hand, and success on the other, will be weak and fraught with exceptions.[12] The Quincy Library Group, for example, did not conform to several of the broad lessons for constructive collaboration extracted by Barb Cestero from a variety of cases. But the group nevertheless succeeded in advancing the common interest, according to the appraisal in the previous chapter.[13] It is unnecessary to have all requisites for success, either actual or alleged, in hand before a community-based initiative can proceed. Every initiative must discover its own requisites as they arise and meet them in a timely fashion by mobilizing resources (including experience) from itself and others. "The ingredients of most successful collaborative efforts," Getches agrees, "cannot be combined according to a strict recipe."[14]

Second, there is a threat that single-interest groups will attempt to co-opt a community-based initiative for their own purposes, if they agree to participate in an initiative at all. Environmentalists, for example, recognize a threat from a mining industry that claims a right to mine on public land under hard rock mining law. "When the mining industry asks, then, for 'collaboration' over a given mining permitting proposal, environmentalists would be well within bounds to refuse to participate, since they know the game is rigged by statute: permission to mine is non-negotiable. All that may be negotiated are 'mitigating measures.' In such instances, negotiation probably implies a battle lost before it is begun."[15] Environmentalists, however, may overlook a reflection of themselves in their image of the opposition. (Different ends often obscure equivalent means in politics.) The game is also rigged by environmental laws and regulations, including the Endangered Species Act, as shown in Chapter 3. The other sides to a local issue may invoke these laws and regulations as good reasons to avoid direct negotiations with environmentalists, or else risk being co-opted by them. Many references to "collaborative conservation" presume that the conservation interest ought to prevail over all other interests without regard to the context. One proposal would explicitly define the criterion for success of watershed groups as "achievement of a specific on-the-ground goal described in terms of improved environmental health."[16] Thus the pursuit of single interests can be carried over from interest-group competition to collaborative initiatives, and "collaboration" thereby can be reduced to just another strategy by which one interest group might prevail over others. In contrast, members of the Quincy Library Group took the interests of other members into account in finding an integrative solution, the Community Stability Proposal: Coates, Jackson, and Nelson each affirmed that it did not compromise the initial interests they brought to the table. Rather, it enabled them to advance each interest and to address their neighbors' interests at the same time.[17]

Third, there is a threat that high-level government officials will attempt to co-opt or impose community-based initiatives from above.

Especially if they lack the motivation or the means to "get on the bus" with others in community-based initiatives, high-level officials will be tempted to "drive the bus" whenever it enters their jurisdictions. Reinventing government is a partial precedent. It began as a variety of successful reforms initiated and implemented voluntarily in many places from the bottom up. It became business as usual when the reforms were distilled into ten general principles and imposed from the top down. The National Performance Review incorporated the principles and rhetoric of reinventing government to produce in just six months in 1993 some 246 recommendations for 21 agencies intended to save $108 billion in five years. This had less to do with reform than with shrinking government to promote the Clinton-Gore administration through popular reductions in the federal budget and civil service employment.[18]

Similarly, by its very name, a program like Community-Based Environmental Protection in the Environmental Protection Agency raises questions about the interests to be served. A local community's interests surely include, but are not exhausted by, the agency's mandate and interest in environmental protection. Such programs may not secure the common interest of the community for another reason as well. In the Upper Clark Fork, experience suggests that "locally based water management probably cannot be imposed from the outside."[19] Additional experience may confirm strict limits on what can be done from afar to resolve local issues. One thing is clear, however: a community-based initiative that is co-opted by any single-interest group, official or unofficial, is a failure if the purpose was to integrate different interests into a consensus on policy. It is also not a success from the broader standpoint of governance reform: there is nothing really new about a single-interest group, even if it is disguised as a collaborative or a community-based initiative.

The historical origins of these threats to community-based initiatives shed additional light on them and on means of coping with them. The threats may be understood in part as expressions of scientific management from the Progressive era as well as expressions of the interest-group politics that overwhelmed this kind of management at the national level. What has survived from scientific initiatives and political reactions long ago tends to be defended, wittingly or not, by attempts to reduce community-based initiatives to general formulas or to avoid, co-opt, or impose them from above.[20] A brief historical overview of the governance of natural resources will provide some context.

Scientific management, in Samuel Hays's famous account, preached a gospel of efficiency that "required new administrative methods, utilizing to the fullest extent the latest scientific knowledge and expert, disinterested personnel." In terms of governance, "the crux of the gospel of efficiency lay in a rational and scientific way of making basic technological decisions through a single, central authority." Conservationists believed that "federal land management agencies should resolve land-use differences among livestock, wildlife, irrigation, recreation, and settler groups." To resolve such differences "through partisan politics, through compromise among competing groups, or through judicial decisions" would be to "defeat the inner spirit of the gospel of efficiency." Thus during Theodore Roosevelt's administration, the "entire program [of conservation leaders] emphasized a flow of authority from the top down and minimized the political importance of institutions which reflected the organized sentiments of local communities."[21]

But efforts to implement scientific management catalyzed political opposition. Hays asserts that "grass-roots groups throughout the country had few positive objectives in common, but they shared violent revulsion against the scientific, calculated methods of resource use favored by the conservationists." These local groups eventually discovered that national pressure groups were their most effective means to affect policy decisions. Eventually, national pressure groups "concerned with single interests . . . joined with administrative agencies in charge of individual programs and congressional committees which dealt with specialized subjects to defeat an integrated approach" by experts in federal land management agencies. In other words, "iron triangles" became the dominant structures despite the aspirations of scientific management to rise above politics on a scientific foundation and on behalf of efficiency. "Single-purpose policies . . . became the predominant pattern because they provided opportunities for grass-roots participation in decision making. They enabled resource users to feel that they had some degree of control over the policies that affected them."[22] Conservationists eventually organized as single-interest groups to compete in kind at the national level. They had few alternatives, until changing social conditions opened a niche for community-based initiatives.

Mark Sagoff has updated this history, emphasizing the tendency of organized interests to engage their own experts to justify conflicting positions on natural resources issues. Thus "scientific analyses and economic assessments fracture along traditional political fault lines, eroding public confidence in science."[23] Sagoff also believes that an iron triangle "now defines environmental policy making it a three-cornered tug-of-war" over particular natural resources issues. "At one vertex of this triangle, the administrative agencies, such as the Forest Service or the BLM [Bureau of Land Management], try to promulgate policies. At the next vertex, the special interests, including industry and national environmental groups, challenge any policy they do not like, often taking the agency to court. At the third vertex, members of Congress intervene with the agency to obtain policies their constituents or contributors desire. Any decision taken at one of these vertices will be appealed and probably blocked at another—and eventually the dispute will wend its way through the judicial system." The iron triangle has become less a concentration of power over particular issues than gridlock among competing powers. Sagoff considers the situation to be "the inevitable result of the overdelegation of legislative authority to the executive branch" through mandates that are typically multiple, conflicting, and ambiguous.

In this context, it is understandable why some agency officials attempt to impose on or co-opt community-based initiatives from above, why some interest-group politicians attempt to co-opt them from inside or to avoid them altogether, and why some experts attempt to reduce them to general requisites and formulas. Intentional or not, these attempts bring community-based initiatives into conformance with what survives from scientific management, with the interest-group reaction to it, and with the structures of governance that express and sustain them.

Community-based initiatives from a broader perspective are responses to the limitations of such structures, as well as potential means of adapting them to present realities. (The Quincy Library Group is the most visible flash point in the confrontation of old and new.) To realize the potential of community-based initiatives, outsiders must respond to these initiatives on their merits. This means taking seriously those proposals from community-based initiatives that will advance common interests and rejecting the rest. When and if this becomes standard practice, more community-based initiatives will arise from a sense of shared opportunity rather than from shared desperation, as is now the case. Cooperation will be necessary, even if conflict will be unavoidable. Journalist Jane Braxton Little explains, "Communities can plan innovative solutions and provide expertise, workers, and infrastructure, but they cannot allocate funds, change laws, or control market forces" on their own. [24]

The following sections review from a broader perspective the policies of the U.S. Forest Service, various environmental interest groups, including the Sierra Club, and the researchers and educators who advise and teach them. The Forest Service and the Sierra Club are particularly interesting because they opposed the Community Stability Proposal of the Quincy Library Group and because they exemplify the difficulties once-perfect organizations tend to have in adapting to changing realities.[25] The purpose is to suggest policy changes that are principled as well as expedient from the standpoints of those involved, and that will help realize the potential of community-based initiatives to advance common interests.

The Forest Service

Forest management in the common interest has been affirmed as the goal of the U.S. Forest Service since the time of the first chief, Gifford Pinchot. Pinchot believed that National Forests should be managed on behalf of "the greatest good for the greatest number."[26] The 1897 Organic Act directed the Forest Service to manage its land for timber production, forest preservation, and watershed protection. But national forests were already being used for a wide variety of additional purposes, including ranching, recreation, fishing, and hunting. When conservationists and others began challenging Forest Service policies, Congress passed the Multiple-Use-Sustained-Yield Act of 1960 to provide additional direction for the agency. Under this act, national forests are to be used for five purposes: outdoor recreation, range, timber, watershed, and wildlife and fish purposes. "Multiple use" is defined in part as management of the various uses in the combination that "will best meet the needs of the American people" and will allow for flexibility to "conform to changing needs and conditions."[27] Multiple-use management is supposed to integrate and balance diverse interests in a given context and be flexible enough to adapt to changing contexts. It is equivalent in principle to management in the common interest.

Michael Dombeck's goal was consistent with the common interest from his first day as chief of the Forest Service in 1997. "Our goal is to increase the Forest Service's capacity and desire to collaborate with all forest users, owners, and interests as a way to improve relationships and resource stewardship."[28] Dombeck also affirms collaborative stewardship, which includes "working with people on the land; using partnerships and collaboration; using science and technology; conservation education; insisting on personal accountability; putting the right people in the right jobs; improving the understanding of how resource management affects economic prosperity; fostering a multi-disciplined, multi-cultural organization; and, adapting to growth while maintaining sustainability."[29] Forest management in the common interest, then, is not a new goal. It has been part of the Forest Service's legal mandate and tradition from its origin up to the present.

What is new is the context in which the Forest Service must now proceed, including the means for advancing common interests given new circumstances. "The Forest Service has been reduced in size while the pressures on the public lands have increased, mostly because the West is the fastest growing region in the country. So we have more pressure on lands with fewer and fewer managers."[30] The way Americans view the agency has also changed. No longer does the Forest Service operate in an environment of unwavering public deference to the professional judgment of its staff. No longer is timber harvest over all other uses acceptable to the American public. Now, the agency must proceed cautiously in an arena where it is watched by more interest groups than ever before. Each year such groups grow more vigilant in examining Forest Service decisions and actions, more sophisticated at navigating the labyrinth of the forest planning process, and more adept at working through Congress and the courts. For example, "Until the mid-1980s, the Forest Service avoided serious disruptions in its timber sales programs from lawsuits based on alleged noncompliance with NEPA. . . . In 1984, the *Mapleton* case was the first in a long string of cases which had the effect of strengthening the EIS requirement."[31] The Forest Service must cope with internal divisions as well. In the words of historian Paul Hirt, "This atmosphere of external vilification and internal dissention [*sic*] is a world apart from that of forty years ago when the Forest Service enjoyed a high degree of public accolade and organizational cohesion."[32]

Historically, the Forest Service did not formally incorporate public participation into its planning process. (There is little room for public participation in the tradition of scientific management.) It reluctantly began to do so in the 1970s, when forced by legal mandate. But even after passage of NEPA, in many cases the public was included only in superficial ways, sometimes merely to leave a "paper trail" that would serve as a defense in case of legal challenges. The current relationship between the Forest Service and community groups differs widely from forest to forest, community to community, and region to region. The various patterns of support and resistance defy easy generalization. It is not accurate to say, as some have suggested, that older employees are resistant to community involvement, and younger employees are supportive.[33] Nor is it the case that longer-term employees fit into one category and shorter-term into another. Agency-community relationships are, in fact, largely dependent on personalities. Individual employees at all levels within the agency have a significant impact on whether (and how) relationships with citizen groups develop. Consider a few cases in point.

Chapter 1 discusses District Ranger Crockett Dumas, who led the Camino Real District of the Carson National Forest in "horseback diplomacy" to learn from traditional Hispanic users of the forest and area environmentalists, and to earn their trust. This led to management on behalf of many local interests rather than a few large operators, an end to protests and appeals of district management decisions, and increased employee time and budget to implement forest restoration projects. Moreover, "Employees have developed a sense of ownership and pride in the program because we had full employee participation from the beginning," states Audrey Kuykendall of the Carson National Forest.[34] Dumas was supported in these efforts by his first supervisor but not his second, and he was investigated twice from Forest Service headquarters in Washington. After Dombeck became chief, Dumas's horseback-diplomacy initiative was relabeled the Northern New Mexico Collaborative Stewardship program, and it was supported by headquarters for an Innovations in American Government Award from the Ford Foundation—which it won in October 1998.

Su Rolle is another exceptional leader in the Forest Service. As Interagency Liaison to the Applegate Partnership in southern Oregon, she helped the partnership survive intact after a series of assaults. The partnership includes representatives of industry, conservation groups, the Bureau of Land Management, the Forest Service, research scientists, and local residents, who collaborate under the motto "Practice trust—them is Us." For Rolle, participation in the partnership was an important step forward in opening up bureaucratic processes. By doing so, she says, "agency personnel gained local knowledge, challenged traditional ways of doing business, generated more ideas and innovations, reached better decisions, and shifted the 'we/they' mentality toward an 'us' perspective with the agencies and communities working together."[35] The partnership was hailed as a model of natural resources management by the Clinton administration. In June 1994, however, the Department of Justice informed Rolle and other officials that their participation in the Applegate Partnership constituted a violation of the Federal Advisory Committee Act (FACA), and they were directed to stop attending meetings. "Everyone was very upset," Rolle says.[36] Relationships between the partnership and the agencies became rocky and distanced. Agency employees resigned from the board but eventually resumed regular participation, in an advisory role only, to comply with FACA.

But these two cases are still exceptions. In Chapter 5, the Quincy Library Group faced a different Forest Service—one that was less open to community participation in its planning process—despite the group's effective role in securing more funding for the local national forests as a step toward implementing the Community Stability Proposal. Why can agency personnel be open to collaboration in some cases, but resistant in others? Several factors help explain the variety of de facto policies toward community-based initiatives in the Forest Service.

Rhetorical support for collaborative stewardship from Chief Dombeck was important, but the effects of that support depended on employees of the service. Before Dombeck, some rangers and forest supervisors who believed in collaborative approaches were reassigned punitively, were fired, or were compelled to leave the Forest Service because their ideas contradicted the dominant view that management decisions ought to be left to the experts.[37] Others stayed with the agency, but conformed to the dominant view and the status quo. Dombeck's support freed these employees to foster open, collaborative relationships with citizens and community groups. Workers who disagreed with collaborative stewardship were free to continue business as usual, within the limits of law and policy as they are enforced. There was no indication that these employees were in danger of losing their jobs or leaving the agency, but their positions could become uncomfortable if collaboration with community-based initiatives becomes the norm. Dombeck's rhetorical support of collaborative stewardship in itself did not change the beliefs or behaviors of Forest Service employees. To do so more effectively the rhetoric must be backed by successful practice of collaborative stewardship in the field and by support from Washington, both sustained over long periods of time.

Another reason for the variety of de facto policies toward community-based initiatives is the decentralization of the Forest Service across 175 national forests and grasslands. This offers a large degree of autonomy to forest supervisors and rangers at the field level. It also helps explain how the chief's official support for collaborative stewardship can encourage some employees and be ignored blatantly by others. Tom Kovalicky, former forest supervisor, says, "When you talk about cultural paradigm changes in an agency like the Forest Service, you have to remember a phenomenon that occurs in a decentralized bureaucracy. Bosses tend to gather around and reward people who act like them. If a forest supervisor has a vision to cut trees and build roads, then those are the kind of employees he or she will beget."[38] Although it is true that the decentralized structure of the Forest Service permits dissent and passive resistance to directives from Washington, this structure offers opportunities as well. It allows for innovation and custom-made collaborations tailored to a specific context. Any successful models may then be diffused for possible adaptation in other ranger districts, forests, or regions.

Tenuous communication and accountability up and down the multiple levels of the Forest Service hierarchy also contribute to the variety of policies toward community-based initiatives. Part of the reason is political, reflecting the growing number of interest groups involved in forest management. Former forest supervisor Orville Daniels explains, "At the national level, there's tremendous chaos. There's almost a vacuum at the top as the people there are so caught up in political battles that they don't know what's going on out in the field."[39] Moreover, field personnel who do not effectively collaborate may have their own political battles with local interest groups, and they may be reluctant to advise their superiors for fear of losing whatever control they have in the field. These political difficulties are compounded by simple information overload. Recent staff cuts leave employees doing the same work that several people used to do, while at the same time the quantity of information coming to agency officials keeps increasing. It is not surprising that it proves difficult to attend to most of it. Major changes in higher-level leadership in a short period of time may have further magnified problems of communication and accountability. This means that some of the multiple directives from Washington to harvest timber, to preserve forest habitats, to collaborate, and so forth, may or may not reach all of the 175 national forests and grasslands, attract attention, or have much effect if they do.

The many laws and regulations governing employees are another significant factor in understanding Forest Service policies toward community-based initiatives. Jack Ward Thomas, former chief of the Forest Service, says, "The combination of laws passed from 1870 to now is a sort of blob. It doesn't work, and we try to go around it to get things done."[40] Former supervisor Daniels elaborates: "People used to see the Forest Service as 'part of us,' but they don't see the agency that way any more. . . . We used to have the time to have coffee with local folks and to be involved deeply in the community. As we became more technically oriented for our work to be legally defensible, we began to put our energy into how to do NEPA, fight appeals, handle administrative legal processes, etc." Daniels concludes that by diverting resources to technical areas, "we severed our relationships with the public."[41] But many employees feel compelled to devote much of their time to these technical issues for fear that they may otherwise violate one of the many regulations to which they could be held accountable.

The Federal Advisory Committee Act in itself is a barrier to collaboration in the Forest Service, as seen in connection with the Applegate Partnership. When passed in 1972, FACA was intended in part to ensure that federal employees obtained balanced advice from a variety of groups and individuals representing diverse sectors of the public. It therefore imposed restrictions on the kinds of interactions federal employees could have with groups claiming to represent a given constituency. The rise in community-based initiatives brought uncertainty over the type and degree of involvement that is legally permissible for Forest Service and other federal employees. According to Su Rolle, interagency liaison with the Applegate Partnership, "It seems that most problems with FACA are perceptual rather than actual." Nevertheless, "there is a great deal of misunderstanding and fear regarding the act." This fear has deterred agency employees from participation in community-based initiatives and prompted them to pull out. Rolle says, "On the average, I receive at least one phone call per week from various agency people (in different agencies) that are needing some encouragement or framework to respond to community groups. In many cases, they were discouraged by staff or their bosses to engage in group associations."[42] The Forest Service's own collaborative stewardship team recommended that the agency "provide positive guidance to field units that encourages collaboration consistent with FACA" and provide assistance in interpreting and applying FACA.[43]

The Forest Service's policy for promoting employees also diminishes the potential for collaborative stewardship in practice. In the service, to move up, you must move out: when employees are promoted, they are transferred. Because a community is only a temporary stop for agency employees, they have less stake in it than the people who expect to live their entire lives there. In addition there is frequent turnover in agency staff, and sometimes a position is left unfilled for up to nine months. Even when the transition is faster, frequent turnover means that upon arrival, new employees must spend considerable time familiarizing themselves with the area, and they rarely develop the kind of local knowledge and contacts that long-term community members have. This tends to undermine trust in the Forest Service and its personnel. Frequent transfer also means that employees do not always finish the projects they start before moving on. Employees often have little motivation to continue projects started by their predecessors because they cannot take full credit for them. They have instead an incentive to start new projects for which they might be recognized and re-warded, perhaps in the form of a promotion and transfer. Of course there are exceptions. Some Forest Service employees care about their local communities, develop local knowledge and contacts, and recognize the public benefits of finishing the job—despite the policy for promotions.

What policy changes might be indicated for the Forest Service? There is no present need to change the multiple-uses mandate from Congress or other authorized goals that are already consistent with advancing the common interest. But to realize these goals in a changing context, the remaining practices of scientific management might be supplemented where appropriate by the evolving practices of collaborative stewardship. The primary task then is to facilitate the evolutionary process already underway. There is a long road ahead, according to Jim Burchfield, who notes that "by the end of [Dombeck's first] year, it was apparent that collaborative stewardship had lost its luster." Among other things, "collaborative stewardship ran into the buzz saw of arrogance" from senior agency personnel, especially scientists, who considered the public incapable of reasoned collaboration.[44] Persistence is warranted under such circumstances, along with some modest policy changes.

First, higher-level management could augment recognition and rewards for agency personnel who have succeeded in advancing the common interest of both place-based communities and the Forest Service through collaborative management. There are precedents to build on. Chief Dombeck promoted Jim Furnish to deputy chief in May 1999. Furnish is known for emphasizing environmental protection and recreation as well as timber harvest.[45] Elizabeth Estill, regional forester and leader of the collaborative stewardship team, always gives the highest award in her region to collaborative projects.[46] Washington headquarter's belated recognition of Crockett Dumas's accomplishments shows how the agency might facilitate further innovation, diffusion, and adaptation of collaborative stewardship practices within the Forest Service. Latent interest among personnel in the field will become active by establishing the expectation that practitioners of collaborative stewardship will *not* be punished after changes in higher-level management. This expectation is likely to be established sooner or later, to the extent that the remaining practices of scientific management are not well adapted to the new context.

Second, the Forest Service might open more opportunities for field personnel to develop their interests in practicing collaborative stewardship. This could include more small workshops for Forest Service personnel, where newcomers to collaborative management would contribute specific problems to be solved and experts would advise on alternative solutions. There could be programs of continuing education for Forest Service personnel interested in investing one to several weeks to learn more about the theory and practice of collaborative management. Third, field personnel and higher-level management in the service might work together to identify and ameliorate specific barriers to collaborative management in agency policies and public laws. Personnel in the field might be granted promotions without transfer, provided they can make good cases for it. It is not inappropriate for field personnel to identify with the communities in which they reside and with the agency that employs them. There can, however, be considerable tension in wearing these two hats. Crockett Dumas is one example. In addition, FACA might be clarified further for agency personnel, and if necessary, amended through the legislative process.

The Forest Service need not mandate collaborative stewardship practices from the top. It need only make good use of its diverse personnel and its decentralized organizational structure to encourage the diffusion and adaptation of successful innovations among field personnel who are in a position to practice the approach and voluntarily accept responsibility for it. A mandate would have little effect where officials in the field do not take responsibility for collaborative stewardship voluntarily and where their accountability to superiors is limited in practice. Expediting the evolution of collaborative stewardship in the Forest Service would be principled in terms of the agency's common-interest goals, and expedient in terms of certain other interests within the agency. These include earning the trust and respect of the public; reducing protests, appeals, and lawsuits in response to management actions by the Forest Service; and using the resources freed up by these developments to help improve environmental, economic, and other conditions in the community, and in the process, morale and job satisfaction in the agency. These developments would serve valid and appropriate interests within the agency, and they would serve the common interest.

Environmental Groups

Realizing the potential of community-based initiatives may also depend on the policies of environmental interest groups. About 140 such groups, for example, opposed the Herger-Feinstein Quincy Library Group Forest Recovery Act of 1998. Over recent decades, the mainstay policies of environmental interest groups have sought to preserve and protect natural resources, including the environment, through a strategy of litigating and of lobbying at the national level.

That strategy contributed to significant advances in the 1960s and 1970s. In the 1970s alone, twenty-three environmental acts were signed into law, providing the legal foundation for aggressive litigation to ensure proper enforcement of the laws.[47] Environmentalists won a series of groundbreaking legal battles through the early 1990s. In 1975, for example, the Fourth Circuit Court ruled in the *Monongahela* case that the 1897 Organic Act prohibited clearcutting on national forests.[48] In 1988, a Seattle judge ordered the Fish and Wildlife Service to reconsider a decision to exclude the northern spotted owl from the threatened species list. The agency listed the owl a year later.[49] Author and journalist Mark Dowie states, "As a result of these acts and other initiatives of the environmental lobby, tens of millions of acres have been added to the federal wilderness system, environmental impact assessments are now required for all major developments, some lakes that were declared dead are living again, and clean air and ground water have become virtual human rights. . . . In addition, several species of animals have been saved from extinction."[50]

But the 1980s brought the Reagan administration, and with it substantial setbacks for the environmental movement. Many loopholes in environmental legislation became apparent, and "industries soon deployed a battalion of lobbyists to Washington to keep them open."[51] By 1991 there were diminishing returns from lobbying. James Dougherty, a vice president of Defenders of Wildlife, observed that "legislative advocacy at the federal level, traditionally the environmental movement's mainstay, now requires an ever-increasing amount of hard work to make significant progress. . . . [Compare] the relatively easy campaign to enact the Superfund law in 1980 with the eleven-year struggle to amend the Clean Air Act in 1990."[52] The effectiveness of litigation dropped off as well. Federal judges who had consistently ruled in favor of the environmental side were gradually replaced by Reagan appointees.[53] In the 1990s, the Clinton administration succeeded the Reagan and Bush years but the election of the anti-environment 104th Congress in 1994 undermined the environmentalists' power base in Washington. Mike Clark, executive director of the Greater Yellowstone Coalition and former president of Friends of the Earth, observed that national groups had spent the past twenty years investing "huge amounts of money [in] national staffs knowledgeable in complex issues who developed contacts with Congress and its staffs." But, he concluded, "those contacts are now destroyed."[54] The strategy of lobbying and litigating no longer met with the same degree of success.

These setbacks had adverse effects on environmental interest groups themselves. The Sierra Club, for example, by 1990 "was in its worst financial shape in twenty years and was forced to pare its payroll by ten percent. The club's membership dropped from 630,000 to 500,000, and it ran a cumulative operating loss of $7 million between 1990 and 1994—in spite of a sixfold increase in foundation funding during the period."[55] Perhaps in response to the threats posed by the 104th Congress, environmental groups began to recover from the decline in membership and funding, but they seemed to be growing only slowly if at all in the mid-1990s.[56] And friction between regional and national interests plagued the environmental movement as a whole. Tension was particularly notable in the Sierra Club and the National Audubon Society, "which, although constitutionally more democratic than other organizations, frequently act without the advice or consent of members or regional chapters. The result is internal splintering that could lead, in both cases, to real organizational schisms."[57] Most of the national environmental groups, according to Mike Clark of the Greater Yellowstone Coalition, "still don't know how to provide field services to groups like us."[58]

In response to adversity, most national environmental groups began to rethink their strategies, hoping to regain the internal support and external power they had enjoyed in previous decades. Before examining some of their responses, it is important to consider why the early successes could not be sustained. Three factors are especially significant.

First, the problems more amenable to national environmental legislation and litigation were rationally addressed earlier, leaving the more difficult problems for later. It was easier to protect endangered species when the bald eagle, a national symbol, was disappearing. It was easier to set aside wilderness areas when clearcutting of forests left visible symbols of environmental devastation. It was easier to curb water and air pollution when rivers caught fire and big industrial plants were belching smoke into a brown cloud for all to see.[59] But after the first Endangered Species Act, the first Wilderness Act, the first Clean Water Act, and so forth, further progress would have to come at the margin. And as the initial working solutions were implemented and began to show results, their costs came into the focus of public attention while the more difficult problems that remained often receded into the background. When protection of the snail darter and the spotted owl

blocked established economic practices, these species began to symbolize for many Americans the exorbitant costs of the Endangered Species Act. Furthermore, the effective regulation of a relative few big industrial polluters leaves millions of less-visible nonpoint sources of air
and water pollution in place. In this way the seeds of adversity were
sown in the earlier successes of the environmental movement.

Second, the national political arena provided more opportunities
for the success of the mainstay environmental strategy in the 1960s
and 1970s. It took some time in the balancing of power for economic
and allied interests to organize effective responses to the rise of environmental regulations. (Among other things, it took time to exploit
shifts in environmental problems and perceptions.) By the time President Reagan took office in January 1981, much of the public was prepared to believe that "In this present crisis, government is not the solution to our problem; government is the problem."[60] The crisis was
economic, not environmental. The growing problems of governance
reviewed in Chapter 1—gridlock, demosclerosis, single-interest politics, the Washington disconnect, and bureaucratic layering, among
others—made it more difficult for national environmental groups or
interest groups of any kind to impose tough, national legislation on
other groups.[61] While the federal government lost some of its capacity
for governance, problems in the governance of natural resources became more numerous and more localized with population growth, social change, and the proliferation of interests in communities in the
West. People representing these different interests increasingly insist
on an effective voice in the natural resources policy issues they face in
their communities. By 1996, the former mayor of Missoula, Dan
Kemmis, was not the only one to conclude that "I do not believe the
federal government has the capacity to manage the West."[62]

Third, the mainstay strategy of lobbying and litigating became more
extreme and narrowly focused over time. Patrick Moore, founder of
Greenpeace, believes that as the environmental movement achieved
many of its original goals, it "moved to the left. Unfortunately, environmentalism is still defined by the media and by our culture as an adversarial role. If you want to remain in that adversarial role while society is
adopting many of your more reasonable positions, you have to become
more extreme in your positions."[63] These tendencies toward extremism
were reinforced by a practical need to inflate environmental threats in
order to mobilize more political and financial support from environmental constituencies. At the same time, the movement narrowed its
focus, alienating the broader base of support it had attracted earlier.
Former environmental lobbyist Don Snow says that "the central prob-

lem with environmentalism is that it lacks a cogent, convincing focus on livelihood, and that has made it vulnerable to Wise Use attacks."[64] Observers have also noted the movement's neglect of the full range of needs and interests of people in Western communities. "When an activist says to reporters, 'I get pretty tired of people shedding tears because they can't make money off public lands,' . . . he's tipping his hand more than he knows."[65] Former Sierra Club lobbyist Rick Johnson says, "We've spent a bunch of years getting really good at bringing lawsuits, dissecting environmental impact statements and eviscerating entire agencies. But one day we turned around and saw that nobody was with us. We need to be speaking for the public—not at the public."[66]

In this changing context, participants in the environmental movement and their supporters have urged reconsideration of the mainstay adversarial strategy. Four leading foundations met with New England environmental groups in 1995 to talk about the future of the movement. In a report titled *New England's Environmental Futures*, they concluded that the adversarial approach, demonizing resource users, would not succeed in today's political climate. "If environmental protection is imposed upon people, we will surely fail. But if it is accomplished with, for, and because of people, we may succeed," said the report.[67] Of course, community-based initiatives provide opportunities for environmentalists to work with, for, and because of the people. "You'll have much greater gain doing this than as a bunch of road warriors who flash into the legislature and put laws onto agencies who have the power of the lion in the Wizard of Oz," says Don Snow. "I mean, how many lawsuits can we file? If you want to save the environment, roll up your sleeves and get working with people who care about that land as much as you do, but who may have different values than you do." This strategy, however, need not replace lobbying and litigating altogether. "It's precisely because of the gains in environmentalism, like the Wilderness Act of 1964, that we're able to have this discussion in the first place," says Snow. "The policy world that the environmentalists helped build gives us the background against which to build consensus."[68]

How have national environmental organizations responded to adversity? The Sierra Club has reinforced the mainstay strategy and actively opposed community-based initiatives. As seen in Chapter 5, the Sierra Club mounted an aggressive lobbying campaign against the Quincy Library Group and the bills in Congress to implement its Community Stability Proposal.[69] Chairman Mike McCloskey criticized collaborative groups more generally in a 1996 memo to the board of directors: "It is troubling that [collaborative] processes tend to de-legitimate conflict as a way of dealing with issues and of mobilizing support. . . . Too much time spent in stakeholder processes may result in demobilizing and disarming our side."[70] The war metaphor suggests that the goal is to overpower and defeat the enemy, not to find common ground through deliberations.[71] This position helps to sustain the flow of resources in a power-balancing context. "The Sierra Club is threatened by local people working out their differences," according to Seth Diamond of the Intermountain Forest Industry Association in Missoula. It "generates resources by fostering and operating in a climate of hostility and polarization. So when people closer to the resources and the issues work out their differences, it becomes difficult to raise funds—and the kind of anger they use to generate those funds."[72]

The Sierra Club has also responded in other ways that reinforce the usual Washington-centered strategy. In the wake of the 1994 elections, when other national groups were beginning to shift resources to emphasize regional and local efforts, the Sierra Club decided to stress the accountability of politicians through electoral politics. "We had taken for granted that Americans who care about the environment were sufficiently concerned about the political process to hold politicians accountable. But it isn't true. They do not hold them accountable. . . . We have to keep the public informed and encourage it to pay attention to politics," said Carl Pope, the Sierra Club's executive director.[73] In 1996, the Sierra Club decided to oppose all commercial logging on federal land. As Dave Foreman, Sierra Club director and founder of Earth First! explains, the no-logging position constricts the support base. "If the Club's position is in fact opposed to all commercial logging, then we have placed ourselves in a difficult strategic position with respect to local communities," Foreman said.[74] It is clear that "the 'no-cut' goal is a no-compromise goal," in the words of forest economist Randal O'Toole.[75] It leaves little room for seeking common ground in cases like the Quincy Library Group, where there is a need to reduce the risk of catastrophic forest fires. The risk was evident when multiple forest fires broke out around the West in 2000.

Is opposition to community-based initiatives consistent with the mission of the Sierra Club? The stated mission is: "To explore, enjoy, and protect the wild places of the earth; To practice and promote the responsible use of the earth's ecosystems and resources; To educate and enlist humanity to protect and restore the quality of the natural and human environments."[76] The "responsible use" of the earth's ecosystems seems to imply a wide variety of human interests, including but not limited to environmental protection and restoration. The desire to "educate and enlist humanity" on behalf of the natural "and human" environments seems to leave room for sustained, non-adversarial inter-actions with people of all kinds, not only members of the Sierra Club and other environmentalists. If so, the group has allowed its mainstay strategy to displace its mission to some extent, transforming the strat-egy into an end in itself. It would be more principled to modify the strategy to allow for selective support of community-based initiatives consistent with the mission statement.

Even if the Sierra Club's mission is narrowly construed as environ-mental protection and restoration alone—regardless of the other inter-ests of people in place-based communities—the organization may still find it expedient in some cases to seek common ground in community-based initiatives. Phil Brick recommends that "where innovative, local plans meet or exceed national standards, environmentalists should be more concerned about results and less worried about precedents that may appear to weaken existing policy regimes." Brick observes in gen-eral that a strategy aimed at national environmental regulations and their enforcement is not sufficient. "National environmental regula-tions can compel change, but these will be shallow and short-lived without a corresponding development of local social and political capi-tal. The history of national civil rights in this country is instructive. Although no one can discount the importance of national civil rights legislation in ending blatant discrimination, real progress in achieving equality is more a function of local social capacity and consent."[77] Sim-ilarly, environmental protection and restoration is more a function of local capacity and consent, given the existing framework of national environmental laws. A modified strategy that selectively includes com-munity-based initiatives could respond to the changing nature of envi-ronmental problems, the declining capacity of the federal government, and the rising power of local communities. Some environmental orga-nizations are moving in that direction.

The Nature Conservancy has begun to emphasize community-based conservation to supplement its traditional strategy, which is buy-ing land. The logic is that if they own it, they can preserve it. In recent years, however, they have recognized that owning land may not be enough, given the interconnectedness of natural systems across human boundaries. Good relations with one's neighbors may also be needed to reduce pollution of the air or water upstream, to minimize harm to wildlife that roam across property boundaries, or to protect and restore the environment in less direct ways. The Nature Conservancy has acted on these insights by investing more in community-based conservation. President and CEO of the conservancy, John Sawhill, believed "that community-based conservation will emerge as the primary vehicle through which the Conservancy delivers our conservation product. . . . We boast today of being a multilocal organization, but the future will find us even more decentralized, even more responsive to the distinct conservation needs of local communities."[78] The conservancy already has established numerous partnerships and collaborative efforts at the community level. The Malpai Borderlands Group, for example, is a citizens' group on the southern border of Arizona and New Mexico that has been collaborating with The Nature Conservancy, agency officials, and university scientists "to see that wildfire once again performs its natural function of keeping these magnificent grasslands free of invading species. The ranchers in this group have also committed themselves to a policy of non-fragmentation of private lands. Now, there is a de facto block of uninterrupted habitat on over a million acres of public and private lands."[79]

The Virginia chapter of the conservancy worked with local landowners to establish a Forest Bank, which will manage forests "to reverse past mismanagement and produce higher quality timber in the future." Chapter director Michael Lipford says, "We knew that The Nature Conservancy would have its greatest impact on the landscape not just by owning more land itself, but by bringing under conservation management land it might never own." The Forest Bank will do just this, and for the long term, "basically forever," he says.[80] In Shady Valley, Tennessee, a chapter of the conservancy has built a partnership with local businesses and civic organizations. "The Nature Conservancy strives not only to work in the communities where it owns preserves, but also to become a valued member of each community," says Conservation Assistant Cindy Pitman. Good relations spurred the volunteer fire department to offer their skills, expertise, and equipment for the prescribed burns that are part of the management plans for Shady Valley. In other parts of Tennessee, the conservancy is working with partners to poll the public before embarking on new conservation efforts. "Behind every conservation success story is a supportive local community," Pitman says.[81]

Other organizations have begun to reach out to local communities, energizing an otherwise waning environmental movement. In the 1995 report on *New England's Environmental Futures*, foundations encouraged environmental advocates to work with traditional users such as hunters, fishers, and farmers. Rick Johnson, like others in the movement, has begun to do just that: build coalitions with hunting and antinuclear organizations, hoping to reach a broader cross-section of the public.[82] The Izaak Walton League has also begun discussing ways to build relationships with the fishing and hunting communities.[83] At a

1995 gathering of forest preservation activists, Steve Holmer of the Western Ancient Forest Campaign (now American Lands), said, "It's very important that we're bipartisan. We can't afford to write off one member."[84] Tarso Ramos, an expert on the wise-use movement, encouraged environmentalists to learn from the wise-users, whose appeal is broad based and populist, tapping into the angst of the times. "You must take these economic issues head on," he said. "It's the only way the environmental movement stands a chance of surviving as a powerful political force in this country. If it stays isolated, the movement threatens to become an agent in its own destruction."[85] The Wilderness Society has done economic analyses along with environmental ones. "If we can't sustain communities around wilderness areas," said its president, Jon Roush, "then we can't have sustainable wilderness areas."[86] There is growing appreciation of the interdependence of the various parts of a community.

Some environmental groups have started to decentralize in pursuit of local strategies. John Flicker of the National Audubon Society explains that "while Audubon has traditionally been a grassroots organization, over the past twenty years we have devoted more resources to building up our capability in Washington." Now, he says, "we are moving into a new era of conservation. We are out of the era of major command and control frameworks and into an era much more focused on solving problems at the state and local level. We need to organize accordingly."[87] Greenpeace, in another example, decentralized its twenty-two regional offices and instructed them to concentrate on local issues.[88] This decentralization opens the way for participation in community-based initiatives by local representatives of environmental organizations.

Environmental organizations clearly have begun to act on the wisdom of Aldo Leopold, whose classic statement of the land ethic still guides principled environmentalists. "To analyze the problem of action," Leopold wrote in 1942, "the first thing to grasp is that government, no matter how good, can only do certain things. . . . The second thing to grasp is that when we lay conservation in the lap of the government, it will always do the things it can, even though they are not the things that most need doing."[89] He gives the example that "[wildlife] sanctuaries are one of the things government can do, but the growth of private ethics and naturalistic management needed to go with them is beyond the powers of government." Leopold suggested that we try self-government as a possible solution to problems of land abuse, but he added: "I do not here refer to such superficial devices as advisory boards, who offer their wisdom to others, or such predatory devices as pressure groups, who exist to seize what they can. I refer rather to social and economic units who turn the light of self-scrutiny on themselves." Perhaps community-based initiatives are the self-scrutinizing units Leopold envisioned to propagate private ethics and naturalistic management, the things that most need doing. The "functions [of government] will become real and important as soon as conservation begins to grow from the bottom up," Leopold concluded, "instead of from the top down, as is now the case."

Leopold conceived the land ethic in general as an enlargement of the internalized constraints needed for cooperation, while recognizing the external constraints of competition. "All ethics so far evolved rest upon a single premise: that the individual is a member of a community of interdependent parts. His instincts prompt him to compete for his place in that community, but his ethics prompt him also to co-operate (perhaps in order that there may be a place to compete for). The land ethic simply enlarges the boundaries of the community to include soils, waters, plants, and animals, or collectively: the land."[90] Perhaps we saw the land ethic in action in the Quincy case, after Nelson and Coates on behalf of local timber and government interests walked into Jackson's law office in November 1992 to find a way out of the timber wars. Jackson and his environmentalist allies chose to cooperate in a search for common ground, rather than allow further competition to harm the Quincy community.

Leopold also believed that "conservation is a state of health in the land-organism. Health expresses the cooperation of the interdependent parts: soil, water, plants, *and people.* . . . When any part lives by depleting another, the state of health is gone."[91] Likewise, the well-being of a democratic community suffers when some of its interdependent parts live by weakening the others. The land ethic is therefore a principled basis within the environmental movement for acceptance of the common interest as the purpose of governance in a democracy. The land ethic is also a principled basis for support of specific proposals from community-based initiatives that advance the common interest. Community-based initiatives, in turn, might be encouraged to propagate the land ethic and the naturalistic management that lie beyond the powers of government.

Researchers and Educators

Researchers and educators also can contribute to realizing the potential of community-based initiatives. They have major roles in harvesting experience for policymakers in and around community-based initiatives and for organized interest groups, and in disseminating the results to students and future policymakers in classrooms around the country. Research and education, however, must go beyond scientific management toward adaptive management if the common interest is to be served. This section critiques research framed in the scientific management tradition and invites consideration of an alternative frame, the policy sciences. An application of the policy sciences suggests how researchers and educators might work with practitioners on the adaptive management of natural resources, including revising priorities for and coordinating operations, research, and education systematically as events unfold.

Scientific management in the Progressive era aspired to rise above politics on a scientific basis for policy purposes. This aspiration is echoed by contemporary researchers in statements like the following: "a primary responsibility of academic inquiry is to promote the examination of information and ideas in a manner guided by precise, reproducible, and presumably value-neutral, criteria and procedures."[92] From this perspective, one immediate problem for inquiry is the riddle of success: evidence from the watershed movement is insufficient to support any definitive conclusions about whether "success" in the form of building trust (or other kinds of civic capacity) contributes to "success" in the form of improved environmental health. Although case studies may be helpful, "a few isolated cases tell us little about the overall movement. Answering this riddle of 'success' requires standardized data on a large number of cases, ideally over many years. Additionally, it requires some consideration of the level of progress that would have resulted had the watershed group not existed, a real complication given the impracticality of control groups for experiments that are highly context-specific."[93] Recognizing such complications and the need for additional expenditures of resources to address them, part of the purpose is "to be able to stand before some of my more academically rigorous colleagues and say, 'I have the proof you've said is lacking.'"

Is such proof relevant to participants in a watershed initiative, the primary policymakers in the watershed movement? Not if they are enlightened participants. First, they would recognize that improved environmental health is not their only interest. Even if it is their primary interest, its multiple components still need to be integrated with their other interests in the watershed if possible, or balanced with them if necessary. Second, they would realize that trust interacts with many factors in shaping the success or failure of their own watershed initiative. These factors include the elements identified as requisite for the

success of collaboratives in various general formulas. Multiple interacting factors shape the outcomes achieved, just as multiple interacting interests affect the outcomes sought. It makes no sense for practical purposes to ignore these interactions. Third, they would recognize
that any imperfect correlation between trust and success in standardized data means that the relationship is contingent at best: it may exist
in some contexts but not in others. Thus enlightened participants
would focus selectively on the handful of contexts most similar to their
own and on models of success in those contexts. The watershed movement overall is not their primary concern.

Such problems of relevance are compounded by matters of timing.
It is seldom prudent or possible to postpone decisions and actions until
rigorous proof becomes available, which is often over many years. The
participants in the Upper Clark Fork Steering Committee were motivated by a shared interest in avoiding the costs and uncertain outcomes
of an imminent battle over water reservations in court, and they acted
without proof that they could build trust or even advance the common
interest. If rigorous proof were required for rational policy decisions
and actions, the world would grind to a halt. Moreover, rigorous proof
tends to become obsolete as events unfold. Policymakers who wait for
such confirmation are vulnerable to "assumption drag," in which decisions and actions are based on assumptions that lag behind unfolding
events and never catch up.[94] There is no reason to believe that whatever
relationship might have existed between measures of trust and success
in 1999 will be the same relationship in 2004 or in 2009. Such relationships change as people learn and adapt to the surprises that are inevitable in a complex world.

Is rigorous proof nevertheless relevant to officials in state or federal
agencies with many watersheds under their jurisdiction?[95] In the tradition of scientific management, they might use an aggregate relationship to specify or rationalize rules that standardize the treatment of
community-based initiatives, as if they were interchangeable, in a program to advance an agency's interests. This would not, of course, eliminate the multiple interests in the community relevant to the success of
each initiative, the multiple factors shaping that success, and their
unique interactions. It would simply ignore them. That relationship
also would not eliminate differences in the meanings of observations
arising from these interactions, despite the standardized meanings imposed by operational definitions of measures. Trust or the lack of it,
for example, may be expressed differently from one case to the next
and over time, and it may have different consequences as well. Under
these circumstances, operational definitions, aggregate relationships,

and standardized treatment of cases do not resolve differences relevant to advancing the common interest. They suppress those differences to the advantage of central authorities pursuing single-policy mandates and to the disadvantage of community-based initiatives striving to find common ground. The criteria and procedures of science in contemporary echoes of scientific management are not value-neutral, as often presumed. They have the effect of sustaining the status quo, not guiding reforms.

More enlightened officials, researchers, and educators will recognize limits to what officials can reliably know about large numbers of community-based initiatives, and they will realize there are limits to what they can effectively impose on initiatives. Such limits appear to be manifest in a brief account of the Resource Advisory Councils established by the Bureau of Land Management and chartered under FACA.[96] Uniform central authority did not guarantee uniform success in two dozen cases. The success of the councils differed considerably and depended on place-specific characteristics, including the voluntary personal commitments of official and non-official participants. More enlightened participants in the process will recognize that successful community-based initiatives can help an agency find innovative policies in the common interest. They will also recognize a valuable asset amid the increasing numbers and complexity of policy issues in our time. And consequently, they will work with successful initiatives selectively when it is mutually advantageous. On a case-by-case basis, it is possible to integrate multiple, independent streams of evidence into knowledge that is contingent on particular configurations of time, place, and culture. This knowledge is dependable as a basis for action, but it is not standardized or universal.

Researchers and educators can move their work beyond scientific management by drawing on the policy sciences. Briefly, the purpose of inquiry for policy scientists is freedom through insight. This means bringing into conscious awareness any internal factors that may have determined choices or decisions unconsciously, or any external factors that may have been overlooked or misconstrued, so that decision makers are free to take them into account.[97] Policy scientists recommend for this purpose:

- *Contextual* inquiry, which means that the significance of any detail is understood in the context of which it is a part. For policy inquiry into community-based initiatives, the relevant context is centered on the individual initiative, not bounded by a statistical sample in which every initiative is presumed

to be equally relevant. Every initiative is unique under a comprehensive description that includes the many factors and interests relevant to its success.[98]

- *Problem-oriented* inquiry, which entails at least a tentative
  commitment to goal values, the clarification of which is an
  essential intellectual task. The authors of this book, for example, are committed to advancing the common interest as a goal
  value; the problem is to help realize the potential of community-based initiatives for advancing the common interest. It is
  a mistake to assume that values can be set aside in the choice
  of research problems, or that concealing values in a cloak of
  neutrality is professionally responsible, or that conscious
  awareness of one's values necessarily compromises the integrity of an inquiry.[99]

- *Multi-method* inquiry, which means that research is not arbitrarily restricted to precise deductive, statistical, experimental, or other "hard" methods. It is not obvious how to measure
  such factors as a clear focus, committed participants, leadership, sound structures, and trust, or whether an attempt to
  do so would have net payoffs.[100] It is not possible to isolate a
  community-based initiative as an experiment, to compare it
  with an identical control group, and thereby to prove rigorously what difference the initiative made. Experimentation, if
  taken literally, obscures the need for context-sensitive methods that are better adapted to policy inquiry in open field settings.[101]

The problem-oriented, contextual, multi-method outlook of the policy sciences has been applied in an array of policy contexts for more
than half a century. And elements of it are being rediscovered by researchers who take seriously the practical requirements of policy.

What are some priorities for harvesting experience for those researchers and educators who share an interest in realizing the potential
of community-based initiatives? The first suggestion is to identify and
correct malfunctions in the processes of innovation, diffusion, and adaptation. All three processes must function well to make the most of
experience: without successful innovations somewhere, good models
for guidance elsewhere are lacking. Without adequate diffusion, the
models are unavailable to those who might use them. And without adaptation, the models available make little difference in practice. Researchers and educators so far, however, have focused almost exclusively on the experience of innovators, both to harvest models worth

adapting and to specify general formulas for success. Hence a complementary focus on the relatively neglected experience of diffusers and
adaptors might pay off the most. Before developing this recommendation in more specific terms, it is worthwhile to consider diffusion and
adaptation in more detail.

When different groups of people face similar problems, or varia-
tions on the same larger problem, they tend to self-organize more or
less spontaneously into networks for the diffusion of information. Innovators are typically motivated to publicize whatever successes they
have realized. Potential adaptors are typically motivated to be informed by the experience of others before making commitments of
their own. And media specialists, among others, are often interested
in making the connections between the demand for relevant information and the supply. The governance of natural resources in the American West is no exception. Harvesting experience from the cases in this
book turned up a number of networks. The following list is far from
exhaustive but nevertheless illustrates the varieties found.

- The Quincy Library Group serves as the center of a network
  to share its own experience. Citizens across the nation have
  sought and received information and advice from the group,
  which has become highly visible through its controversial lobbying in Washington.[102]
- The Lead Partnership Group is a consortium of bioregional
  watershed and community-based groups from northern California and southern Oregon, including the Quincy Library
  Group. It appears to be organized by region, rather than by a
  specific resource such as water or forests.
- The Community Stewardship Exchange, a website operated
  by the Sonoran Institute in Tucson, "includes information,
  contacts and examples to promote community-based strategies that preserve and protect the ecological integrity of protected lands and at the same time meet the economic aspirations of adjoining landowners and communities."[103]
- *High Country News*, published biweekly most of the year
  in Paonia, Colorado, is self-described as "A Paper for People
  who Care about the West." For that general audience, it
  includes occasional and sometimes detailed reports on
  community-based initiatives, many of which are cited in this
  book.[104]
- *Chronicle of Community*, published two or three times a year
  since 1996 by the Northern Lights Institute in Missoula, serves

as "both a theory and practice journal of participatory processes. Each edition includes [material] on the theory side of community-building and consensus-based decision making; and direct reportage on living events in the field."[105]

- The Natural Resources Law Center at the University of Colorado, Boulder, publishes reports and holds conferences that serve a networking function for academics and practitioners involved in natural resources policy. A series of recent reports have focused on community-based watershed management and alternative problem-solving strategies.[106]

- *Communities and Forests* is the newsletter of the Communities Committee of the Seventh American Forest Congress, published by the Udall Center at the University of Arizona, in part to "disseminate lessons learned from local forest communities to others." The committee strives to "ensure local community well-being and the long-term sustainability of forested ecosystems" through improvements in economic and political structures.[107]

- Officers of about three dozen private foundations have organized themselves through the Internet for a continuing conversation about community-based initiatives. The discussion includes reports on individual initiatives and comparative analyses of why they succeed or fail, which are relevant to identifying good investments.[108]

- *Eco-Watch Policy Dialogues* is a web site of the U.S. Forest Service for discussion of national and regional issues. Forest Service employees are encouraged to "use this site as a medium to garner broader participation in development of emerging policy and program guidance, as well as to serve as an integration point for public comment."[109]

It may be worthwhile to contact people involved in the diffusion process to clarify *who* says *what, how,* to *whom,* and with what *effects,* through selected networks or kinds of networks, in order to identify possible gaps.[110] The existence of web sites accessible through the Internet is, of course, an important new factor in the diffusion process. In contrast to the Progressive era, policy intelligence can now flow horizontally, from community to community, as easily as it can flow vertically from national centers to local communities.

This list suggests a structure of multiple, specialized, overlapping networks. Control over the diffusion of information is distributed among different kinds of organizations, ranging from community-based initiatives themselves to think tanks, newspapers, and academic centers, to nongovernmental organizations and a federal agency. In principle, this helps many different participants find a network for diffusing their perspectives. The content of information disseminated is specialized geographically by locale and region; by forest and water resources; and by practical, academic, and funding purposes. This helps anyone with an interest manage the flood of information by tapping into one or several networks most relevant to his or her interests. At the same time there are overlaps among the networks. Information on community-based initiatives in forestry, for example, is distributed by several different networks and may be picked up from any one of them. Where such overlaps exist, the overall structure is more reliable than any one of the component networks: even if one or more of the components fails, the word still gets out.[111] These are among the many benefits of a structure that evolves network-by-network from the bottom up, which is different from a single entity designed at the top and handed down. But with little inquiry into actual experience in this structure, these benefits may be more hypothetical than real: structures help shape but do not determine functions.

The evolution of such structures can easily leave gaps. For the purpose of realizing the potential of community-based initiatives, for example, it is not clear that the networks diffuse information with sufficient frequency and coverage to alert most of the people who are otherwise motivated and able to take the initiative on problems in their own communities. *High Country News* probably comes closest, but the circulation may be rather small compared to the coverage needed. National newspapers and television networks have all but ignored community-based initiatives, although some have mentioned briefly the Quincy Library Group's controversial activities in Washington and the prestigious Innovations in American Government award won by the Northern New Mexico Collaborative Stewardship Program.[112] The unrealized possibilities are suggested by national media coverage of President Clinton's visit to the Jackie Robinson Academy in Long Beach, California, in 1996 to publicize a school uniform policy that had helped reduce school crime by 36 percent in its first year. Within eighteen months, more than half of the urban school districts in the country had adopted a school uniform policy voluntarily. The publicity helped, along with a pamphlet the president instructed the U.S. Department of Education to send to all school districts at the time of his visit to Long Beach.[113]

Policy inquiry to identify and correct malfunctions in the processes of innovation, diffusion, and adaptation might begin with the experience of adaptors and potential adaptors.[114] Their experience has not been clearly distinguished from innovators' experience, or examined in sufficient detail, despite their growing numbers and significance. Attention has been focused instead on the experience of a few early innovators who proceeded in the absence of well-developed models. An initial sample of adaptors could be identified by contacting the most visible innovators for leads to communities who have contacted them for information or advice. The most visible innovators in forest management, for example, might include the Quincy Library Group, the Applegate Partnership, and the Northern New Mexico Collaborative Stewardship Program. Then the adaptors might be interviewed separately to clarify how to improve the three processes for maximum effect from their standpoints. To illustrate:

- Researchers might identify what information about *innovations* elsewhere adaptors have actually used in what forms, and what information they think they need. Perhaps the models and formulas already available do not meet the needs of most adaptors. Further policy research on innovation might focus more selectively on adaptors' needs—for example, on new models that provide different answers to the main constitutive questions, old models that have worked in different contexts, and anomalous models that challenge what we know. Researching large numbers of cases as if they were equally significant for policy purposes would yield mostly redundant information at unnecessary expense.
- Researchers might identify what networks or other sources the adaptors have found and used in the *diffusion* process, and what additional sources they think they need. Perhaps the existing networks are satisfactory, or perhaps they need to be publicized to connect with additional adaptors, or perhaps some additional networks and sources need to be set up. Further policy research on diffusion might focus more selectively on the adaptors' needs—possibly needs for advisors, workshops, or other interactive sources to supplement publications in order to access more quickly and selectively the information most relevant to their own circumstances.
- Finally, researchers might identify what resources, in addition to knowledge and information, are necessary to initiate and sustain action in the *adaptation* process. Finding a facilitator, funding a newsletter, or mobilizing political support outside the initiative may be the key at various stages. Researchers

have a professional interest in promoting more research. But action based on what is already known (including the establishment of continuing education programs) may be the key to realizing the potential of community-based initiatives.[115]

A second suggestion for policy inquiry goes beyond the innovation, diffusion, and adaptation of community-based initiatives to their external relations with potential supporters and opponents. This is the arena of reform politics. One priority is a comprehensive appraisal of the various assessments of the Quincy Library Group. The Quincy Library Group is probably the single most important precedent for shaping external support of or opposition to community-based initiatives: it is the most visible initiative, thanks to controversy and resulting press coverage; and it may set the pattern for future conflicts (where they cannot be avoided) with established interest groups unwilling to cooperate with community-based initiatives. The application of existing, common-interest criteria for the appraisal function[116] would go a long way toward discrediting incomplete or incompetent appraisals of the Quincy Library Group, reducing the scope of reasonable disagreement and providing a more comprehensive and dependable assessment of the significance of community-based initiatives for potential supporters and opponents to consider. Another priority is to monitor (and to criticize and correct insofar as practical) inflated claims of success for community-based initiatives, premature or otherwise unfounded claims of failure, and the co-optation of such initiatives by established agencies or interest groups. Neither co-optation nor inflated or unfounded claims serve the common interest, but they can be expected to occur in any political arena. Finally, another priority might be continuing counterpart seminars on the U.S. Forest Service, the Sierra Club, and similar organizations that are important in the future of community-based initiatives. Such a seminar may be designed to serve as an independent source of intelligence and appraisal on policy decisions for the organization in question and for the public at large.[117] The seminar may improve their capacity to learn and adapt.

Priorities will change as events continue to unfold in ways that cannot be reliably anticipated or controlled—because researchers, educators, and decision makers learn from their experience and adjust their overt behavior accordingly.[118] (These adjustments will also cause indices and relationships to decay, reducing rigorous proofs of generalizations to descriptions of historical contexts.) Unless comprehensive maps of the past and possible futures of community-based initiatives are continually updated, the rational choice of priorities for realizing the potential of community-based initiatives is out of the question. The need for updating comprehensive maps is dramatized in the story of the drunkard's search. As told by Abraham Kaplan, it is "the story of the drunkard searching under a street lamp for his house key, which he had dropped some distance away. Asked why he didn't look where he had dropped it, he replied, 'It's lighter here!' "[119] Every researcher or educator has conceptual and theoretical frameworks that work like the street lamp, arbitrarily constraining the search for a solution to the practical problem at hand. So does every policy maker for that matter. Calls for interdisciplinary research, interagency coordination, and sometimes interest-group alliances recognize the limitations of specialized perspectives that shed only a little light on a given situation. The persistence of such calls indicates difficulties in overcoming these limitations. There is consequently a critical need to pool intelligence from multiple perspectives for updating comprehensive maps and revising priorities as events unfold in natural resources policy and governance.

Hence, a third suggestion is to organize a coordinating committee for these purposes, with researchers and educators taking the lead. The default alternative to a coordinating committee is exclusive reliance on the "invisible hand" that is supposed to secure the common interest through competition among particular interests. Sometimes that hand succeeds, but the growing crisis in governance indicates that it, too, has limitations under present social conditions. A committee could supplement the invisible hand by facilitating cooperation among different interests to advance the common interest. Consider some initial and tentative specifications for a coordinating committee designed to realize the purposes outlined above.[120]

- *Participants*. Each invited participant might represent at least one important perspective on the governance of natural resources and bring some capabilities for improving policy or governance through operations, research, or education. Taken together, participants would cover as much of the natural resources area as possible, within a practical constraint of about fifteen participants. A stable core is essential. Some turnover can be expected as events unfold, however, allowing for new core participants and one-time visitors to address the most important priorities.
- *Perspectives*. The relevant perspectives would be based on personal experience in the natural resources area in various capacities as a participant in or supporter of community-based

initiatives, including innovators, adaptors, and funders; as a reporter, editor, or publisher in a diffusion network; as an official from a field office or headquarters of a government agency; as a member of an interest group, local or national; or as a researcher or educator. An outside observer with a broader perspective on policy and governance should be considered.

- *Organization*. The participants would convene annually for a workshop of two or three days' duration. (Between workshops, self-selected groups of participants would work informally to follow-up priorities of mutual interest.) Three annual workshops would be sufficient to make an informed decision to continue or not. For efficiency and continuity, a neutral organization would host the workshops at the same location each year. An alternative would be to rotate the host organization among those represented by participants in order to share in the costs and benefits of serving as host.
- *Resources*. The coordinating committee would require funds sufficient to support three annual workshops comprising about fifteen participants each, including modest honoraria for short papers and white papers. Participants acting alone or in self-selected groups would seek funds and any other resources required to follow-up important priorities on their own. Some important resources (like time, expertise, or authority) may be made available to participants by their own organizations.
- *Procedures*. For reading in advance of the first workshop, each participant would prepare a short paper on the relevant past and possible futures of natural resources policy and governance in the American West, along with a list of priorities for improving them. (See the suggestions above and Chapter 1 for partial examples.) These papers would put participants' perspectives on the table for discussion at the outset. For subsequent workshops, short papers would emphasize what is new. White papers might be commissioned on a few key priorities.
- *Outcomes*. The outcome of each workshop would be a report that includes the short papers and white papers, as revised by their authors in light of workshop discussions, and a summary of those discussions prepared by the host organization or a facilitator. At a minimum, the summary would include a comprehensive map of the evolving context and current priorities, distinguishing what is controversial from what is a matter of

consensus. The report would be published for use by the participants and by broader audiences.

- *Effects*. The participants individually or in self-selected groups would take responsibility for following-up any priorities of particular interest. Coordination for operations, research, or education would occur informally through the structures represented by the participants and by others who use the annual report. The reports would guide reform efforts, in competition with available alternatives, including defenses of scientific management, symbolic innovations (buzz words) as substitutes for action, and rebellion as "solutions" to natural resources problems.

This design assumes that participants would be drawn by opportunities to summarize their individual perspectives concisely, to learn more about other perspectives, and to compare them—as a supplement to (not a substitute for) their on-going activities in operations, research, or education. The workshop reports could be used to plan and justify changes in those activities. Appraisals would emphasize the extent to which the coordinating committee makes a positive difference in the relevant perspectives and continuing activities of the participants themselves and any others involved in natural resources policy and governance. Changes in participants' perspectives can be monitored through their working and revised short papers for each annual workshop. Changes in their activities may be tracked through projects to follow-up priorities from the workshops. Broader influence on the operations of community-based initiatives, foundations, agencies, and interest groups, and on research and education may be detected, even if they are confounded by other sources. Such effects would depend in large part on the diverse perspectives, knowledge, and other assets (including status) that participants bring to the committee, and on their capacity to cooperate over a suitable period of time.

A coordinating committee along such lines would amount to an exercise in adaptive management, based on a larger concept of "science" than its predecessor, scientific management. According to a leading theorist, C. S. Holling, adaptive management is grounded in "a science of the integration of parts" that is distinguished from the traditional "science of parts." In the latter, "the goal is to narrow uncertainty to the point where acceptance of an argument among scientific peers is essentially unanimous. It is appropriately conservative and unambiguous, but it achieves this by being incomplete and fragmentary." In contrast, the science of the integration of parts is "fundamentally interdisciplinary and combines historical, comparative, and experimental approaches at scales appropriate to the issues. . . . It is a stream of investigation that is fundamentally concerned with integrative modes of inquiry and multiple sources of evidence. This stream has the most natural connection to related ones in the social sciences that are historical, analytical, and integrative. It is also the stream that is most relevant for the needs of policy and politics." The second stream recognizes limits on what can we know. "The premise of this second stream is that knowledge of the system we deal with is always incomplete. Surprise is inevitable. Not only is the science incomplete, but the system itself is a moving target, evolving because of the impact of management and progressive expansion of the scale of human influences on the planet."[121] In the management of such systems, then, it is essential not only to pursue goals through action, but also to update understandings of the evolving system continuously and to provide flexibility for adapting to surprises. This is the essence of adaptive management.[122] A coordinating committee on community-based initiatives and the initiatives themselves can be designed for adaptive management. Bureaucracies cannot be redesigned for adaptive management, without giving up their bureaucratic core, including the impersonal application of fixed and unambiguous rules to standardized cases. It would make little sense to wait years for rigorous proof of incomplete and fragmentary relationships from the traditional science of the parts, or to rely on this information alone for policy purposes.

Holling is not the only researcher who has begun to converge on the contextual, problem-oriented, and multi-method outlook of the policy sciences.[123] There are additional examples from environmental policy that emphasize the importance of evolving contexts. In the second environmental science envisioned by the social psychologist Paul Stern, "The most important point is probably that human beings are continually responsive to interventions . . . so that it will never be possible to write a cookbook for behavior change. It is absolutely essential to treat interventions as dynamic and to monitor and revise them continually."[124] In global change research, the anthropologist Steve Rayner and Elizabeth Malone asked how society can face profound change at an accelerating rate if, as they contend, decision makers cannot predict the unpredictable. "The answer may be to focus on building responsive institutional arrangements that monitor change and maximize the flexibility of populations to respond creatively and constructively to it."[125] In research on tragedies of the commons, political scientist Elinor Ostrom views humans "as fallible, boundedly rational, and norm-using. In complex settings, no one is able to do a complete analysis before actions are taken, but individuals learn from mistakes and are able to craft tools—including rules—to improve the structure of the repetitive situations they face."[126] Indeed, when large numbers of boundedly rational "agents" in computer simulation models are programmed to act on their fallible "internal models" and to learn from their mistakes in interacting with each other, the models confirm that complex adaptive systems "continue to evolve, and they steadily exhibit new forms of emergent behavior. History and context play a critical role" in understanding their behavior.[127]

Are existing intellectual tools adequate for adaptive management— including a coordinating committee for updating and using comprehensive maps to clarify priorities for operations, research, and education? The question arises because Holling wrote that answers to practical environmental and renewable resource issues are "not simple or consistent because we have just begun to develop the concepts, technology, and methods that can deal with the generic nature of the problems."[128] It would be more accurate to say that adequate (although always improvable) intellectual tools are not well known or applied in various specializations, especially those that are relatively new to the contextual, problem-oriented, multi-method outlook.

The need for such tools was anticipated long ago by social scientists who observed (rather than assumed) how human beings actually make decisions, in order to improve human rationality in practice. From his observations, Harold Lasswell developed the maximization postulate as the logical foundation for empirical inquiry in the policy sciences. The postulate holds that "living forms are predisposed to complete acts in ways that are perceived to leave the actor better off than if he had completed them differently. The postulate draws attention to the actor's own perceptions of the alternative act completions open to him in a given situation."[129] But no one is omniscient: the actor's own perceptions are somewhat mistaken, somewhat different from the perceptions of others, and subject to change through new insight and experience. Similarly, Herbert Simon formulated the principle of bounded rationality, emphasizing human cognitive constraints relative to the complexity of real-world problems. The first consequence of the principle is that "the intended rationality of an actor requires him to construct a simplified model of the real situation in order to deal with it. He behaves rationally with respect to this model, and such behavior is not even approximately optimal with respect to the real world."[130] Both Lasswell and Simon emphasized that the "internal models" (or perspectives) on which we act are not to be fixed, or given, or assumed for purposes of inquiry. They must be clarified through empirical inquiry into particular contexts, guided by the best-available conceptual and theoretical tools used as heuristics. The perspectives of all involved in community-based initiatives are an important part of harvesting experience.

In his 1956 Presidential Address to the American Political Science Association, Lasswell claimed that the conceptual and theoretical tools distilled from the main tradition of political and social thought by policy scientists were already adequate. In particular, he claimed that "our intellectual tools have been sufficiently sharp" to make largely correct appraisals of the consequences of science-based technologies for policy. He drew the inference that "within a rich theoretical tradition, the most significant task is to construct a continuing institutional activity by which central theory is related continuously to events as they unfold."[131] This is the distinctive purpose of the coordinating committee suggested above. The reference to "a rich theoretical tradition" presumes the primary purpose of policy inquiry is not rigorous proof of scientific generalizations for academics, but freedom through insight for decision makers. This freedom undermines generalizations and predictions made from generalizations when decision makers modify their overt behavior in light of their revised "internal models" or perspectives. As more specializations become more contextual, problem-oriented, and multi-method in outlook, they will develop their own intellectual tools to implement the same basic outlook.[132] Any attempt to standardize the tools across specializations would be both futile and unnecessary: in principle at least, many equivalent sets of tools can serve the purposes of policy inquiry, and it is possible to translate one set into another. This translation can be done with ease from a less comprehensive to a more comprehensive set, but with difficulty the other way around.

Finally, it is important to recognize that progress depends not only on empirical inquiry into particular contexts guided by adequate intellectual tools, but also on the local knowledge of participants in the initiatives.[133] Examples of local knowledge from previous chapters include the Wyoming ranchers' understanding of how to prevent transmission of brucellosis from wildlife to cattle, based on their first-hand experience in the Jackson Hole area; and irrigators' understanding of the unique hydrology of the Upper Clark Fork basin, based on their first-hand experience in the basin and later confirmed by professional hydrologists after it was questioned. Consider also the local knowledge gained by Michael Jackson, Michael Yost, and Steve Evans as they walked through the national forests around Quincy prior to the genesis of the Community Stability Proposal. Members of the Quincy Library Group later discovered, through similar observations, that certain areas had been misidentified as old growth in the Sierra Nevada Ecosystem Report.

It is time to open up natural resources management to laypersons with local knowledge, and to open up the concept of science itself insofar as policy is concerned. Scientists who believe that "policy must be scientific to be effective" might agree with Abraham Kaplan. "But to say scientific is not to speak [only] of the paraphernalia and techniques of the laboratory; it is to say realistic and rational—empirically grounded and self-corrective in application. Policy is scientific when it is formed by the free use of intelligence on the materials of experience."[134] This adaptation of science to policy purposes would reintegrate modern science with a much older science of the concrete, which is based on experience in particular contexts. The anthropologist Lévi-Strauss stated, "This science of the concrete . . . was no less scientific and its results no less genuine [than the exact natural sciences]. They were achieved ten thousand years earlier and still remain at the basis of our own civilization."[135]

In this chapter we have been harvesting experience from the case studies and other relevant sources to suggest how and why particular policies might be modified to help realize the potential of community-based initiatives. It is worthwhile in conclusion to step back from the particular policies of those most directly involved—participants in community-based initiatives and their supporters, organized interest groups, and researchers and educators—to review what may be at stake in the larger context.

If the diagnosis of current problems of governance in Chapter 1 is approximately correct, more of the same appears to be unsustainable. More social groups will be differentiated and interconnected through science-based technologies. More groups will organize themselves in and around government agencies to protect their interests through law and public policy. As competition intensifies on more policy issues, and more policy areas become congested, more groups will have to commit additional resources to realize smaller gains. The accumulation of such structural constraints over the past century, however, has already been sufficient to impede the process of finding common ground in more and more policy areas. The structural constraints on common-interest policies show up in gridlock, demosclerosis, single-issue politics, a Washington disconnect, and public distrust of government, among other problems of governance—and in growing pressures for constitutive reforms that cannot be discounted or ignored indefinitely. Some of these reforms, especially campaign finance reforms, are worth pursuing to help constrain special interests, even if they address symptoms rather than causes and raise questions of political feasibility and constitutionality. Other reform efforts—including more ballot initiatives, more violence, and the quest for a strong man to set aside politics— will create more problems than they solve. In short, there are reasons to project that problems of governance will worsen.

Americans may have no better alternative than harvesting experience on a continuous basis to realize the potential of community-based initiatives. We may have little choice as the proliferation of complex issues runs up against the time-and-attention constraints of a fixed twenty-four-hour day, forcing national leaders to leave more decisions to smaller communities by default. We are well aware that the processes of innovating, diffusing, and adapting community-based initiatives in natural resources and other policy areas are no panacea for constitutive reform: they are subject to various malfunctions, they are perceived (mistakenly or not) as threats by some established agencies and interest groups, and their aggregate contribution to constitutive reform cannot be predicted with any precision or confidence, particularly as the horizon extends a few years or more into the future.

Yet it is clear that each new community-based initiative need not start from scratch or repeat the mistakes of the past; researchers already have been harvesting experience for their policy purposes. And it is clear that each established interest group need not respond with a reflexive defense of an unsustainable structure of governance. Some have already accepted collaboration with community-based interests as expedient or principled. Limited predictability need not be taken as a reason for inaction. As Kaplan argued decades ago, "A mature man does not demand ironclad guarantees from God or nature, and seldom even from other men; and surely he does not deceive himself with illusions of certitude. . . . There is profound wisdom in the Americanism that in this world nothing is certain but death and taxes. We do not always remember that [Benjamin] Franklin wrote these words in a passage appraising the prospects of survival of the newly adopted Constitution. The courage of the men who established our republic was no whit lessened by their realistic perspectives on politics as a succession of calculated risks."[136] If enough contemporary Americans act with courage, in good faith, and with eyes open, we may be able to minimize the human and natural costs of a transformation in governance that appears to be unavoidable. And we may be able to create new structures of governance more capable of clarifying and securing common interests amid the multiplying complexity of society in the twenty-first century.

Notes

Chapter 1. Problems of Governance

1. Both Little Thunder and Fox are quoted in Patricia Walsh, "The Slaughter of Bison Opens Old Wounds," *High Country News* (June 9, 1997), p. 6.

2. James Brooke, "Yellowstone Bison Herd Cut in Half over Winter," *New York Times* (Apr. 13, 1997), p. 18.

3. This Interim Bison Management Plan and others like it become policies when they are authorized and implemented. Usage of "plan" and "management" under these circumstances is probably a legacy of scientific management from the Progressive era and is still preferred because the connotations are more scientific and less overtly political than the alternatives, "policy" and "politics."

4. Todd Wilkinson, "No Home on the Range," *High Country News* (Feb. 17, 1997), p. 9.

5. All three are quoted in Wilkinson, "No Home on the Range," pp. 1, 9, and 1, respectively.

6. Wilkinson, "No Home on the Range," p. 8.

7. Brooke, "Yellowstone Bison Herd Cut in Half over Winter."

8. For a more complete and detailed account of the bison management case, see Chapter 4. A concise source on this background is a draft report by the Montana Consensus Council, *Bison in the Greater Yellowstone Area: A Situation Assessment and Suggested Work Plan and Ground Rules* (Helena, Mont.: June 25, 1997).

9. Previously, the National Park Service had turned Yellowstone bison loose in the summer, rounded them up and fed them hay in the winter, and eventually processed some of them in the service's slaughterhouse in the Lamar Valley. Scott McMillion, "For Bison, It's Deja Vu All Over Again," *High Country News* (Feb. 17, 1997), p. 11.

10. APHIS Veterinary Services, "APHIS' Commitment to Resolving the Brucellosis Problem at Yellowstone," *Backgrounder* (Dec. 1994), p. 2.

11. 42 U.S.C. Sec. 4331(a) and Sec. 4332(2)(C). The Council on Environmental Quality provides information on NEPA at http://ceq.eh.doe.gov/nepa.

12. Sarah Van de Wettering, "NEPA: Environmental Analysis or Paralysis?" *Chronicle of Community* 3 (Spring 1999), p. 26. Many of the articles cited from *Chronicle of Community*, but not this one, have been republished in Philip Brick, Donald Snow, and Sarah Van de Wettering, eds., *Across the Great Divide: Explorations in Collaborative Conservation in the American West* (Washington, D.C.: Island, 2001).

13. Quoted in Todd Wilkinson, "Will the Bison Killing Resume Next Winter?," *High Country News* (June 9, 1997), p. 6.

14. Quoted in Jeff Gearino, "State Claims Right to Doctor Refuge Elk," *Casper Star-Tribune* (Feb. 19, 1998), pp. A1, A12.

15. Editors, "Bison Report Offers a Chance to Speak Up," *Bozeman Daily Chronicle* (June 18, 1998), p. 4.

16. *Draft Environmental Impact Statement (EIS) for the Interagency Bison Management Plan for the State of Montana and Yellowstone National Park* (Denver, Colo.: National Park Service, State of Montana, U.S. Forest Service, U.S. Animal & Plant Health Inspection Service, 1998). The draft EIS was released on June 5 and published in the *Federal Register* on June 18, 1998.

17. From the author's notes of a presentation at the Workshop on Governance and Natural Resources: New Models for the Twenty-first Century, Jackson, Wyo., Sept. 2–4, 1998. The workshop was organized by the Northern Rockies Conservation Cooperative in Jackson and funded by the Henry P. Kendall Foundation of Boston.

18. For details on litigation over bison management in greater Yellowstone, see Chapter 4.

19. *Record of Decision for Final Environmental Impact Statement and Bison Management Plan for the State of Montana and Yellowstone National Park* (Dec. 20, 2000). See also the multivolume *Bison Management Plan for the State of Montana and Yellowstone National Park: Final Environmental Impact Statement* (U.S. Department of the Interior, National Park Service, Aug. 2000).

20. *Record of Decision*, p. 43, which also notes that 2,974 commentors demanded that public lands "either be set aside for wildlife, or that they be used for bison and not cattle if there is a conflict"; and that 849 commentors "indicated the modified preferred alternative was . . . not a cost-effective approach to managing the risk of transmission. Several asked for a cost-effective plan, and noted the easiest way to achieve this was by managing cattle, not bison."

21. The Montana Consensus Council, *Bison in the Greater Yellowstone Area*, p. 5, concurs that "The agreement [of the Working Group] received little or no attention from public officials." The chairman of the Greater Yellowstone Interagency Brucellosis Committee was unaware of the Working Group's plan at the Symposium entitled "Where the Buffalo Roam: Finding the Common Ground," Buffalo Bill Historical Center, Cody, Wyo., Aug. 8–9, 1997.

22. Bison Management Citizen's Working Group, *Management of Yellowstone Bison*, with covering letter to Superintendent Robert D. Barbee, Yellowstone National Park (Bozeman, Mont.: May 15, 1991).

23. From a letter, dated Jan. 31, 1997, addressed to President Clinton, Secretary of Agriculture Glickman, Secretary of the Interior Babbitt, and Governor Geringer of Wyoming. The letter was signed by representatives of the Jackson Hole Alliance, the Greater Yellowstone Coalition, the Wyoming Wildlife Federation, and five ranchers, including the former U.S. Senator from Wyoming, Cliff P. Hansen.

24. Compare Robert A. Dahl, *After the Revolution?* (New Haven: Yale University Press, 1970), p. 26: "If . . . I believe that the personal choices of others have

equal dignity with my own and we must all therefore be counted as political equals, then I may choose to accept authority as legitimate if it expresses the personal choices of the greatest number in our association."

25. Harold D. Lasswell, "The Public Interest: Clarifying Principles of Content and Procedure," in Carl J. Friedrich, ed., *The Public Interest: Nomos V* (New York: Atherton, 1962), p. 60. Of course, all claims are not equally valid in terms of the evidence or equally appropriate in terms of larger goals of the body politic.

26. Thus "community-based initiative" here is restricted to a "community of place," defined by a shared territory that is local in scope and includes many different interests (e.g., economic growth *and* conservation *and* others). What has elsewhere been called a "community of interest" is called here an "interest group," defined by a shared interest (e.g., economic growth *or* conservation) pursued across territorial boundaries. There is little really new about interest groups in American politics, apart from their proliferation over recent decades.

27. As conceived here, a "community-based initiative" can be further distinguished from related concepts that are often used to refer to the same phenomena but to emphasize different characteristics. The most important of these is "collaborative conservation," which emphasizes collaborative strategies to realize conservation interests and thereby de-emphasizes strategies other than collaboration and interests other than conservation. See, for example, Donald Snow, "What Are We Talking About?" *Chronicle of Community* 3 (Spring 1999), pp. 33–37; Barb Cestero, *Beyond the Hundredth Meeting: A Field Guide to Collaborative Conservation on the West's Public Lands* (Tucson: Sonoran Institute, 1999); and the National Academy of Public Administration, *Resolving the Paradox of Environmental Protection: A Report to Congress* (Washington, D.C.: National Academy of Public Administration, 1997), especially p. 107.

28. The approach taken here draws upon core works in the policy sciences, most notably Harold D. Lasswell and Myres S. McDougal, *Jurisprudence for a Free Society: Studies in Law, Science, and Policy* (New Haven and Dordrecht: New Haven Press and Martinus Nijoff, 1992); Myres S. McDougal, Harold D. Lasswell, and W. Michael Reisman, "The World Constitutive Process of Authoritative Decision," in Myres S. McDougal and W. Michael Reisman, eds., *International Law Essays* (Mineola, N.Y.: Foundation, 1981), pp. 191–286; and Harold D. Lasswell, *A Pre-View of Policy Sciences* (New York: Elsevier, 1971). The preface to *A Pre-View* notes the origins of the policy sciences in the pragmatism of John Dewey. For an introduction, see Robert B. Westbrook, *John Dewey and American Democracy* (Ithaca, N.Y.: Cornell University Press, 1991). For background on the next section, see also Lasswell, "The Public Interest," and Abraham Kaplan, *American Ethics and Public Policy* (New York: Oxford University Press, 1963).

29. "At net cost to the community as a whole" is an important consideration in distinguishing special interests from common interests. Exclusive common interests are of much greater importance to some members of the community than to others, but nevertheless of some importance to all. Inclusive common interests are of considerable importance to all community members. See Lasswell and McDougal, *Jurisprudence for a Free Society*, p. 360.

30. APHIS Veterinary Services, *Backgrounder* (Dec. 1994).

31. Compare Aldo Leopold, *A Sand County Almanac: And Sketches from Here and There* (New York: Oxford University Press, 1989), pp. 203–204: "All ethics so far evolved rest upon a single premise: that the individual is a member of a community of interdependent parts. . . . The land ethic simply enlarges the boundary of the community to include soils, waters, plants, and animals, or collectively: the land." This concept of a "community" is also similar to Dewey's concept of a "pub-

lic" as developed by Westbrook, *John Dewey and American Democracy*, in chapter 9, "The Phantom Public." A community in this sense is *not* defined by the jurisdictional boundaries that frustrate governance amid the increasing number of interdependent parts in modern society.

32. McDougal, Lasswell, and Reisman, "The World Constitutive Process," p. 206, affirm that "whenever value consequences in significant degree are involved for more than one participant, the common interest is at stake."

33. See, for example, Timothy P. Duane, "Community Participation in Ecosystem Management," *Ecology Law Quarterly* 24 (1997), pp. 771 ff. This application of the principle of affected interests is addressed in Chapter 5.

34. These judgments of competence and economy in participation may be mistaken, but in a free society we make them for ourselves and for those with whom we identify.

35. Dahl, *After the Revolution*, pp. 64, 66.

36. Ibid., p. 102.

37. On the dynamics of issue and community expansion, see Harold D. Lasswell and Abraham Kaplan, *Power and Society: A Framework for Political and Social Inquiry* (New Haven: Yale University Press, 1950), pp. 103–107; and E. E. Schattschneider, *The Semisovereign People: A Realist's View of Democracy in America* (Hinsdale, Ill.: Dryden, 1975). Like Dahl and other realists, Schattschneider emphasizes the importance for democracy of competence and economy in the making of policy decisions.

38. See Richard J. Bernstein, *Beyond Objectivism and Relativism* (Philadelphia: University of Pennsylvania Press, 1985). It should be noted that "relativism" in the title refers to a radical relativism that assumes anything goes if no one knows for sure, not the disciplined relativism of pragmatists such as Abraham Kaplan.

39. For a more comprehensive set of tests compatible with these three, see Lasswell's working criteria for appraisal of decision processes in *A Pre-View of Policy Sciences*, pp. 85–87; and McDougal, Lasswell, and Reisman, "The World Constitutive Process," pp. 219–21.

40. N. F. Cheville and D. R. McCullough, *Brucellosis in the Greater Yellowstone Area: Executive Summary* (Washington, D.C.: National Research Council, 1997). The report, however, also concluded that under future circumstances "it is likely that brucellosis can be eliminated from [the Park] without loss of large numbers of bison or loss of genetic diversity." Evidently, the science of bison management is inconclusive, and may be employed selectively by different interest groups for their own purposes.

41. McDougal, Lasswell, and Reisman, "The World Constitutive Process," p. 202. See also Robert E. Goodin, "Institutionalizing the Public Interest: The Defense of Deadlock and Beyond," *American Political Science Review* 90 (June 1996), pp. 331–43.

42. McDougal, Lasswell, and Reisman, "The World Constitutive Process," p. 207.

43. This would amount to goal displacement in the technical sense: what were means (the tests) displace the original ends (judgments about the common interest). The operational definition of standard measures to replace judgments of the common interest would be an example.

44. The notion of bounded rationality and its implications are developed at length in the works of Herbert A. Simon. For an introduction, see his *Reason in Human Affairs* (Stanford: Stanford University Press, 1983).

45. This fallacy is exposed at length in Bernstein, *Beyond Objectivism and Relativism*.

46. Letter of July 9, 1998 to workshop participants from Peyton Curlee, executive director, Northern Rockies Conservation Cooperative, Jackson, Wyoming.

47. The discussion is reconstructed from notes taken by the author and by Christine H. Colburn at the Workshop on Governance and Natural Resources: New Models for the Twenty-first Century.

48. Lasswell, *A Pre-View of Policy Sciences*, p. 89. Explosive protest is not far-fetched in natural resources policy. A pipe bomb blew a hole in the office of Forest Service District Ranger Guy Pense in Carson City, Nevada in March 1995. Several months later a van in the driveway of his home was dynamited. See also Charles McCoy, "Catron County, N.M., Leads a Nasty Revolt over Eco-Protection," *Wall Street Journal* (Jan. 3, 1995), p. 1.

49. Developers exclude other interests as a matter of principle when they presume that their economic interest should prevail regardless of the context. So do environmentalists when they presume that their conservation interest should prevail regardless of the context. On the pathology of managing for a single target variable according to a particular interest, see Lance H. Gunderson, C. S. Holling, and Stephen S. Light, eds., *Barriers and Bridges to the Renewal of Ecosystems and Institutions* (New York: Columbia University Press, 1995), p. 8. On puritanism as pushing any virtue so far that it becomes a vice, see Richard A. Shweder, "Puritans in High-Top Sneakers," *New York Times* (Sept. 27, 1993), p. A13.

50. Robert A. Dahl, *The New American Political (Dis)Order* (Berkeley: Institute of Governmental Studies, University of California, 1994), p. 5. On the limitations of this Madisonian system for governance in the American West, see Daniel Kemmis, *Community and the Politics of Place* (Norman: University of Oklahoma Press, 1990), and Hanna J. Cortner and Margaret Moote, *The Politics of Ecosystem Management* (Washington, D.C.: Island, 1999).

51. Dahl, *The New American Political (Dis)Order*, p. 9.

52. Carl J. Friedrich, quoted in Lasswell and Kaplan, *Power and Society*, p. 243.

53. Richard L. Merritt, *Symbols of American Community, 1735–1775* (New Haven: Yale University Press, 1967).

54. Robert Wiebe, *The Search for Order, 1877–1920* (New York: Hill and Wang, 1967), p. xiii.

55. Stephen Skowronek, *Building a New American State: The Expansion of National Administrative Capacities, 1877–1920* (Cambridge: Cambridge University Press, 1982), p. 30.

56. Ibid., p. 16.

57. Wiebe, *The Search for Order*, p. xiv.

58. Skowronek, *Building a New American State*, p. 287.

59. Ibid., p. 14. See also David Osborne and Ted Gaebler, *Reinventing Government: How the Entrepreneurial Spirit Is Transforming the Public Sector* (Reading, Mass.: Addison-Wesley, 1992), especially pp. 12–16.

60. Harold D. Lasswell, "The Garrison State," *American Journal of Sociology* 46 (1941), p. 458. This article is one of several works on the skill revolution, a construct of the world revolution of our time. For an introduction, see Ronald D. Brunner and William Ascher, "Science and Social Responsibility," *Policy Sciences* 25 (1992), pp. 295–331, beginning at p. 303.

61. Lasswell, "The Garrison State," p. 458.

62. Paul Slovic, "Perceived Risk, Trust, and Democracy," *Risk Analysis* 13 (1993), pp. 675–82.

63. See Thomas Petzinger, Jr., *The New Pioneers: The Men and Women Who*

Are Transforming the Workplace and the Marketplace (New York: Simon & Schuster, 1999). Compare Petzinger's summary (p. 17) with Wiebe's summary (quoted in the text) of the bureaucratic order rising a century ago: "The new pioneers celebrate individuality over conformity among their employees and customers alike. They deploy technology to distribute rather than consolidate authority and creativity. They compete through resilience instead of resistance, through adaptation instead of control. In a time of dizzying complexity and change, they realize that tightly drawn strategies become brittle while shared purpose endures." See also Gifford Pinchot and Elizabeth Pinchot, *The End of Bureaucracy and the Rise of the Intelligent Organization* (San Francisco: Berrett-Koehler, 1993).

64. From the transcript published in the *Washington Post* (Jan. 21, 1981), p. A34.

65. From the transcript published in the *Washington Post* (Jan. 24, 1996), p. A13.

66. Thomas E. Mann, "Is the Era of Big Government Over?" *Public Perspective* 9 (February/March 1998), p. 27. See p. 30 in the same issue on "Confidence in the National Government Has Not Rebounded in the Nineties" for data. On current problems in governance, in addition to the works cited below, see John E. Chubb and Paul E. Peterson, eds., *Can the Government Govern?* (Washington, D.C.: Brookings Institution, 1989); Ronald D. Brunner, "Myth and American Politics," *Policy Sciences* 27 (1994), pp. 1–18; and C. Eugene Steuerle et al., *The Government We Deserve: Responsive Democracy and Changing Expectations* (Washington, D.C.: Urban Institute, 1998).

67. James L. Sundquist, ed., *Beyond Gridlock? Prospects for Governance in the Clinton Years—and After* (Washington, D.C.: Brookings Institution, 1993).

68. Jonathan Rauch, *Demosclerosis: The Silent Killer of American Government* (New York: Times Books, 1994), p. 18. Rauch relies on his own reporting and on Mancur Olson, *The Rise and Decline of Nations* (New Haven: Yale University Press, 1982).

69. Dale Bumpers, "How the Sunshine Harmed Congress," *New York Times* (Jan. 3, 1999), p. 9. The effects of openness are explored further in Neal Gabler, "Behind the Political Curtain," *New York Times* (Dec. 10, 2000), sec. 4, p. 1.

70. Robert J. Samuelson, "Washington Disconnected," *Washington Post National Weekly Edition* (Jan. 11, 1999), p. 26. See also Frank Rich, "All the Presidents Stink," *New York Times Magazine* (Aug. 15, 1999), pp. 42 ff., which refers to "the Great Disconnect of '98, in which those hermetically sealed in the Beltway bubble expressed daily shock and bafflement that the great unwashed did not follow their moral example and political prognostications by guillotining a President who soiled his office."

71. Quoted in David S. Broder, "Jerry Ford's Sense," *Washington Post* (June 16, 1999), p. A37.

72. Mann, "Is the Era of Big Government Over?" p. 29.

73. Herbert Kaufman, *Are Government Organizations Immortal?* (Washington, D.C.: Brookings Institution, 1976), p. 66. This work presents data on a sample of federal agencies that excluded the Department of Defense, the U.S. Postal Service, and more than fifty independent agencies for reasons of practicality or representativeness. The sample included 421 agencies that existed in 1923 or were created in the fifty years between 1923 and 1973. Only twenty-seven of the agencies in the sample were terminated by 1973. Kaufman concludes, however, with a section on "How Little Is Known"—a conclusion affirmed in general in Patrick D. Larkey, Chandler Stolp, and Mark Winer, "Theorizing about the Growth of Government: A Research Assessment," *Journal of Public Policy* 1 (May 1981), pp. 157–220.

74. Kaufman, *Are Government Organizations Immortal?* p. 67.

75. Ibid., table 6, p. 48, and fig. 4, p. 62.

76. Rauch, *Demosclerosis,* p. 17.

77. The society grew modestly and steadily through the 1960s. Rauch, *Demosclerosis,* p. 42; Fig. 5, p. 43; and Fig. 1, p. 39. On the expansion of international interest groups, from about 6,000 in 1990 to about 26,000 in 1999, see "The Non-Governmental Order," in *Economist* (Dec. 11, 1999), pp. 20–21; on the expansion of their activities, see "Sins of the Secular Missionaries," in *Economist* (Jan. 29, 2000), pp. 25–27.

78. Rauch, *Demosclerosis,* p. 47.

79. *The United States Government Manual 1998/1999* (Washington, D.C.: Government Printing Office, June 1998), p. 311.

80. Ibid., p. 316.

81. Ibid., p. 136.

82. APHIS Veterinary Services, p. 1.

83. *The United States Government Manual,* p. 121.

84. The counterparts of the U.S. Fish and Wildlife Service are the Wyoming Department of Game and Fish, the Idaho Department of Fish and Game, and the Montana Department of Fish, Wildlife, and Parks. The latter lost jurisdiction over brucellosis in wildlife to the Montana Department of Livestock in 1995. The counterparts of agencies within the U.S. Department of Agriculture are the Montana Department of Livestock, the Idaho Department of Agriculture, and the Wyoming Livestock Board.

85. Jim Geringer et al., *Memorandum of Understanding Creating the Greater Yellowstone Interagency Brucellosis Committee* (1995), Part Ic.

86. *The United States Government Manual,* p. 96.

87. Of course these are not the only interest groups involved. For example, the Fund for Animals, a major litigator in bison management, did not support the Citizens' Plan. Organized ranching and farming interests in bison management tend to work relatively quietly through sympathetic government agencies and officials.

88. From the written comments of Jeanne-Marie Souvigney at the symposium "Where the Buffalo Roam: Finding the Common Ground," p. 1.

89. For an introduction to FACA, see Thomas Brendler, "The Federal Advisory Committee Act," *Chronicle of Community* 1 (August 1996), pp. 44–47. See also Stephen P. Croley and William F. Funk, "The Federal Advisory Committee Act and Good Government," *Yale Journal of Regulation* 14 (1997), pp. 461 ff. The author is indebted to Erica Adshead for a seminar paper on FACA.

90. George Cameron Coggins, Charles F. Wilkinson, and John D. Leshy, *Federal Public Land and Resources Law,* 3d ed. (Westbury, N.Y.: Foundation, 1993), p. 8. See also Jeffrey L. Pressman and Aaron B. Wildavsky, *Implementation: How Great Expectations in Washington are Dashed in Oakland* (Berkeley: University of California Press, 1973), and the work of Charles Lester on coastal management in California.

91. George Cameron Coggins, Charles F. Wilkinson, and John D. Leshy, *Public Land and Resources Law,* 3d ed. (Westbury, N.Y.: Foundation, 1997), p. iii.

92. Lasswell and McDougal, *Jurisprudence for a Free Society,* p. 26.

93. Ronald C. Moe, "The 'Reinventing Government' Exercise: Misinterpreting the Problem, Misjudging the Consequences," *Public Administration Review* 54 (March–April 1994), p. 112. This is a vigorous defense of the administrative management paradigm in opposition to "reinventing government" as proposed by Os-

borne and Gaebler, and partially incorporated into the National Performance Review led by Vice President Gore in 1993.

94. They are listed and very briefly summarized in Appendix E, pp. 750–61, of volume one of the final EIS (August 2000), titled *Bison Management for the State of Montana and Yellowstone National Park*.

95. Mark Sagoff, "The View from Quincy Library: Civic Engagement in Environmental Problem Solving," in Robert K. Fullinwider, ed., *Civil Society, Democracy, and Civic Renewal* (Lanham, Md.: Rowman & Littlefield, 1999), pp. 151–83, at p. 164. As Osborne and Gaebler observe, *Reinventing Government*, p. 12: "It is hard to imagine today, but 100 years ago the word *bureaucracy* meant something positive . . . something to take the place of the arbitrary exercise of power." Emphasis in the original. See also Pinchot and Pinchot, *The End of Bureaucracy*.

96. Bureau of Reclamation, *How to Get Things Done: Decision Process Guidebook* (Summer 1998), p. 22.

97. On scientific management in the Progressive era, see Samuel P. Hayes, *Conservation and the Gospel of Efficiency: The Progressive Conservation Movement, 1890–1920* (Cambridge: Harvard University Press, 1959).

98. Coggins, Wilkinson, and Leshy, *Federal Public Land and Resources Law*, p. 8.

99. Daniel Lewis, "The Trailblazer," *New York Times Magazine* (June 13, 1999), p. 52. See also U.S. General Accounting Office, *Forest Service Decision-Making: A Framework for Improving Performance*, GAS/RCED-97-71 (Washington, D.C.: U.S. General Accounting Office).

100. On yesterday's Forest Service, see Herbert Kaufman, *The Forest Ranger: A Study in Administrative Behavior* (Baltimore: Johns Hopkins University Press, 1960).

101. Constitutional amendments are a rough gauge of the demand for constitutive reforms and for resistance to them. According to Dale Bumpers in the op-ed cited, "more constitutional amendments have been offered in the past 32 years (5,449) than in the first 173 years of our history, virtually all of them ill-conceived, trivial and politically driven. To the Senate's credit, not one has been approved by the required two-thirds vote in the past 24 years."

102. David D. Chrislip, "Transforming Politics," *Chronicle of Community* 2 (Autumn 1997), pp. 28–35, evaluates "collaborative initiatives" along with campaign reform and other prominent proposals for constitutive reform.

103. Dahl, *The New American Political (Dis)Order*, p. 16. For reasons explained below, Dahl refers to the structure as "the fragmented plebiscitary order."

104. For a promising proposal to reduce candidates' demands for campaign contributions, see Max Frankel, "You Can't Dam the Money," *New York Times Magazine* (Feb. 20, 2000), pp. 25–26.

105. David S. Broder, "A Battle of Bank Accounts," *Washington Post* (July 7, 1999), p. A19.

106. David S. Broder, "Escape from the Term Limits Trap," *Washington Post* (Feb. 19, 1997), p. A21.

107. *Buckley v. Valeo*, 424 U.S. 1 [1976]. See also Daniel R. Ortiz, "Constitutional Restrictions on Campaign Finance Regulation," in Anthony Corrado et al., eds., *Campaign Finance Reform: A Sourcebook* (Washington, D.C.: Brookings Institution, 1997), pp. 63–92.

108. Rauch, *Demosclerosis*, p. 164.

109. Congressional Budget Office, *Using Performance Measures in the Federal Budget Process* (Washington, D.C.: Congressional Budget Office, July 1993), p. ix.

110. Ibid., p. xii.

111. Donald F. Kettl and John J. DiIulio, eds., *Inside the Reinvention Machine: Appraising Governmental Performance* (Washington, D.C.: Brookings Institution, 1995), pp. 64–65.

112. Mann, "Is the Era of Big Government Over?" p. 29.

113. Mary Walton, *The Deming Management Method* (New York: Perigee Books, 1986), p. 36.

114. W. Edwards Deming, quoted in Mary Walton, "Doing Without Performance Appraisals," in *Deming Management at Work* (New York: Perigee Books, 1991), p. 219.

115. James C. Collins and Jerry I. Porras, *Built to Last: Successful Habits of Visionary Companies* (New York: HarperBusiness, 1997), p. 55.

116. V. F. Ridgway, "Dysfunctional Consequences of Performance Measures," *Administrative Science Quarterly* 1 (1956), pp. 240–47. Of course, quantitative performance measures can be useful if supplemented by qualitative understanding of the particular context and by judgment in application.

117. Walter Lippmann, *Public Opinion* (New York: Free Press, 1965), p. 233, first published in 1922. On the co-optation of scientific management by political interests in and outside the Forest Service, and by timber production interests in particular, see Paul W. Hirt, *A Conspiracy of Optimism: Management of the National Forests since World War Two* (Lincoln: University of Nebraska Press, 1994).

118. The three decades with the highest number of statewide initiatives on the ballot are the 1910s (290), 1980s (276), and 1990s (323), according to M. Dane Waters, "A Century Later—The Experiment with Citizen-Initiated Legislation Continues," *Public Perspective* 10 (December–January 1998), p. 128. The decades with the lowest number are the 1940s (133), 1950s (108), and 1960s (79). On the evaluation of ballot initiatives, see Peter Schrag, *Paradise Lost: California's Experience, America's Future* (New York: New Press, 1998).

119. The rise of militias prompted a new edition of David H. Bennett, *The Party of Fear: The American Far Right from Nativism to the Militia Movement* (New York: Vintage Books, 1995).

120. Sean Wilentz, "Bombs Bursting in Air, Still," *New York Times Magazine* (June 25, 1995), pp. 40–41.

121. William Schneider, "Wooing Ross Perot's Voters for 1996," *National Journal* (Jan. 16, 1993), p. 166.

122. Rauch, *Demosclerosis*, p. 193.

123. Jody Powell, press secretary to President Carter, quoted in Sundquist, *Beyond Gridlock?* p. 22.

124. Dahl, *The New American Political (Dis)Order*, p. 2. Emphasis in the original.

125. Ibid., pp. 1, 2. Emphasis in the original.

126. At the most general level, see propositions about the probability, direction, and form (partial incorporation) of ideological change in world politics, in Harold D. Lasswell, Daniel Lerner, and Ithiel de Sola Pool, *The Comparative Study of Symbols: An Introduction* (Stanford: Stanford University Press, 1952), ch. 1. For examples of the pattern in various policy areas, see Ronald D. Brunner, "Decentralized Energy Policies," *Public Policy* 28 (Winter 1980), pp. 71–91; Osborne and Gaebler, *Reinventing Government;* Hedrick Smith, *Rethinking America: A New Game Plan from the American Innovators: Schools, Business, People, Work* (New York: Random House, 1995); and Lisbeth B. Schorr, *Common Purpose: Strengthening Families and Neighborhoods to Rebuild America* (New York: Anchor Books, 1997).

127. Donald Snow, "What Are We Talking About?" p. 34.

128. Donald Snow, "Coming Home," *Chronicle of Community* 1 (Autumn 1996), pp. 40–43, at p. 41.

129. Snow, "What Are We Talking About?" p. 34.

130. Snow's characterizations of the book in "Coming Home," p. 41.

131. Douglas Kenney, *Resource Management at the Watershed Level: An Assessment of the Changing Federal Role in the Emerging Era of Community-Based Watershed Management*, Report to the Western Water Policy Review Advisory Commission (Boulder, Colo.: Natural Resources Law Center, October 1997), p. 1. For more on the scope of the collaborative movement, see Cestero, *Beyond the Hundredth Meeting;* Julia M. Wondolleck and Steven L. Yaffe, *Making Collaboration Work: Lessons from Innovation in Natural Resource Management* (Washington, D.C.: Island, 2000); and Philip Brick, Donald Snow, and Sarah Van de Wettering, eds., *Across the Great Divide: Explorations in Collaborative Conservation and the American West* (Washington, D.C.: Island, 2001), which reprints many of the articles from *Chronicle of Community* cited here.

132. Kemmis spoke at the Boulder, Colorado, public library, Jan. 31, 1998, in a conversation sponsored by the Center of the American West of the University of Colorado.

133. See Brunner, "Decentralized Energy Policies," and the congressional hearings cited there, for more on this case and on the Energy 1990 case in Seattle, in which consensus on a policy that advanced the common interest of a place-based community also followed a heated conflict won by environmentalists.

134. See "More Talk, Less Tension over Timber," in a special section by the Ford Foundation in *Governing* (1998), p. A16, announcing the awards. The author is grateful for seminar papers on this case by Zoe Miller and by Donna Walrath Tucker and colleagues, whose work on the case continues.

135. Hedrick Smith, "Preparing Students for the World of Jobs," *New York Times* (Apr. 20, 1995), p. A19. For more on this case and others like it, see Smith's book cited above.

136. In "Coming Home," p. 40, Snow emphasizes the limitations of collaborative groups: "consensus-based processes are not an unconditional good, are apt to be effective in only limited circumstances, are terribly inadequate in many issues (perhaps the majority of issues) now affecting the West's natural environment, and are necessarily undergirded by the conflict-ridden, traditional political debate which these very processes of consensus seem designed to replace." Other kinds of community-based initiatives might compensate for such limitations within the same constraints.

137. This account is adapted from Ronald D. Brunner and Tim W. Clark, "A Practice-Based Approach to Ecosystem Management," *Conservation Biology* 11 (February 1997), pp. 48–58, and based on Lasswell, Lerner, and Pool, *The Comparative Study of Symbols*.

138. Compare Smith, "Preparing Students for the World of Jobs," which generalizes a strategy for educational policy that could be generalized further to natural resources: "With notable successes in hand, the educational challenge today is to capitalize on our best models, to disseminate the best ideas of America's innovators and replicate them nationwide."

139. The beginning of a backlash may be detected, for example, in Douglas Kenney, "Are Community-Based Watershed Groups Really Effective?" *Chronicle of Community* 3 (Winter 1999), pp. 33–37.

140. This point is developed in Ronald D. Brunner, "Predictions and Policy Decisions," *Technological Forecasting and Social Change* 62 (1999), pp. 73–78.

141. Pinchot and Pinchot, *The End of Bureaucracy*, p. 7.

142. George Cameron Coggins, "Of Californicators, Quislings, and Crazies: Some Perils of Devolved Collaboration," *Chronicle of Community* 2 (Winter 1998), pp. 27–33, at p. 30.

143. Ibid., p. 33.

144. Ibid., p. 28.

145. Michael McCloskey, "Concerns Over the Push to Do Business Collaboratively," Remarks at a forum in Missoula, Montana, on Mar. 5, 1997.

146. Ibid.

147. Michael McCloskey, "The Skeptic: Collaboration Has Its Limits," *High Country News* 28 (May 13, 1996).

148. Ibid.

149. In "Abandoned by the Roadside," *Chronicle of Community* 3 (Autumn 1998), pp. 31–36, at p. 32; Jim Burchfield likewise complains that "Collaborative stewardship [in the Forest Service] has been shamefully and narrowly portrayed as a replacement for decision-making procedures, opening it to unrelenting criticism, especially from environmental interests."

150. Coggins, "Of Californicators, Quislings, and Crazies," p. 27. McCloskey, however, concludes his "Concerns Over the Push to Do Business Collaboratively" with the observation that "under the right circumstances, CP [collaborative processes] might be a useful tool."

151. Quoted in Lasswell and Kaplan, *Power and Society*, p. 107n.

152. The revival of politics and the public order is sometimes assumed to depend on the revival of civil society. The relationship tends to be reversed, however, where citizens in community-based initiatives assert themselves in policy decisions important enough to justify investments of their time, attention, and other resources. On civil society, see E. J. Dionne, Jr., ed., *Community Works: The Revival of Civil Society in America* (Washington, D.C.: Brookings Institution, 1998).

153. In *The New American Political (Dis)Order*, p. 22, Dahl argues against major reforms from the top down because "judgments about alternatives still rest too heavily on speculation to justify major constitutional revamping."

154. To describe these structures, we have adapted the main constitutive categories and questions from Lasswell and McDougal, *Jurisprudence for a Free Society*, pp. 1137–38 and elsewhere. Participants: Who was authorized to participate in which decisions in the initiative? Perspectives: What basic policies were sought? What interests of participants were relevant to those policies? Situations: How were interactions among participants organized? Resources: How was authority distributed among them? How were resources obtained? Strategies: How were resources used by participants to influence policy outcomes? Outcomes: What were the policy decisions affected? Effects: For what intended and unintended effects were participants responsible and accountable? The categories may also be used to compare structures of governance.

155. An appraisal of policy outcomes is necessary to complete an appraisal of a decision-making structure. Outcomes and structures are interdependent but only to some extent. Other factors do matter. Hence an appraisal of one is no adequate substitute for an appraisal of the other.

156. Gerald Mueller, "Lesson from the Clark Fork" (Remarks of Gerald Mueller to the Northwestern University Dispute Resolution Center, colloquium, Apr. 5, 1995), p. 3.

Chapter 2. Water Management and the Upper Clark Fork Steering Committee

1. Norman Maclean, *A River Runs Through It and Other Stories* (Chicago: University of Chicago Press, 1976).

2. For an overview of research and projects on the Upper Clark Fork, see United States Environmental Protection Agency, *Clark Fork–Pend Orille Basin Water Quality Study* (1993).

3. "Water" judges are appointed to hear water cases in the state of Montana. Other Western states have similar systems to manage heavy loads of cases focused on interpretations of earlier water decisions, state statutes, and rights and allocation. A decision by a water judge can be appealed to the appellate court.

4. MCA 85-2-338.

5. Hydropower generation is one exception, because it was considered a beneficial use. Hydropower producers in the Upper Clark Fork basin could apply for rights to water that would then remain in the streambed.

6. Interview with Audrey Aspholm, Mar. 12, 1999, Anaconda, Mont.

7. *Irwin v. Phillips*, 1855: 5 Cal. 140, 146. See also Charles F. Wilkinson, *Crossing the Next Meridian* (Washington, D.C.: Island, 1992).

8. John Wesley Powell, who traveled down the Colorado River in 1869, noted that the Mormons in Utah were an exception. They shared their water according to supply and need. The traditional "acequia" distribution systems of Hispanic communities in parts of the southwest were also temporary exceptions to prior appropriation. Wallace Stegner, *Beyond the Hundredth Meridian* (New York: Penguin Books, 1954).

9. Wilkinson, *Crossing the Next Meridian*.

10. As early as 1901, dams were providing hydropower for industries in the Upper Clark Fork basin. Upper Clark Fork Steering Committee, *Upper Clark Fork River Basin Water Management Plan* (1994); Wilkinson, *Crossing the Next Meridian*.

11. James D. Crammond, "Leasing Water Rights for Instream Flow Uses: A Survey of Water Transfer Policy, Practices, and Problems in the Pacific Northwest," *Environmental Law* 26 (Spring 1996), pp. 225–63; Karen A. Russell, "Wasting Water in the Northwest: Eliminating Waste as a Way of Restoring Stream Flows," *Environmental Law* 27 (Spring 1997), pp. 151–201.

12. In *Winters v. United States*, the judge ruled that "the indians [*sic*] had command of the lands and the waters—command of all their beneficial use, whether kept for hunting, and grazing roving herds of stock, or turned to agriculture and the arts of civilization," even though homesteaders were the first to divert water for consumptive use. 207 U.S. 564 (1908).

13. Upper Clark Fork Steering Committee, *Water Management Plan*; Gerald Mueller, "Lesson from the Clark Fork" (Remarks of Gerald Mueller to the Northwestern University Dispute Resolution Center, colloquium, Apr. 5, 1995); Interview with Jim Dinsmore, July 29, 1998, Drummond, Mont.

14. The actual distribution of water is self-monitored by water rights owners except in times of low flow. Self-monitoring, combined with the tremendous financial and human resources that would be necessary to keep track of water allocation in such a large state, make it impossible for state water resource managers to know exactly what water users are doing all of the time. The Montana Power Company engages in informal decision making in water allocation. The company holds senior rights on the downstream dam of Upper Clark Fork, but does not insist that its full rights be met since a "call" on this water would result in expensive litigation that would harm many of its customers. If the utility were to demand

that its share of instream flow make it to their dams, junior rights holders up the river would have to stop irrigating.

15. Interview with Mike Mclane, July 30, 1998, Helena, Mont.

16. C. Von Reichert and James Sylvester, "Population Dynamics in Montana," *Montana Business Quarterly* 35 (January 1997), p. 10.

17. Paul E. Polzin, "Montana's Communities in 2010," *Montana Business Quarterly* 35 (April 1997), p. 2; Von Reichert and Sylvester, "Population Dynamics in Montana."

18. Holland and Hart, L.L.P., "Employment Figures Paint a Rosy Picture," *Montana Employment Law Letter* 2 (November 1997), p. 10.

19. Low stream flows increase the concentration of nutrients and other pollutants. In turn, high instream levels can dilute nutrients, and instantly improve water quality if the amount of pollutants remains constant.

20. U.S. Environmental Protection Agency, *Clark Fork–Pend Orille Basin Water Quality Study*.

21. MWC 85–2.

22. Interview with Ole Ueland, Mar. 12, 1999, Silver Bow, Mont.

23. Under prior appropriation, water had to be put to beneficial use in order for the right to be secured. The reservations acknowledged that the water would not actually be put to use until some future time, providing a legal protection for that right until the water could be used beneficially. Montana Department of Natural Resources and Conservation (DNRC), "Water Rights in Montana" (December 1997). Available from DNRC, P.O. Box 201601, Helena, Mont., 59620–1601.

24. Interview with Stan Bradshaw, July 30, 1998, Helena, Mont.; Interview with Mike Mclane, July 30, 1998.

25. Interview with Mike Mclane, July 30, 1998; Telephone interview with Donald Snow, Jan. 12, 2001.

26. Interview with Dennis Workman, Mar. 12, 1999, Missoula, Mont.

27. Interview with Holly Franz, July 29, 1998, Helena, Mont.

28. The water reservations that DFWP and Granite Conservation applied for were not "wet" water, which meant that a reservation did not guarantee delivery of water because the mainstem and tributaries were largely overallocated. The only years that their reservation might be fulfilled would be those of high precipitation.

29. Interview with Donald Snow, Mar. 13, 1999, Missoula, Mont.; Donald Snow, "Montana's Clark Fork: A New Story for a Hardworking River," in Philip Brick, Donald Snow, and Sarah Van de Wettering, eds., *Across the Great Divide: Exploration in Collaborative Conservation in the American West* (Washington, D.C.: Island, 2001.)

30. Interview with Stan Bradshaw, July 30, 1998.

31. Upper Clark Fork Basin Water Allocation Task Force meeting summaries, Oct. 5, 1990; Dec. 3–4, 1990; Jan. 15–16, 1991; Feb. 5–6, 1991; Mar. 7, 1991; May 7, 1991.

32. Upper Clark Fork Steering Committee, *Upper Clark Fork Water News*, vols. 1(1)–3(1).

33. The exception to the closure also included expansion of zero-consumption hydropower generation and storage for beneficial uses. Upper Clark Fork Steering Committee, *Water Management Plan*, p. 4.

34. Interview with Jim Dinsmore, July 29, 1998.

35. Upper Clark Fork River Basin Steering Committee, *Report to the 1999 Montana Legislature*, 1999.

36. Interview with Joe Aldegaire, July 31, 1998, Missoula, Mont.

37. Flood irrigation in the spring in the Flint Creek watershed fills natural

alluvial aquifers, which "store" flows during heavy run-off and release them in drier months. DNRC; *Flint Creek Return Flow Study*, Montana Bureau of Mines and Geology Open-File Report 364, 1997.

38. To bring Western waters in compliance with this challenging water quality standard, the Environmental Protection Agency required states to create their own TMDL plans and to implement them within ten years. Because TMDL-compliance requires attention to nonpoint source pollution, such as run-off from a pasture or a suburban lawn, it is going to be one of the most difficult water quality standards to meet.

39. Avista owns a dam on the border of Idaho and Montana. The state began negotiating with Avista because of concerns that if the company put a call on its water, individuals and conservation districts that have rights junior to those of Avista could be required to stop irrigating, drain storage dams, and the like. Mike Mclane of DNRC reported regularly to the committee on the proceedings, and when the negotiations failed, the committee suggested that the state could not abandon the issue because of the level of public interest. As a result, a piece of legislation was drafted by the governor's office that would put in place mechanisms for basin-wide planning.

40. Donald Snow, "River Story: A New Chapter for Montana's Clark Fork," *Chronicle of Community* 1 (Autumn 1996), pp. 18–25; Janet Maughan, "Taming Troubled Waters: How Mediation Triumphed over Confrontation in Shaping the Future of Montana's Storied Clark Fork River," in the Ford Foundation's 1994 summer report.

41. NAPA's positive appraisal is hindered by some misinformation about the leasing program and other details of the committee's process. National Academy of Public Administration, "Making Environmental Decisions in the Upper Clark Fork River Watershed," in *Resolving the Paradox of Environmental Protection: An Agenda for Congress, EPA, and the States* (Washington, D.C.: National Academy of Public Administration, 1997).

42. Jennifer H. Smalley, *An Overview of Water Planning in Four Western States*, 1993. Available from Western Network, 616 Don Gaspar, Santa Fe, N.M., 87501.

43. Interview with Ole Ueland, Mar. 12, 1999.

44. Because their water rights are already unfulfilled for much of the year, the Granite Conservation District reservations would have posed a serious threat to the ample instream flow required for hydropower production.

45. DNRC, "Water Rights in Montana," p. 19.

46. A lessee must prove that changing a consumptive use to an instream use will not have a negative impact on any other water rights. Furthermore, if the lease results in a lawsuit, the lessee must carry the financial burden of the objector.

47. Interview with Audrey Aspholm, Mar. 12, 1999.

48. Well-diggers in the basin were concerned that the plan's original ground-water proposition would, in some cases, needlessly limit their work and that of their clients. Interview with Vivian Brooke, Mar. 15, 1999, Missoula, Mont.

49. Interview with Gerald Mueller, July 28, 1998, Missoula, Mont.

50. Interview with Holly Franz, July 29, 1998.

51. Interview with Land Lindbergh, July 31, 1998, Ovando, Mont.

52. Interview with Jim Dinsmore, July 29, 1998.

53. Interview with Dennis Workman, Mar. 12, 1999.

54. Montana DNRC and DEQ have given the committee funding to continue its work on allocation issues and begin VNRP efforts. An EPA groundwater grant, secured through DNRC, will help the committee as it continues to explore the link between ground and surface water in the basin.

55. Upper Clark Fork River Basin Steering Committee, *Report to the 1999 Montana Legislature.*

56. Interview with Stan Bradshaw, July 30, 1998.

57. Interview with Mike Mclane, July 30, 1998.

58. Interview with Land Lindbergh, July 31, 1998.

59. Interview with Donald Snow, Mar. 13, 1999.

60. For more on social capital and its significance, see Robert Putnam, *Making Democracy Work: Civic Traditions in Modern Italy* (Princeton, N.J.: Princeton University Press, 1993); Michael Woolcock, "Social Capital and Economic Development: Toward a Theoretical Synthesis and Policy Framework," *Theory and Society* 27(2): 1998, pp. 151–208; Anthony Bebbington, "Capitals and Capabilities: A Framework for Analyzing Peasant Viability, Rural Livelihoods, and Poverty," *World Development* 27(12): 1999, pp. 2021–44.

61. Interview with Land Lindbergh, July 31, 1998.

62. Interview with Dennis Workman, Mar. 12, 1999.

63. Interview with Gerald Mueller, July 28, 1998.

64. Interview with Dennis Workman, Mar. 12, 1999.

65. Interview with Stan Bradshaw, July 30, 1998.

66. Interview with Holly Franz, July 29, 1998.

67. Because a call by Avista would require any water user with junior rights to immediately halt their water use, the negotiations between the state and Avista attracted significant attention and concern among basin residents throughout the Clark Fork. The legislation was introduced by the governor, but as of February 2001 had not yet been through the legislature.

68. Interview with Dennis Workman, Mar. 12, 1999.

69. J. Durgan Smith, *Geomorphology Flood-Plain Tailings, and Metal Transport in the Upper Clark Fork Valley, Montana,* (Montana: USEPA/USGS, 1998); Duncan Adams, "Colorado-Based Geomorphologist Makes Recommendations for Montana River," *Montana Standard,* Butte, Mar. 13, 2000.

70. Interview with Donald Snow, Mar. 13, 1999.

71. Douglas Kenney, "Are Community-Based Watershed Groups Really Effective?" *Chronicle of Community* 3 (Winter 1999), pp. 33–37; David Getches, "Some Irreverent Questions About Watershed-Based Efforts," *Chronicle of Community* 2 (Spring 1998), pp. 28–34; David Chrislip, "Transforming Politics," *Chronicle of Community* 2 (Autumn 1997), pp. 28–35.

72. Kenny, "Are Community-Based Watershed Groups Really Effective?," p. 33.

73. Interview with Dr. Vicki Watson, Mar. 11, 1999, Missoula, Mont.

74. See Reed D. Benson, "The Role of Streamflow Protection in Northwest River Basin Management," *Environmental Law* 26 (Spring 1996), pp. 175–224.

75. Interview with Donald Snow, Mar. 13, 1999.

Chapter 3. Wolf Recovery in the Northern Rockies

1. Denise Casey and Tim Clark (comp.), *Tales of the Wolf: Fifty-One Stories of Wolf Encounters in the Wild* (Moose, Wyo.: Homestead Publishing, 1996), p. xiii.

2. United States Fish and Wildlife Service, *Record of Decision and the Reintroduction of Gray Wolves to Yellowstone National Park and Central Idaho; Final Environmental Impact Statement* (United States Department of the Interior, Fish and Wildlife Service, 1994), pp. 3–4.

3. The following historical sources were relied on for this chapter: John J. Craighead, "Yellowstone in Transition," in Robert B. Keiter and M. S. Boyce, eds.,

The Greater Yellowstone Ecosystem (New Haven, Conn.: Yale University Press, 1991); John Weaver, "The Wolves of Yellowstone," *Natural Resources Report*, no. 14 (U.S. Department of the Interior, National Park Service, 1978); Hank Fischer, *Wolf Wars* (Helena, Mont.: Falcon, 1995); Alston Chase, *Playing God in Yellowstone* (San Diego, Calif.: Harcourt Brace Jovanovich, 1987).

4. Craighead, "Yellowstone in Transition," p. 27.
5. Casey and Clark, *Tales of the Wolf*, p. 87.
6. Weaver, "The Wolves of Yellowstone," p. 7.
7. 30 U.S.C. Sec. 22.
8. Chase, *Playing God in Yellowstone*, pp. 16–17.
9. Fischer, *Wolf Wars*, pp. 17–18.
10. Ibid., pp. 20–21.
11. 16 U.S.C. Sec. 1.
12. Weaver, "The Wolves of Yellowstone," p. 8.
13. Chase, *Playing God in Yellowstone*, p. 23.
14. A. S. Leopold, S. A. Cain, C. M. Cottam, I. N. Gabrielson, and T. L. Kimball, "Wildlife Management in the National Parks," *Trans. North Am. Wildl. Conf.* 24 (1963), pp. 28–45.
15. Weaver, "The Wolves of Yellowstone," pp. 5, 16.
16. Ibid., pp. 20–22.
17. Fischer, *Wolf Wars*, pp. 49–51.
18. USFWS, *The Reintroduction of Gray Wolves to Yellowstone National Park and Central Idaho*, pp. 6–32 to 6–35.
19. Fischer, *Wolf Wars*, pp. 86–96.
20. Hank Fischer, "Wolf Fans Pick up Financial Burden," *Defenders* (Summer 1998), p. 26.
21. 42 U.S.C. Sec. 4332(2)(c).
22. Fischer, *Wolf Wars*, pp. 103–105.
23. Interview with Tom Dougherty, National Wildlife Federation Rocky Mountain office director, June 10, 1998, Boulder, Colo.
24. Interview with Tom Dougherty, June 10, 1998; Fischer, *Wolf Wars*, pp. 122–25.
25. Fischer, *Wolf Wars*, p. 129.
26. Interview with Tom Dougherty, June 10, 1998.
27. Fischer, *Wolf Wars*, p. 135.
28. Ibid., p. 136.
29. Ibid., p. 140.
30. Hank Fischer, "Discord over Wolves," *Defenders* (July/August 1991), p. 39.
31. Interview with Steven Fritts, USFWS biologist, June 8, 1998, Denver, Colo.
32. Personal communication with Ed Bangs, Oct. 27, 1999.
33. Ibid.
34. USFWS, *Reintroduction of Gray Wolves*, p. 2–26.
35. 40 C.F.R. Sec. 1501.7.
36. 40 C.F.R. Sec. 1502.14.
37. *Congressional Record*, Senate, Oct. 31, 1991, S15674.
38. USFWS, *Reintroduction of Gray Wolves*, p. 1–12.
39. Personal communication with Ed Bangs, Nov. 16, 1999.
40. Personal communication with Ed Bangs, Oct. 27, 1999.
41. Ibid.
42. 50 C.F.R. Pt. 17. Civil penalties for violating ESA can range up to $25,000 for each violation, while criminal penalties include fines of up to $50,000 and imprisonment of up to one year, or both. 16 U.S.C. Sec. 1540.

43. 16 U.S.C. Sec. 1539(j)(1).

44. Telephone interview with Larry Kruckenberg, special assistant for policy, Wyoming Game and Fish Department, July 9, 1998.

45. Telephone interview with Curt Mack, Nez Percé biologist, June 29, 1998.

46. *Wyoming Farm Bureau Federation et al. v. Babbitt*, Civil Case No. 94-CV-286-D (D. Wyo. 1997).

47. *Wyoming Farm Bureau Federation et al. v. Babbitt*, 199 F.3d 1224 (10th Cir. 2000).

48. USFWS, *Rocky Mountain Wolf Recovery 1999 Annual Report*, www.r6.fws.gov/wolf/annualrpt99/.

49. Fischer, "Wolf Fans Pick Up Financial Burden."

50. USFWS, *1996 Annual Report of the Rocky Mountain Interagency Wolf Recovery Program;* Edward E. Bangs, Steven H. Fritts, Joseph A. Fontaine, Douglas W. Smith, Kerry M. Murphy, Curtis M. Mack, and Carter C. Niemeyer, "Status of Gray Wolf Restoration in Montana, Idaho, and Wyoming," *Wildlife Society Bulletin* 26(4): 1998, pp. 785–98; USFWS, *Rocky Mountain Wolf Recovery 1999 Annual Report;* USFWS, *Rocky Mountain Wolf Recovery 2000 Annual Report*, www.r6.fws.gov/wolf/annualrpt00/.

51. See www.r6.fws.gov/wolf/.

52. Bangs et al., "Status of Gray Wolf Restoration in Montana, Idaho, and Wyoming," pp. 792–93.

53. Ibid., p. 796.

54. An MSU-Billings poll conducted in October 1998 found over 60 percent of Montana residents polled opposed the removal of wolves from Yellowstone and the surrounding ecosystem (www.msubillings.edu/cati/poll98.html). In a National Wildlife Federation poll, 50 percent of Wyoming residents and 54 percent of Idaho residents polled opposed removal of wolves from Yellowstone and Idaho (www.nwf.org/nwf/wolves/wolfpoll.html).

55. Bangs et al., "Status of Gray Wolf Restoration in Montana, Idaho, and Wyoming," p. 790.

56. *Wyoming Farm Bureau v. Babbitt*, 199 F.3d 1224.

57. Laura Sands, "Crying Wolf! A Farm Organization's Effort To Help May Be More of a Hindrance," *Beef Today* (April 1998), www.farmjournal.com.

58. Leo Hargrave, "Wolves Are Not a Big Problem," *Billings Gazette* (June 22, 1997), p. 8C.

59. Telephone interview with Hank Fischer, May 19, 1998.

60. Personal communication with Ed Bangs, Oct. 2, 2001.

61. 16 U.S.C. Sec. 1531.

62. 16 U.S.C. Secs. 1532, 1538.

63. 16 U.S.C. Sec. 1533.

64. Ibid. Any advisory committee subject to FACA must be open to the public and may not conduct any meeting absent a designated federal officer or employee. 5 U.S.C. App.2.

65. 16 U.S.C. Sec. 1533.

66. 16 U.S.C. Sec. 1535.

67. 42 U.S.C. Sec. 4321.

68. 40 C.F.R. Secs. 1501–1506.

69. *Robertson v. Methow Valley Citizens Council*, 490 U.S. 332 (1989).

70. Interview with Tom Dougherty, June 10, 1998; interview with Steve Fritts, June 3, 1998; Fischer, *Wolf Wars*, pp. 135–37.

71. Interview with Steven Fritts, June 3, 1998.

72. Telephone interview with Hank Fischer, Nov. 29, 1999.

73. They included APHIS/Animal Damage Control, Idaho Department of Fish and Game, Wyoming Game and Fish Department, Montana Department of Fish, Wildlife, and Parks, Wind River tribe, Nez Percé tribe, Shoshone-Bannock tribes, Alberta Wildlife Branch, Canadian Parks Service, BLM, Minnesota Department of Natural Resources, Alaska Department of Fish and Game, British Columbia Ministry of Environment, Wisconsin Department of Natural Resources, and the University of Montana.

74. Fischer, *Wolf Wars*, p. 109.

75. Ibid., p. 111.

76. Personal communication with Ed Bangs, June 18, 1999.

77. Ibid.

78. Fischer, *Wolf Wars*, p. 146.

79. Personal communication with Ed Bangs, June 18, 1999.

80. Fischer, *Wolf Wars*, p. 143.

81. Personal communication with Ed Bangs, June 18, 1999.

82. Telephone interview with Larry Bourrett, Wyoming Farm Bureau, July 15, 1998.

83. Doug Honnold, "Wolves, Bears, and the Spirit of the Wild: Asking the Right Questions," in Robert B. Keiter, ed., *Reclaiming the Native Home of Hope* (Salt Lake City: University of Utah Press, 1998), p. 129.

84. Personal communication with Ed Bangs, Oct. 27, 1999.

85. Ibid.

86. Defenders of Wildlife Wolf Compensation Trust Web site, www.defenders.org.

87. Telephone interview with Hank Fischer, Nov. 29, 1999.

88. Fischer, "Wolf Fans Pick Up Financial Burden."

89. Ibid.

90. Ben Long, "Respecting Predators in our Changing West," *Defenders* (Winter 2000–2001), p. 16.

91. Ed Bangs, July 3, 2000, letter to Andrea Lococo, Fund for Animals, www.r6.fws.gov.

92. Telephone interview with Hank Fischer, Nov. 29, 1999.

93. Todd Wilkinson, "No Home on the Range," *High Country News* (Feb. 17, 1997).

94. Interview with Tom Dougherty, June 10, 1998.

95. Hank Fischer, "Moving Past the Polarization: Wolves, Grizzly Bears, and Endangered Species Recovery," in Keiter, ed., *Reclaiming the Native Home of Hope*, pp. 123–24.

96. Paul Larmer, "Idaho Grizzly Plan Shifts into Low Gear," *High Country News* (Nov. 9, 1998).

97. Telephone interview with Hank Fischer, Nov. 29, 1999.

98. *Record of Decision Concerning Grizzly Bear Recovery in the Bitterroot Ecosystem, Federal Register*, 65:223 (Nov. 17, 2000), pp. 69644–49).

99. Dan Gallagher, "Bear Program Violates Sovereignty, Idaho Says," *Daily Camera* (Jan. 21, 2001).

100. *Federal Register*, 66:121 (June 22, 2001).

Chapter 4. Bison Management in Greater Yellowstone

1. It would be more difficult to justify lethal control of bison inside a national park than outside it. Thus the political situation in Grand Teton National Park, with cattle grazing allotments inside, differs from Yellowstone.

2. National Park Service, State of Montana et al., *Draft Environmental Impact Statement for the Interagency Bison Management Plan for the State of Montana and Yellowstone National Park* (Denver, Colo.: National Park Service, State of Montana, U.S. Forest Service, U.S. Animal and Plant Health Inspection Service, 1998); U.S. Department of Interior, U.S. Department of Agriculture, *Record of Decision for Final Environmental Impact Statement and Bison Management Plan for the State of Montana and Yellowstone National Park* (Dec. 20, 2000).

3. Robert B. Keiter and Peter H. Froelicher, "Bison, Brucellosis, and Law in the Greater Yellowstone Ecosystem," *Land and Water Law Review* 28 (1993), pp. 1–75; Robert B. Keiter, "Greater Yellowstone's Bison: Unraveling of an Early American Wildlife Conservation Achievement," *Journal of Wildlife Management* 61 (1997), pp. 1–11.

4. John A. Baden and Donald Leal, *The Yellowstone Primer: Land and Resource Management in the Greater Yellowstone Ecosystem* (San Francisco: Pacific Research Institute for Public Policy, 1990).

5. David Dary, *The Buffalo Book: The Full Saga of the American Animal* (Athens, Ohio: Swallow Press, 1989).

6. Larry Barness, *Heads, Hides, and Horns: The Compleat Buffalo Book* (Fort Worth: Texas Christian University Press, 1985); Dary, *The Buffalo Book;* Valerius Geist, *Buffalo Nation: History and Legend of the North American Buffalo* (Stillwater: Voyager, 1986).

7. David D. Smitts, "The Frontier Army and the Destruction of the Buffalo: 1855–1883," *Western Historical Quarterly* 25:3 (1994), pp. 312 ff.

8. Mary Meagher, "Bison," in *Big Game of North America, Ecology and Management: A Wildlife Handbook* (Stackpole Books, 1978), pp. 123–33.

9. Quoted in Paul Schullery, *Yellowstone's Ski Pioneers: Peril and Heroism on the Winter Trail* (Worland: High Plains, 1995), p. 108.

10. Aubrey L. Haines, *The Yellowstone Story: A History of Our First National Park*, vol. 1 (Boulder: Colorado Associated University Press, 1977).

11. Rosalie Little-Thunder, "To Chris Kelley of the Church Universal and Triumphant; Response to Your Bison E-mail" (www.wildrockies.org/Buffalo/speak/rosalie2.html, 1997).

12. Norm Bishop, Paul Schullery et al., *Yellowstone's Northern Range: Complexity and Change in a Wildland Ecosystem* (Mammoth Hot Springs, Wyo.: National Park Service, 1997).

13. Haines, *The Yellowstone Story*, p. 73.

14. Richard West Sellars, *Preserving Nature in the National Parks: A History* (New Haven: Yale University Press, 1997), p. 380; Haines, *The Yellowstone Story*, vol. 2, p. 543.

15. Haines, *The Yellowstone Story;* Barness, *Heads, Hides, and Horns.*

16. Mary Meagher, "Yellowstone's Free Ranging Bison," *Naturalist* 36 (1985), pp. 20–27.

17. Paul Nicoletti and Michael J. Gilsdorf, "Brucellosis—The Disease in Cattle," in E. Tom Thorne, Mark S. Boyce, Paul Nicoletti, and Terry J. Kreeger, eds., *Brucellosis, Bison, Elk, and Cattle in the Greater Yellowstone Area: Defining the Problem, Exploring Solutions* (Jackson: Wyoming Game and Fish Department for the Greater Yellowstone Interagency Brucellosis Committee, 1997), pp. 3–6.

18. Granville H. Frye and Terry J. Kreeger, in *Brucellosis, Bison, Elk, and Cattle in the Greater Yellowstone Area*, pp. 79–85.

19. Mary Meagher, "Brucellosis and the Yellowstone Bison" (Yellowstone National Park: U.S. Department of Interior, National Park Service, 1972); Mary

Meagher, "Yellowstone's Bison: A Unique Wild Heritage," *National Parks and Conservation Magazine* (May 1974), pp. 9–14.

20. Granville H. Frye and Bob R. Hillman, "National Brucellosis Eradication Program," in *Brucellosis, Bison, Elk, and Cattle in the Greater Yellowstone Area*.

21. Yellowstone National Park, *Wyoming Brucellosis Workshop Planning: Summary of Information* (Yellowstone National Park: U.S. Department of Interior, National Park Service, 1996), p. 2; Bishop, Schullery et al., *Yellowstone's Northern Range*.

22. Bishop, Schullery et al., *Yellowstone's Northern Range*.

23. Paul Schullery, "Drawing the Lines in Yellowstone: The American Bison as Symbol and Scourge," *Orion* 5 (1986), pp. 33–45.

24. Jim Robbins, "After a One-Hundred-Year Hiatus, Bison-Hunting Season Is Set to Begin," *New York Times* (Nov. 11, 1985), p. A12; Anonymous, "Shades of Buffalo Bill," *Time* 133 (Feb. 20, 1989), p. 41.

25. Anonymous, "Regional News," BC cycle (Bozeman, Mont., Apr. 9, 1985), Lexis-Nexis.

26. Jim Robbins, "Bison Hunt Is Over but Debate Lives," *New York Times* (Apr. 6, 1986), p. 31.

27. The Fund lost the suit. Anonymous, "Judge Won't Block Killing of Wild Bison," AM cycle (Dec. 3, 1985), Lexis-Nexis.

28. Alan Kesselheim, "Life Amid the Ghost Trees," *Backpacker* (April 1985), pp. 42–50, 126.

29. John D. Varley and Paul Schullery, "The Yellowstone Fires," *Encyclopedia Britannica Yearbook of Science and the Future* (1991), pp. 131–43.

30. Christine Bertelson, "Park's Winter Kill Aids Grizzly Bear," *St. Louis Post-Dispatch* (May 14, 1989), p. 10A; David Kingham, "Many Die or Are Killed by Hunters When They Seek Food Outside the Park; Expanded Winter Range Called Vital to Yellowstone Elk, Bison," *Los Angeles Times* (United Press International, Apr. 2, 1989), p. 30.

31. Robert Ekey, "Park Rangers May Shoot Female Bison: Concern About Disease Prompts Yellowstone Plan," *Washington Post* (Oct. 4, 1990), p. A3.

32. Quoted in Pat Morrison, "Humble Germ Pits Nature, Ranchers in a 'Range War,'" *Los Angeles Times* (July 22, 1990), p. A1.

33. State of Montana (Montana Fish, Wildlife, and Parks); U.S. Department of Interior (Yellowstone National Park); U.S. Department of Agriculture (Gallatin National Forest), *Yellowstone Bison: Background and Issues*, May 1990.

34. Ben Brown, "Fund for Animals Goes to Court for Bison," *USA Today* (Dec. 6, 1990), p. 9C; Associated Press, "Safe Range Proposed for Bison Roaming outside Yellowstone," *Casper Star Tribune* (July 30, 1991), p. B1; Interview with Jeanne-Marie Souvigney, July 13, 1998, Bozeman, Mont.

35. The group submitted the proposal with a letter to Yellowstone National Park superintendent Bob Barbee. Signatories to the letter included local rancher John Ragsdale; Jim Richard of the Montana Wildlife Federation; Kara Rickets of the Greater Yellowstone Association of Conservation Districts; Michael Scott of The Wilderness Society; Jeanne-Marie Souvigney of the Greater Yellowstone Coalition; Leroy Ellig, the retired Fish, Wildlife, and Parks regional supervisor who initiated the group; Edward Francis, a local landowner and member of the Royal Teton Ranch; and Robert S. Gibson, retired forest supervisor.

36. Author's notes from the *Where the Buffalo Roam: Finding Common Ground* symposium, Cody, Wyo., Aug. 8–9, 1997.

37. Yellowstone National Park, *Wyoming Brucellosis Workshop Planning:*

Summary of Information on Yellowstone National Park (U.S. Department of Interior, National Park Service, 1996).

38. J. Lee Alley, "Brucellosis Committee Report," 1995 Reno United States Animal Health Association Meeting (Reno, Nev., 1995).

39. Ibid.

40. This account of DOL is based in part on an interview with Arnold Gertonson, Sept. 24, 1998.

41. Yellowstone National Park, "Wyoming Brucellosis Workshop Planning."

42. Settlement Agreement (Helena, Mont.: Department of Interior, Department of Agriculture, and the State of Montana, 1995).

43. Yellowstone National Park, "Wyoming Brucellosis Workshop Planning."

44. An Environmental Assessment, a cursory analysis of the potential environmental and social effects of a proposed government action, is often completed to determine the necessity of completing a full Environmental Impact Statement.

45. Settlement Agreement.

46. National Park Service and State of Montana, *Interim Bison Management Plan* (Aug. 9, 1996), p. 1.

47. Jeanne-Marie Souvigney, "Comments of Jeanne-Marie Souvigney," from *Where the Buffalo Roam: Finding Common Ground* symposium, Cody, Wyo., Aug. 8–9, 1997.

48. Mike Finley and John Mak, "Finding of No Significant Impact: Interim Bison Management Plan" (Aug. 5, 1996).

49. The plaintiffs included the Intertribal Bison Cooperative, Defenders of Wildlife, the Greater Yellowstone Coalition, the Jackson Hole Alliance for Responsible Planning (now Jackson Hole Conservation Alliance), and David A. Ritchie. Defendants included Secretary of Interior Bruce Babbitt, Acting Deputy Director of the National Park Service Dennis Galvin, Superintendent of Yellowstone National Park Michael Finley, Secretary of Agriculture Dan Glickman, Chief of the U.S. Forest Service Michael Dombeck, Administrator Terry Medley of APHIS, Governor Marc Racicot of Montana, Executive Officer Laurence Peterson of the Montana Department of Livestock, Director Patrick J. Graham of Montana Fish, Wildlife, and Parks, and the Montana State Department of Fish, Wildlife, and Parks. Two separate lawsuits were filed, both to initiate an injunction against killing bison until the completion of an EIS. Both lawsuits were lost by the plaintiffs, and the two cases were combined for the judge to rule on the merits of the cases (Interview with Jeanne-Marie Souvigney, May 10, 1999, Bozeman, Mont.).

50. Interview with Jim Angell, May 6, 1999, Bozeman, Mont.

51. Doug Peacock, "The Yellowstone Massacre," *Audubon* (June 1997), p. 40.

52. National Park Service, State of Montana et al., *Draft Environmental Impact Statement for the Interagency Bison Management Plan for the State of Montana and Yellowstone National Park.*

53. Ibid.

54. Anonymous, "The Great Bison Break-Out," *Economist* (February 1997), p. 28.

55. Anonymous, "Emergency Bison Protection Plan Proposed," *U.S. Newswire* (Jan. 30, 1997), National Desk, Environment and agriculture writers, Lexis-Nexis; Louis Sahagun, "Yellowstone Bison Roam into Deadly Battle; Environment; Fear of Disease Has Led to Slaying of 733 Animals. U.S. Offers Plan to Slow the Killing," *Los Angeles Times* (Jan. 31, 1997), p. A1; Todd Wilkinson, "Winter and Park Service Pact Threaten Yellowstone Bison," *Christian Science Monitor* (Jan. 22, 1997), p. 3.

56. Anonymous, "End to Bison Killing Near Park Sought," *Fort Worth Star-Telegram* (Feb. 28, 1997).

57. Jackson-area ranchers, Franz Camenzind, Mike Clark, Lloyd Dorsey, "Brucellosis Management in Wyoming: Letter to President Clinton, Secretaries Glickman, Babbitt, and Governor Geringer," Jan. 31, 1997.

58. Peacock, "The Yellowstone Massacre."

59. Low-risk animals include bulls, yearlings, calves, and cows that have live calves and which passed all birth membranes. (R. M. Nervig and Carl Bausch, "Letter to Joan Arnoldi Regarding Low Risk Bison," Oct. 17, 1997. This letter can be found on p. 369 of the 1998 draft EIS.)

60. Bruce Smith and Thomas Roffe, "A Political Disease Brucellosis," *Bugle* (Summer 1992), pp. 71–80; E. Tom Thorne, "Presentation: Bovine Brucellosis and Bison, Elk, and Cattle in the Greater Yellowstone Area," (AMK Ranch, Wyo., June 25, 1998); Scott McMillion, "Feds Say 'Low-Risk' Bison Should be Allowed to Wander," *Bozeman Daily Chronicle* (Apr. 22, 1998), p. A1.

61. Interview with Patrick Collins, Feb. 10, 1999, Washington, D.C.

62. Arnold A. Gertonson, Letter to Deputy Administrator Joan Arnoldi, Feb. 19, 1998; Arnold A. Gertonson, Letter to other state veterinarians, Feb. 19, 1998; Scott McMillion, "Racicot Knocks Federal Official's Bison Comments," *Bozeman Daily Chronicle* (May 5, 1999), p. 3.

63. Meghan Fay, "Groups Slam Bison EIS for Inadequacies," Bison Advocacy Project, Ecology Center, Wild Rockies InfoNet, 1998.

64. *Draft Environmental Impact Statement*, table 9, p. 113.

65. Letter from the undersecretary for marketing and regulatory programs of the Department of Agriculture, the undersecretary for natural resources and environment of the Department of Agriculture, and the assistant secretary for Fish, Wildlife, and Parks of the Department of Interior to Governor Marc Racicot, Dec. 13, 1999, Washington, D.C., p. 1.

66. U.S. Department of Interior and U.S. Department of Agriculture, *Record of Decision for Final Environmental Impact Statement and Bison Management Plan for the State of Montana and Yellowstone National Park*, p. 21; See also "Mediator to Enter Bison Dispute," *Billings Gazette* (Feb. 4, 2000), obtained from http://www.wildrockies.org/Buffalo/press99/releas07.html.

67. These lawsuits include one filed in 1985 by the Fund For Animals (the Fund) to force the Park to prevent bison migrations; one in 1989 by the Parker Land and Cattle Company seeking compensation from the Park for allowing wildlife infected with brucellosis to wander out of Park boundaries and infect its herds (a claim never proved); one in 1990 by the Fund to prevent the killing of bison that migrate out of the Park, and an appeal; another in 1991 by the Fund to halt the killing; one in 1993 by the Fund against the U.S. Department of Agriculture for failing to assess the environmental impacts of using bison in a brucellosis-transmission study; one in 1995 filed by the State of Montana against the Park and APHIS; one in 1996 and another in 1997 by a group of conservation and tribal organizations to halt the implementation of the Interim Plan; one in 1996 by the National Wildlife Federation to obtain information about brucellosis control from APHIS; one in 1997 by the Fund to halt the implementation of the Jackson Bison Management Plan; and one in 1998 by the state of Wyoming to allow wardens from the Wyoming Game and Fish Department to vaccinate elk and bison on the National Elk Refuge.

68. See Greystone, *Content Analysis of Public Comment for the Interagency Bison Management Plan for the State of Montana and Yellowstone National Park*

(Greenwood Village, Colo.: Department of Interior, National Park Service, Department of Agriculture, U.S. Forest Service and Animal and Plant Health Inspection Service, State of Montana, March 1999).

69. Greystone, *Content Analysis of Public Comment for the Interagency Bison Management Plan;* Brodie Farquhar, "Montana Pleased, Greens Glum over Final Bison Plan," *Casper Star Tribune* (Dec. 21, 2000), pp. A1, A12.

70. Donald S. Davis, Joe W. Templeton et al., "Brucella abortus in Captive Bison: Serology, Bacteriology, Pathogenesis, and Transmission to Cattle," *Journal of Wildlife Diseases* 26 (1990), pp. 360–71.

71. Interview with Jeanne-Marie Souvigney, May 10, 1999.

72. American Buffalo Foundation, Defenders of Wildlife et al., "Buffaloed by Fear," *Denver Post* (Feb. 7, 1999).

73. Farquhar, "Montana Pleased, Greens Glum over Final Bison Plan."

74. Clarence J. Siroky, "Prepared Testimony by Clarence J. Siroky, State Veterinarian, Montana Department of Livestock before the Senate Energy and Natural Resources Committee Subcommittee on Parks, Historic Preservation, and Recreation Senate Hearing for Senate Bill 745," Mar. 7, 1996.

75. Jim Hagenbarth et al., "The Cattle Industries of the Greater Yellowstone Area," in *Brucellosis, Bison, Elk, and Cattle in the Greater Yellowstone Area,* pp. 154–60.

76. Interview with Brian Severin, Sept. 25, 1998, Gardiner, Mont.

77. Greystone, *Content Analysis of Public Comment for the Interagency Bison Management Plan.*

78. Michael Satchell, "A Discouraging Word for the Buffalo," *U.S. News and World Report* 121 (Sept. 30, 1996), p. 61.

79. Cat Urbigkit, "Geringer Warns States to Avoid Brucellosis Disaster," *Jackson Hole Guide* (Pinedale, Wyo., Mar. 12, 1997).

80. Paul Hutchinson, "Blood on the Snow; Buffalo Slaughter Raises Commotion," *Denver Post* (Feb. 23, 1997), p. A1.

81. Telephone interview with James Holt.

82. Interview with Gloria Wells-Norlin, Bozeman, Mont., Apr. 6, 1999.

83. DOL spent $162,425 in FY1998, and $369,648 in FY1996 and 1997. These figures are contained in Robert S. Tallerico, Letter from Robert S. Tallerico, associate fiscal analyst, to Rep. Bob Raney regarding bison control funding, Montana Legislative Branch, Oct. 5, 1998, and in George H. Harris, "Bison Fiscal Report FY1999 to Date: Montana Department of Livestock," Centralized Services Division, Feb. 16, 1999.

84. Interview with Mike Philo, Bozeman, Mont., Aug. 7, 1999.

85. General Accounting Office, "Many Issues Unresolved in the Yellowstone Bison-Cattle Brucellosis Conflict," October 1992, GAO/RCED-93-2; General Accounting Office, "Issues Concerning the Management of Bison and Elk Herds in Yellowstone National Park," July 10, 1997, GAO/RCED-97-200, p. 17.

86. Norman F. Cheville and Dale McCullough, *Brucellosis in the Greater Yellowstone Area* (Washington, D.C.: National Academy, 1998), pp. 7, 9.

87. This state of affairs has been called "collective administrative anarchy" in Arnold Rogow and Harold Lasswell, *Power, Corruption, and Rectitude* (Englewood Cliffs, N.J.: Prentice-Hall, 1963), p. 23.

88. Interview with Jason Campbell, Oct. 1, 1998, Helena, Mont.; and interview with Brad Mead.

89. Siroky, Prepared Testimony; Clint Peck, "Bison, Brucellosis, and Bureaucrats," *Farmer-Stockman* (mid-February 1997), pp. 5–10.

90. Cheville and McCullough, *Brucellosis in the Greater Yellowstone Area,* p. 186.

91. *Greater Yellowstone Interagency Brucellosis Committee Interagency Action Plan,* May 2, 1997, Jackson, Wyo., p. 1.

92. This information can be found in Jim Geringer, Phillip E. Batt et al., *Memorandum of Understanding Creating the Greater Yellowstone Interagency Brucellosis Committee* (Wyoming, Idaho, Montana: U.S. Department of Interior, U.S. Department of Agriculture, 1995).

93. From author's notes at the GYIBC meeting, Sept. 17, 1998, Gardiner, Mont.

94. Interview with Terry Terrell, Sept. 17, 1998, Gardiner, Mont.

95. Author's notes, GYIBC meeting, May 19, 1999, Jackson, Wyo.

96. Interview with Patrick Collins, Feb. 10, 1999.

97. Ibid.

98. Interview with Marian Cherry, July 1, 1999, Bozeman, Mont.

99. Phone interview with Jim Berkley, U.S. Environmental Protection Agency, Apr. 10, 1999.

100. Montana State Legislature, Senate Bill no. 312, passed Apr. 10, 1995; Montana State Legislature, Senate Bill no. 352, passed Apr. 27, 1995.

101. U.S. Congress, Senate Bill no. 745, introduced May 3, 1995.

102. Interview with Jeanne-Marie Souvigney, July 13, 1998, Bozeman, Mont.

103. Letter from the Bison Management Citizen's Working Group to Superintendent Robert D. Barbee, May 15, 1991.

104. Souvigney, "Comments of Jeanne-Marie Souvigney," p. 2.

105. Interview with Peyton Curlee-Griffin, June 16, 1998, Jackson, Wyo.

106. Ranchers graze cattle next to bison in the Jackson Hole area, although they have not experienced infection in their herds. Jurisdiction is more complicated because bison migrate from Grand Teton National Park into the National Elk Refuge, which is administered by the U.S. Fish and Wildlife Service, in addition to national forest and private land. And finally, the elk in the refuge have a high rate of brucellosis infection, because elk feeding grounds in Wyoming facilitate transmission of the disease among them.

107. Interview with Peyton Curlee-Griffin, June 17, 1998, Jackson, Wyo.

108. Interview with Joe Bohne, June 26, 1998, Jackson, Wyo.

109. The groups include: American Buffalo Foundation, Defenders of Wildlife, Gallatin Wildlife Association, Greater Yellowstone Coalition, Idaho Wildlife Federation, Intertribal Bison Cooperative, Jackson Hole Conservation Alliance, Montana Audubon, Montana River Action Network, Montana Wilderness Association, Montana Wildlife Federation, National Parks and Conservation Association, National Wildlife Federation, Natural Resources Defense Council, The Wilderness Society, Wyoming Wildlife Federation, Bench Ranch, Wyoming Wear, and Yellowstone Raft Company (Interview with Jeanne-Marie Souvigney, Mar. 30, 1999).

110. Interview with Jon Catton, Mar. 16, 1999, Bozeman, Mont.

111. Greystone, *Content Analysis of Public Comments for the Interagency Bison Management Plan;* interview with Jeanne-Marie Souvigney, May 10, 1999. Twenty-nine comments were also received opposing the plan.

112. American Buffalo Foundation, Defenders of Wildlife et al., "The Citizens' Plan to Save Yellowstone Buffalo" (Bozeman, Mont., 1998), p. 7.

113. This information can be found on the Greater Yellowstone Coalition's web site. The address is http://hosts2.in-tch.com/www.greateryellowstone.org/happened.html.

114. Interview with Jeanne-Marie Souvigney, Mar. 30, 1999.

115. National Park Service, State of Montana et al., "Draft Environmental Impact Statement," p. i.

116. Hagenbarth et al., "The Cattle Industries of the Greater Yellowstone Area."

117. Cheville and McCullough, *Brucellosis in the Greater Yellowstone Area*, p. 7.

118. Joel Berger and Steven L. Cain, "Reproductive Synchrony in Brucellosis-Exposed Bison in the Southern Greater Yellowstone Ecosystem and in Noninfected Populations," *Conservation Biology* 13 (1999), pp. 357–66.

119. J. Robb Brady, "A Senseless Slaughter in Montana," *Post Register* (Feb. 9, 1999).

120. Arnold Gertonson, "Testimony on H.R. 631" (1999).

121. Hagenbarth et al., "The Cattle Industries of the Greater Yellowstone Area," p. 158.

122. U.S. General Accounting Office, *Packers' and Stockyards' Programs: USDA's Response to Studies on Concentration in the Livestock Industry* (April 1997, GAO/RCED-97-100).

123. Anonymous, "Ranchers Rush to Halt 'Unfair' Canadian Stampede," *Jackson Hole Daily* (Oct. 13, 1999), p. 5.

124. Larry Peterson, "Memo re: Governor's Briefing Canadian Border Inequities," Sept. 25, 1998.

125. Charles E. Hanrahan and Mary L. Dunkley, "U.S. Agricultural Trade: Trends, Composition, Direction, and Policy" (Washington, D.C.: Congressional Research Service, Mar. 11, 1998). Report number 98-258ENR.

126. Interview with Brad Mead.

127. Anonymous, "Department of Livestock Mulls More Lenient Bison Policy," *Casper Star Tribune* (Jan. 10, 1999), p. B1; Interview with Patrick Collins, Feb. 10, 1999.

128. Settlement Agreement, p. 3.

129. U.S. Department of Interior and U.S. Department of Agriculture, *Record of Decision for Final Environmental Impact Statement and Bison Management Plan for the State of Montana and Yellowstone National Park*, p. 22.

130. Hutchinson, "Blood on the Snow; Buffalo Slaughter Raises Commotion."

131. Interview with Franz Camenzind, June 19, 1998, Jackson, Wyo.

132. Interview with Matt Ferrari, May 26, 1999, Bozeman, Mont.

133. Bishop, Schullery et al., *Yellowstone's Northern Range*, p. 148.

134. Elinor Ostrom, Johanna Burger et al., "Revisiting the Commons: Local Lessons, Global Challenge," *Science* 284 (1999), pp. 278–82.

135. Interview with Brian Severin, Sept. 25, 1998.

136. Interview with Karen Kovacs, Feb. 10, 1999, Washington, D.C.

Chapter 5. Forest Policy and the Quincy Library Group

1. George Cameron Coggins, Charles F. Wilkinson, and John Leshy, *Federal Public Land and Resources Law*, 3d ed. (Westbury, N.Y.: Foundation, 1993), ch. 2.

2. The Central Pacific Railroad was completed in 1869 and the Western Pacific Railroad in 1910.

3. Geri Bergen and Paul F. Barker, *Tahoe National Forest Land and Resource Management Plan* (Nevada City, Cal.: Pacific Southwest Region, USDA Forest Service, 1990), section I, pp. 1–2. Geri Bergen is a forest supervisor, and Paul Barker is a regional forester.

4. The Creative Act of 1891, which authorized the president to create forest reserves, also protected watersheds on forest reserves. The Organic Act of 1897 was the basic charter of the Forest Service and recognized commercial timber harvesting as the second purpose of the agency. Committee of Scientists, *Sustaining the People's Lands: Recommendations for Stewardship of the National Forests and Grasslands into the Next Century* (Washington, D.C.: U.S. Department of Agriculture, Mar. 15, 1999), pp. 6–7; see also Charles F. Wilkinson, *Crossing the Next Meridian* (Washington D.C.: Island, 1992), pp. 122–24.

5. Quoted in Wilkinson, *Crossing the Next Meridian*, p. 129.

6. Before World War II, annual harvests averaged 1 billion board feet (bbf) and first exceeded 2 bbf in 1940; 4 bbf in 1951; 8 bbf in 1959; and 12 bbf in 1966. Bureau of the Census, *Historical Statistics of the United States*, Series L 15–23 (1970), p. 534. (Cited in Coggins, Wilkinson, and Leshy, *Federal Public Land*, p. 606.)

7. Wilkinson, *Crossing the Next Meridian*, p. 132.

8. From discussion at the "Workshop on Governance and Natural Resources: New Models for the Twenty-first Century," Jackson, Wyo., Sept. 2–4, 1998.

9. Frank Clifford, "Coalition's Olive Branch Saves Economy, Forest," *Los Angeles Times* (Nov. 15, 1995), p. A1.

10. Wilkinson, *Crossing the Next Meridian*, p. 145.

11. Telephone interview with Michael Yost, Feb. 8, 1999.

12. Quoted in Ed Marston, "The Timber Wars Evolve into a Divisive Attempt at Peace," *High Country News* 29 (Sept. 29, 1997).

13. Dan Smith and Hal Beatty, members, Plumas Sierra Citizens for Multiple Use, quoted in "Two Groups Square-off on Proposed Forest Plans," *Feather River Bulletin* (Mar. 12, 1986).

14. Jane Braxton Little, "Plumas Rallies behind Maximum Timber Harvests," *Feather River Bulletin* (May 7, 1986).

15. Ibid.

16. Paul F. Barker, *Record of Decision: Final Environmental Impact Statement, Plumas National Forest Land and Resource Management Plan* (Aug. 26, 1988).

17. Telephone interview with Michael Yost, Feb. 8, 1999.

18. Wilkinson, *Crossing the Next Meridian*, p. 160.

19. Ibid., p. 162.

20. Ibid.

21. On the Lassen, 200 million board feet were harvested in 1987, while only 117 million board feet were harvested in 1991. On the Tahoe, 119.4 million board feet were offered in 1987, and only 28 million board feet in 1991. The source of these figures for all three forests is D. Stone, "Overview of Budget, Staff and Outputs," Plumas National Forest (Dec. 11, 1995).

22. Telephone interview with Ron Stewart, deputy chief for programs and legislation, USFS, July 30, 1998.

23. Quoted in Tom Philp, "Fallout from a Logging Consensus in the Sierra," *Sacramento Bee* (Nov. 9, 1997), p. F1.

24. Bill Coates, "Finding Common Ground: Restoring a Small-Town Economy and National Forests to Health," 1995, www.QLG.org.

25. Philp, "Fallout from a Logging Consensus in the Sierra."

26. This is Jackson's account, as quoted in Marston, "The Timber Wars Evolve into a Divisive Attempt at Peace," p. 9.

27. Telephone interview with Michael Yost, Feb. 8, 1999.

28. Interview with Tom Nelson, Feb. 19, 1999, Quincy, Cal.

29. Telephone interview with Michael Yost, Feb. 8, 1999.

30. Centers for Water and Wildland Resources, *Summary of the Sierra Nevada Ecosystem Project Report* (Davis, Cal.: University of California, Davis, 1996).

31. Ibid.

32. Quincy Library Group, *Community Stability Proposal* (February 1997), pp. 1–2, available from the QLG web site at www.qlg.org.

33. Mark Sagoff, "The View from Quincy Library: Civic Engagement in Environmental Problem Solving," in Robert K. Fullinwider, ed., *Civil Society, Democracy, and Civic Renewal* (Landham, Md.: Rowman and Littlefield, 1999), pp. 151–83, gives a detailed description on p. 167: "On 10 July 1993, the Quincy Library Group presented its management plan at a town hall meeting attended by about 150 individuals representing every view, interest, and position in the surrounding communities." Marston, "Timber Wars Evolve into a Divisive Attempt at Peace," p. 9, states that the meeting took place in the Spring and that the number of attendees was 250.

34. Interview with Linda Blum, Feb. 17, 1999, Quincy, Cal., and interview with John Preschutti and Neil Dion, Feb. 17, 1999, Blairsden, Cal.

35. Leonard Atencio, Data General Message, Jan. 9, 1994, 3:11 p.m., www.qlg.org. Emphasis in the original.

36. For more on scientific management, see the discussion in Chapter 6 and the references to Samuel Hays, *Conservation and the Gospel of Efficiency: The Progressive Conservation Movement, 1890–1920* (Cambridge: Harvard University Press, 1959).

37. Telephone interview with Ron Stewart, July 30, 1998.

38. Interview with George Terhune, Feb. 19, 1999, Quincy, Cal.

39. Interview with Rose Comstock, Feb. 17, 1999, Quincy, Cal.

40. Michael DeLasaux, "Quincy Library Group Retrospective and Update," p. 2. Michael DeLasaux is a natural resources advisor to Cooperative Extension.

41. Jane Braxton Little, "National Groups Object to Grassroots Power in D.C.," *High Country News* 29 (Mar. 31, 1997).

42. George and Pat Terhune, "QLG Case Study," Case Study Prepared for the Workshop on *Engaging, Empowering, and Negotiating Community: Strategies for Conservation and Development*, Oct. 8–10, 1998, sponsored by the Conservation and Development Forum, West Virginia University, and the Center for Economic Options.

43. Ibid.

44. The Federal Advisory Committee Act is intended to prevent any one interest group from gaining unfair influence with agency decision makers. Judicial interpretations of the act have been conflicting and unclear. For a discussion of FACA and its application to community-based initiatives, see Thomas Brendler, "The Federal Advisory Committee Act," *Chronicle of Community* 1 (August 1996), pp. 44–47.

45. Interview with Tom Nelson, Feb. 19, 1999.

46. The Herger-Feinstein Quincy Library Group Forest Recovery Act, 16 U.S.C. 2104, Sec. 401(l). For the political story, see Jane Braxton Little, "Forest Plan Powers through Congress," *High Country News* (Aug. 4, 1997); and Jon Margolis, "How a Foe Saved the Quincy Library Group Bacon," *High Country News* (Sept. 29, 1997).

47. Interview with Missy Nemeth, staff for Congressman Vic Fazio, July 2, 1998. See also an editorial, "Boxer Caves: Switch on Logging Bill a Political Gesture," *Sacramento Bee* (Dec. 19, 1997), p. B8.

48. For example, Representatives Helen Chenoweth, Wally Herger, and Don Young, who were all strong Republican supporters of the QLG bill, receive signifi-

cant campaign contributions from forestry and forest products industries. Senator Boxer and Rep. George Miller (both Democrats) do not receive substantial contributions from the timber industry, but environmentalist groups are among the top contributors to their campaigns. (www.opensecrets.org/home/index.asp).

49. The Herger-Feinstein Quincy Library Group Forest Recovery Act, 16 U.S.C. 2104, Sec. 401. The subsections quoted are, respectively, a, h(1), k(1), and k(2).

50. Interview with Dave Peters, pilot project manager for the Herger-Feinstein QLG Act, USFS, Feb. 18, 1999, Quincy, Cal.

51. United States Forest Service, USDA, "Notice of Intent to Prepare an Environmental Impact Statement," *Federal Register* 63 (Dec. 21, 1998).

52. Telephone interview with Dave Peters, June 8, 1999.

53. Record of Decision, Herger-Feinstein Quincy Library Group Act Final EIS, Aug. 20, 1999.

54. The Quincy Library Group, "Appeal by the Quincy Library Group of the Final EIS and Record of Decision for the Herger-Feinstein Quincy Library Group Forest Recovery Act," Nov. 4, 1999, and Bradley Powell, regional forester, "Decision Summary," Mar. 28, 2000.

55. "Conservationists Appeal Quincy Decision," *Sierra Nevada Forest Protection Campaign Save Our Sierra*, Oct. 18, 1999, and Bradley Powell, Regional Forester, "Decision Summary," Mar. 28, 2000.

56. The QLG Act specified that all resource management activities required in the act must be consistent with CASPO interim guidelines "or the subsequently issued guidelines, whichever are in effect."

57. Record of Decision, Sierra Nevada Forest Plan Amendment Environmental Impact Statement, Jan. 2001.

58. Telephone interview with Linda Blum, Feb. 9, 2001.

59. Telephone interviews with Jay Watson, Feb. 9, 2001; Louis Blumberg, Feb. 9, 2001; and Barbara Boyle, Feb. 14, 2001.

60. George and Pat Terhune, "QLG Case Study," p. 5.

61. Telephone interview with Rose Comstock, Aug. 7, 1998.

62. The regional groups include the Klamath Forest Alliance and the Sierra Nevada Campaign. The national groups include the National Audubon Society, which is in opposition to its Plumas chapter.

63. Jim Carlton, "Business Coalition Protests U.S. Plan to Greatly Increase Logging in the West," *Wall Street Journal* (Aug. 12, 1999), p. A2.

64. Atencio, Data General Message. Emphasis in the original.

65. Jane Braxton Little, "Forest Service Called Sluggish," *Sacramento Bee* (Apr. 29, 1994), p. B1.

66. Quoted in Ed Marston, "We May Be Seeing the Devolution of the Environmental Movement," *High Country News* 29 (Sept. 29, 1997), p. 9.

67. Madrid and Connaughton are quoted in Marston, "The Timber Wars Evolve into a Divisive Attempt at Peace," p. 12.

68. Telephone interview with Dave Stone, Sept. 24, 1998.

69. Interview with Dave Peters, Feb. 18, 1999.

70. Michael Yost, "The Quincy Library Group Has Green Credentials," a letter to *High Country News* (Dec. 27, 1997). The QLG refused the offer, even though the activists threatened to "get ugly" according to Yost.

71. Debbie Sease, "Sierra Club Legislative Director Testimony on Quincy Library Group Bill," Senate Subcommittee on Forests and Public Lands, Committee on Energy and Natural Resources, concerning S. 1028 and H.R. 858, July 24, 1997.

72. Louis Blumberg, "Testimony of Louis Blumberg, Assistant Regional Direc-

tor, The Wilderness Society, California/Nevada Office," Mar. 5, 1997, Washington, D.C., p. 3.

73. Erin Noel, Sierra Nevada Forest Protection Campaign; David Edelson, Natural Resources Defense Council; and Scott Hoffman Black, Sierra Nevada Forest Protection Campaign; for Friends of the River, Natural Resources Defense Council, Forest Issues Group, the Center for Sierra Nevada Conservation, Pacific Rivers Council, and The Wilderness Society, "Comments on the Notice of Intent to Prepare an Environmental Impact Statement Pursuant to the Quincy Library Group Act," Jan. 19, 1999, p. 1.

74. Sease, "Sierra Club Legislative Director Testimony on Quincy Library Group Bill."

75. Interview with Steve Holmer, American Lands, July 1, 1998.

76. Telephone interviews with Jay Watson, Feb. 9, 2001; Louis Blumberg, Feb. 9, 2001; and Barbara Boyle, Feb. 14, 2001.

77. Sease, "Sierra Club Legislative Director Testimony on Quincy Library Group Bill." See also Blumberg, "Testimony of Louis Blumberg, Assistant Regional Director, The Wilderness Society, California/Nevada Office," p. 96.

78. The Audubon Society, letter to senator, Sept. 17, 1997.

79. Quoted in Cassandra Sweet, "Plan to Log Dead Trees Comes under Fire," Associated Press, Oct. 21, 1997.

80. The Wilderness Society, "Quincy Library Bill No Solution, but the Bill Became Law Despite Conservationist Efforts to Defeat It," *Conservation Coast to Coast*, October 1998.

81. Interview with Steve Holmer, July 1, 1998.

82. From the *Community Stability Proposal* available on the QLG web site.

83. Senate report 105–138, Nov. 4, 1997.

84. Sec. 401 (a) and (b). Of course, acts of Congress are not infallible specifications of the common interest of the national community. No alternative specifications are authorized in the Constitution, however, apart from Supreme Court decisions that are not supposed to be democratic.

85. George and Pat Terhune, "QLG Case Study," pp. 6–7.

86. Quincy Library Group, *Community Stability Proposal*, p. 2.

87. Even a conservation director of the Sierra Club, Bruce Hamilton, acknowledges exceptions. "While the Club has a position that advocates an end to all commercial logging on public lands, private use and noncommercial logging for ecological restoration purposes is allowable." See his letter to *High Country News* (Mar. 26, 2001), p. 15.

88. Plumas Corporation, "The QLG Economic Baseline," December 1995.

89. Ronald E. Stewart, deputy chief, Programs and Legislation, USFS, in a letter to Senator Diane Feinstein, Oct. 22, 1997.

90. Jane Braxton Little, "A Year Later, Quincy Forest Plan Leaves Saws Mostly Silent," *Sacramento Bee*, Aug. 21, 2000, p. A1.

91. The Quincy Library Group, "Concerns and Responses about the Quincy Library Group Bill," http://www.qlg.org/pub/bill/misperfacts.htm.

92. Senator Diane Feinstein, letter to the Honorable Barbara Boxer, Dec. 4, 1997; Philip G. Langley, "Quality Assessment of Later Seral Old-Growth Forest Mapping," *Sierra Nevada Ecosytem Project Report*, vol. 2, ch. 22, pp. 663–69; Jerry F. Franklin and Jo Ann Fites-Katifinan, "Assessment of Late-Successional Forests of the Sierra Nevada," *Sierra Nevada Ecosytem Project Report*, vol. 2, ch. 21, pp. 627–62.

93. Little, "A Year Later, Quincy Forest Plan Leaves Saws Mostly Silent," p. A1.

94. The Forest Service plans to construct "Strategically Placed Area Treatments" (SPLATs), zones of thinning intended to slow the progress of a wildfire, as part of the SNCF. Unlike DFPZs, they are nonlinear, but like DFPZs, they have never actually been constructed, though the theory is well-developed.

95. Interview with Steve Holmer, July 1, 1998.

96. Yost, "The Quincy Library Group Has Green Credentials."

97. Telephone interviews with Jay Watson, Feb. 9, 2001; Louis Blumberg, Feb. 9, 2001; Barbara Boyle, Feb. 14, 2001; confirmed by David Edelson, Feb. 15, 2001.

98. Sagoff, "The View from Quincy Library," p. 164.

99. Quoted in Philp, "Fallout from a Logging Consensus in the Sierra."

100. Quoted in Little, "A Year Later, Quincy Forest Plan Leaves Saws Mostly Silent," p. A1.

101. Ibid.

102. Jane Braxton Little, "Sawmill Closing for Good this Time," *Sacramento Bee*, Feb. 23, 2001, p. B1.

103. George and Pat Terhune, "QLG Case Study," p. 16. The authors hastened to add that "QLG anticipated some trends [in Forest Service management], but did not necessarily create them."

104. Jonathan Kusel, Lee Williams, Diana Keith, and Participating Lead Partnership Groups, *A Report on All-Party Monitoring and Lessons Learned from the Pilot Projects*, September 2000, Forest Community Research, The Pacific West National Community Forestry Center, Technical Report 101–2000, p. 7.

105. See Little, "A Year Later, Quincy Forest Plan Leaves Saws Mostly Silent," p. A1.

106. Don Young, Dianne Feinstein, Wally Herger, Larry E. Craig, Larry Combest, Mike Thompson, and George Radanovich; Letter to Mike Dombeck, chief, United States Forest Service; Mar. 31, 1999, www.qlg.org. Emphasis in original.

107. Telephone interview with Duane Gibson.

108. Telephone interview with George Terhune, Mar. 16, 2001.

109. Interview with Rose Comstock, Feb. 17, 1999.

110. Interview with John Preschutti, Feb. 17, 1999.

111. Telephone interview with Michael Yost, Feb. 8, 1999.

112. George and Pat Terhune, "QLG Case Study," p. 8.

113. Jane Braxton Little, "Quincy Library Group Bars Outsiders," *High Country News* (Apr. 26, 1999).

114. The following quotations are from Debra Moore, "Quincy Library Group: Who Are They?" *Feather River Bulletin* (Sept. 17, 1997), p. 2.

115. Tom Nelson, Testimony before Senate Subcommittee on Forests and Public Lands, Committee on Energy and Natural Resources, concerning S. 1028 and H.R. 858, July 24, 1997.

116. Interview with Tom Nelson, Feb. 19, 1999.

117. Interview with Harry Reeves, Feb. 17, 1999, Quincy, Cal.

118. Interview with Linda Blum, Feb. 17, 1999.

119. George and Pat Terhune, "QLG Case Study," p. 5.

120. Telephone interview with Michael Yost, Feb. 8, 1999.

121. Yost, "The Quincy Library Group Has Green Credentials."

122. Interview with Rose Comstock, Feb. 17, 1999.

123. Ibid.

124. Interview with Tom Nelson, Feb. 19, 1999.

125. QLG P2C2 meeting, Feb. 18, 1999, Quincy, Cal., and interview with Linda Blum, Feb. 17, 1999.

126. Interview with Linda Blum, Feb. 17, 1999.

127. "Who Should Determine the Fate of a Forest?" *San Francisco Chronicle,* June 15, 1997.

128. Sease, "Sierra Club Legislative Director Testimony on Quincy Library Group Bill," p. 41.

129. Timothy P. Duane, "Community Participation in Ecosystem Management," *Ecology Law Quarterly* 24 (1997), p. 796.

130. Louis Blumberg and Darrell Knuffke, "Count Us Out," *Chronicle of Community* 2 (Winter 1998), pp. 41–44, at p. 42.

131. Robert A. Dahl, *After the Revolution?* (New Haven: Yale University Press, 1970), ch. 2.

132. Sierra Nevada Forest Protection Campaign, Fact Sheet, "Vote No on the Quincy Logging Bill S. 1028 and/or S. 1079."

133. Kusel et al., *A Report on All-Party Monitoring,* p. 8. See also Little, "Quincy Group Bars Outsiders."

134. The Audubon Society, letter to senator, Sept. 17, 1997. See also Sease, "Sierra Club Legislative Director Testimony on Quincy Library Group Bill," July 24, 1997.

135. Barb Cestero, *Beyond the Hundredth Meeting: A Field Guide to Collaborative Conservation on the West's Public Lands* (Sonoran Institute, July 1999), p. 77.

136. Duane, "Community Participation in Ecosystem Management," p. 792.

137. 16 U.S.C. 2104, Sec. 401(l).

138. After he retired as Forest Service chief, Jack Ward Thomas told a reporter for *High Country News* that "he (Thomas) disliked almost everything about the Quincy Library Group, especially the fact that Sierra Pacific Industry was involved, and that Thomas' political boss, Secretary of Agriculture Dan Glickman, was backing it." Marston, "The Timber Wars Evolve into a Divisive Attempt at Peace," p. 10.

139. Importantly, residents of Quincy did not have the luxury of waiting; each successive month of inaction left them feeling more desperate about the economic stability in their community. In contrast, national environmental groups did not feel the same sense of urgency. On the contrary, inaction from the perspective of environmental groups was viewed as a success.

140. Among the opponents are Blumberg and Knuffke. In "Count Us Out," p. 42, they lay out a set of "rules for successful consensus processes," the first of which "is that *all* stakeholders must be at the table as early on as possible." Among the other proponents, presumably, is Duane. In "Community Participation in Ecosystem Management," he uses theories of communicative rationality to develop principles of participation that are applied as rules.

141. Cestero, *Beyond the Hundredth Meeting,* p. 76.

142. Ibid., p. 16.

143. Dale Bosworth, for Ron Stewart, Leonard Atencio, Wayne Thornton, and John Skinner, Memo to All Employees, Lassen, Plumas, and Tahoe National Forests, Jan. 21, 1994.

144. *Lead Partnership Group Newsletter,* vol. 1, no. 1, March 1997, p. 1.

145. Ibid.

146. Telephone interview with Lynn Jungwirth, Feb. 12, 2001. For details about the pilot projects and lessons learned, see Kusel et al., *A Report on All-Party Monitoring.*

147. Interview with Gerry Gray, American Forests, July 6, 1998, Washington, D.C.

Chapter 6. Harvesting Experience

1. "Policy" need not be limited to the public policies of government agencies. In the policy sciences, the term is understood inclusively as any projected program of goal values and action alternatives for realizing them. "Alternatives" includes sequences of actions, or strategies.

2. See Ronald D. Brunner, J. Samuel Fitch, Janet Grassia, Lyn Kathlene, and Kenneth R. Hammond, "Improving Data Utilization: The Case-Wise Alternative," *Policy Sciences* 20 (1987), pp. 365–94, which reviews theory and presents some experimental results on alternative forms. See also Harold D. Lasswell, "The Study of Political Elites," in Harold D. Lasswell and Daniel Lerner, eds., *World Revolutionary Elites* (Cambridge: M.I.T. Press, 1965), pp. 27–28: "The demand to take responsibility in the common interest is transmitted when . . . exemplified in the conduct of teachers, parents, public leaders, and similarly influential people. Models speak louder than maxims, but maxims provide guides to individual and concerted action."

3. Adapted from Harold D. Lasswell and Myres S. McDougal, *Jurisprudence for a Free Society: Studies in Law, Science, and Policy* (New Haven and Dordrecht: New Haven Press and Martinus Nijoff, 1992), pp. 1137–38. See also Myres S. McDougal, Harold D. Lasswell, and W. Michael Reisman, "The World Constitutive Process of Authoritative Decision," in Myres S. McDougal and W. Michael Reisman, eds., *International Law Essays* (Mineola, N.Y.: Foundation, 1981), pp. 191–286.

4. For example, compare for purposes of application the ten general principles for reinventing government and the specific cases used to illustrate those principles in David Osborne and Ted Gaebler, *Reinventing Government* (Reading, Mass.: Addison-Wesley, 1992).

5. Each model can be summarized in a page or two, a whole chapter, or at greater length. The optimum level of detail will vary for different audiences and different purposes. So will the medium: it is not to be assumed that print is the only or the most important medium. As noted below, further research is needed to clarify the most effective forms for communicating harvested experience.

6. The Wolf Management Committee is an advisory committee rather than a community-based initiative because it was composed largely of officials representing the diverse interests of their agencies rather than the diverse interests of a local community. The Greater Yellowstone Interagency Brucellosis Committee in Chapter 4 was composed exclusively of agency representatives.

7. Hank Fischer, "Wolf Fans Pick up Financial Burden," *Defenders* (Summer 1998), pp. 26–27, at p. 27.

8. This point is illustrated in C. T. Walbridge, "Genetic Algorithms: What Computers Can Learn from Darwin," *Technology Review* (January 1989), pp. 47–52. On the structure of evolutionary processes, see Herbert A. Simon, "The Architecture of Complexity," in his *The Sciences of the Artificial* (Cambridge: M.I.T. Press, 1969), pp. 84–118.

9. David H. Getches, "Some Irreverent Questions about Watershed-Based Initiatives," *Chronicle of Community* 2 (Spring 1998), pp. 28–34, at p. 34. Similar but less easily summarized "Ingredients for Success" can be found in Donald Snow, "What Are We Talking About?," *Chronicle of Community* 3 (Spring 1999), pp. 33–37. "The ingredients of a constructive collaborative process" are abstracted from cases in Barb Cestero, *Beyond the Hundredth Meeting: A Field Guide to Collaborative Conservation on the West's Public Lands* (Tucson, Ariz.: Sonoran Institute, 1999),

beginning on p. 72. See also Julia M. Wondolleck and Steven L. Yaffee, *Making Collaboration Work: Lessons from Innovation in Natural Resource Management* (Washington, D.C.: Island, 2000).

10. According to the conjunction rule of probability, the probability of requisites A and B occurring together (the conjunction) is less than or equal to the probability of A or the probability of B. Thus as more requisites C, D, E . . . are added to the conjunction, the probability of the conjunction decreases.

11. On these complexities of leadership, see Garry Wills, "What Makes a Good Leader?" *Atlantic Monthly* (April 1994), pp. 64 ff.

12. Skeptics are invited to consider the number of perfect correlations discovered among nontrivial variables in the social sciences. Moreover, the rare strong correlation tends to disappear as the number of cases becomes more inclusive or the context expands.

13. In contrast, Cestero concludes in *Beyond the Hundredth Meeting*, p. 76, that the Quincy Library Group "is not a positive model," because it failed to conform to her general lessons. This is goal displacement, in that her original goal (constructive conservation) is displaced by the means of realizing the goal (the general lessons), as if the relationship between the two were perfect. But if the relationship is imperfect, the means do not always or necessarily realize the goals, and the goals may be advanced by other means, as in the Quincy case. In a world of imperfect relationships, there is always a need to examine (not merely assume) the extent to which the goals were realized.

14. Getches, "Some Irreverent Questions about Watershed-Based Initiatives," p. 34.

15. Snow, "What Are We Talking About?," p. 36.

16. Douglas S. Kenney, "Are Community-Based Watershed Groups Really Effective?," *Chronicle of Community* 3 (Winter 1999), pp. 33–37, at p. 34. In contrast, the Sonoran Institute has a common-interest orientation. Consider the statement of its executive director, Luther Propst, in the preface to Cestero, *Beyond the Hundredth Meeting*, p. iii: "The Sonoran Institute hopes that this report will contribute to preserving the ecological integrity of our precious natural world while also respecting and enhancing humanity's social, economic, and spiritual well-being and our own sense of place in the web of life." Similarly, Aldo Leopold, in *A Sand County Almanac: And Sketches from Here and There* (New York: Oxford University Press, 1989), p. 224, urges us to "quit thinking about decent land-use as solely an economic problem." But in doing so, he does not reject economic considerations: "Examine each question in terms of what is ethically and esthetically right, as well as what is economically expedient."

17. They affirmed this toward the end of a video titled "The Local Forest: A Solution to the Timber Wars" (The Earth Island Films and Summit Films, 1994), produced by Roger Brown and directed by Nicholas Brown.

18. Compare Al Gore, *Creating a Government That Works Better and Costs Less: Report of the National Performance Review* (New York: Times Books, 1993), with Osborne and Gaebler, *Reinventing Government*, and with Donald F. Kettl and John J. DiIulio Jr., eds., *Inside the Reinvention Machine: Appraising Governmental Reform* (Washington, D.C.: Brookings Institution, 1995).

19. Gerald Mueller, "Lessons from the Clark Fork" (Remarks of Gerald Mueller to the Northwestern University Dispute Resolution Center Dinner Colloquium, Apr. 5, 1995), p. 4.

20. To the extent they fall short of outright restriction, such responses are forms of defense through partial incorporation, a mechanism reviewed in Harold

D. Lasswell, Daniel Lerner, and Ithiel de Sola Pool, *The Comparative Study of Symbols: An Introduction* (Stanford: Stanford University Press, 1952), pp. 5–6.

21. The quotations are from Samuel P. Hays, *Conservation and the Gospel of Efficiency: The Progressive Conservation Movement, 1890–1920* (Cambridge: Harvard University Press, 1959), pp. 266, 271, and 272.

22. Ibid., pp. 272–73, 275.

23. Mark Sagoff, "The View from Quincy Library: Civic Engagement in Environmental Problem-Solving," in Robert K. Fullinwider, ed., *Civil Society, Democracy, and Civic Renewal* (Lanham, Md.: Rowman and Littlefield, 1999), pp. 151–83, at p. 160. See also Harold D. Lasswell, "Must Science Serve Political Power," *American Psychologist* 25 (1970), pp. 117–23. The remaining quotations in this paragraph are from Sagoff, "The View from Quincy Library," p. 158.

24. Jane Braxton Little, "The Woods: Reclaiming the Neighborhood," *American Forests* (Winter 1998), p. 41. Of course, the Quincy Library Group did succeed in changing the law, but the Herger-Feinstein Quincy Library Group Forest Recovery Act of 1998 was highly restricted in geographic scope and time, and expressly did not modify existing environmental laws.

25. For more on such organizations, see Garry D. Brewer, "Perfect Places: NASA as an Idealized Institution," in Radford Byerly, Jr., ed., *Space Policy Reconsidered* (Boulder, Colo.: Westview, 1989), pp. 157–73.

26. Charles F. Wilkinson, *Crossing the Next Meridian* (Washington, D.C.: Island, 1992), p. 127.

27. George Cameron Coggins, Charles F. Wilkinson, and John D. Leshy, *Federal Public Land and Resources Law*, 3d ed. (Westbury, N.Y.: Foundation, 1993), p. 622.

28. Michael Dombeck, quoted in Al Todd, "Collaborative Planning and Stewardship," USDA Forest Service S&PF (Washington, D.C., 1997).

29. Alan Polk, USDA Forest Service Public Affairs Office, "New Forest Service Chief Outlines Plan To Move Agency into Twenty-first Century" (Jan. 6, 1997).

30. Daniel Kemmis, quoted in "The Lubrecht Conversations," *Chronicle of Community* 3 (Autumn 1998), p. 13.

31. Robert L. Glicksman and George Cameron Coggins, in *Modern Public Land Law in a Nutshell* (St. Paul, Minn.: West, 1995), pp. 191–92.

32. Paul W. Hirt, *A Conspiracy of Optimism: Management of the National Forests since World War Two* (Lincoln: University of Nebraska Press, 1994), p. xvi.

33. C. L. Rawlins, "Forest Service: Villain and Scapegoat," *High Country News* 25 (Sept. 6, 1993), p. 1.

34. E. Lynn Burkett, "Forest Service Ranger District Wins $100,000 for Model Community Program," News Release from the U.S. Forest Service National Media Desk (Oct. 22, 1998). This account also draws on seminar papers by Zoe Miller and by Donna Tucker Walrath.

35. Su Rolle, Interagency Liaison for Forest Service and Bureau of Land Management, Applegate Adaptive Management Area and Applegate Partnership, "Applegate Partnership."

36. Su Rolle, telephone interview, June 28, 1999. This account is also based on a telephone interview with Jack Shipley, an Applegate Partnership founder, June 29, 1999; and on Kathie Durbin, "The Progress of Freewheeling Consensus Jeopardized as Feds Pull Back," *High Country News* 26 (Oct. 17, 1994), p. 2.

37. Todd Wilkinson, "Breaking an Agency of Its Old Ways," *High Country News* 30 (Apr. 27, 1998).

38. Todd Wilkinson, "Will Dombeck Sock It to Rebellious Supervisors?" *High Country News* 30 (Apr. 27, 1998), p. 1.

39. Orville Daniels, quoted in "The Lubrecht Conversations," p. 8.

40. Jack Ward Thomas, quoted in "The Lubrecht Conversations," p. 9. As noted in Chapter 1, some are immobilized by the complex of laws. Others may consider the complex "workable." The point is that the complexity itself encourages diverse perceptions and responses.

41. Daniels, quoted in "The Lubrecht Conversations," p. 8.

42. Su Rolle, Interagency Liaison, Medford, Oreg., "FACA: Proposed Rule-Making" (July 8, 1997), pp. 1, 3. For guides to FACA, see Thomas Brendler, "The Federal Advisory Committee Act: What You Need To Know," in *Chronicle of Community* 1 (Autumn 1996), pp. 44–47; and the appendix in Cestero, *Beyond the Hundredth Meeting*, pp. 79–80.

43. *Report of the Collaborative Stewardship Team, 1998* (May 28, 1998), p. 2.

44. Jim Burchfield, "Abandoned by the Roadside," *Chronicle of Community* 3 (Autumn 1998), pp. 31–36, at pp. 31, 34.

45. Jeff Barnard, "New Forest Official Plans Changes: Deputy Chief in Northwest Says Timber is a Low Priority," *Boulder Daily Camera* (May 20, 1999).

46. Elizabeth Estill, telephone interview, July 1, 1999.

47. Mark Dowie, *Losing Ground: American Environmentalism at the Close of the Century* (Cambridge: M.I.T. Press, 1995), p. 33.

48. This ruling induced Congress to enact the National Forest Management Act in 1976. See Glicksman and Coggins, *Modern Public Land Law in a Nutshell*, p. 189.

49. Wilkinson, *Crossing the Next Meridian*, p. 163.

50. Dowie, *Losing Ground*, p. 33.

51. Wilkinson, *Crossing the Next Meridian*, p. 66.

52. James Dougherty, quoted in Dowie, *Losing Ground*, p. 193.

53. Dowie, *Losing Ground*, p. 37.

54. Mike Clark, quoted in Phil Shabecoff, "D.C.'s Green Power-Brokers Look for New Home," *High Country News* 27 (Nov. 13, 1995).

55. Dowie, *Losing Ground*, p. 175.

56. Shabecoff, "D.C.'s Green Power-Brokers Look for New Home." See also Gary Lee, "Environmental Groups Launch Counterattack after Losses on Hill," *Washington Post* (Aug. 19, 1995), p. A6.

57. Dowie, *Losing Ground*, p. 261.

58. Quoted in Shabecoff, "D.C.'s Green Power-Brokers Look for New Home."

59. "The [Cuyahoga] river catching fire brought national attention and ridicule to Cleveland, but it also proved to be the instrumental rallying point in the passage of the Clean Water Act of 1972," according to Steven R. Davis of the U.S. Forest Service, who describes himself as "a lone federal employee working at the grass-roots level to help the Cuyahoga." Quoted in Francis X. Clines, "Navigating the Renaissance of the Ohio River That Once Caught Fire," *New York Times* (Jan. 23, 2000), p. 12.

60. This was the most memorable line in his first inaugural address, from the transcript published in the *Washington Post* (Jan. 21, 1981), p. A34. The rise of sentiments against environmental regulations in and around the Reagan administration also mobilized environmentalists in the balancing of power.

61. Cases in point are the gutting of President Carter's National Energy Plan in 1977–1978 and the defeat of the Clinton administration's national healthcare

plan in 1994. Compare these outcomes with the outcome of President Johnson's Great Society initiatives in the mid-1960s.

62. Quoted in Lisa Jones, "Howdy, Neighbor! As a Last Resort, Westerners Start Talking to Each Other," *High Country News* 28 (May 13, 1996).

63. Patrick Moore, quoted in John Elvin, "A Green Activist Changes Colors," *Insight on the News* (Oct. 14, 1997).

64. Donald Snow, "The Pristine Silence of Leaving it All Alone," *Northern Lights* (Winter 1994), pp. 10–16.

65. William deBuys, "Separating Sense from Nonsense in New Mexico's Forests," *High Country News* 28 (Feb. 5, 1996). In the ellipses, deBuys gives the source of the embedded quote, *New Mexican* (Nov. 5, 1995).

66. Rick Johnson, quoted in Heather Abel, "Greens Prune Their Message to Win the West's Voters," *High Country News* 28 (Oct. 14, 1996).

67. Quoted in Scott Allen, "The Greening of the Movement; Big Money Is Bankrolling Select Environmental Causes," *Boston Globe* (Oct. 19, 1997), p. A1.

68. Snow is quoted in Jones, "Howdy, Neighbor!"

69. See especially Debbie Sease, "Sierra Club Legislative Director Testimony on Quincy Library Group Bill," Testimony before the Senate Subcommittee on Forests and Public Lands, Committee on Energy and Natural Resources, concerning S. 1028 and H.R. 858 (July 24, 1997).

70. Mike McCloskey, "The Skeptic: Collaboration Has Its Limits," *High Country News* 28 (May 13, 1996).

71. Other environmentalists also perceive themselves as engaged in a war. In 1995, Brock Evans, then vice president of the Audubon Society, said, "We're going to fight wise use and we're going to beat them. They can be beaten. We've faced groups like this before." Quoted in Kathie Durbin, "Forest Activists Retrench and Grope for Support," *High Country News* 27 (Feb. 20, 1995).

72. Quoted in Jones, "Howdy, Neighbor!"

73. Quoted in Shabecoff, "D.C.'s Green Power-Brokers Look for New Home."

74. Dave Foreman, quoted in Alex Barnum, "Battle over Legacy of John Muir Logging Vote Cuts to Heart of Sierra Club Dispute," *San Francisco Chronicle* (Apr. 20, 1996), p. A1.

75. Randal O'Toole, "Beyond the Hundredth Paradigm" (Thoreau Institute, 1999).

76. The "Sierra Club Mission Statement" can be found at http://www.sierraclub.org/policy/mission.html.

77. Phil Brick, "Of Imposters, Optimists, and Kings: Finding a Niche for Collaborative Conservation," *Chronicle of Community* 2 (Winter 1998), pp. 34–38, at pp. 35, 36.

78. John Sawhill, in a January 1988 report to members, quoted in Brick, "Of Imposters, Optimists, and Kings," p. 36.

79. Dan Dagget, "It's UnAmerican, or at Best UnWestern, but Cooperation Works," *High Country News* 27 (Oct. 16, 1995).

80. Michael Lipford, "From the Director," *Virginia Chapter News* (July 12, 1999), http://tncnt.tnc.org:70/newstory.

81. Cindy Pitman, Conservation Assistant, Tennessee Chapter, The Nature Conservancy, "The Human Context of Stewardship," *Tennessee Science and Stewardship*, http://tncnt.tnc.org:70/newstory.

82. See Allen, "The Greening of the Movement," on the Environmental Futures report and Abel, "Greens Prune Their Message to Win the West's Voters," on Rick Johnson.

83. Gary Lee, "Environmental Groups Launch Counterattack after Losses on Hill," *Washington Post* (Aug. 19, 1995), p. A6.

84. Steve Holmer, quoted in Durbin, "Forest Activists Retrench and Grope for Support."

85. Tarso Ramos, quoted in Durbin, "Forest Activists Retrench and Grope for Support."

86. Quoted in Shabecoff, "D.C.'s Green Power-Brokers Look for New Home."

87. Flicker quoted in Lee, "Environmental Groups Launch Counterattack after Losses on Hill."

88. Lee, "Environmental Groups Launch Counterattack after Losses on Hill."

89. Aldo Leopold, "Land Use and Democracy," *Audubon* 44 (September/October 1942), pp. 259–65, at p. 262. The following quotations can be found at pp. 263, 264, and 265.

90. Aldo Leopold, *A Sand County Almanac*, pp. 203–204.

91. Leopold, "Land Use and Democracy," p. 265. Emphasis added. "Of Imposters, Optimists, and Kings" by Phil Brick elaborates, or perhaps rediscovers, many of the practical implications of Leopold's land ethic.

92. Douglas Kenney, *Analysis of Institutional Innovation in the Natural Resources and Environmental Realm: The Emergence of Alternative Problem-Solving Strategies in the American West* (Boulder: Natural Resources Law Center, University of Colorado Law School, 1999), p. 7. It is far from clear what, if anything, might qualify as value-neutral criteria. Improvement in environmental health is not value-neutral, nor is the advancement of science, even though they may be taken as given among environmentalists and scientists, respectively.

93. Kenney, "Are Community-Based Watershed Groups Really Effective?," p. 35. The following quotation is from p. 37 of the same article. For a similar approach, see William D. Leach, Neil W. Pelkey, and Paul A. Sabatier, "Conceptualizing and Measuring Success in Stakeholder Partnerships," a paper circulated at the Annual Research Conference of the Association for Public Policy Analysis and Management, Seattle, Nov. 2–4, 2000.

94. For a theory of assumption drag, see William Ascher, *Forecasting: An Appraisal for Policy Makers and Planners* (Baltimore: Johns Hopkins University Press, 1978), including the foreword by Harold D. Lasswell.

95. In a personal communication (Mar. 9, 2000), Dr. Kenney responded that rigorous proof of generalizations may matter to federal or state agencies in a position to adopt a given policy over a range of watersheds or other places, even if it is not directly relevant to participants in the initiatives themselves. He also affirmed, however, that the most obvious generalization supported by the evidence is that the success of each initiative depends upon the context.

96. Cestero, *Beyond the Hundredth Meeting*, pp. 50–55.

97. As Harold D. Lasswell observed in *The Political Writings of Harold D. Lasswell* (Glencoe, IL: Free Press, 1951), p. 524, "it is the growth of insight, not simply the capacity of the observer to predict the future of an automatic compulsion, or of a non-personal factor, that represents the major contribution of the scientific study of interpersonal relations to policy." On the policy sciences as contextual, problem-oriented, and multi-method, see Harold D. Lasswell, *A Pre-View of Policy Sciences* (New York: Elsevier, 1971), p. 4, and many other sources in the policy sciences.

98. If only 50 dichotomous variables were relevant, there would be 2^{50} possible conjunctions of them—a number well in excess of the number of actual initiatives. Hence most cells in this 50-dimensional space would be empty, and the remainder would likely be represented by only one case.

99. Compare Harold D. Lasswell, "The Policy Orientation," in Daniel Lerner and Harold D. Lasswell, eds., *The Policy Sciences* (Stanford: Stanford University Press, 1951), pp. 3–15, at p. 14: "The policy approach does not mean that the scientist abandons objectivity in gathering or interpreting data, or ceases to perfect his tools. The policy emphasis calls for the choice of problems which will contribute to the goal values of the scientist, and the use of scrupulous objectivity and maximum technical ingenuity in executing the projects undertaken."

100. Compare Lasswell, "The Policy Orientation," p. 8: "The richness of the context in the study of interpersonal relations is such that it can be expressed only in part in quantitative terms."

101. Nevertheless, experimentation is still taken literally by some scientists, even those who question how much scientific rigor is attainable in open field settings. Kai N. Lee, "Appraising Adaptive Management," *Conservation Ecology* 3 (September 1999), online, makes a dubious distinction between experiments in the field and trial-and-error. Among psychologists who have adapted experimentation to policy reforms and discovered the importance of context, see Donald T. Campbell, "Reforms as Experiments," in F. Caro, ed., *Readings in Evaluation Research* (N.Y.: Russell Sage Foundation, 1969), pp. 233–61; and Lee J. Cronbach, "Beyond the Two Disciplines of Scientific Psychology," *American Psychologist* 30 (1975), pp. 116–27. Harold D. Lasswell considered prototyping an intermediate method between experimentation and policy intervention in "Experimentation, Prototyping, Intervention," in *The Future of Political Science* (N.Y.: Atherton, 1963), pp. 95–122.

102. The Quincy Library Group maintains its own web site at www.QLG.org.

103. The address is www.sonoran.org/front.html. For more on the Sonoran Institute, see Cestero, *Beyond the Hundredth Meeting*, and Sarah B. Van de Wetering, "Fresheners," *Chronicle of Community* 3 (Autumn 1998), pp. 43, 45.

104. It is available online at www.hcn.org. On diffusion via newsletters see Ed Marston, "The Working West: Grassroots Groups and Their Newsletters," *High Country News* (May 11, 1998), pp. 1 ff.

105. Northern Lights Research and Education Institute, "A Brief Sketch of Projects and Activities from 1985 to the Present" (Missoula, Mont.: May 1999), p. 6. Van de Wetering, "Fresheners," is an occasional feature that updates information resources for community-based initiatives in the *Chronicle*.

106. Douglas S. Kenney, *Resource Management at the Watershed: An Assessment of the Changing Federal Role in the Emerging Era of Community-Based Watershed Management*, Report to the Western Water Policy Review Advisory Commission (Boulder: Natural Resources Law Center, University of Colorado Law School, October 1997); Douglas S. Kenney, *Analysis of Institutional Innovation in the Natural Resources and Environmental Realm*; and Douglas S. Kenney, *Arguing about Consensus: Examining the Case against Western Watershed Initiatives and Other Collaborative Groups Active in Natural Resources Management* (Boulder: Natural Resources Law Center, University of Colorado Law School, 2000).

107. *Communities and Forests* 2 (Fall 1998), p. 8.

108. For example, a report by Brett KenCairn on "Criteria for Evaluating Community-based Conservation/Natural Resource Partnership Initiatives" was distributed via internet on Jan. 22, 1999.

109. From a Forest Service memo of Dec. 14, 1998, on Eco-Watch Dialogues to Regional Foresters, Station Directors, Area Directors, and W.O. Staff Directors. The site is www.fs.fed.us/eco/eco-watch/ecowatch.html.

110. The italicized cues suggest, respectively, the importance of control analysis, content analysis, media analysis, audience analysis, and effects analysis for a

contextual understanding of an act of communication. See Harold D. Lasswell, "The Structure and Function of Communication in Society," in Wilbur Schramm, ed., *Mass Communications*, 2d ed. (Urbana: University of Illinois Press, 1960), pp. 117–30.

111. See Martin Landau, "Redundancy, Rationality, and the Problem of Duplication and Overlap," *Public Administration Review* (July/August 1969), pp. 346–58.

112. The authors are indebted to Janine Wingard for a seminar paper on media coverage. On the award, see "More Talk, Less Tension over Timber," in a Special Section Sponsored by the Ford Foundation of *Governing* (1998), p. A16.

113. Alison Mitchell, "President Acts on School Attire," *New York Times* (Feb. 25, 1996), p. 1; Tamar Lewin, "More Public School Pupils Now Don Uniforms," *New York. Times* (Sept. 25, 1997), p. A1. However, publicity prior to the consolidation and success of a community-based initiative can make it unnecessarily vulnerable to internal dissension and external opposition.

114. There is some guidance from experience in other policy areas and from theory. Relevant sources include Lisbeth B. Schorr, *Common Purpose: Strengthening Families and Neighborhoods to Rebuild America* (N.Y.: Anchor Books, 1997); Ronald D. Brunner, "Decentralized Energy Policies," *Public Policy* 28 (Winter 1980), pp. 71–79; the section on international development in Ronald D. Brunner and William Ascher, "Science and Social Responsibility," *Policy Sciences* 25 (1992), pp. 295–331: and Ronald D. Brunner and Roberta Klein, "Harvesting Experience: A Reappraisal of the U.S. Climate Action Plan," *Policy Sciences* 32 (1999), pp. 133–61. See also Paul L. Doughty, "Vicos: Success, Rejection, and Rediscovery of a Classic Program," in E. M. Eddy and W. L. Partridge, eds., *Applied Anthropology in America*, 2d ed. (N.Y.: Columbia University Press, 1987), pp. 433–59. More generally, see the criteria for the appraisal of decision processes (especially the intelligence and appraisal functions) in Harold D. Lasswell, *A Pre-View of Policy Sciences*, pp. 86–93; and Everett M. Rogers, *Diffusion of Innovations*, 4th ed. (New York: Free Press, 1995).

115. Compare George E. Brown, Jr., then chairman of the Committee on Science, Space, and Technology of the U.S. House of Representatives, in "The Objectivity Crisis," *American Journal of Physics* 60 (September 1992), pp. 779–81: "The fact is, we already have much of the knowledge and many of the technologies necessary to decrease population growth, increase energy efficiency, reduce and recycle wastes, and improve public health and education throughout the world. The real problem, of course, is implementation: adapting our social and economic systems so that they are capable of assimilating and using this information and hardware."

116. See Harold D. Lasswell, *A Pre-View of Policy Sciences*, pp. 93–97.

117. For more on decision seminars, see Lasswell, *A Pre-View of Policy Sciences*, pp. 142–55.

118. Ronald D. Brunner, "Alternatives to Prediction," in Daniel Sarewitz, Roger A. Pielke, Jr., and Radford Byerly, Jr., eds., *Prediction: Science, Decision-Making, and the Future of Nature* (Washington, D.C.: Island, 2000), pp. 199–213.

119. Abraham Kaplan, *The Conduct of Inquiry: Methodology for Behavioral Science* (San Francisco: Chandler, 1964), p. 11.

120. For comparisons, see the Committee of Scientists, *Sustaining the People's Land: Recommendations for Stewardship of the National Forests and Grass Lands into the Next Century* (Washington, D.C.: U.S. Department of Agriculture, Mar. 15, 2000); and Gerald J. Gray, Maia J. Enzer, and Jonathan Kusel, eds., *Understanding*

Community-Based Forest Ecosystem Management: An Editorial Synthesis of an American Forest Workshop, Bend, Oreg., June 1998 (Washingon, D.C.: American Forests, 2000).

121. This and preceding quotations can be found in C. S. Holling, "What Barriers? What Bridges?," in Lance H. Gunderson, C. S. Holling, and Stephen S. Light, eds., *Barriers and Bridges to the Renewal of Ecosystems and Institutions* (N.Y.: Columbia University Press, 1995), pp. 3–34, at p. 13.

122. Paraphrased from Holling, "What Barriers? What Bridges?," p. 14.

123. On the convergence hypothesis, see Lasswell, *A Pre-View of Policy Sciences*, p. 8. For more on convergence by Holling and his coeditors, see the first author's review of *Barriers and Bridges to the Renewal of Ecosystems and Institutions*, in the *Journal of Wildlife Management* 61 (1997), pp. 1437–39.

124. Paul C. Stern, "A Second Environmental Science: Human-Environment Interactions," *Science* 260 (June 25, 1993), pp. 1897–99, at p. 1898.

125. Steve Rayner and Elizabeth L. Malone, "Zen and the Art of Climate Maintenance," *Nature* 390 (Nov. 27, 1997), pp. 332–34, at p. 332.

126. Elinor Ostrom, "Coping with Tragedies of the Commons," *Annual Review of Political Science* 2 (1999), pp. 493–535, at p. 496.

127. John H. Holland, "Complex Adaptive Systems," *Daedalus* 121 (Winter 1992), pp. 17–30, at p. 20. Holling and Ostrom are well aware of the connections between their work and work on complex adaptive systems.

128. Holling, "What Barriers? What Bridges?," p. 33. Gunderson, Holling, and Light, *Barriers and Bridges to the Renewal of Ecosystems and Institutions*, p. 530, go further to call for "conceptual reconfigurations" and for "new myths, words and meanings in our language, and quickly." In his *Analysis of Institutional Innovation in the Natural Resources and Environmental Realm*, p. v, Kenney also raises questions about tools for academic research: "new techniques and concepts are needed to evaluate alternative institutional arrangements in a more consistent, comprehensive and rigorous manner than is typically observed."

129. Lasswell, *A Pre-View of Policy Sciences*, p. 16. The postulate was introduced as "economical behavior" in Harold D. Lasswell and Abraham Kaplan, *Power and Society: A Framework for Political Inquiry* (New Haven: Yale University Press, 1950), p. 69. The manuscript for this book was finished by the end of 1945, according to its preface, p. vi.

130. Herbert A. Simon, *Models of Man* (N.Y.: John Wiley & Sons, 1957), p. 199.

131. Harold D. Lasswell, "The Political Science of Science: An Inquiry into the Possible Reconciliation of Mastery and Freedom," *American Political Science Review* 50 (December 1956), pp. 961–79, at pp. 961 and 965, respectively. The major statement of central theory at the time was Lasswell and Kaplan, *Power and Society*.

132. A case in point is the Institutional Analysis and Development (IAD) framework, which includes seven clusters of boundary rules to restructure the action situations faced by resource appropriators. See Ostrom, "Coping with Tragedies of the Commons."

133. Research into particular contexts would be the priority even if we had rigorously proved general laws of behavior. As Herbert Simon observed in "Human Nature in Politics: The Dialogue of Psychology with Political Science," *American Political Science Review* 79 (1985), pp. 293–304, at p. 301, even "the natural sciences . . . get only a little mileage from their general laws. Those laws have to be fleshed out by a myriad of facts, all of which must be harvested by laborious empir-

ical research." Thomas Kuhn makes essentially the same point in *The Structure of Scientific Revolutions,* 3d ed. (Chicago: University of Chicago Press, 1996), pp. 188–89.

134. Abraham Kaplan, *American Ethics and Public Policy* (N.Y.: Oxford University Press, 1963), p. 92.

135. Claude Lévi-Strauss, *The Savage Mind* (Chicago: University of Chicago Press, 1966), p. 16.

136. Kaplan, *American Ethics and Public Policy,* pp. 96–97.

Index